BEST OF
LIVING DESIGN

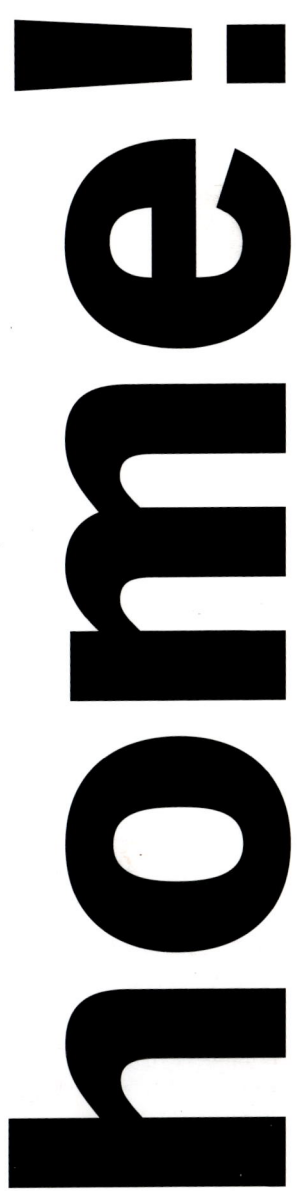

home!

Imprint
The Deutsche Nationalbibliothek lists this publication in the Deutsche Nationalbiografie;
detailed bibliographical data are available in the internet at http://dnb.dnb.de.

ISBN 978-3-03768-129-9
© 2013 by Braun Publishing AG
www.braun-publishing.ch

The work is copyright protected. Any use outside of the close boundaries of the copyright law, which has not been granted permission by the publisher, is unauthorized and liable for prosecution. This especially applies to duplications, translations, microfilming, and any saving or processing in electronic systems.

1st edition 2013

Selection of projects & layout: Michelle Galindo
Graphic concept: Michaela Prinz

All of the information in this volume has been compiled to the best of the editor's knowledge. It is based on the information provided to the publisher by the architects' and designers' offices and excludes any liability. The publisher assumes no responsibility for its accuracy or completeness as well as copyright discrepancies and refers to the specified sources (architects' and designers' offices). All rights to the photographs are property of the photographer (please refer to the picture credits).

BEST OF LIVING DESIGN

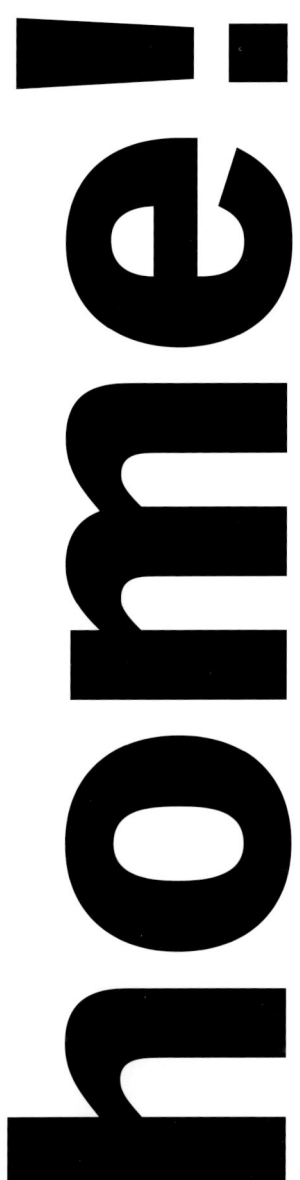

home!

BRAUN

6 Preface

Adelaide
10 Mini to the Max |
Troppo Architects,
Enoki (interiors)

Barcelona
18 Glazed Apartment |
Sergi Pons

Berlin
22 August 68 |
Oskar Fabian
Architecture Studio

32 Villas and Apartments
Ensemble in Grunewald |
Wiegand/Hoffmann
Architektur & Intérieurs

Brooklyn
38 Prospect Heights Residence |
Workstead

Cáceres
44 Estate in Extremadura |
Àbaton Arquitectura

Dniepropetrovsk
52 House in Ukraine |
Yakusha design

Emeryville
58 Benoit Residence |
Peter Benoit

Falmouth
66 Corkellis House |
Linea Studio/Kathryn Tyler

Kirchheim
74 Con&Vent House |
Alexander Brenner
Architekten

London
78 Little Venice Apartment |
Openstudio Architects

84 Tex-Tonic House |
Paul McAneary Architects

Los Angeles
92 Hollywood House |
Walker Workshop
Design Build

100 Nakahouse |
XTEN Architecture

Marseille
108 Le Prado |
Padovani Maurice

Monfumo
118 Chiavelli Residence |
Filippo Caprioglio –
Caprioglio Associati
Studio di Architettura

Montreal
126 Parisien / Raymond
Residence |
Naturehumaine

Muxbal, Guatemala City
132 Casa Luz |
Paz arquitectura

New York
140 Cameron Loft |
SchappacherWhite

148 Transformer | Studio Garneau

154 Krastev/Nikolova Residence | su11 architecture + design

Norfolk
160 Stable Acre | David Kohn

Osaka
170 House in Uenoshiba | Fujiwaramuro Architects

Österlen
176 Summerhouse Skåne | LASC Studio

Pyrgos Kallistis, Santorini Island
186 Villa Fabrica | Palimpsest | Architects + Engineers office

San Sebastián
196 San Sebastián Apartment | Mikel Irastorza

São Paulo
206 idalga 727 | Sub Estúdio

212 Apartment on Oscar Freire Street | Felipe Hess

220 Abbade Apartment | WHYDESIGN / Guto Requena, Maurício Arruda and Tatiana Sakurai

226 Harmonia Apartment | WHYDESIGN / Guto Requena, Maurício Arruda and Tatiana Sakurai

Shenzhen
234 House of the Tree | Kokaistudios

Stuttgart
240 House Strauss | Alexander Brenner Architekten

Tijuana
246 Casa del Mar | graciastudio

Tinos Island, Cyclades
256 Vacation House in Tinos | Zege architects / Marilyn Katsaris (interiors)

Toronto
266 Block Townhouse | Cecconi Simone

Vacallo
274 Casa Rizza | Studio Inches architettura

Vedbæk
280 Vedbæk House | Norm. Architects

Wilton
290 The Wilton Residence | UXUS Design

302 Architects Index
304 Picture Credits

Preface

Home! Best of Living Design unleashes a set of contemporary interior designs, presenting a mix collection of contemporary and mid-century ambients: from loft-like interiors where the lines between public and private spheres are blurred, to stark boundaries where unusual ideas and innovative solutions are implemented in the interior. The integration of the surroundings, the combination of materials, as well as the organization of the interior space is a major task for the designers. This volume features a global spectrum of contemporary styles, from rustic minimalism to urbane eclecticism. From small wonders, with a cool palette and clean-lined furnishing, charming craftsmanship style houses with updated interiors. Other interiors are handled with flare, with a few dramatic flourishes, and vivacious colors as a combination with print patterns, creating a space packed with personality. The rural, suburban and urban locations lend multiple possibilities for creative designs and styles. Some of the interiors are a relaxing escape from the stresses of city life – in a surprisingly sophisticated setting in the countryside, while others are the perfect balance of old-charm and modern-day simplicity in urban cities.

The work of the interior designers featured in this book reveals how function and style can co-exist under the same roof. While the functional demands are relatively flexible and rather unrestricted, the creative potential seems almost limitless. The selected projects testify the variety of inspirational design possibilities for contemporary living spaces. Simple and unparalleled solutions are the language of many of these private interiors. The warm lighting brings in a "very homely" feel to the design and unique lamp shades, furniture-designed pieces, snug-looking rugs, a blend of various types of chairs and plenty of accessories give the rooms a unique trademark look.

The wide array of interiors presents authentic dwellings, with love for detail, and zest for individual expression. The interior concept of *Estate in Extremadura* in Cáceres, Spain was influenced by the

location. Ábaton Arquitectura was commissioned to transform an abandoned stable into a family home. The interior design of this rural home consisted in the implementation of sustainability systems to solve problems relating to the electricity and water supply of the area. The supporting walls in the interior were replaced by light metal pillars and the haylofts in the upper area were converted into bedrooms. The stone exterior of this charming house is complemented by the rustic, Scandinavian style interior.

Another interior concept was based on a streamlined-macho theme and inspired by a photo of a ceiling in a Finnish lodge. *Hollywood House* from around 1916, by Walker Workshop Design Build, designed for a bachelor man, subtly embraces the gentlemen's-club aesthetic (dark colors, lots of wood) by refracting it through a minimalist lens. The look is especially evident in the living room, where spindly wooden skeletons of vintage Danish modern chairs have been stained a deep brown and thickly reupholstered in dark leather with three skulls hanging on the wall.

Finally, the interior concept of *Vedbæk House* by Norm. Architects was inspired by the cool and relaxed atmosphere of a fisherman's cottage, built in 1860 outside Copenhagen for a young family. This carved out exceedingly cozy, light-filled home has an aesthetic component, too – worn wood and strewn sheepskins. Its sloping ceilings, sculptural spiral staircase, and "lots of irregular little steps and corners and twisted angles" make this renovated house feel much more spacious than it is. The low ceiling in the sitting and dining room is pierced with skylights to give a sense of verticality, a move inspired by traditional Japanese temples, as well as to create a rhythm of light and dark and "spaces within a space".

Home! Best of Living Design rounds up a diverse and enticing selection of private homes' interiors from around the world, some of today's most exceptional and inspiring interiors. A global spectrum of contemporary styles, featuring an array of décor from solidly classical to the ultimate in contemporary glamour.

Glazed steel structure provides the **interior** with **warmth** and brightness **of natural daylight**

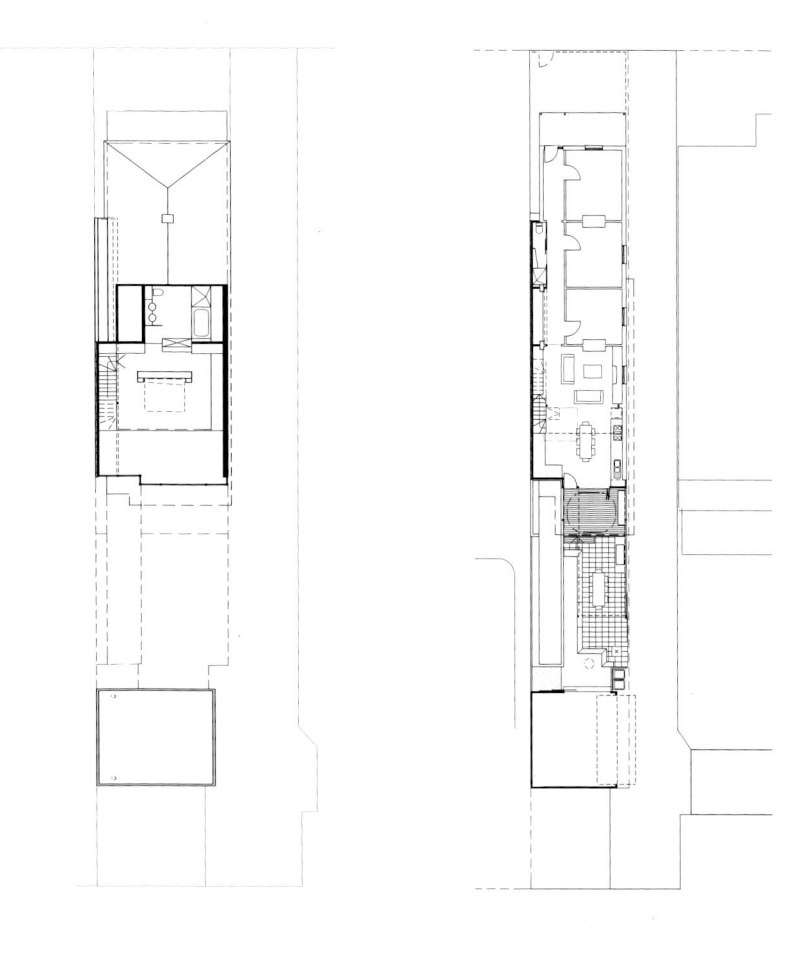

Glazed Apartment | Barcelona | Sergi Pons

The white space plays with **citrus** yellow and contrasts **with the concrete amber-tinted floor.**

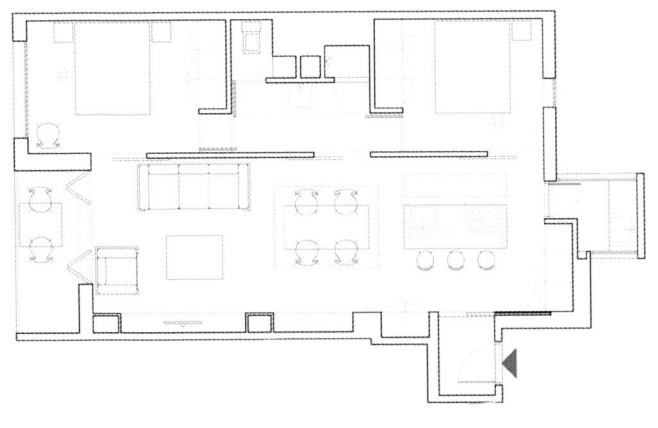

Mirror, mirror on the wall!

August 68 | Berlin | Oskar Fabian Architecture Studio

Villas and Apartments Ensemble in Grunewald | Berlin | Wiegand/Hoffmann Architektur & Intérieurs

Cosmopolitan interior with tailormade design: English, Italian and French furniture, wallpapers and mosaics

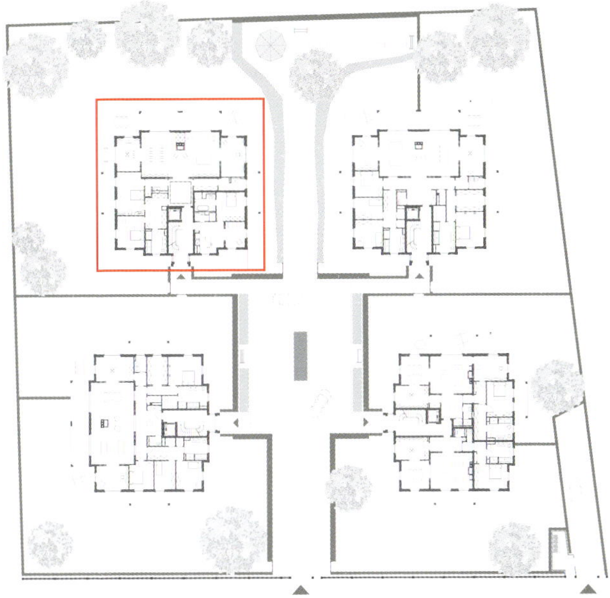

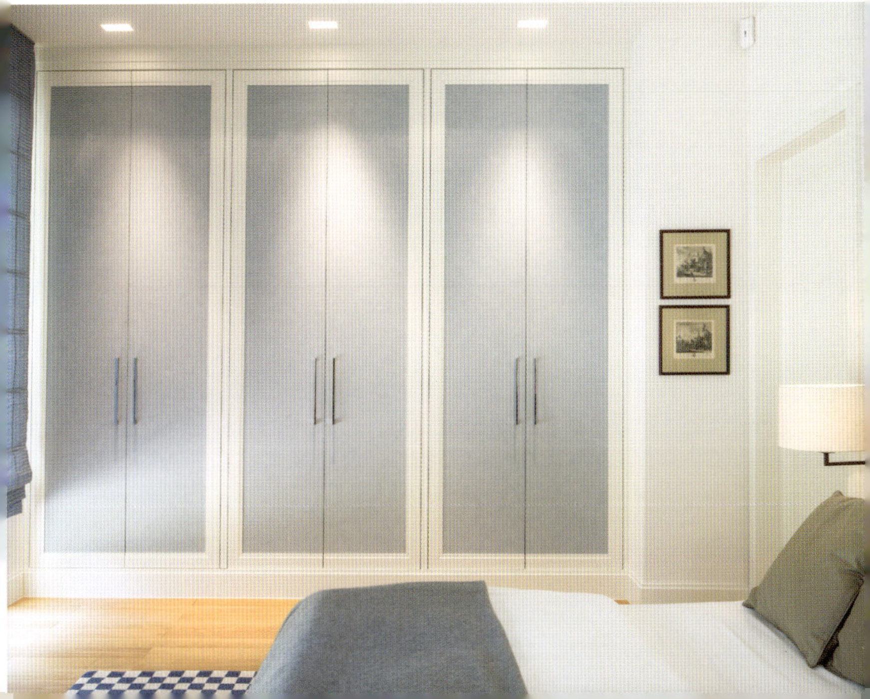

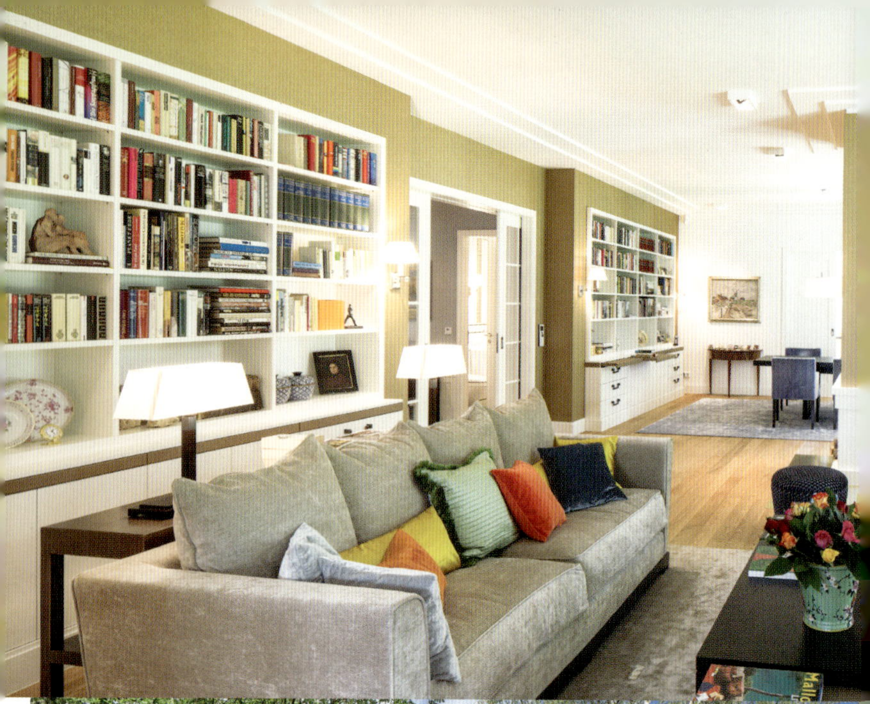

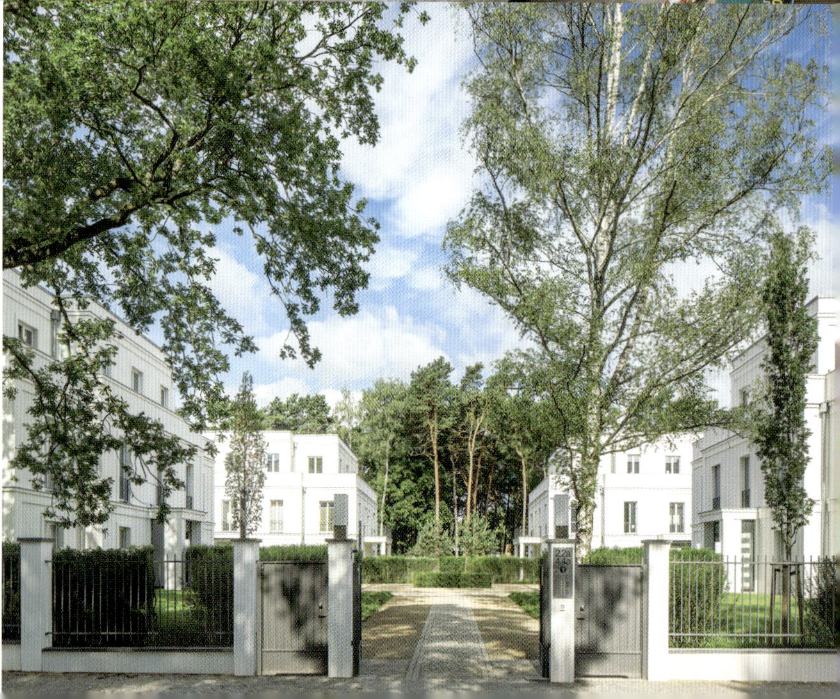

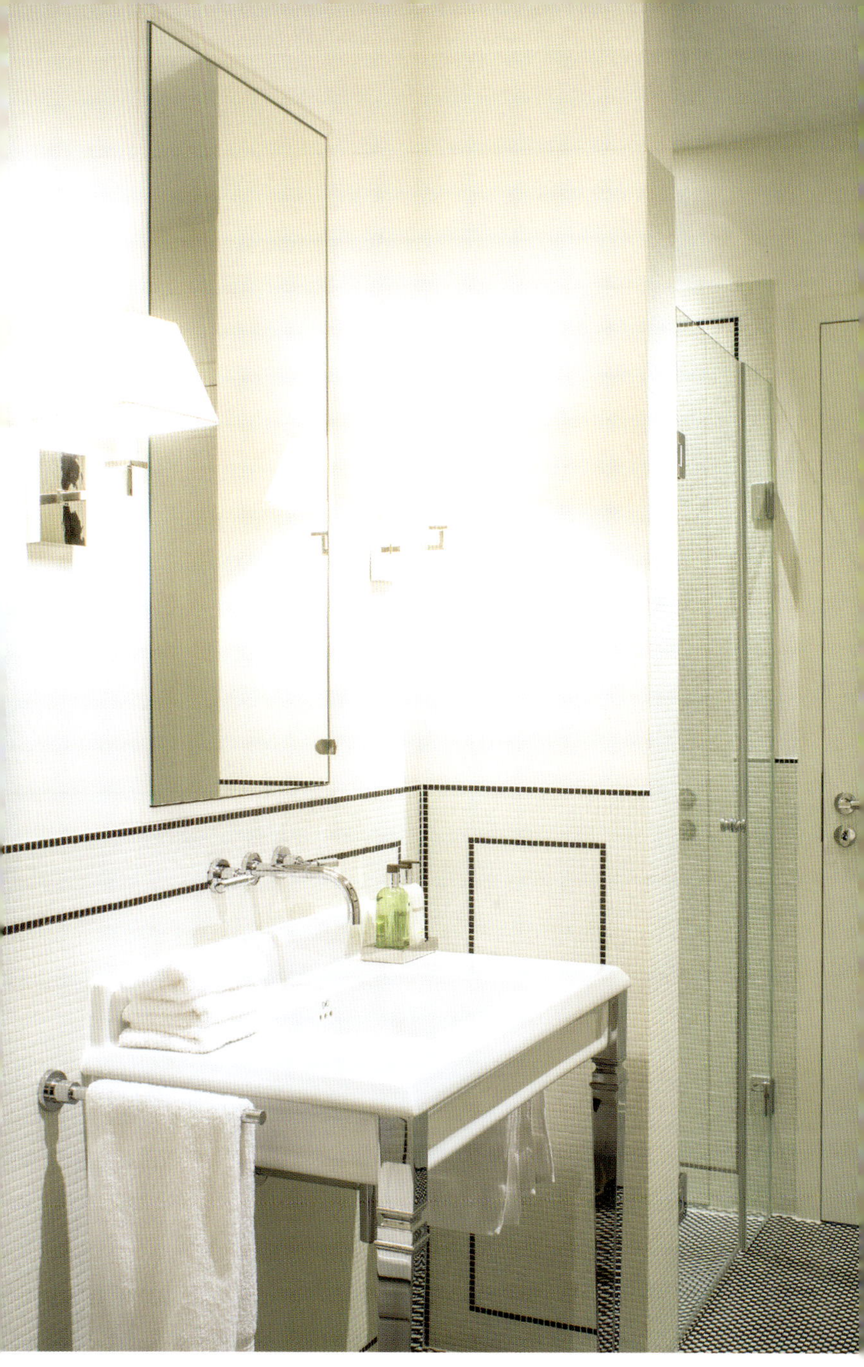

Rich wood and colorful brass create a sense of grace and punctuate a backdrop to the bustle of everyday life.

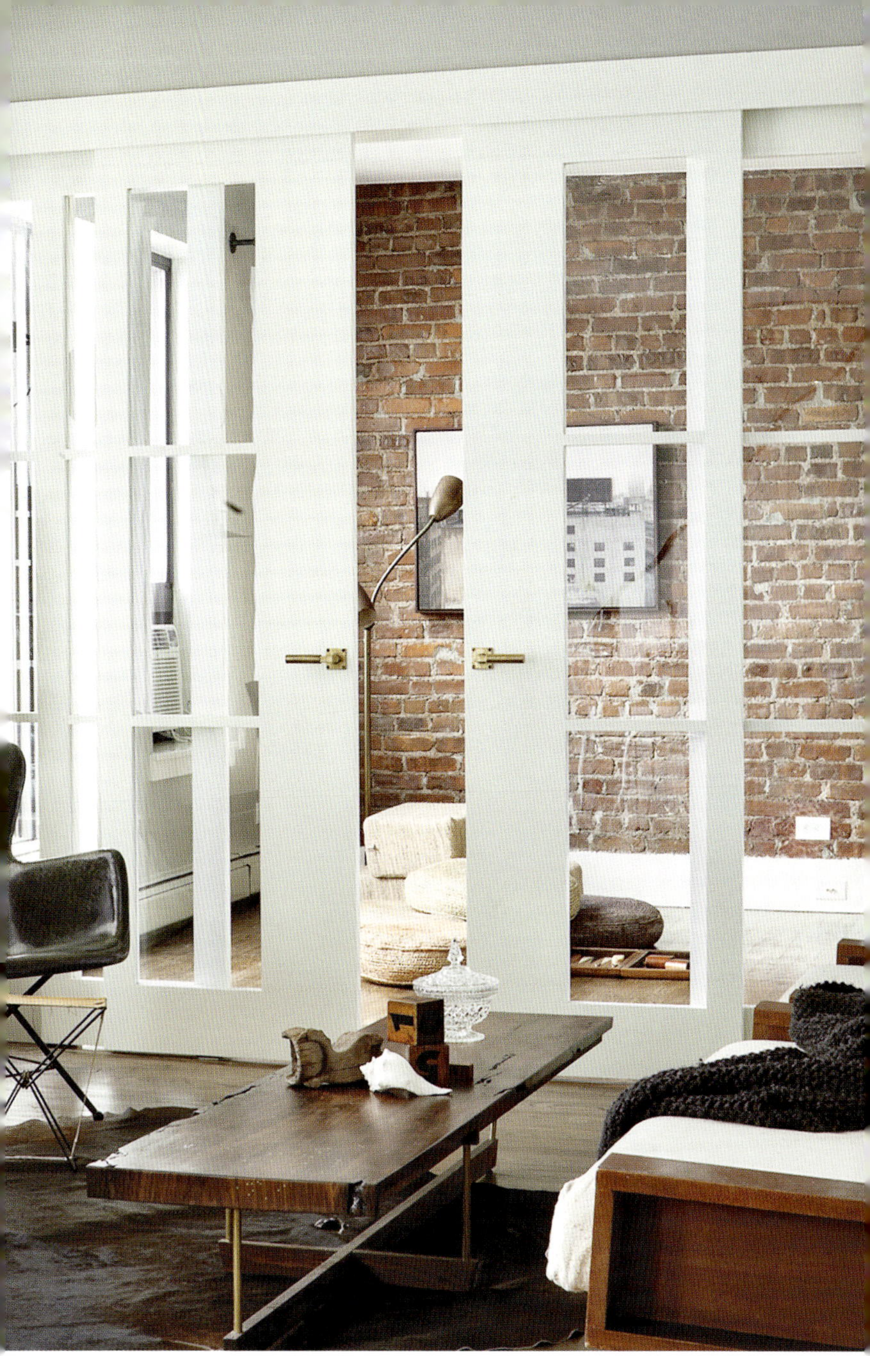

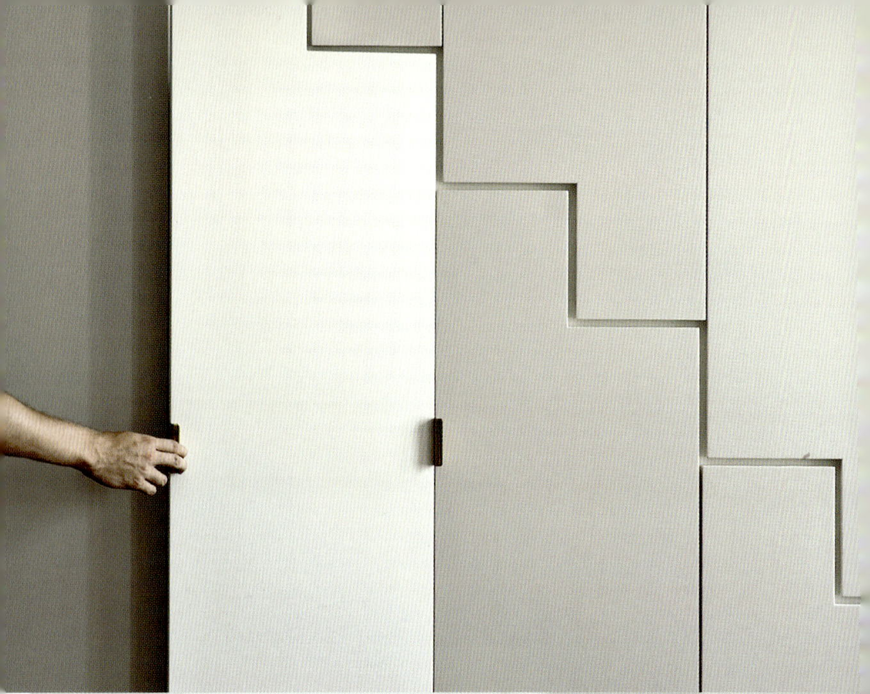
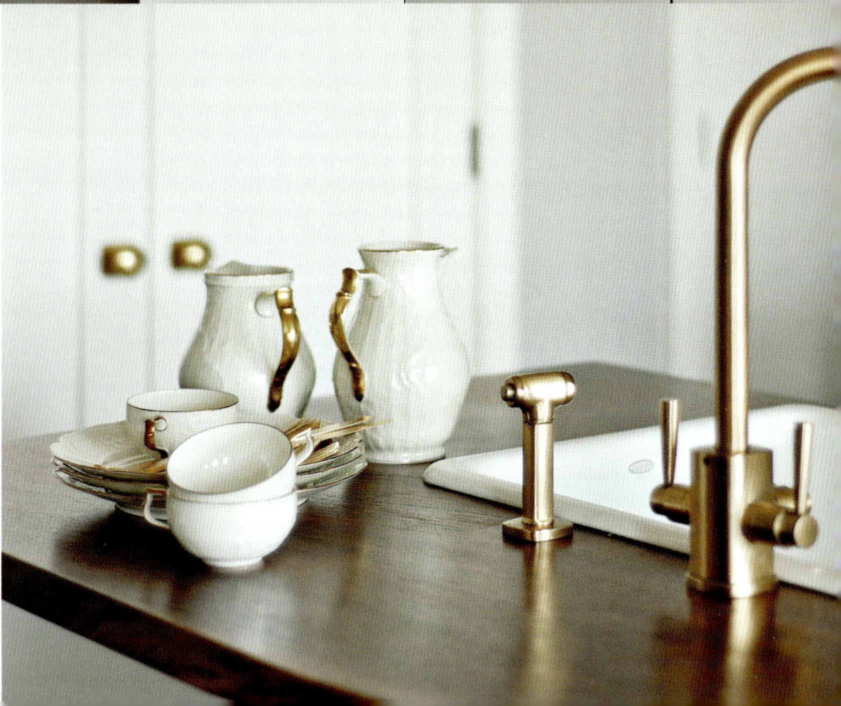

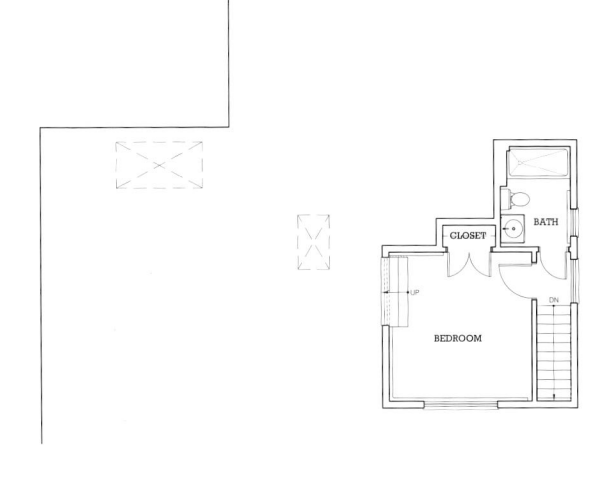

Upper Floor

- CLOSET
- BATH
- BEDROOM
- UP
- DN

Main Floor

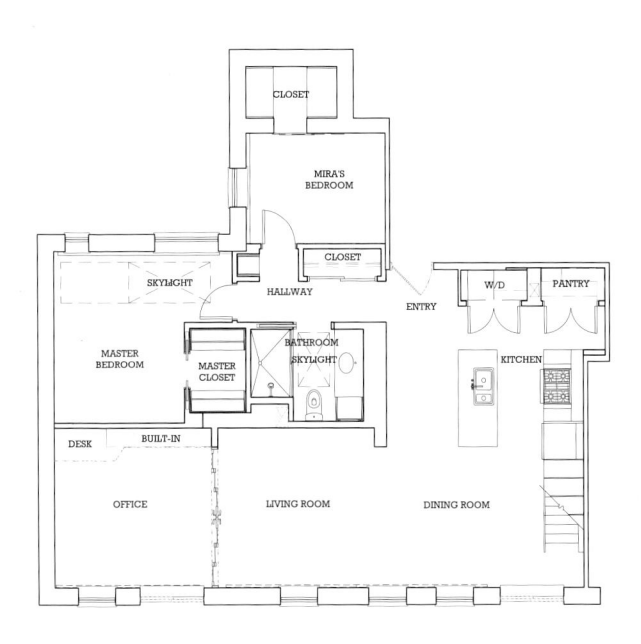

- CLOSET
- MIRA'S BEDROOM
- CLOSET
- HALLWAY
- ENTRY
- W/D
- PANTRY
- SKYLIGHT
- MASTER BEDROOM
- MASTER CLOSET
- BATHROOM
- SKYLIGHT
- KITCHEN
- DESK
- BUILT-IN
- OFFICE
- LIVING ROOM
- DINING ROOM

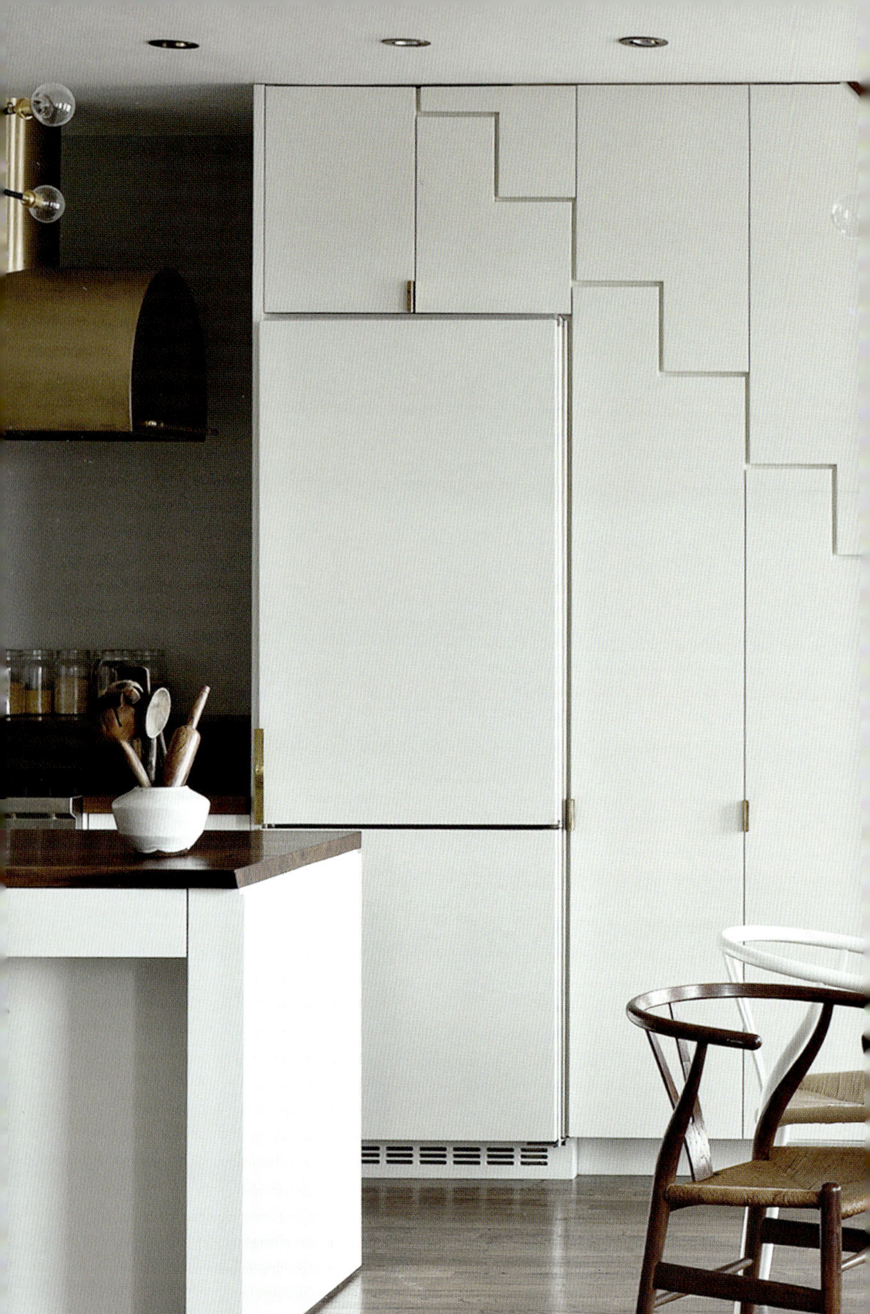

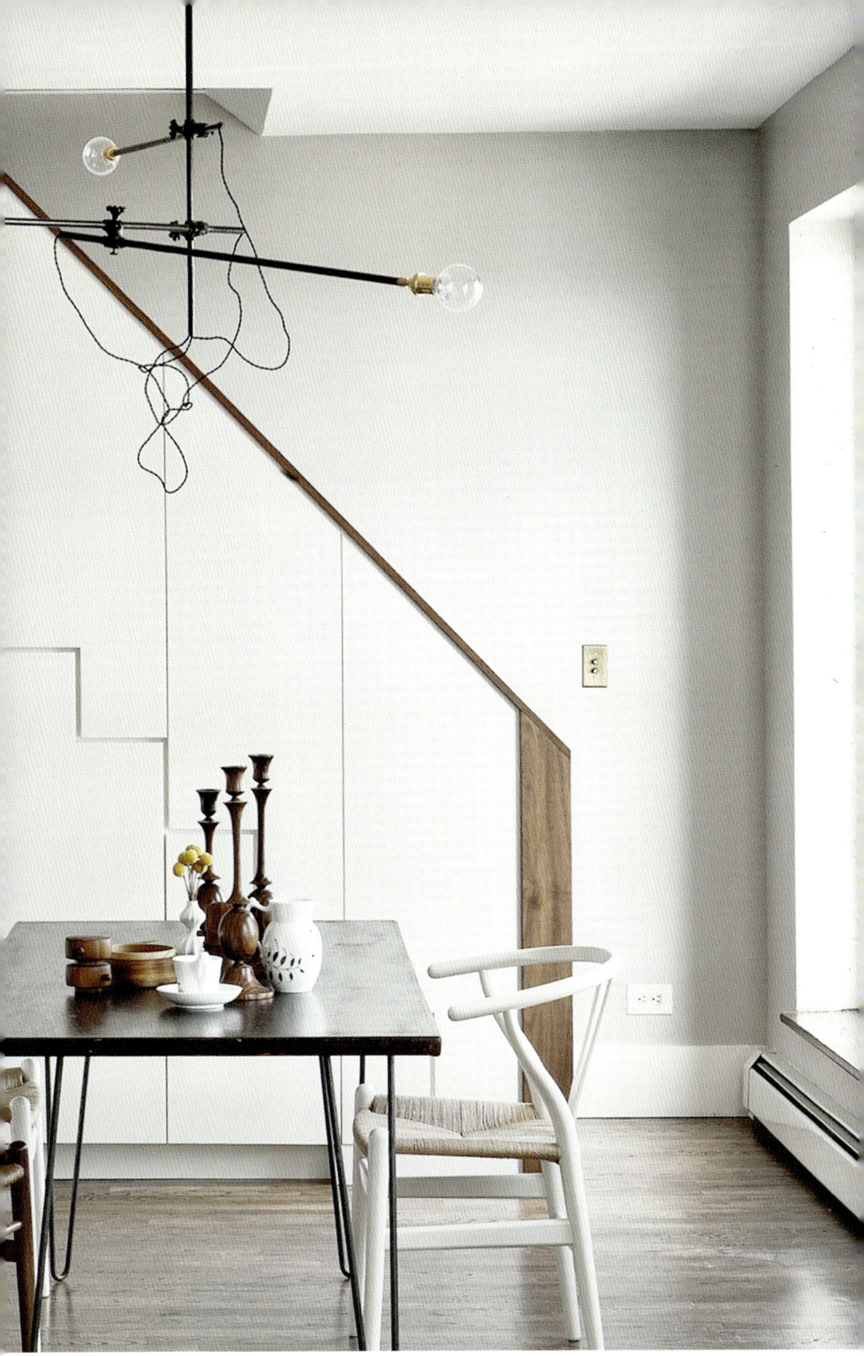

44 | **Estate in Extremadura** | Cáceres | Àbaton Arquitectura

An abandoned stable converted into a family home with water elements in its interior

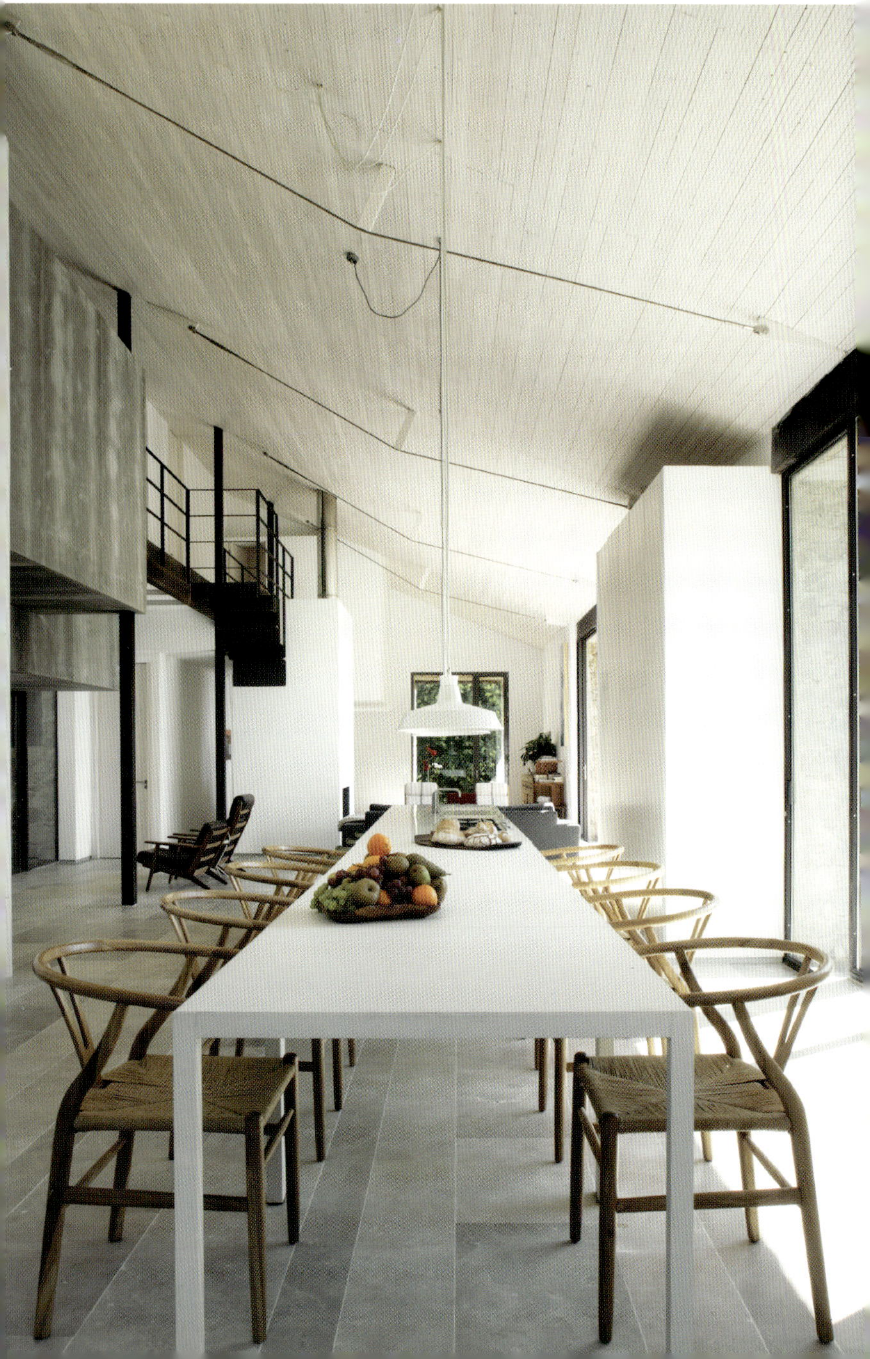

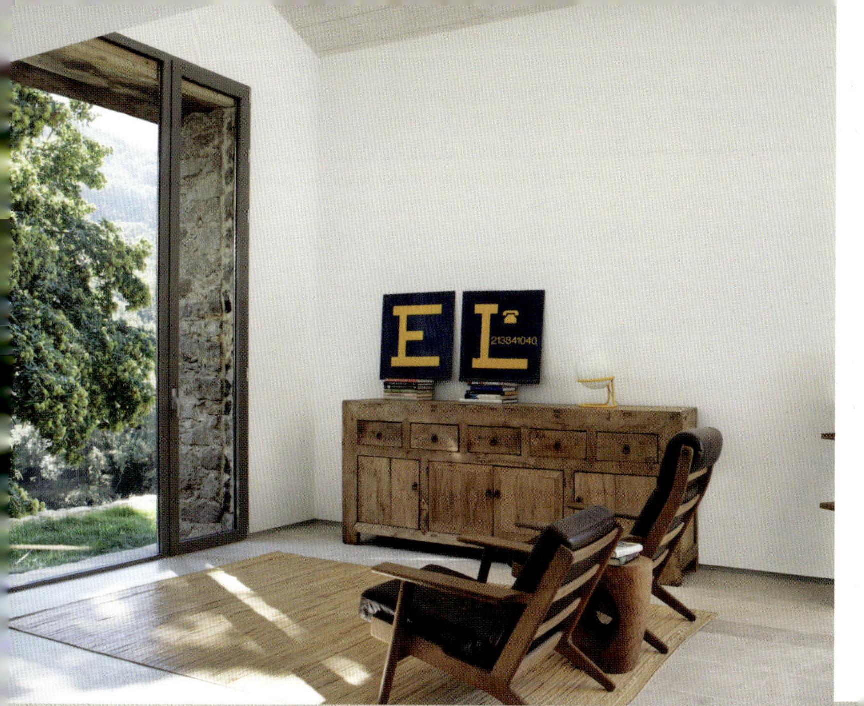
E
L
21384104O

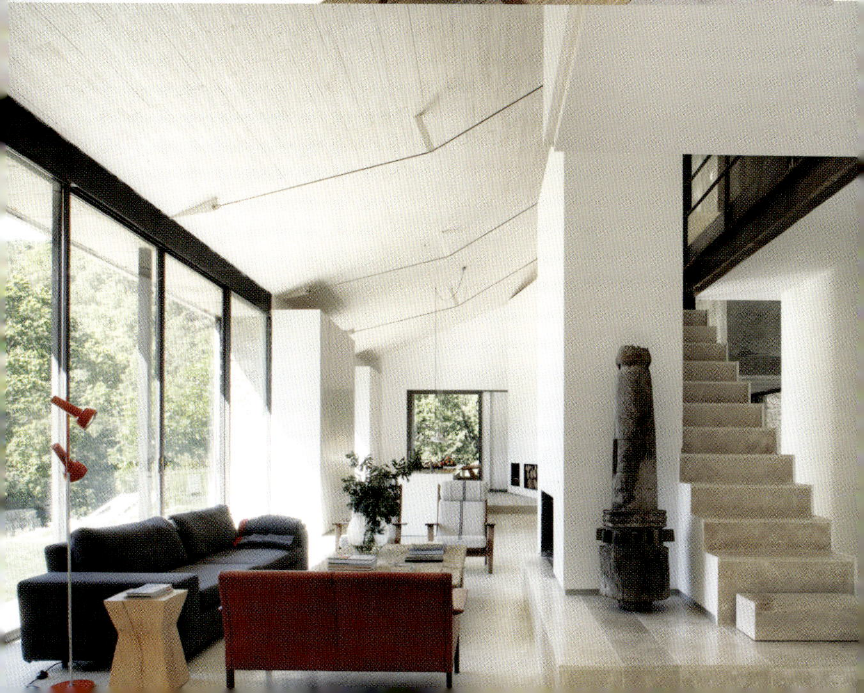

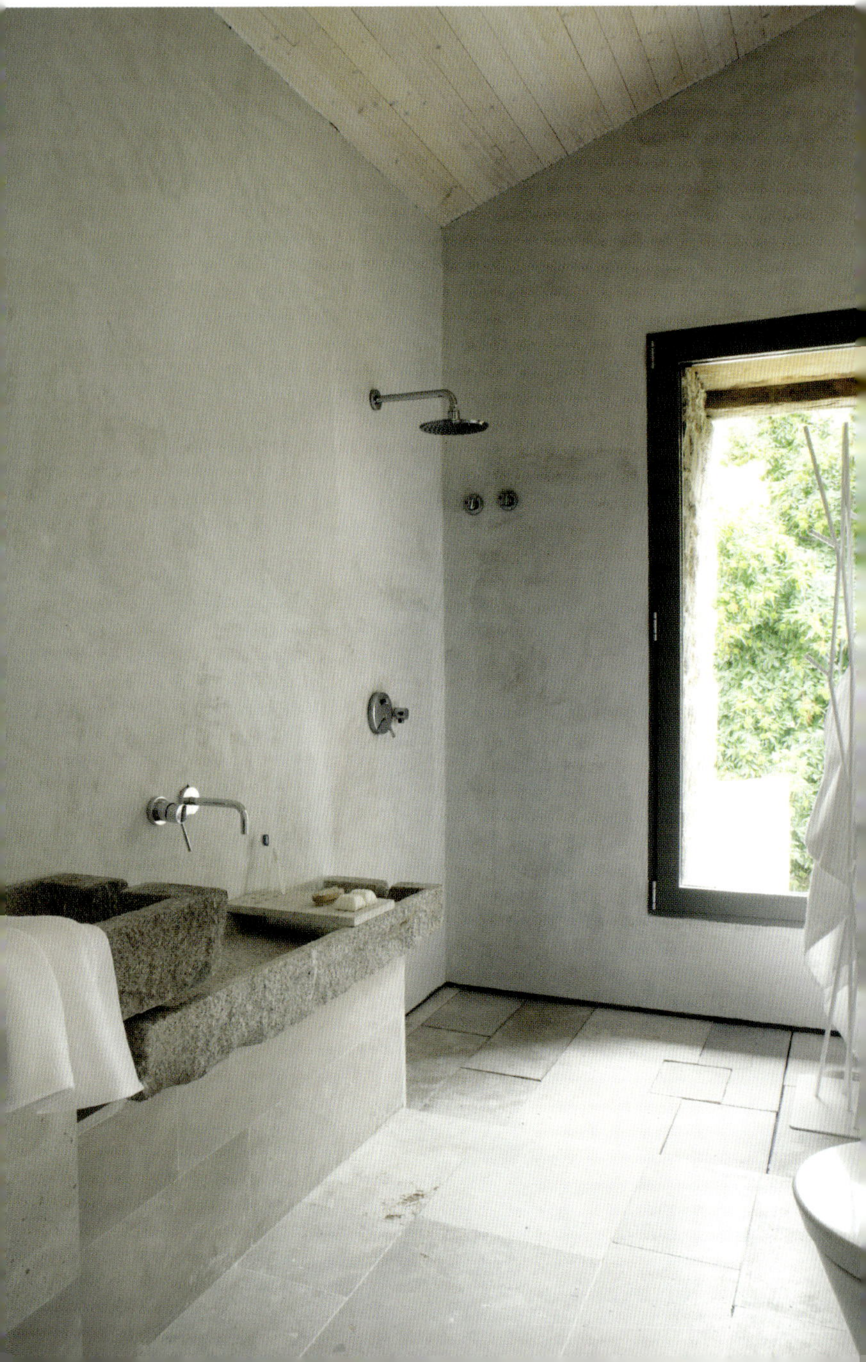

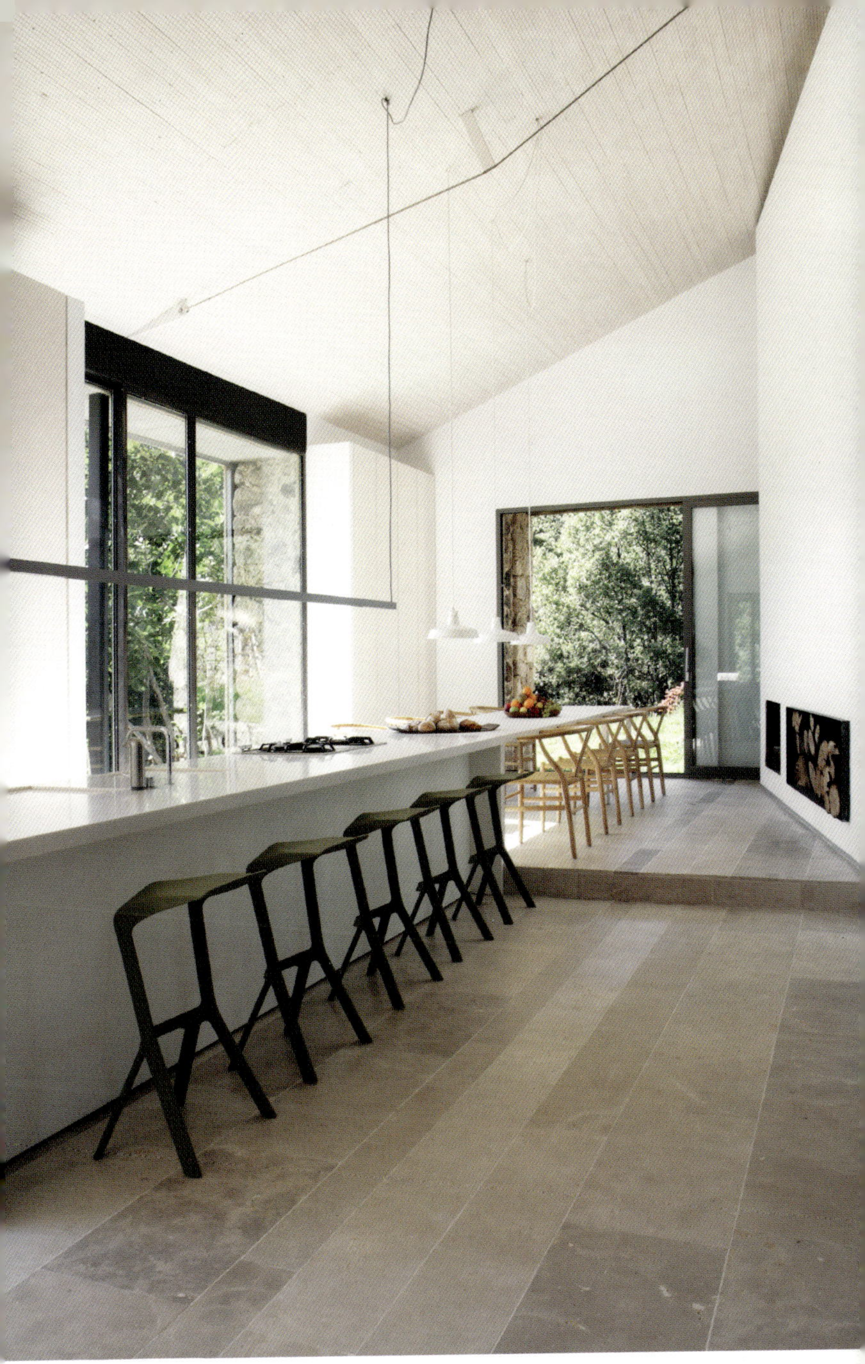

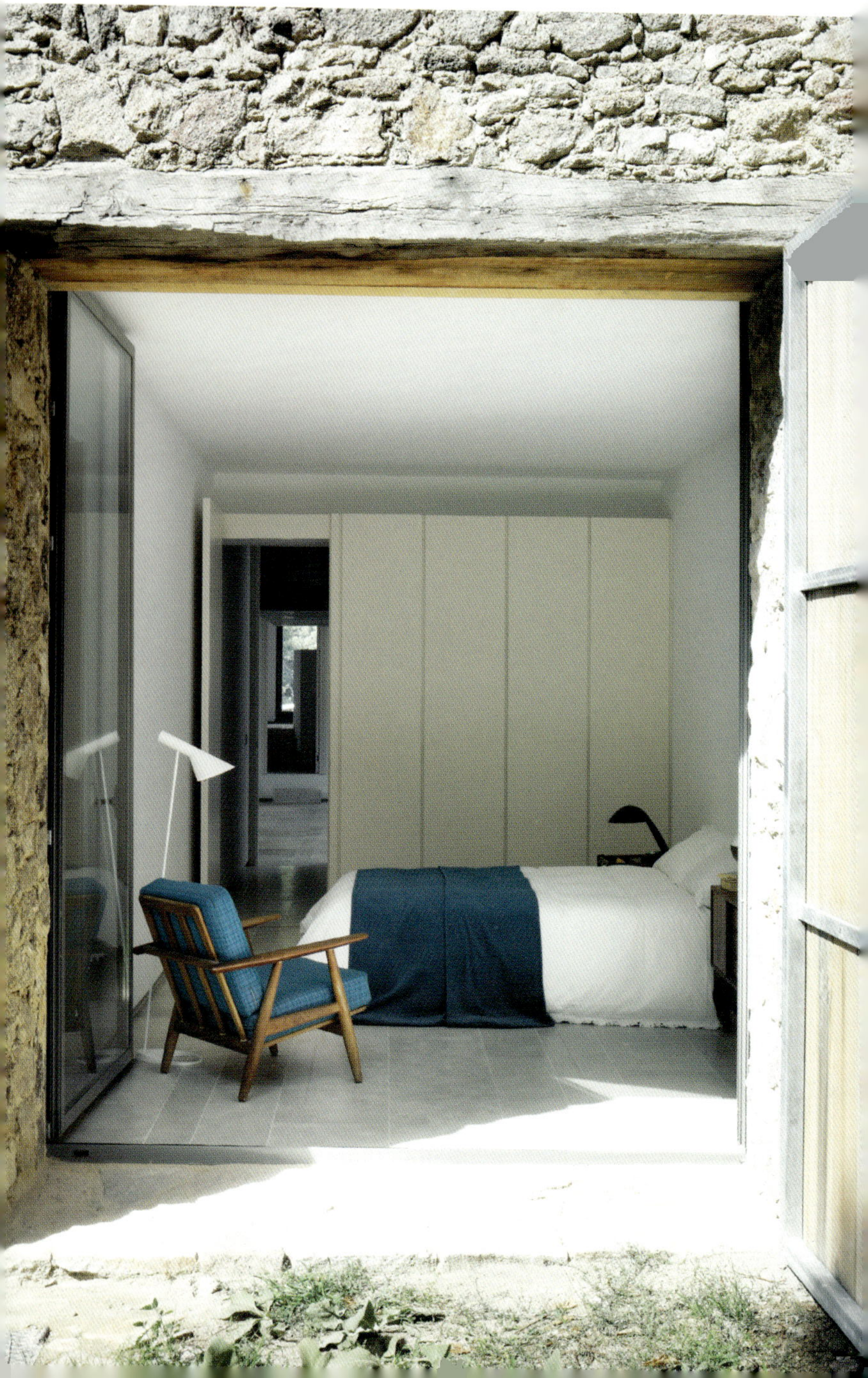

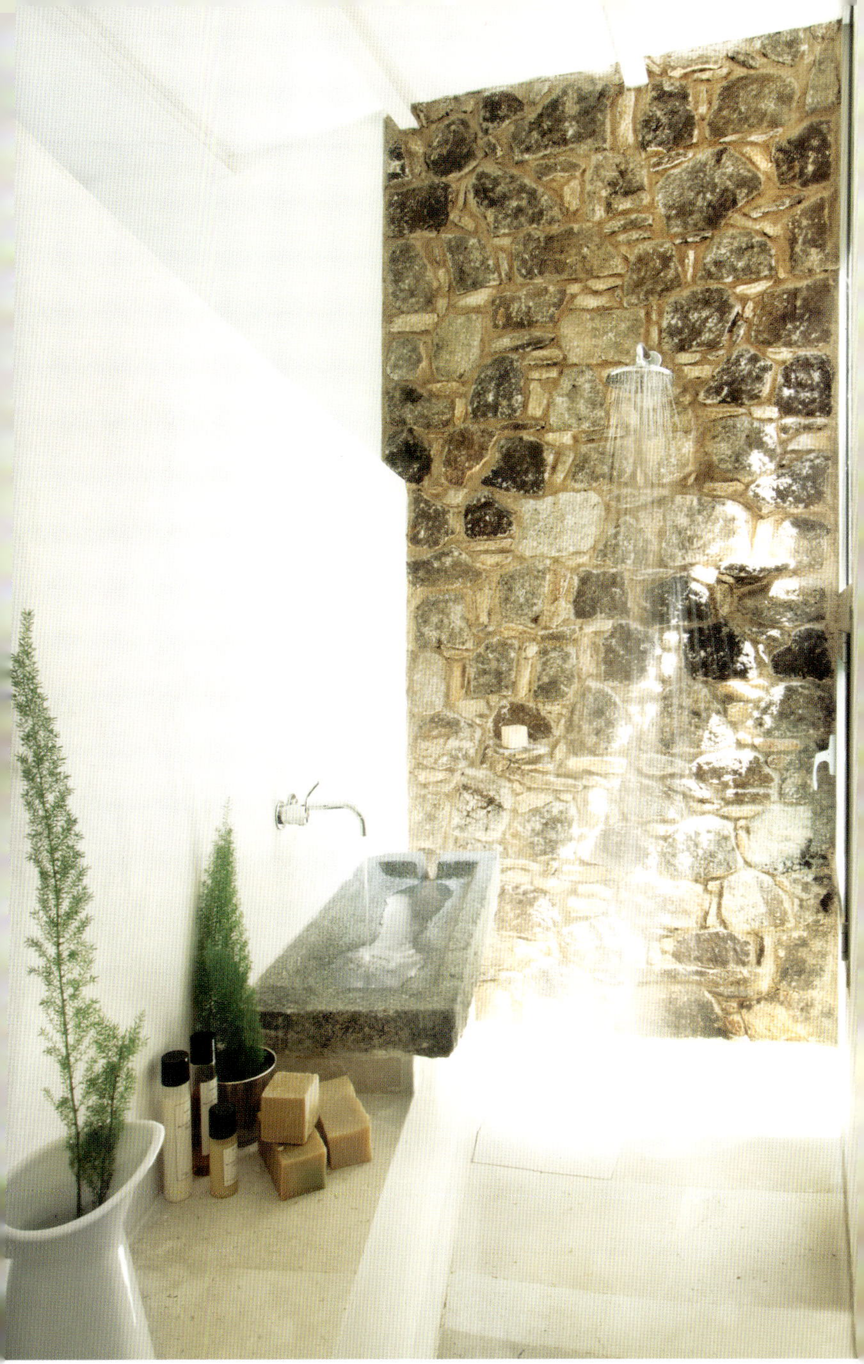

House in Ukraine | Dniepropetrovsk | Yakusha design

Contemporary interior in a Bavarian style house

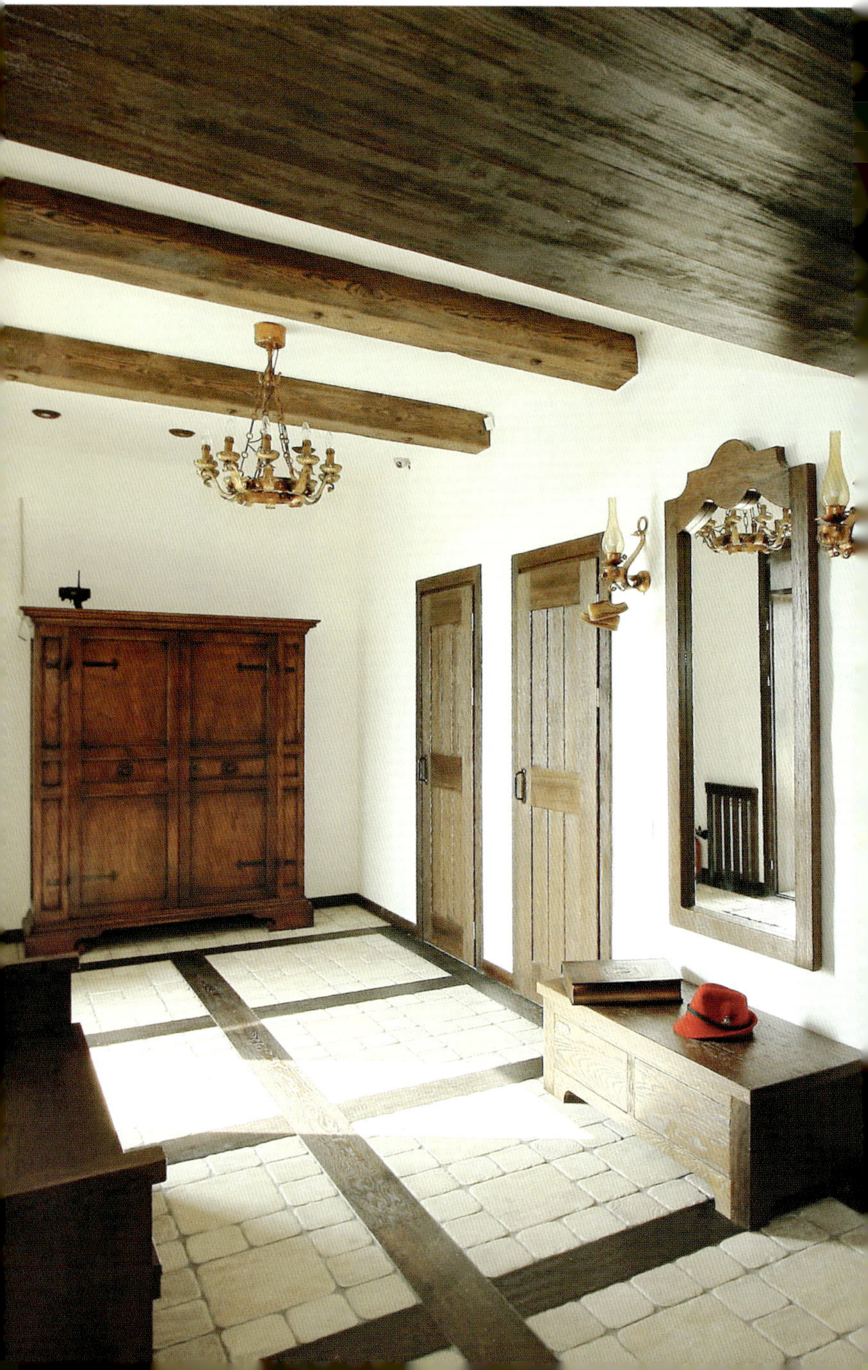

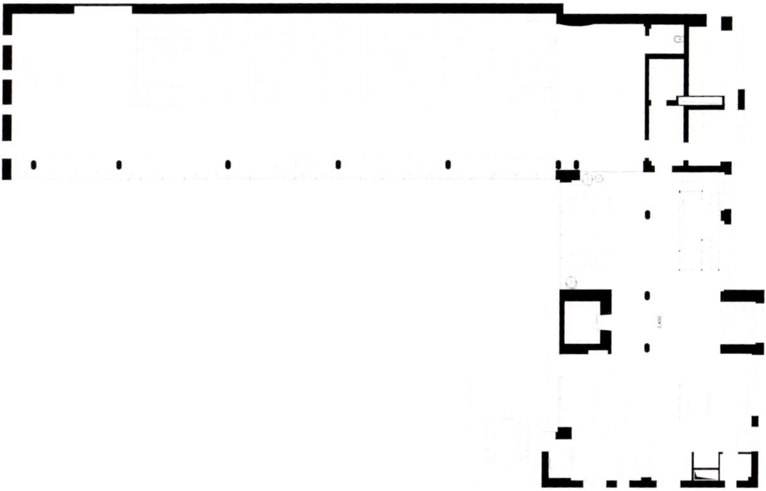

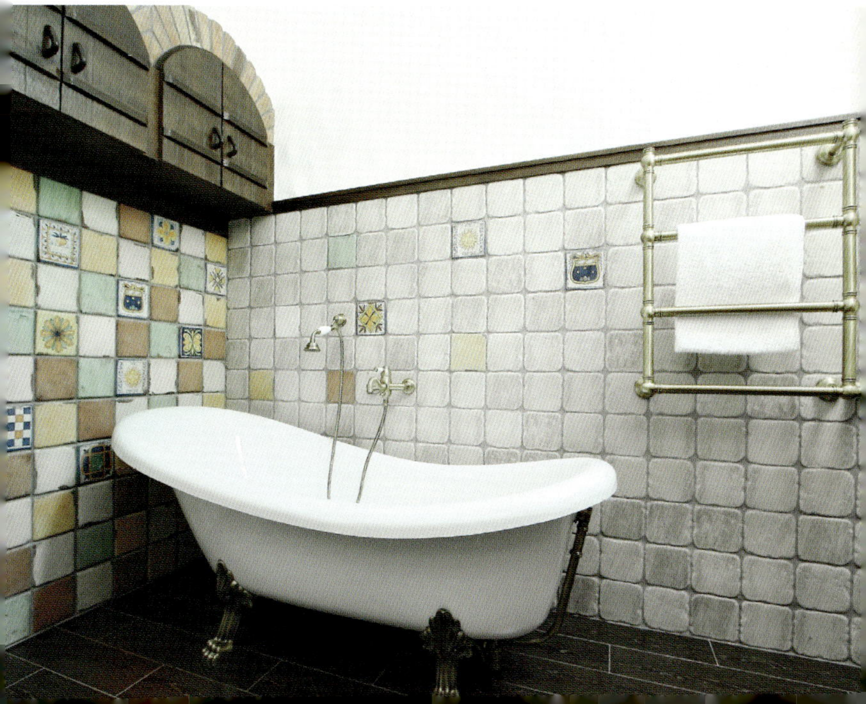

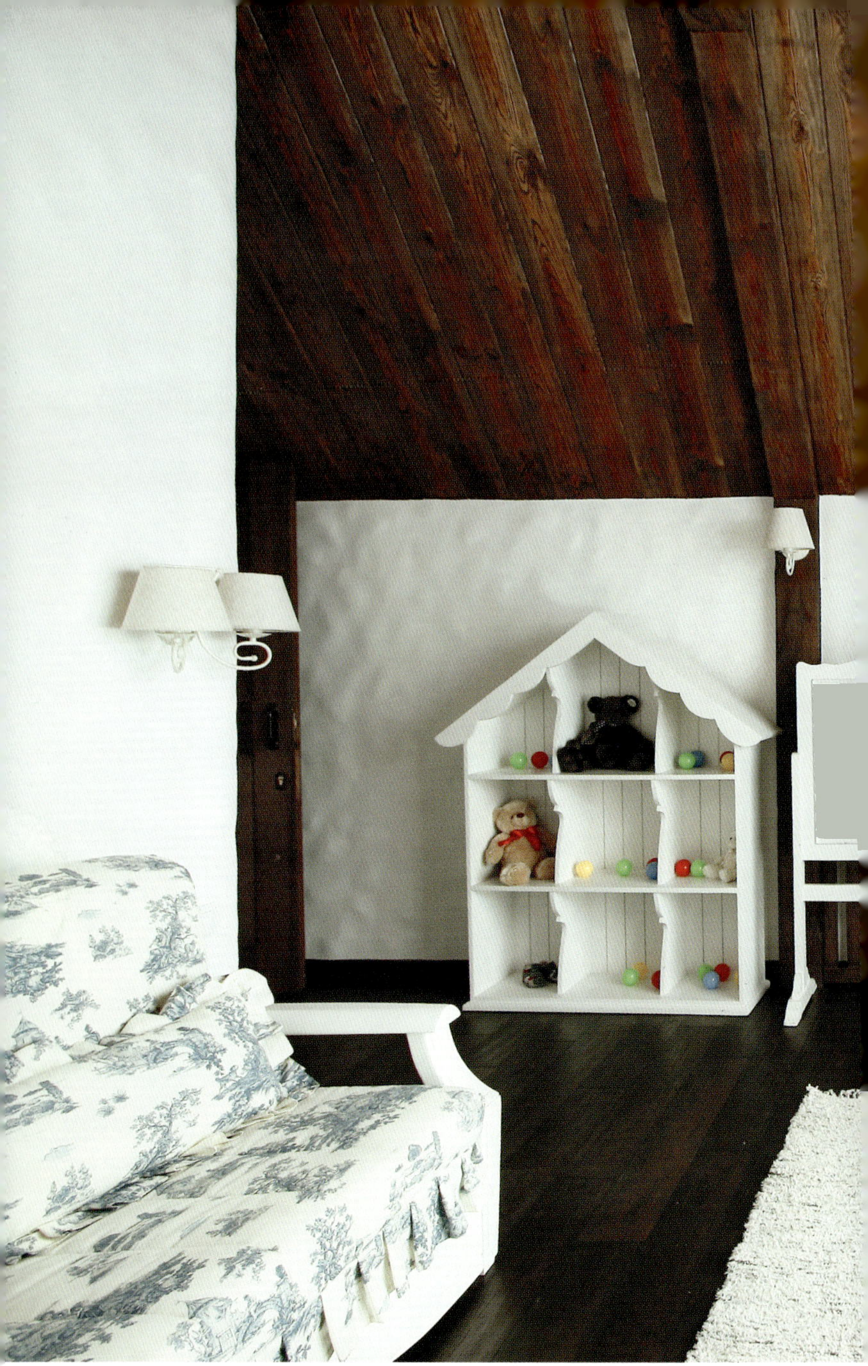

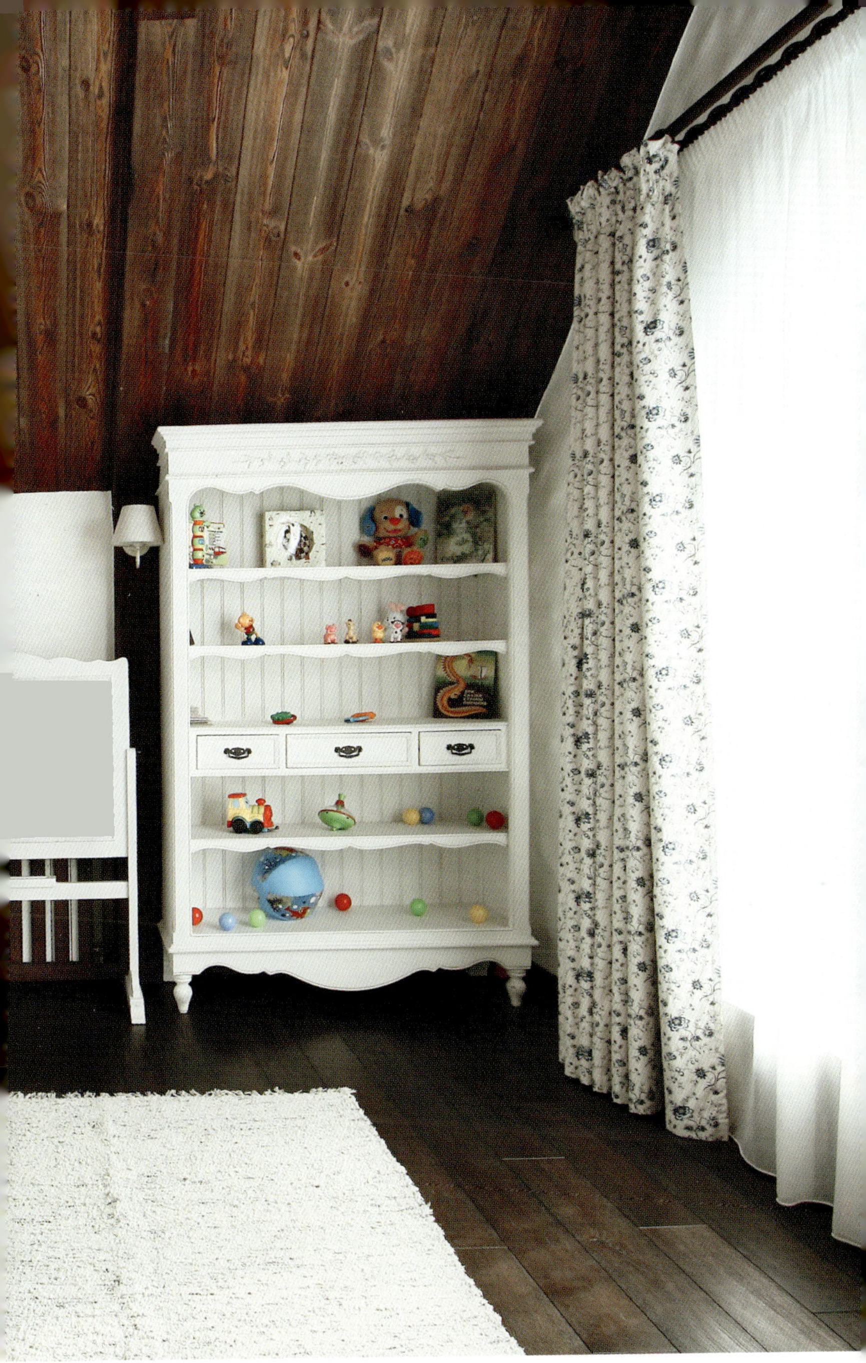

58 | **Benoit Residence** | Emeryville | Peter Benoit

A sunlit masterwork space completely customized

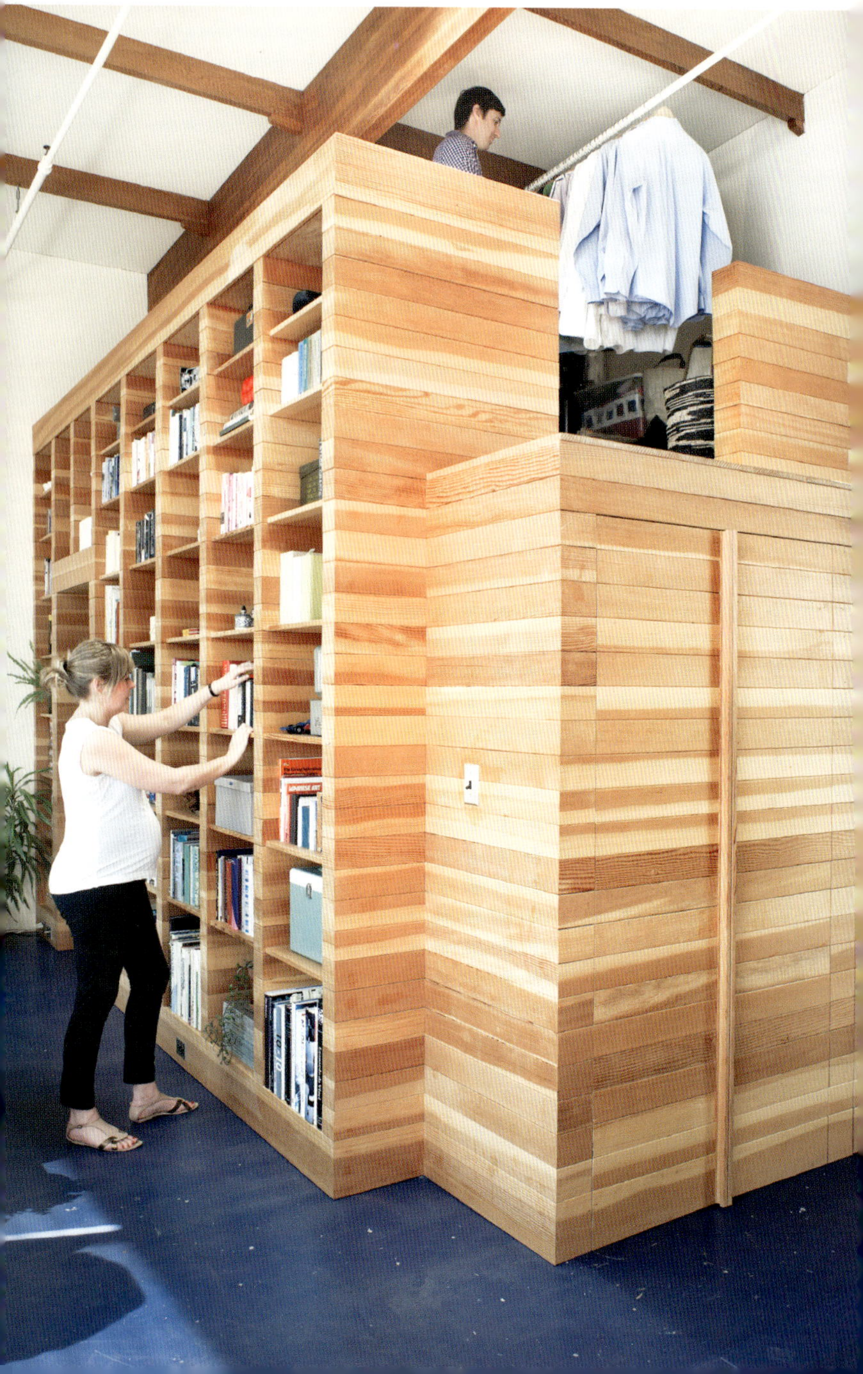

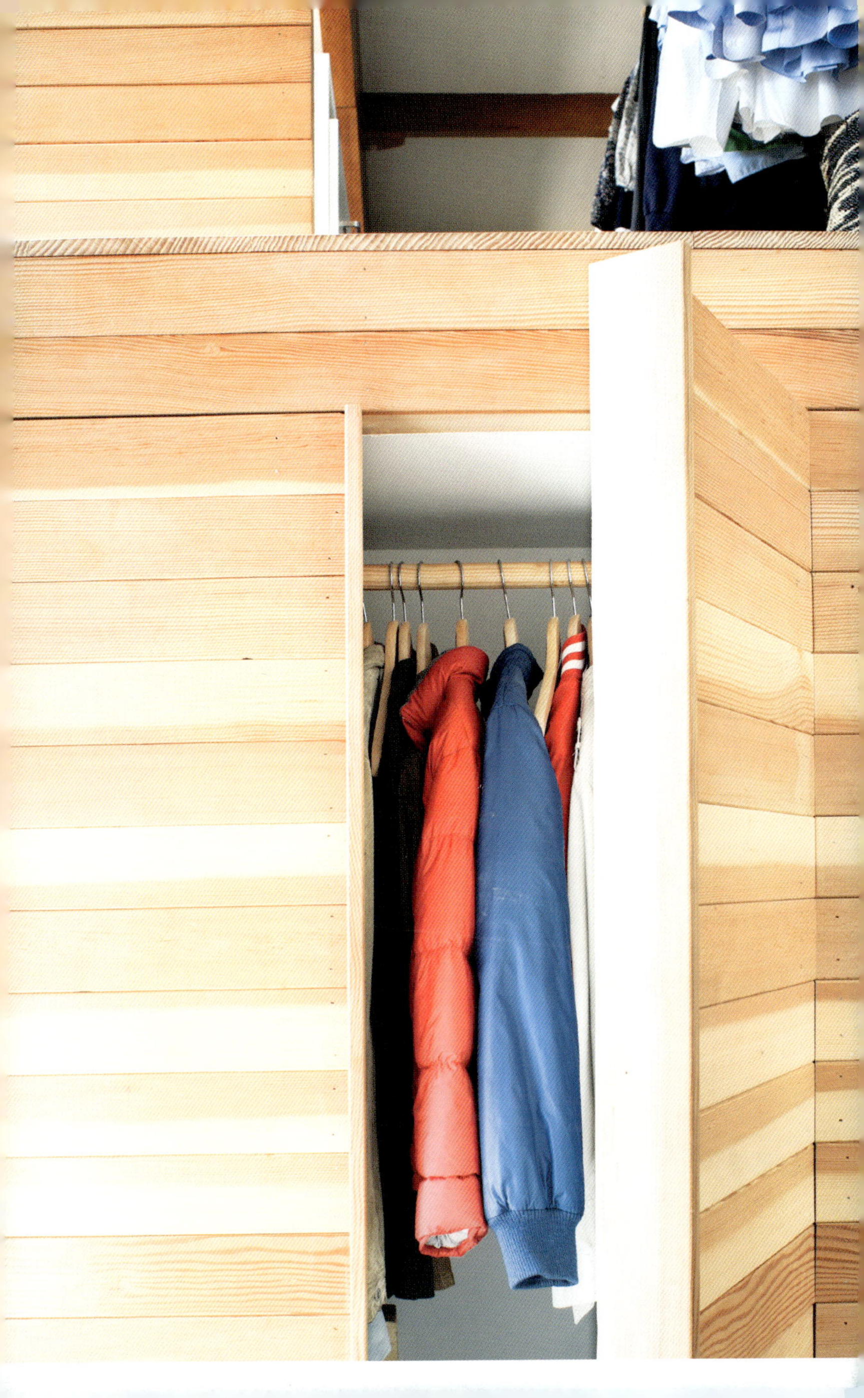

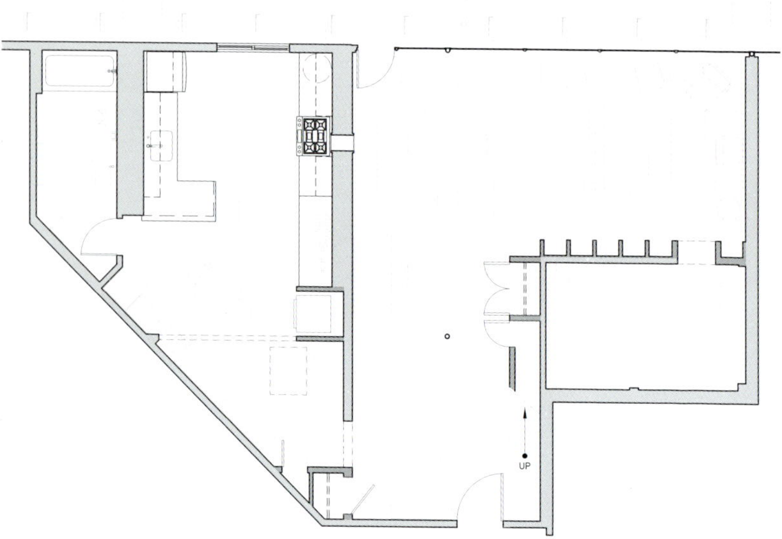
UP

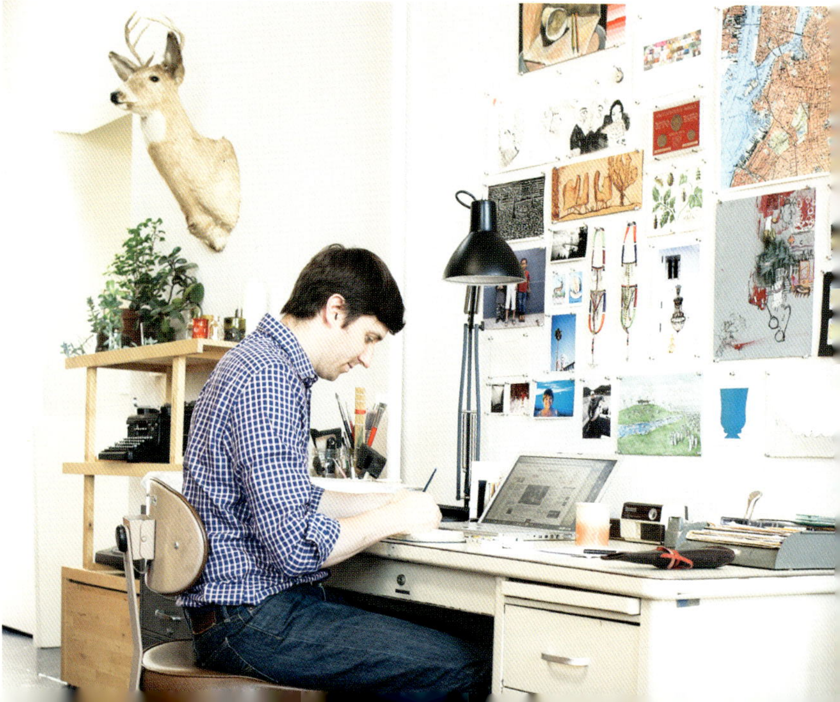

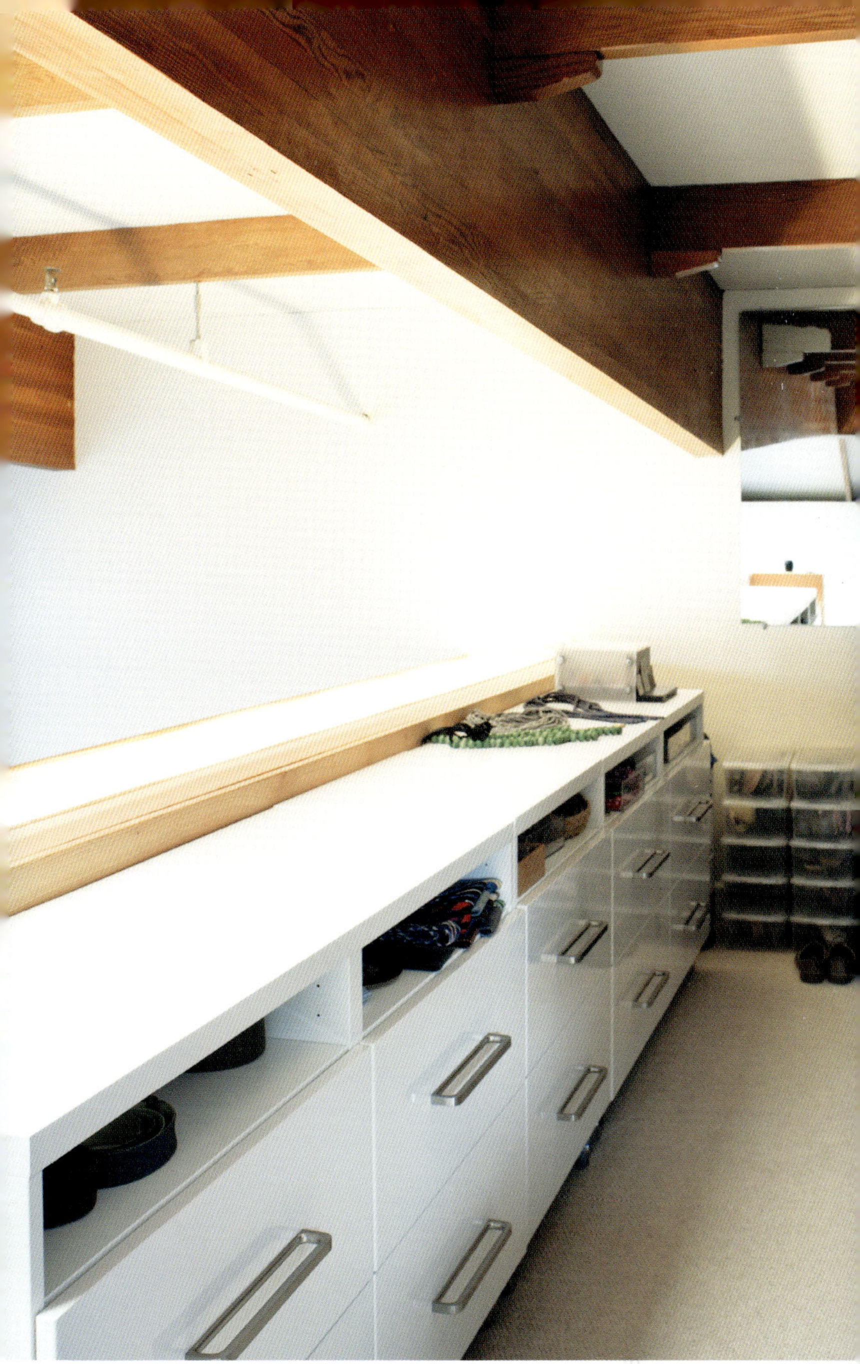

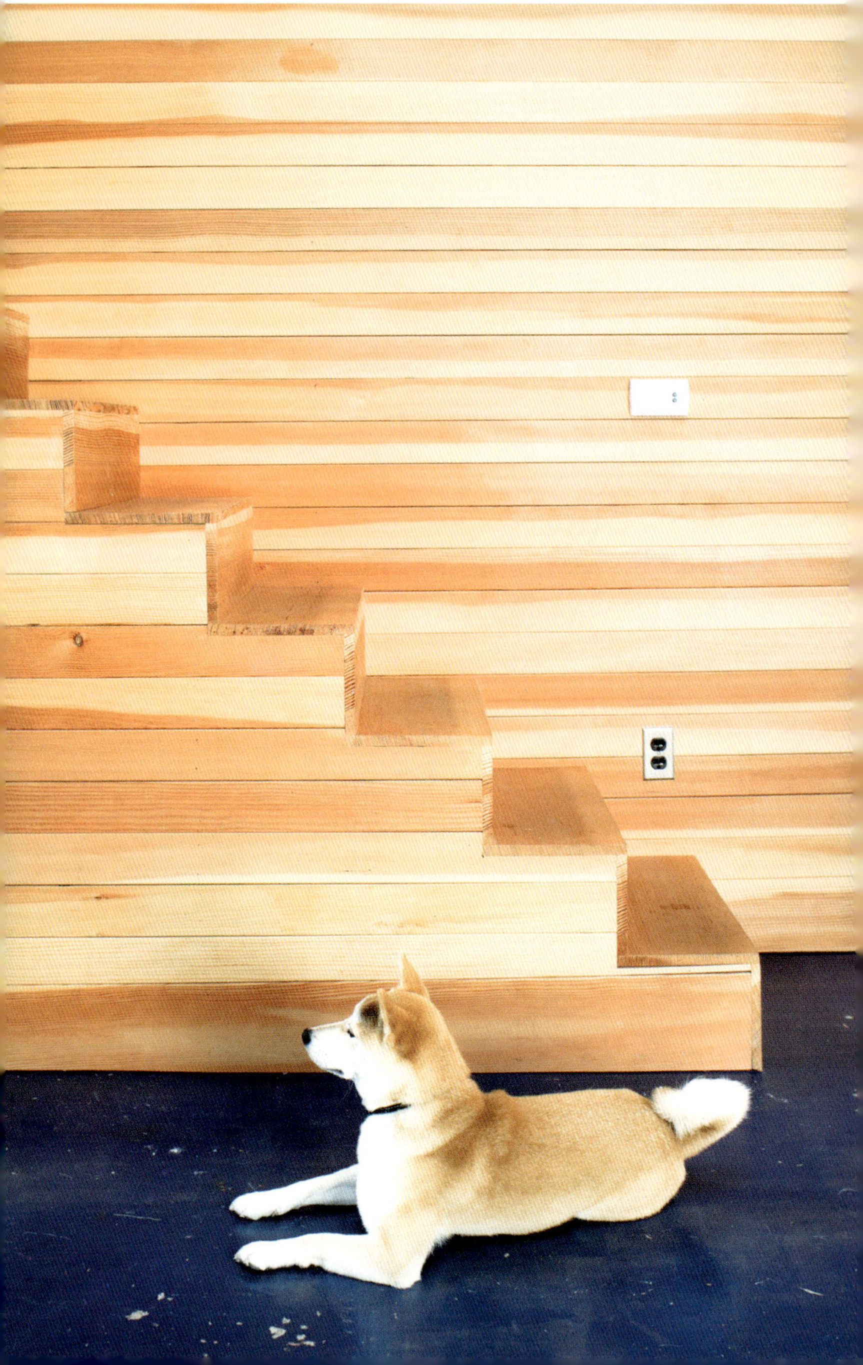

atlas folio
Denmark
GERMAN SHEPHERD
SPAIN
SPAIN
Valley of the Dolls
ABCD
THE BIG DIG
WOOD DESIGN

Vintage pieces provide balance and simplicity to the interior.

Corkellis House | Falmouth | Linea Studio/Kathryn Tyler

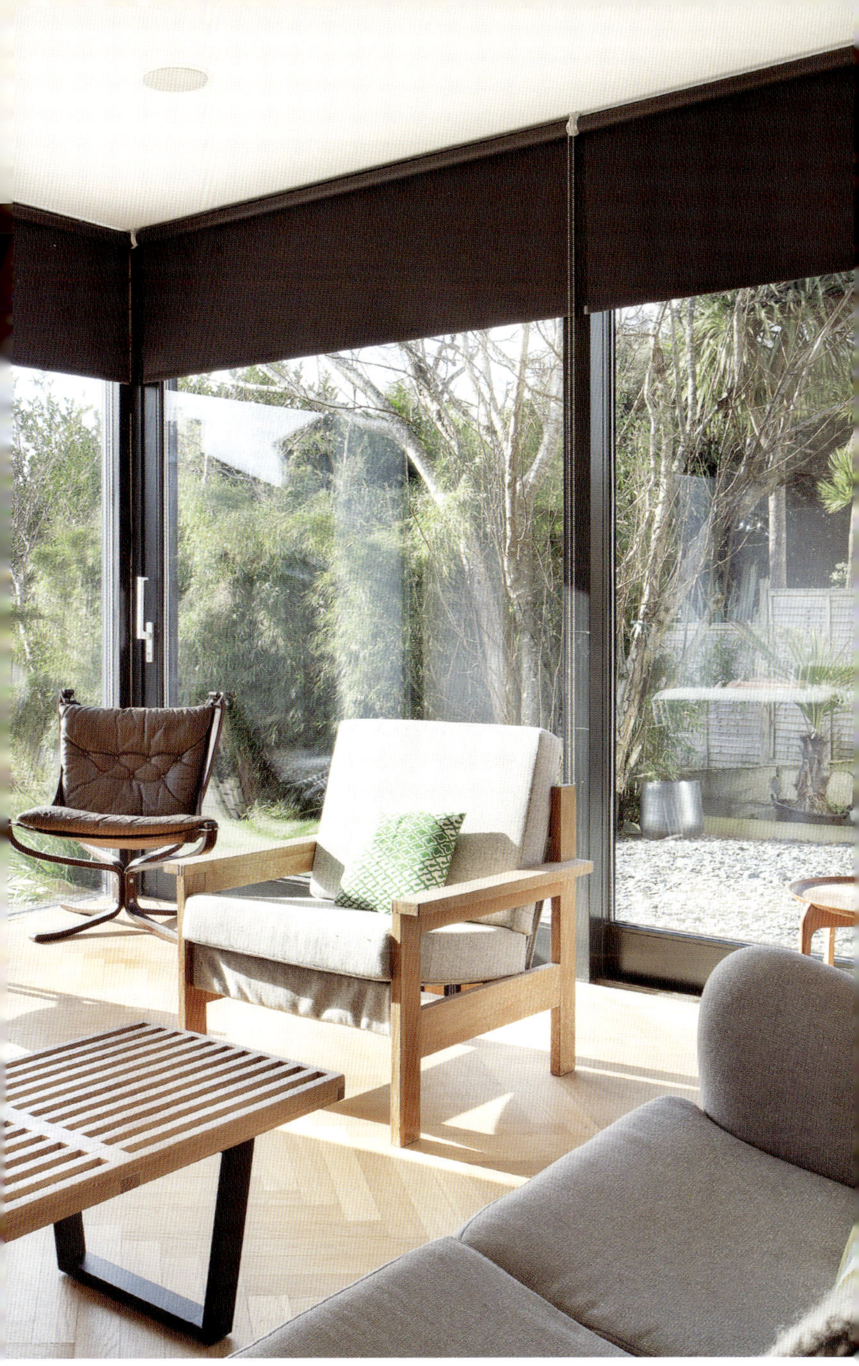

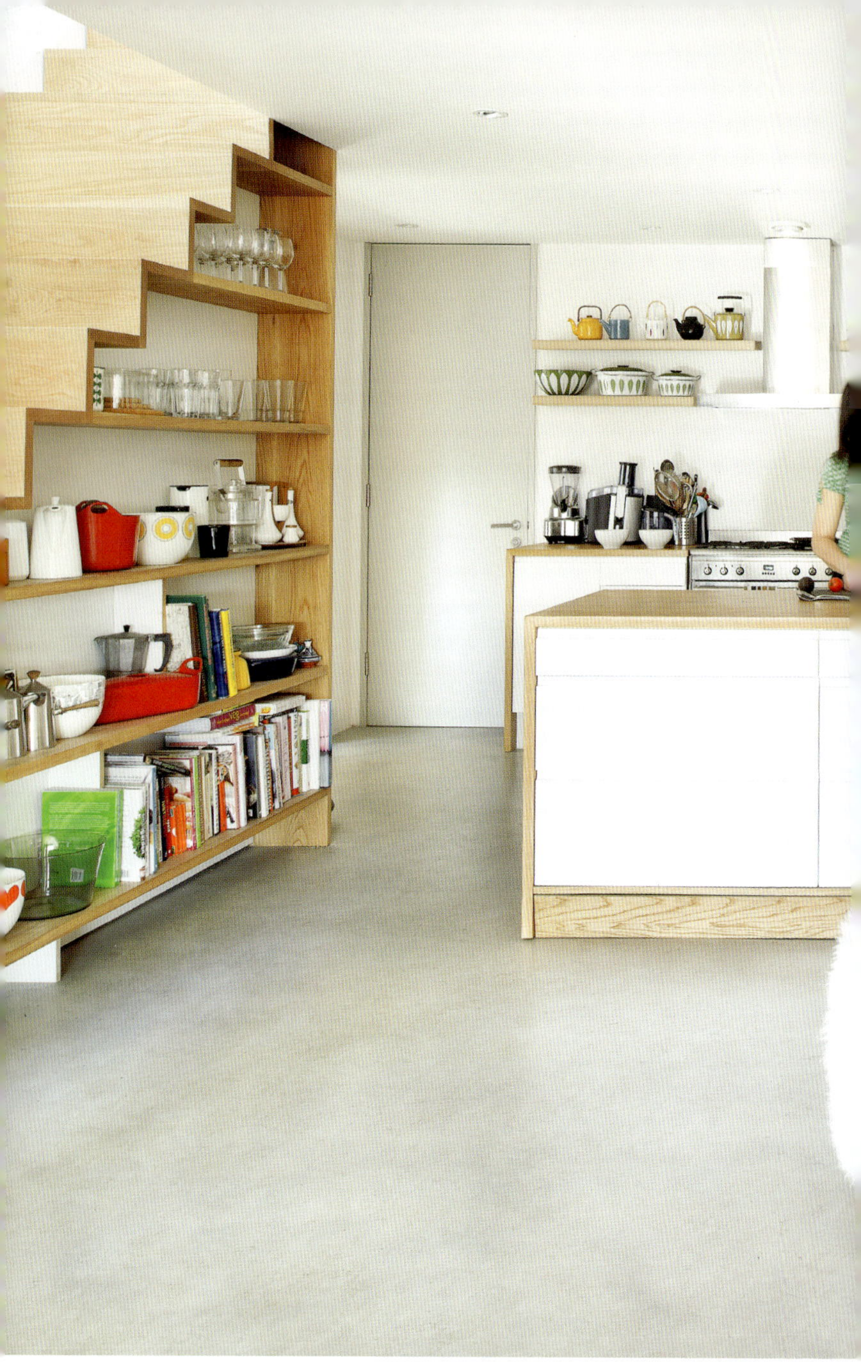

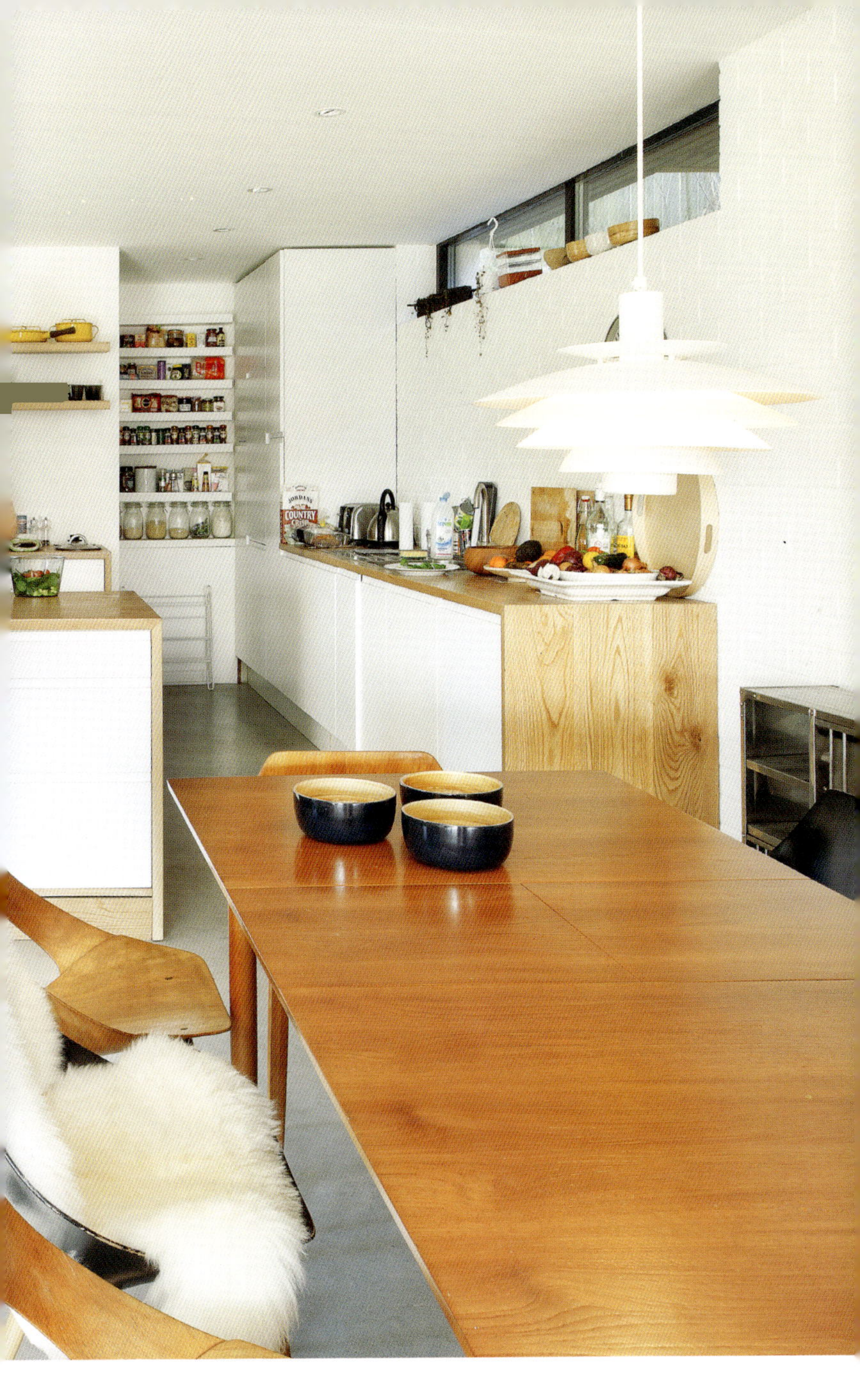
COUNTRY

Ellsworth
Kelly
The
Detroit
Institute
of
Arts
June 25 – August 11

Arts Council
exhibition of
reproductions:
the human figure
in European
painting
Ecole
de
Paris

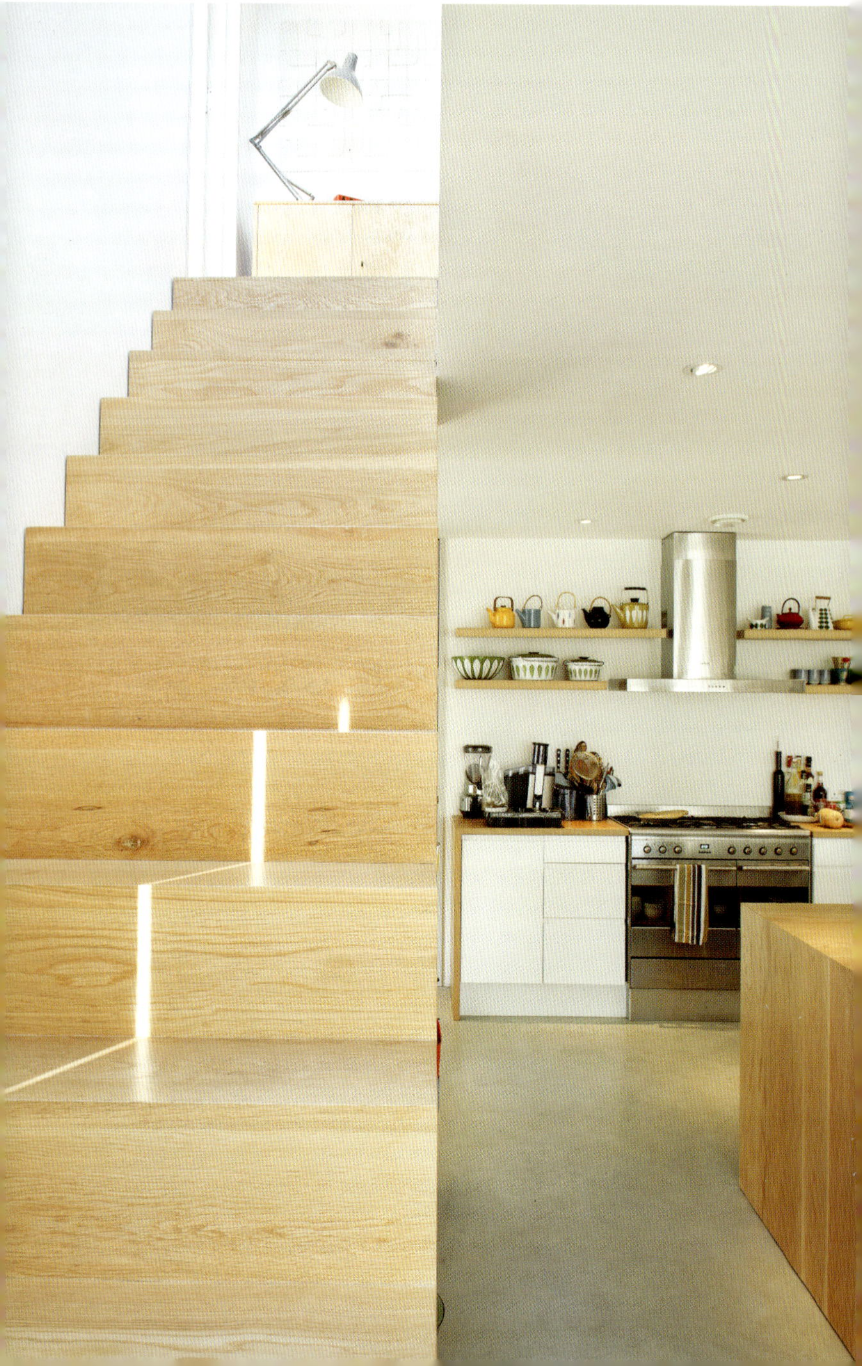

Landscape in western art
20th century Drawings
new prints
Brueghel
Canaletto
Modern Gouaches and Watercolours
Arts Council exhibition of reproductions: the human figure in European painting
Ecole de Paris

74 | **Con&Vent House** | Kirchheim | Alexander Brenner Architekten

Monastic composition for two families within protective walls

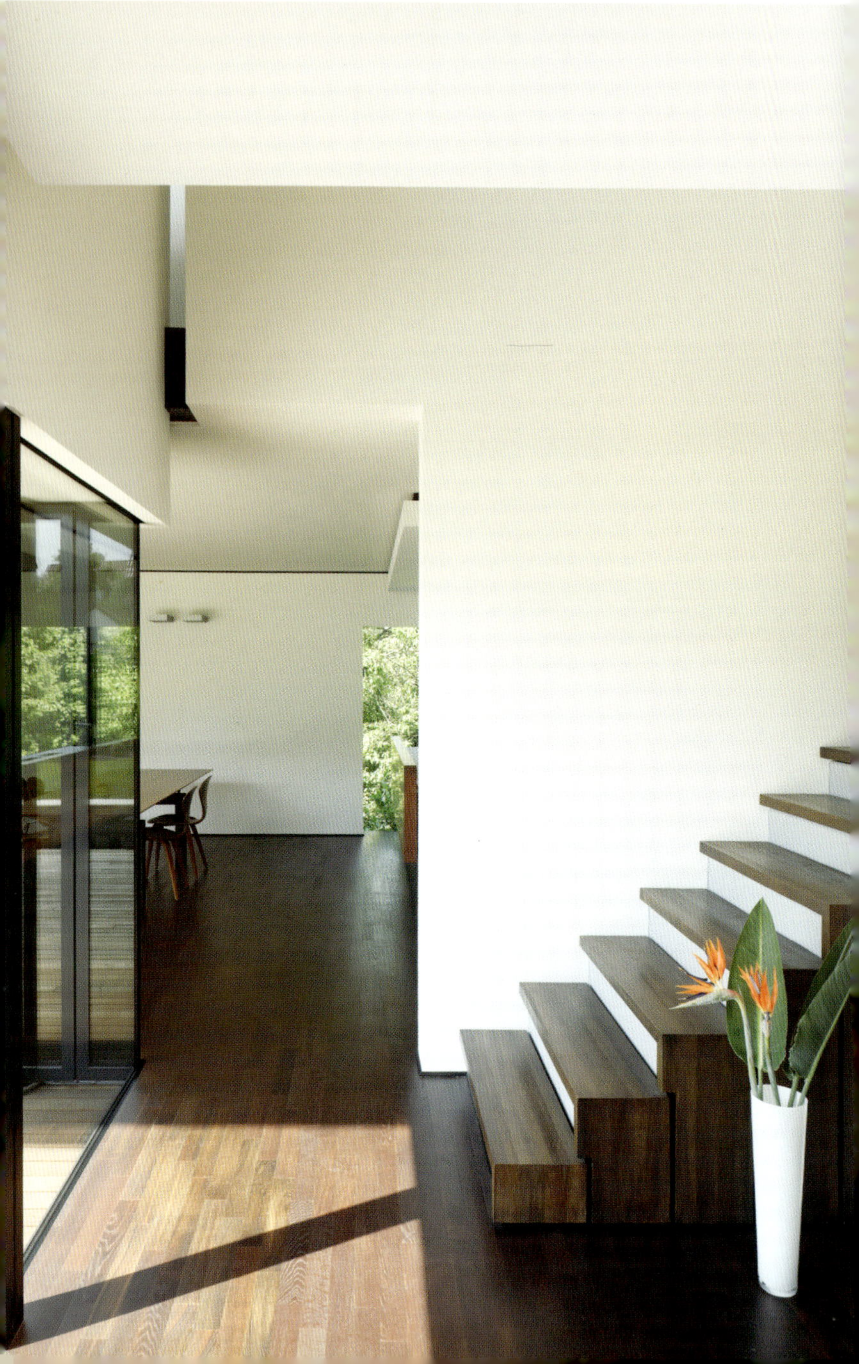

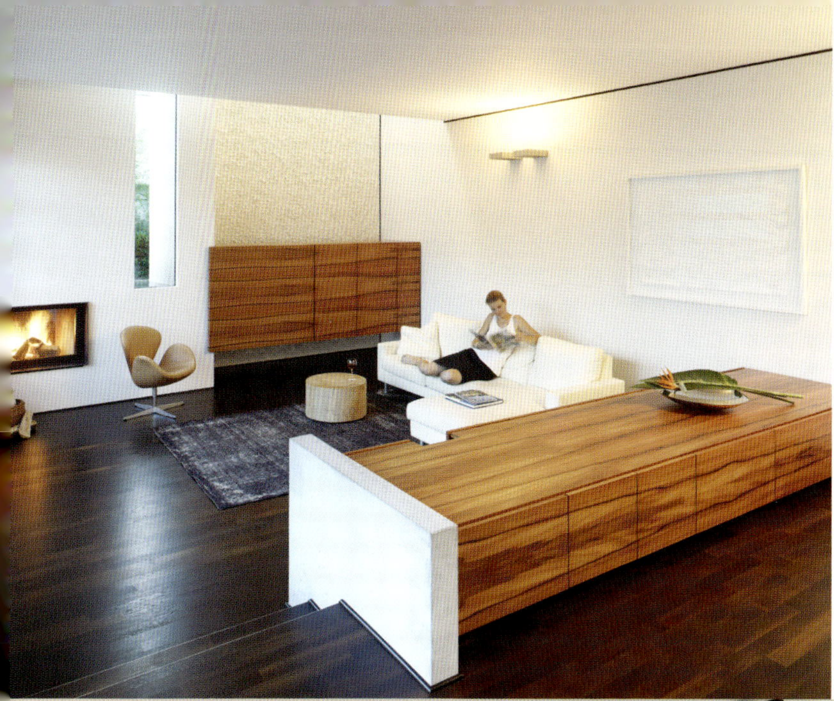

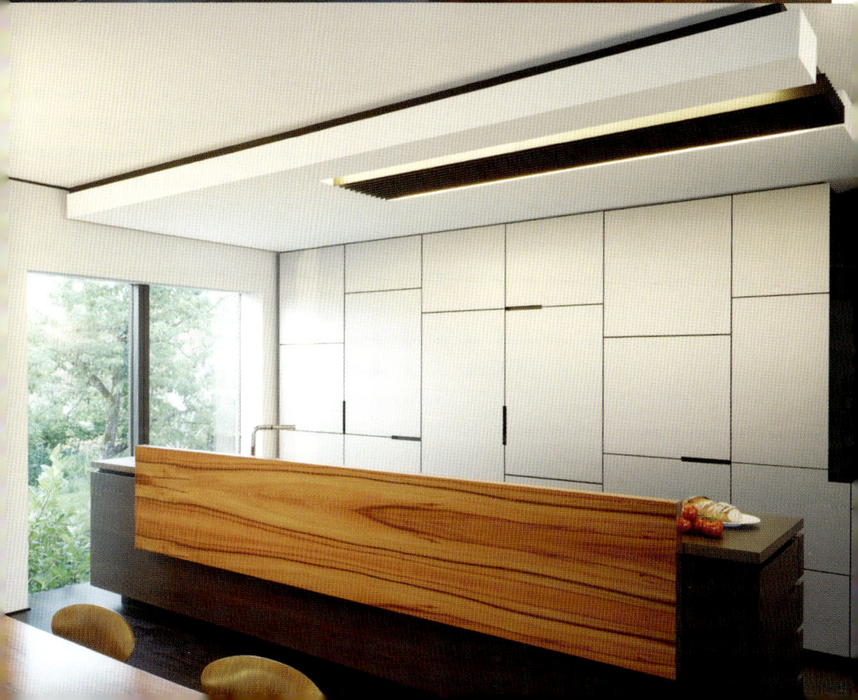

Interior with spatial fluidity and emphasis on natural materials

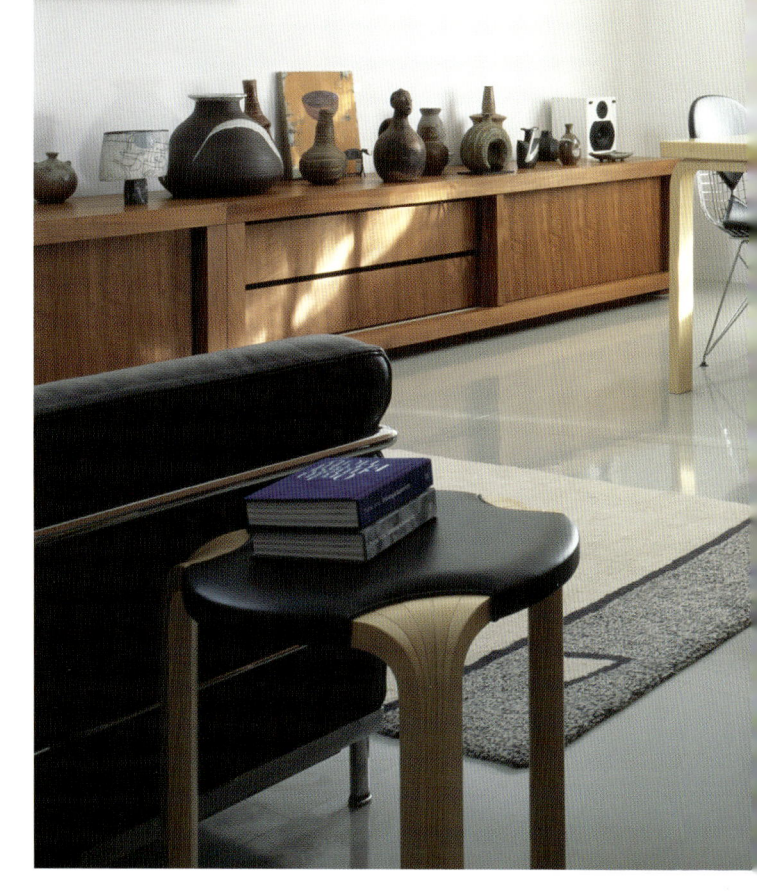

Little Venice Apartment | London | Openstudio Architects

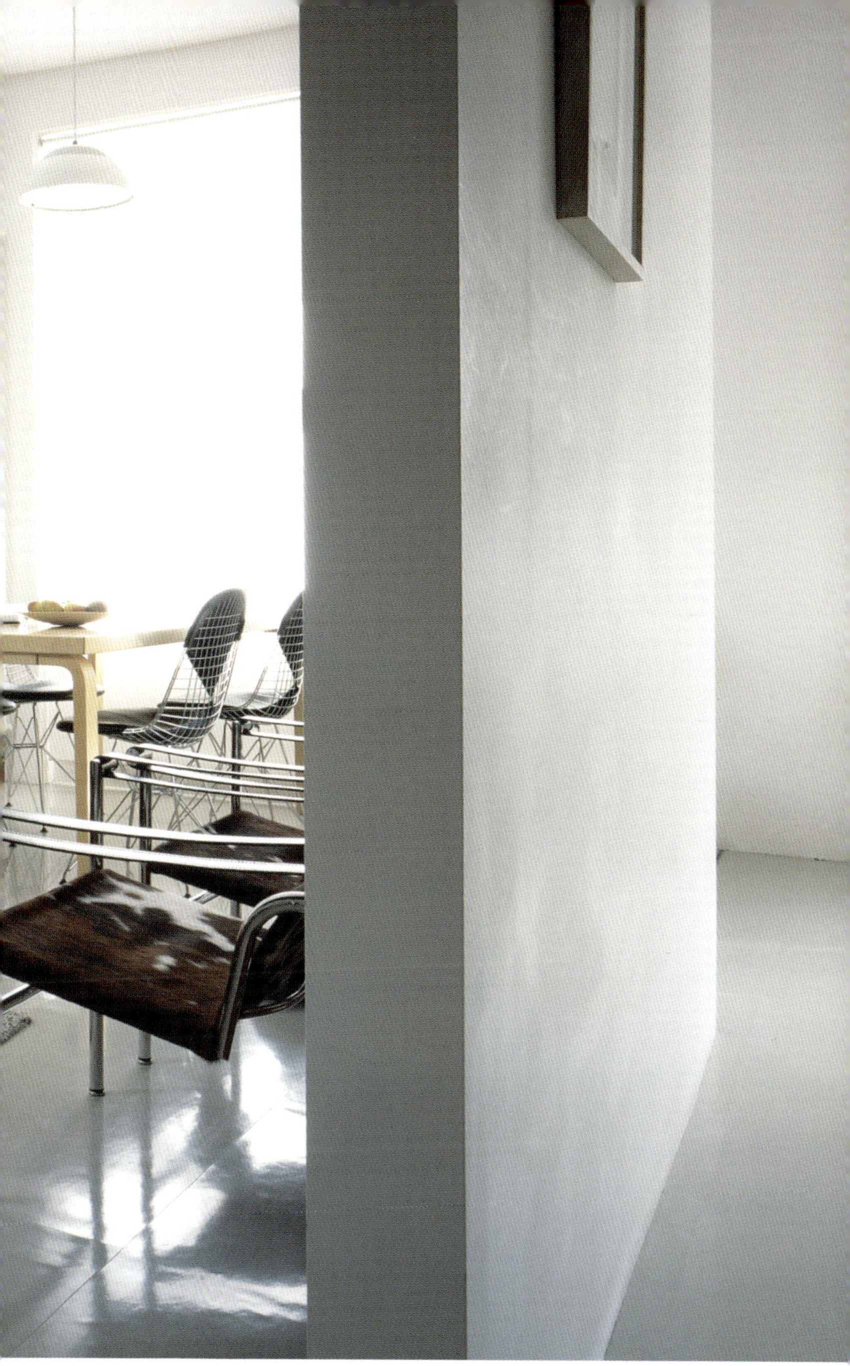

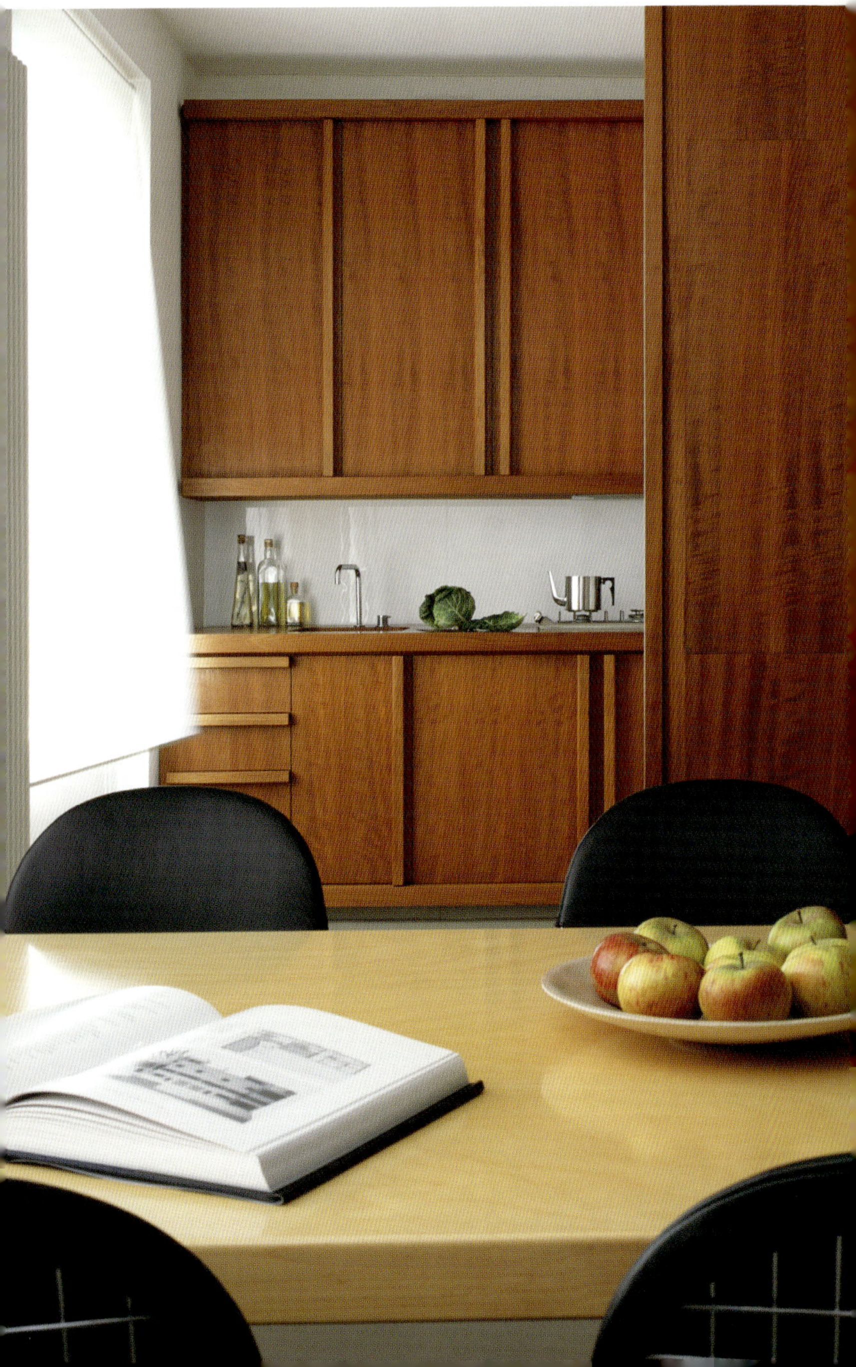

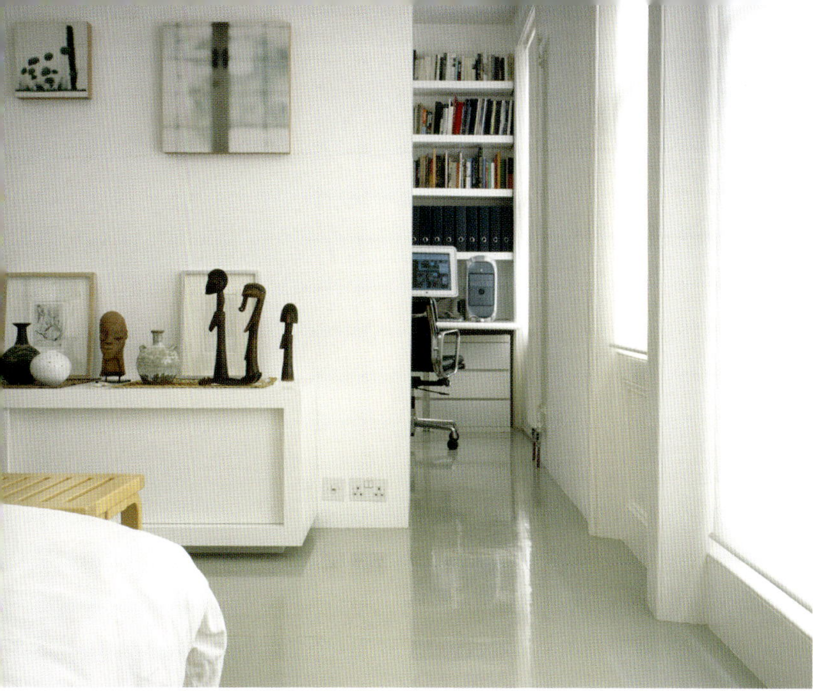

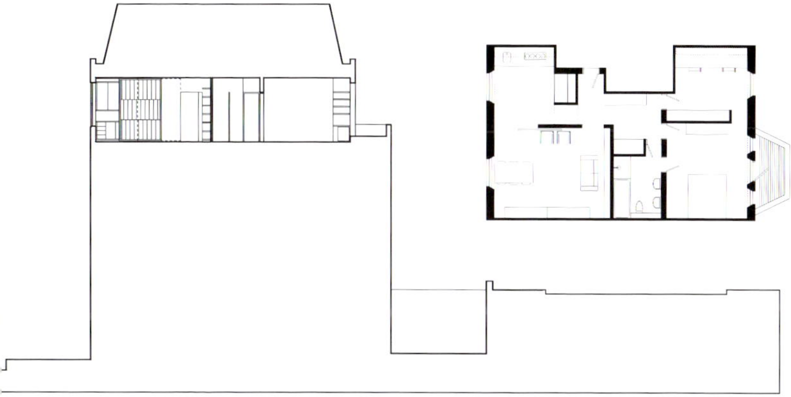

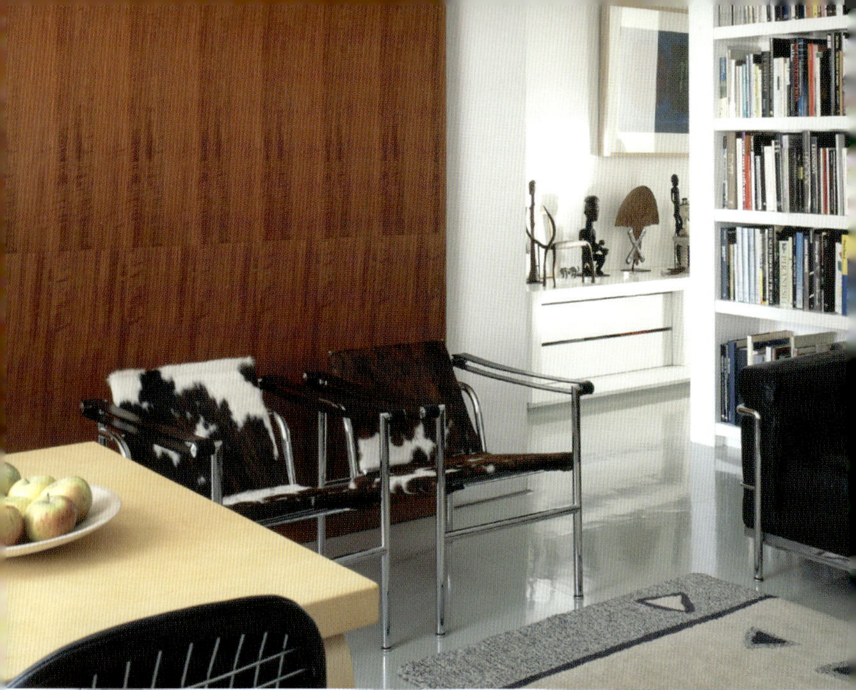

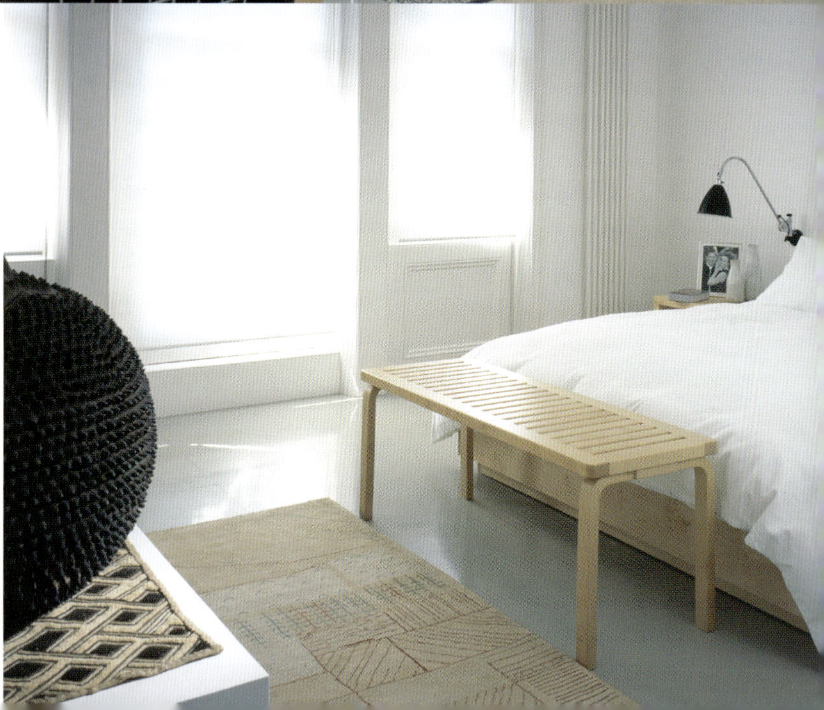

EGYPT
THE RENZO PIANO LOGBOOK
Shin Takamatsu
VENTURI SCOTT BROWN & ASSOCIATES
MORPHOSIS

Tex-Tonic House | London | Paul McAneary Architects

Loft-like space with natural tectonics **through new details and a** new material type of **cast timber bronze**

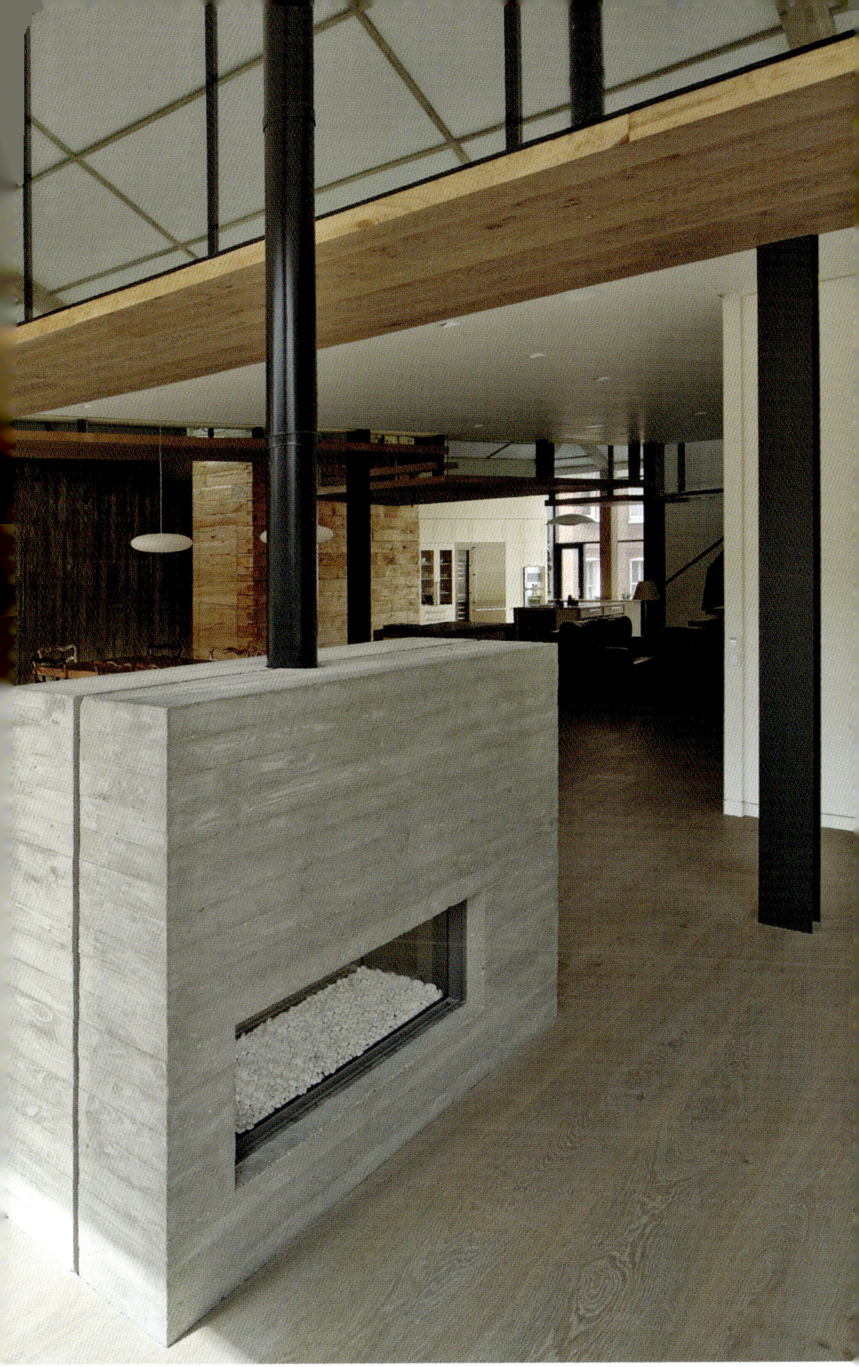

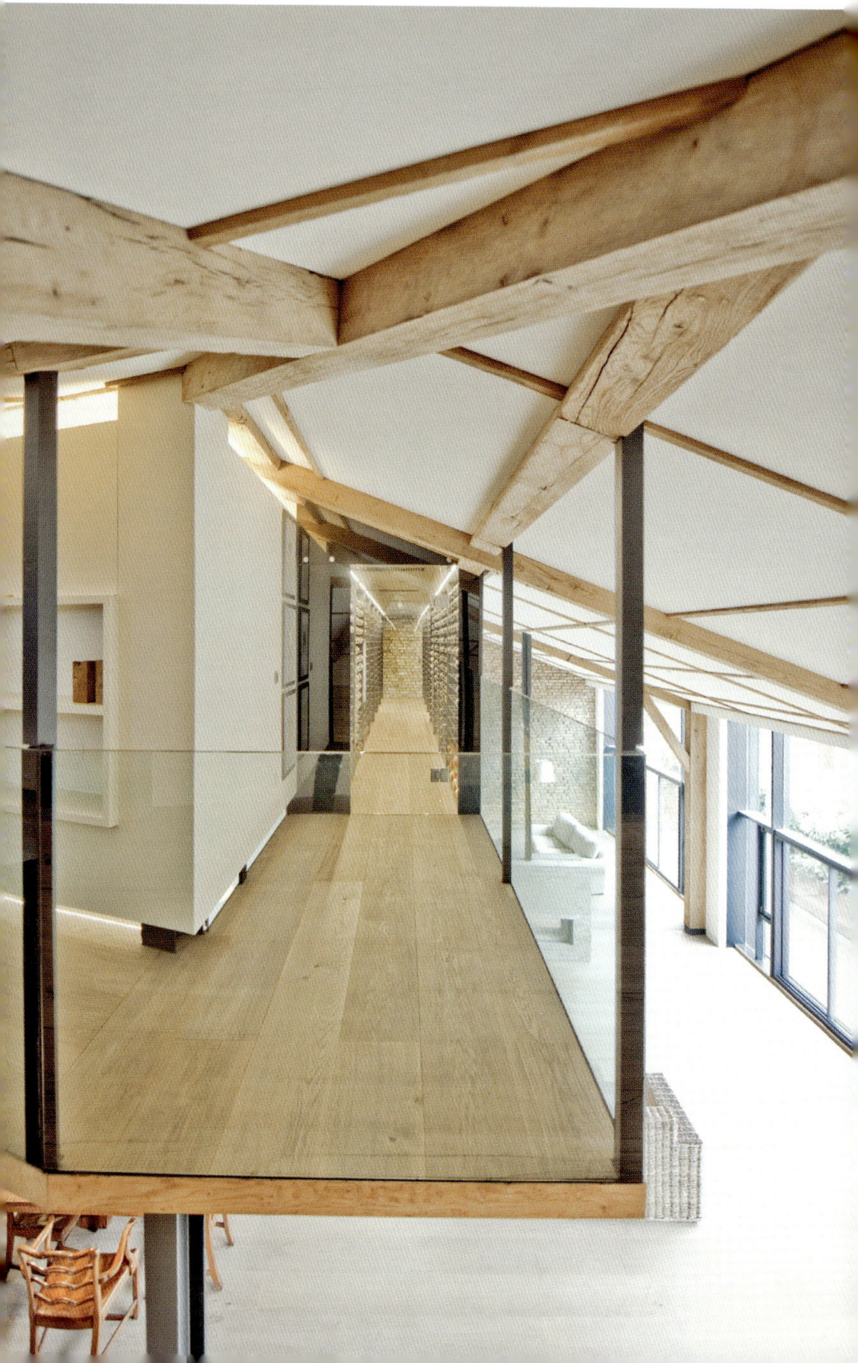

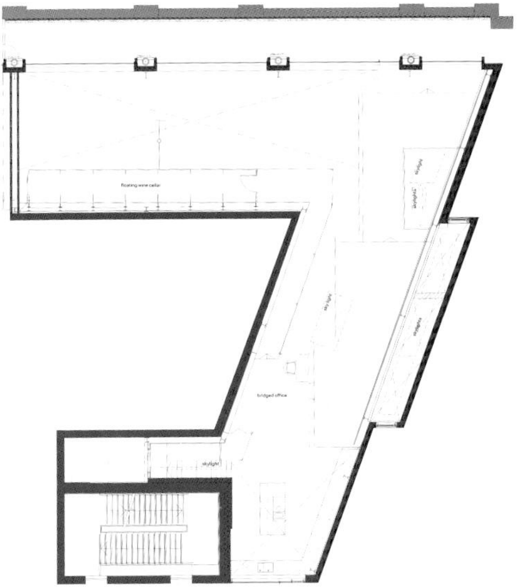

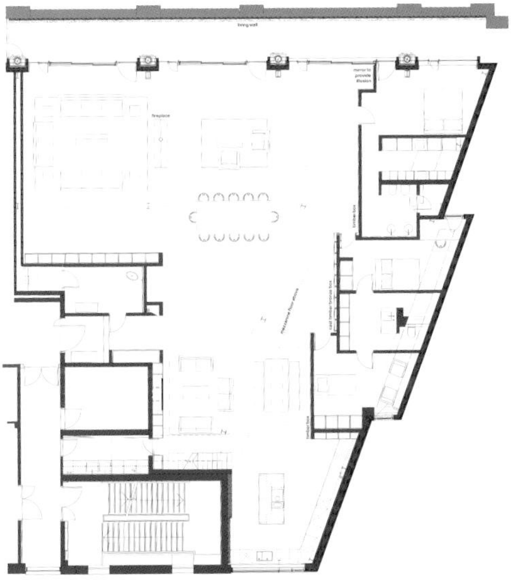

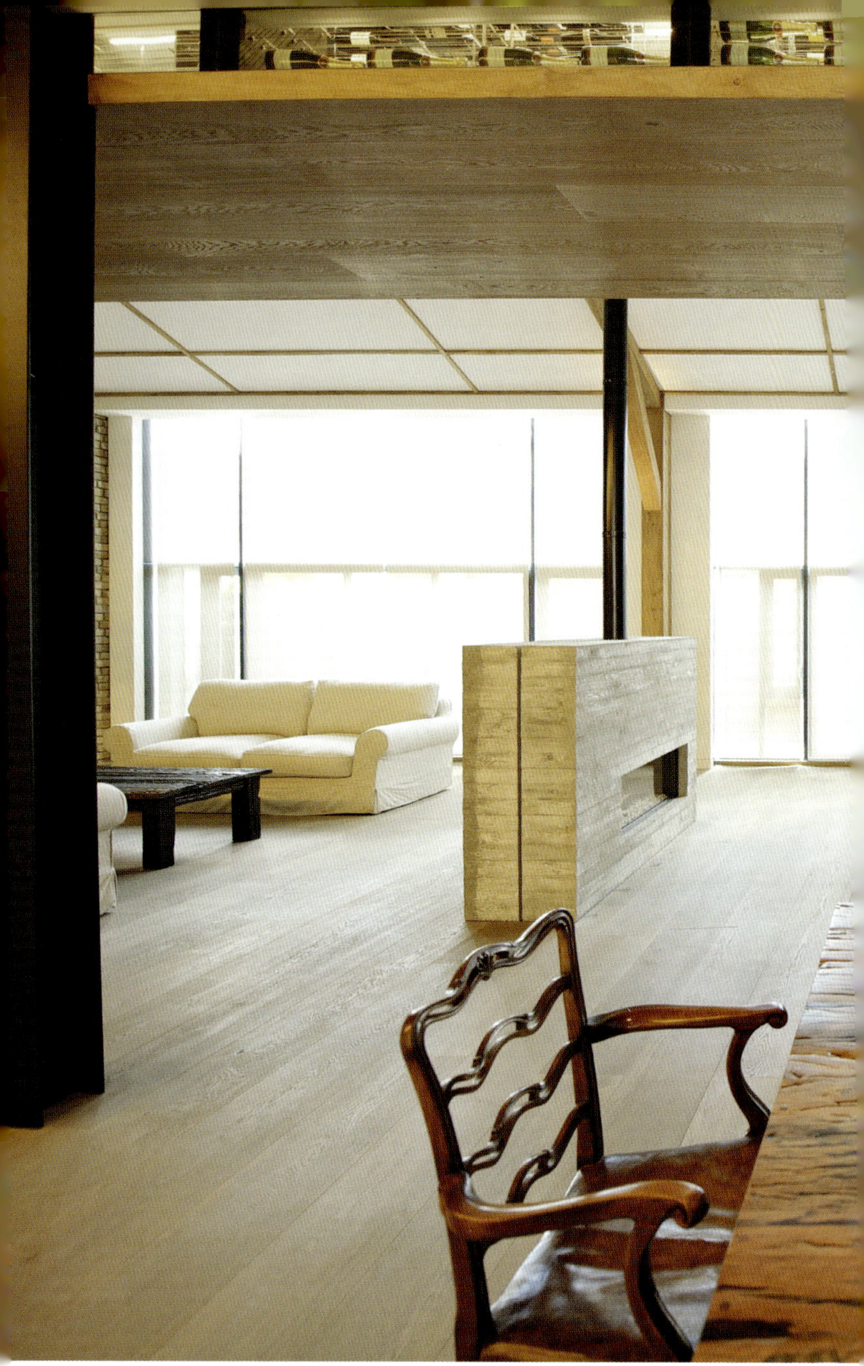

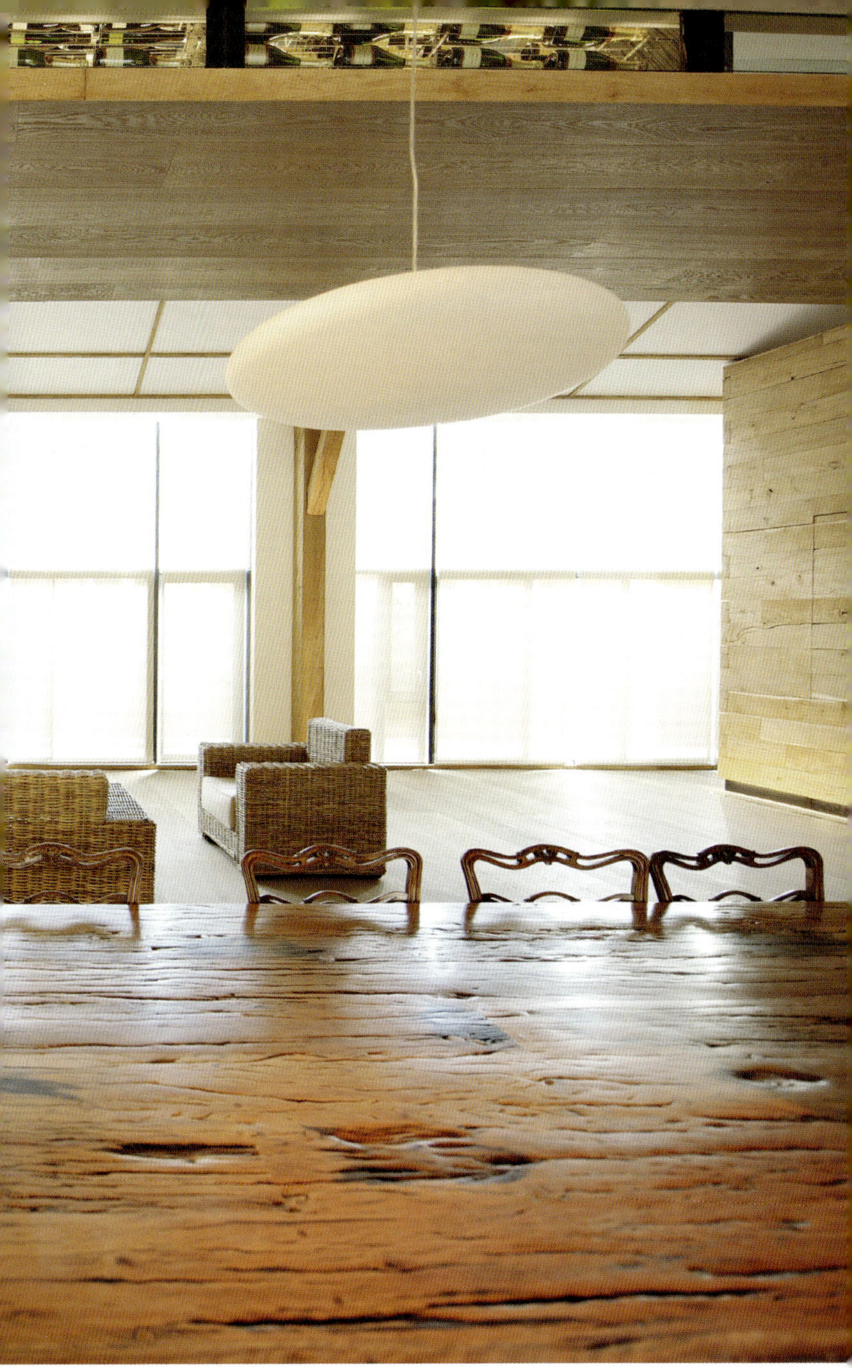

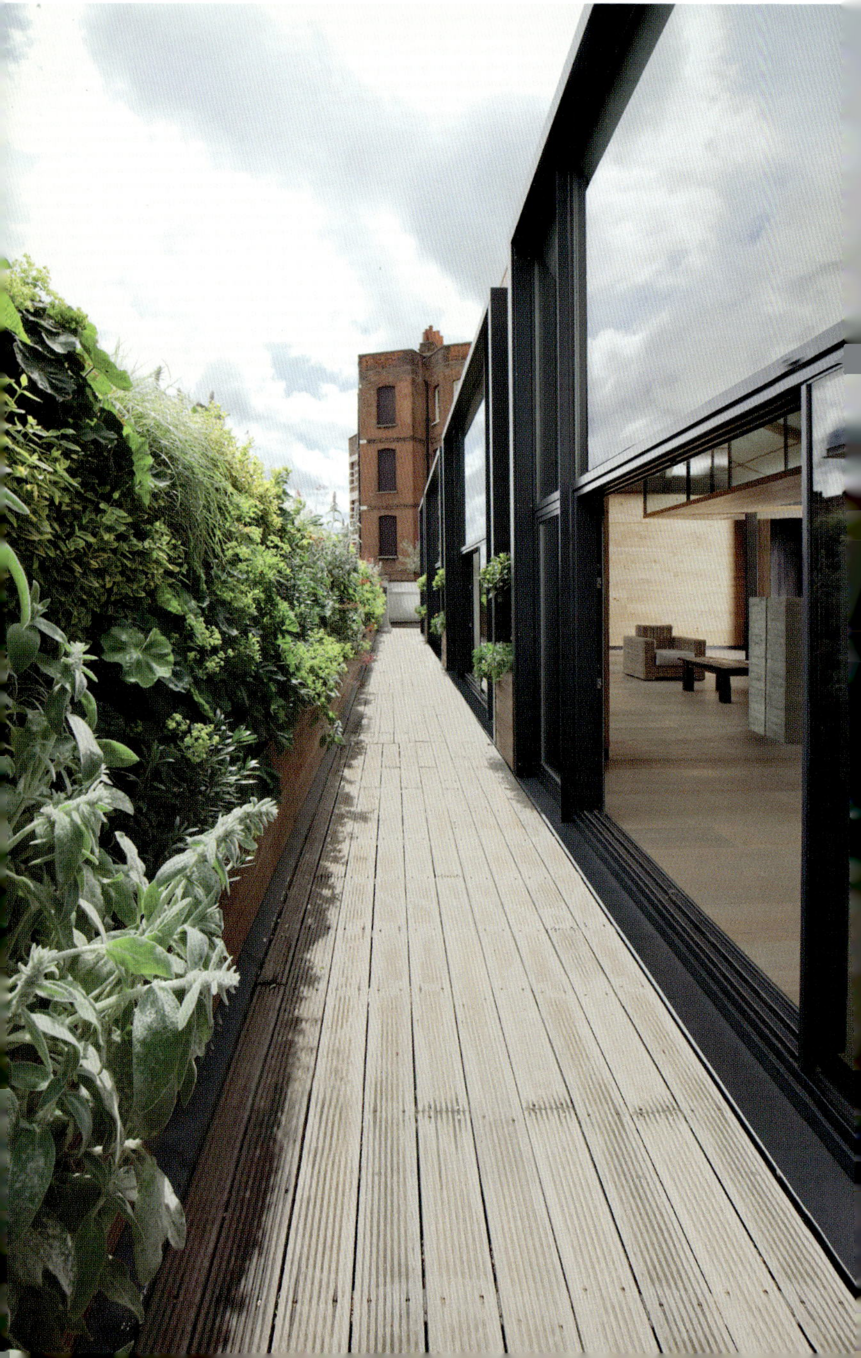

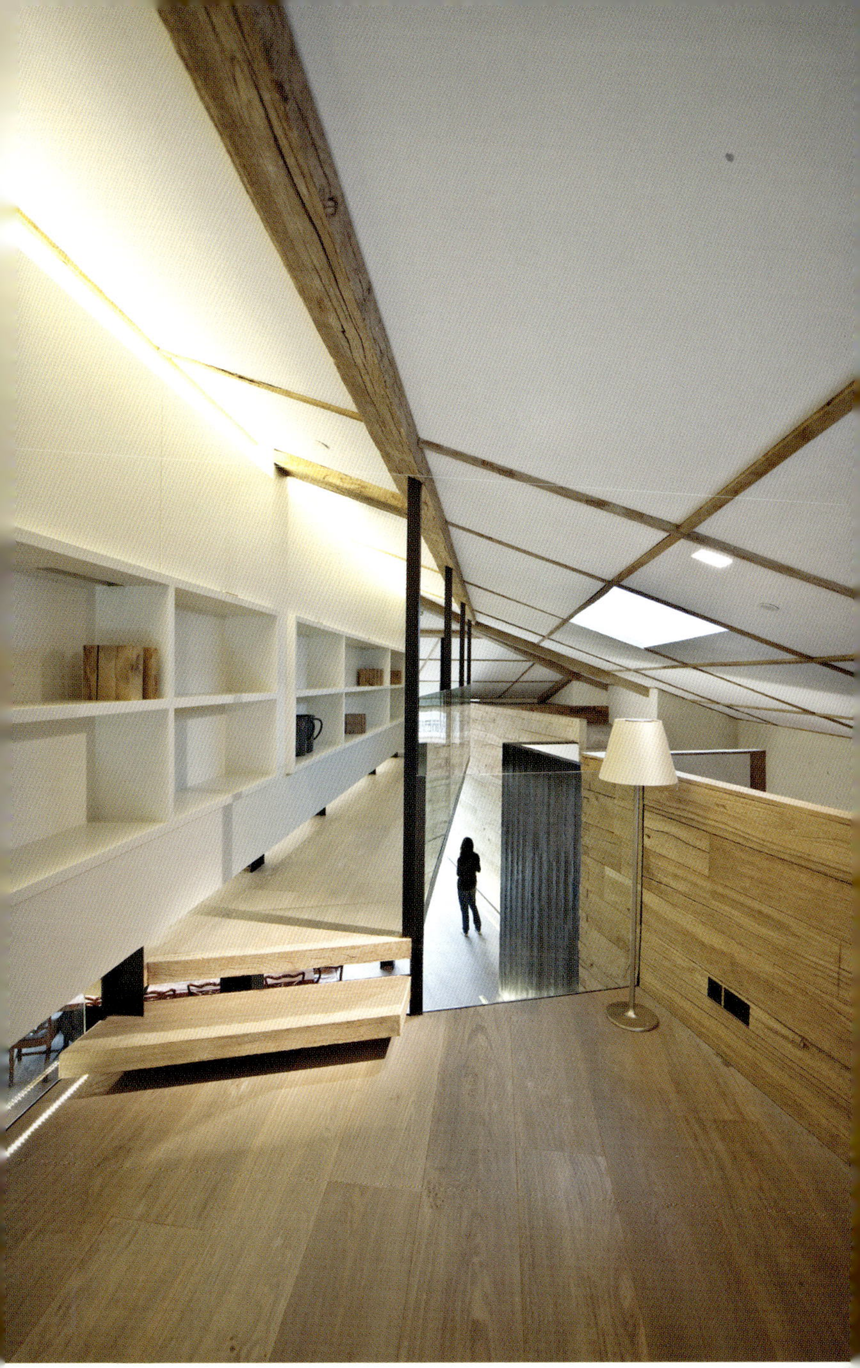

92 | **Hollywood House** | Los Angeles | Walker Workshop Design Build

Wood-filled modern bungalow with volumetric skylight at cor...

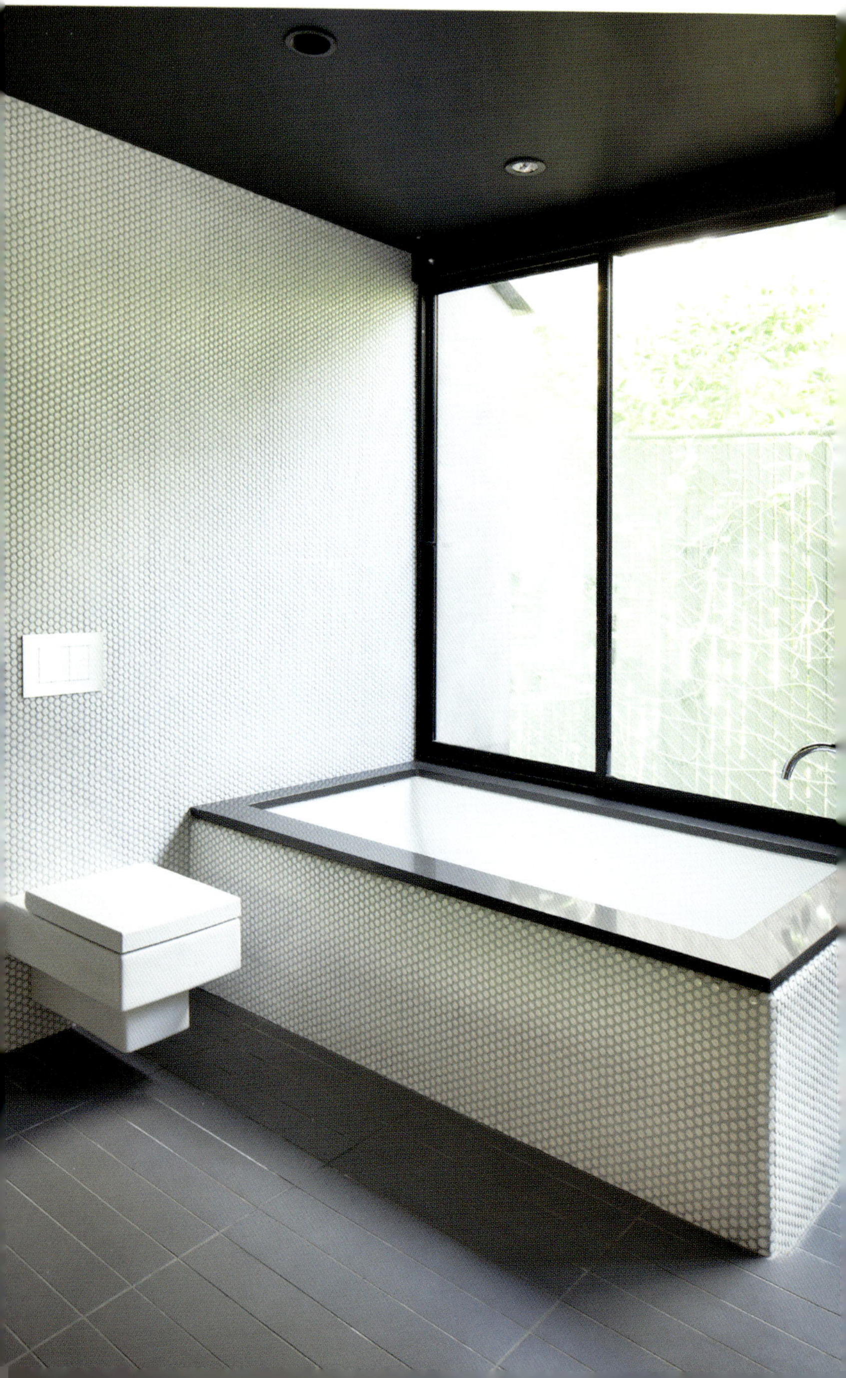

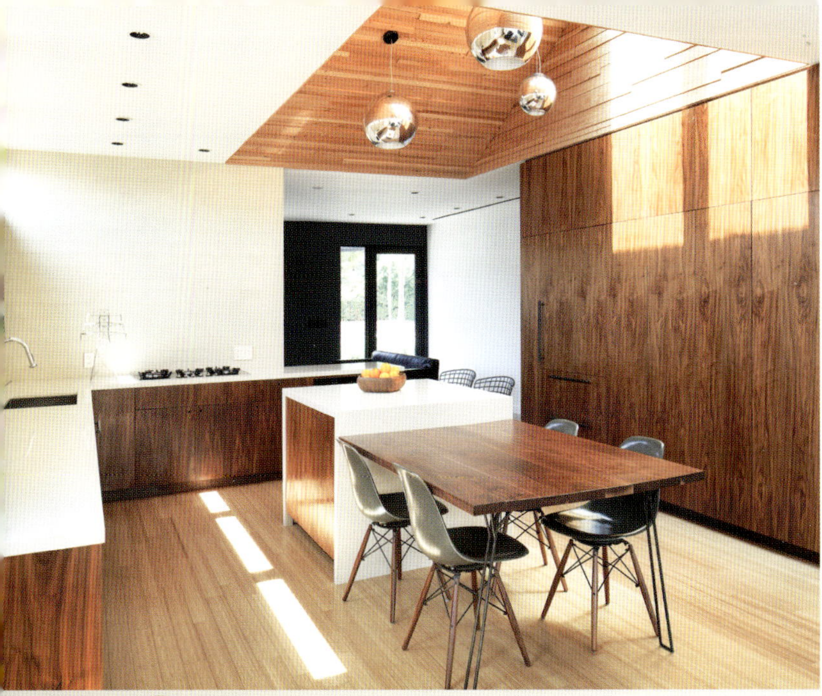

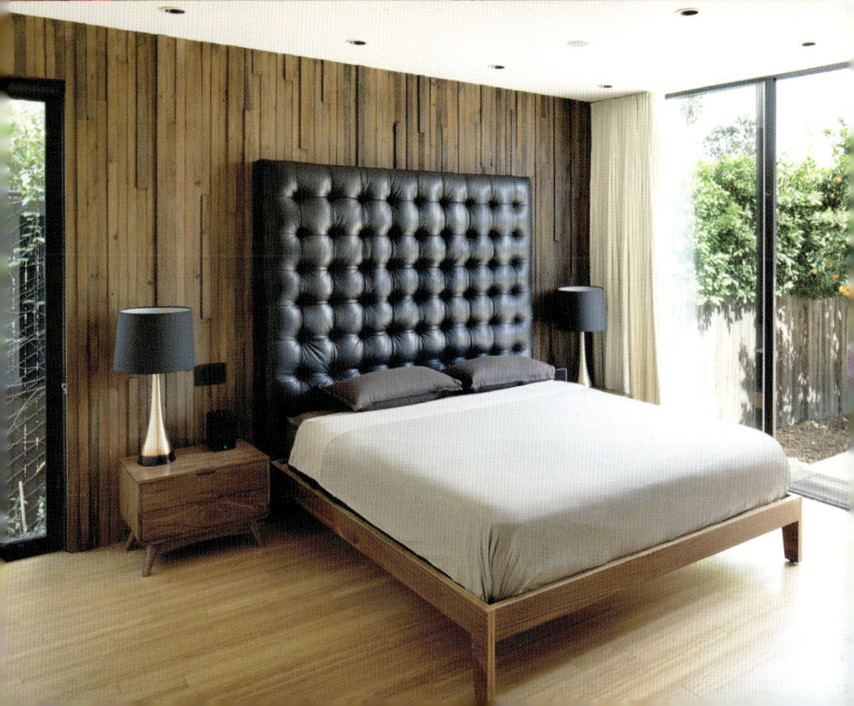

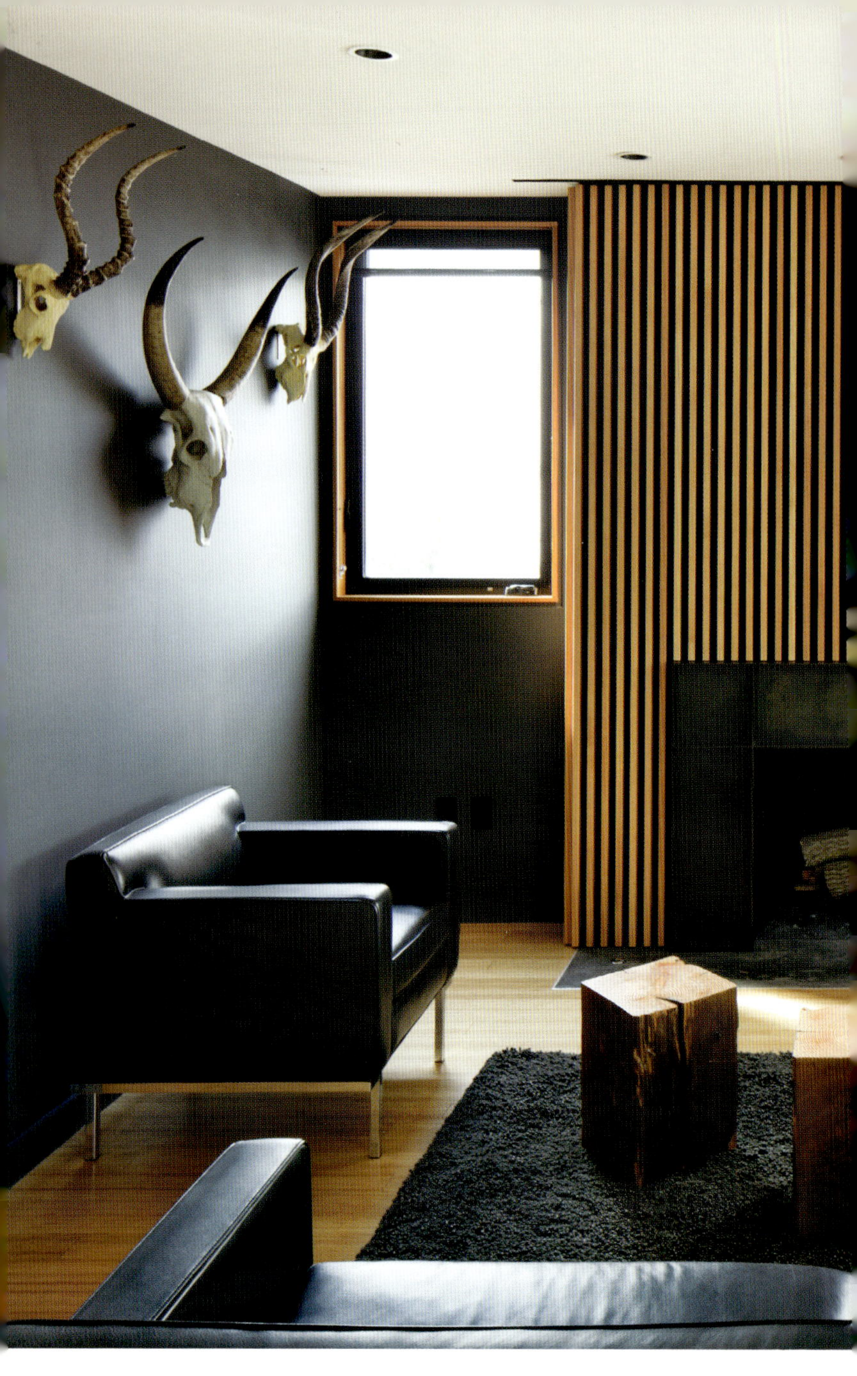

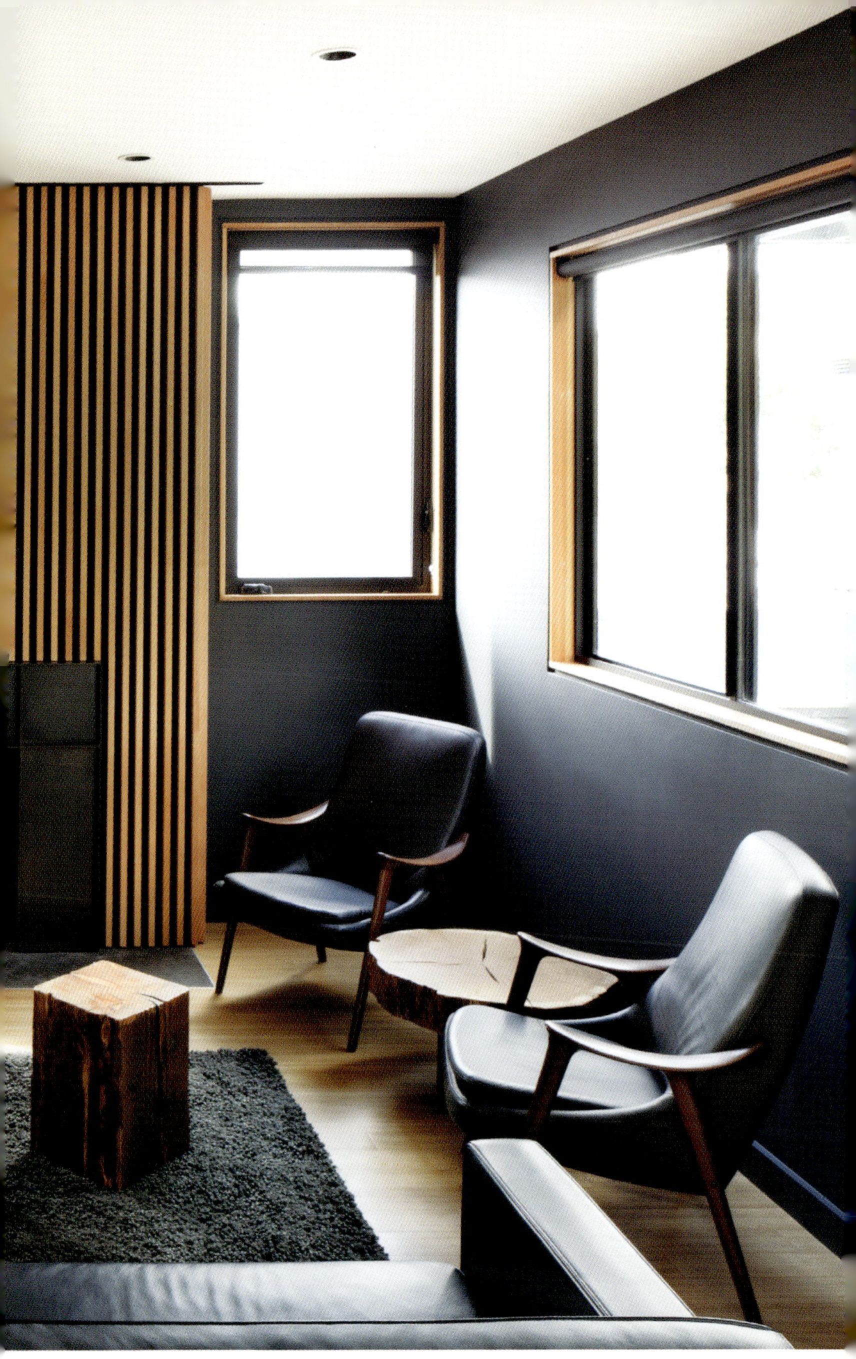

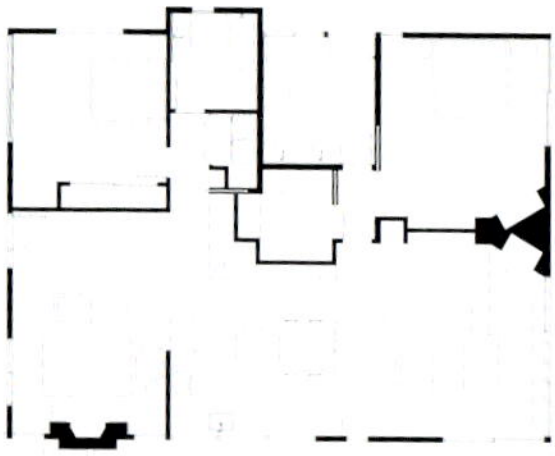

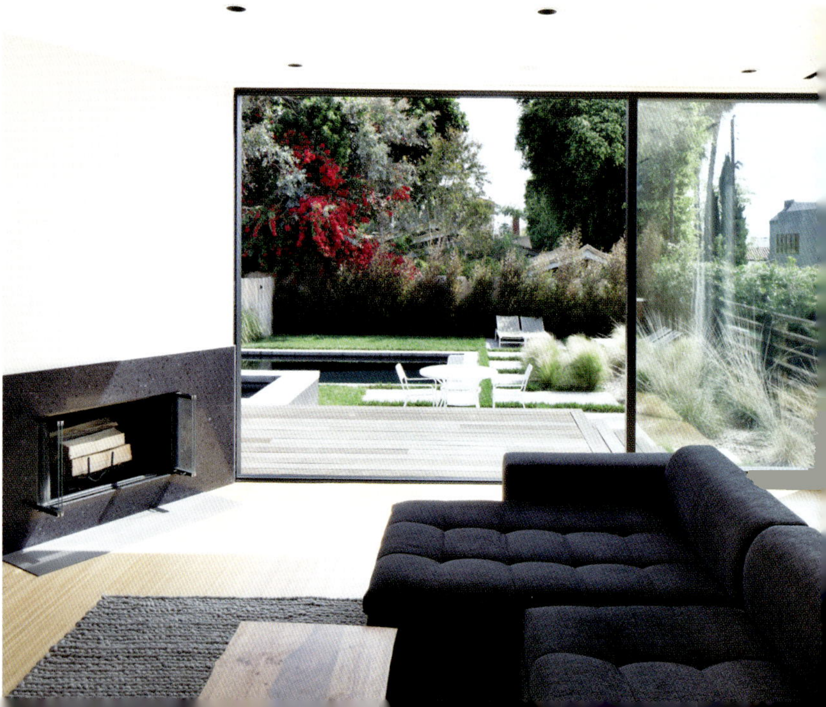

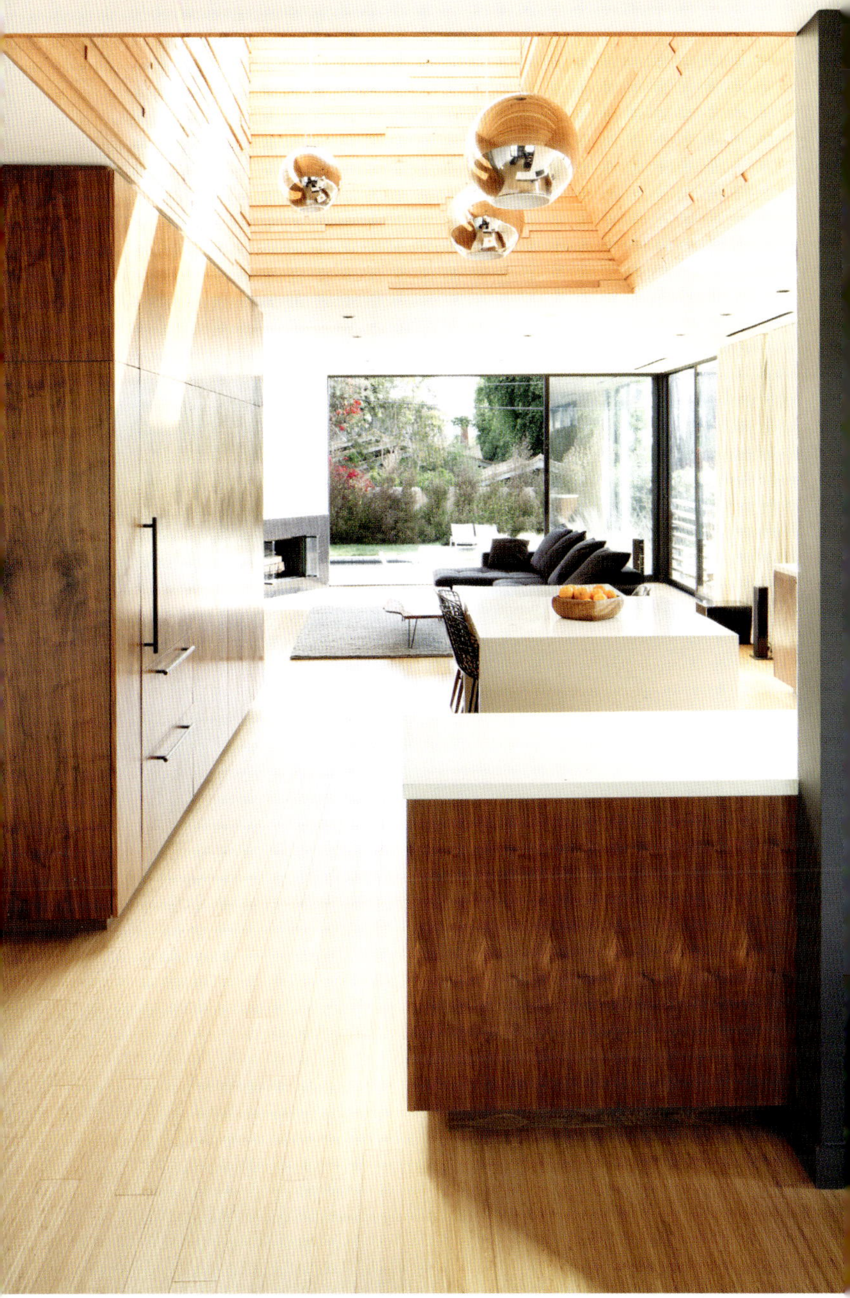

Nakahouse | Los Angeles | XTEN Architecture

White surfaces blend the rooms together, creating a heightened, abstract atmosphere.

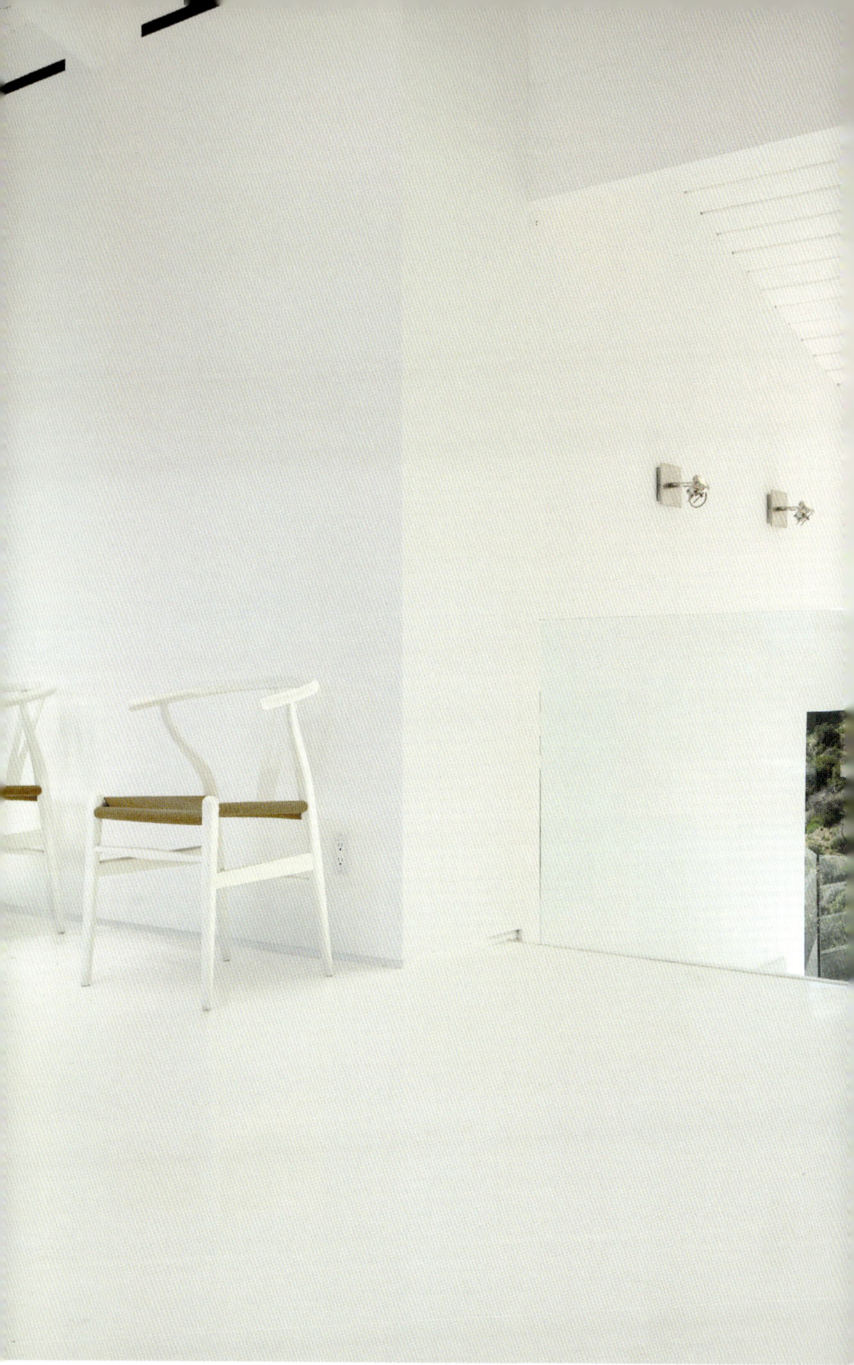

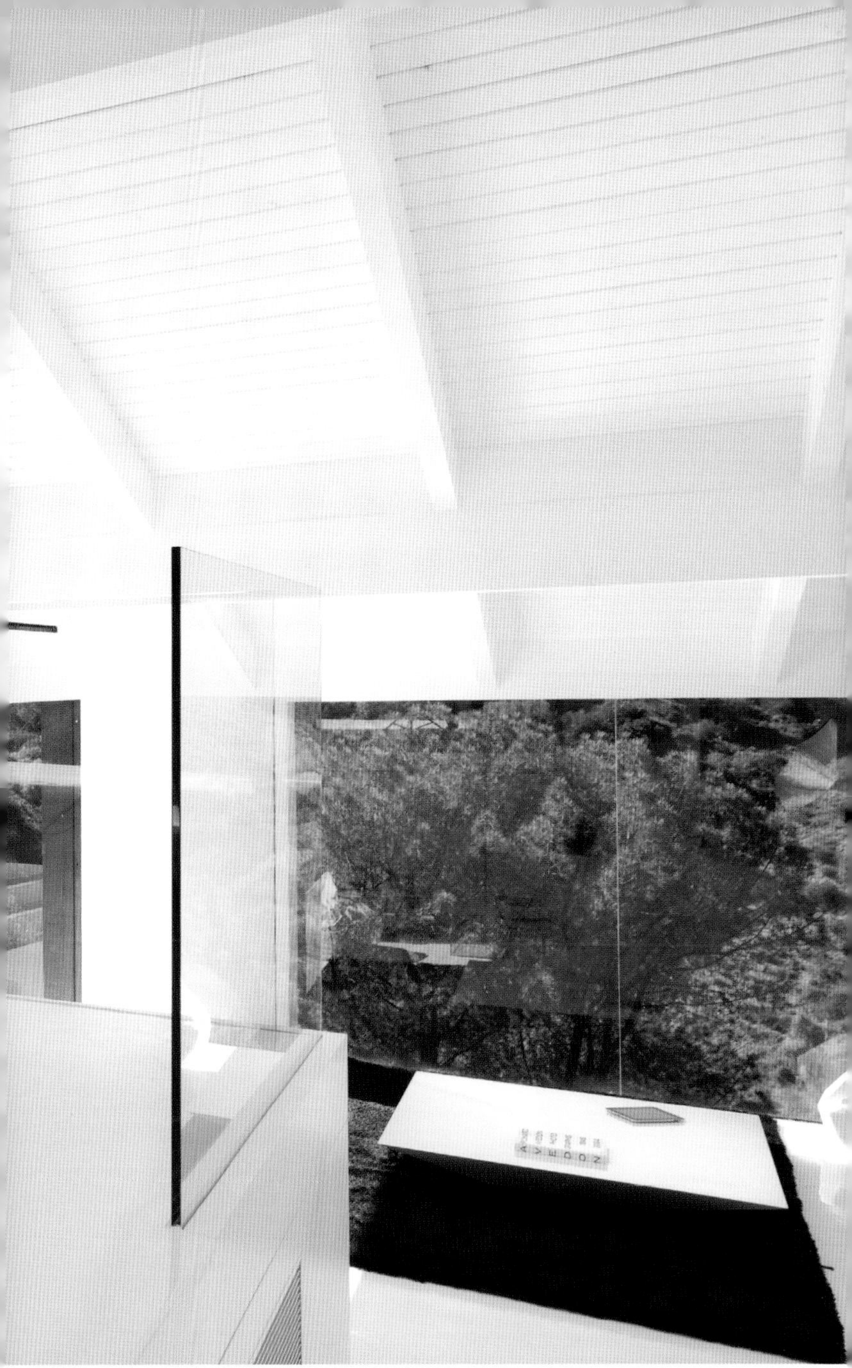

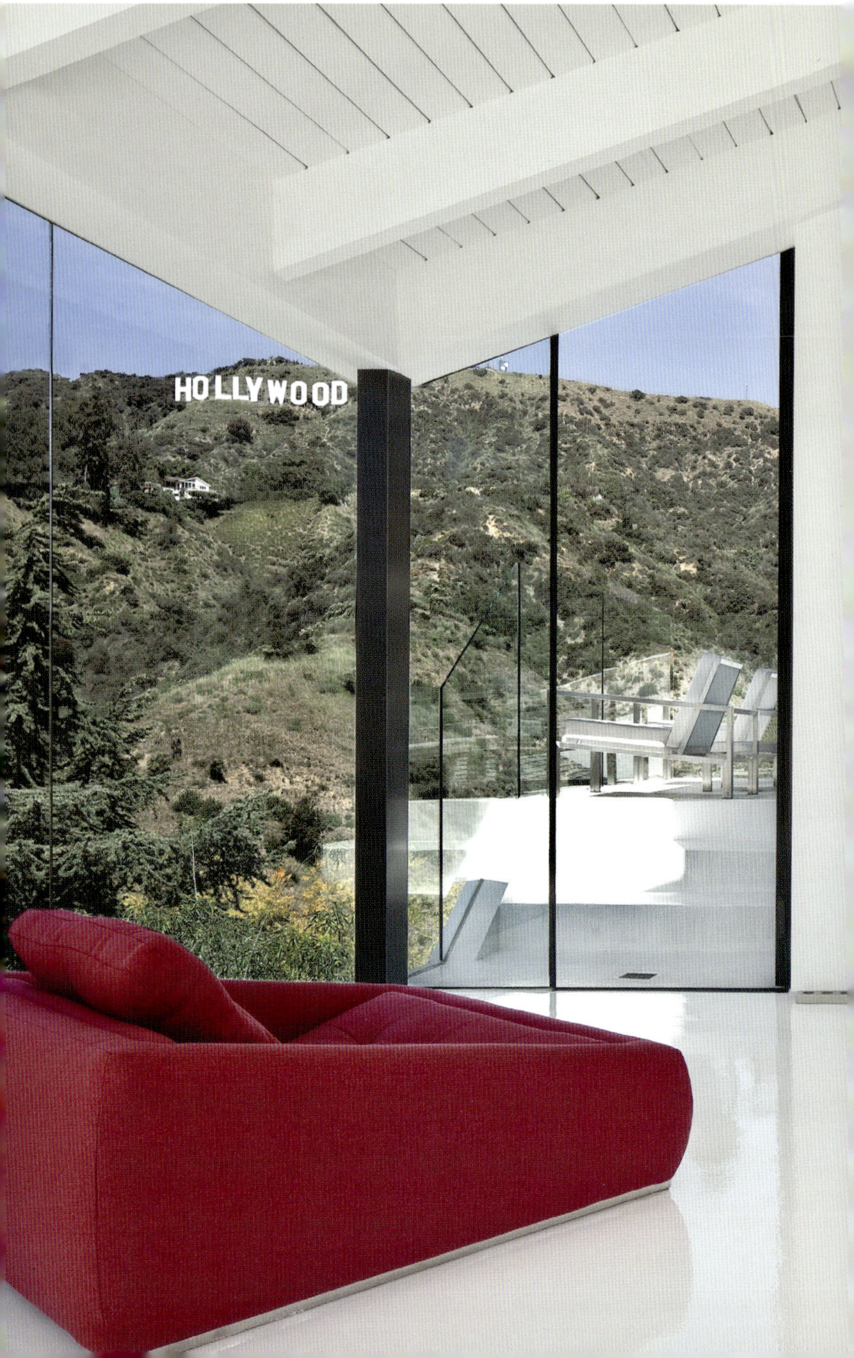
HOLLYWOOD

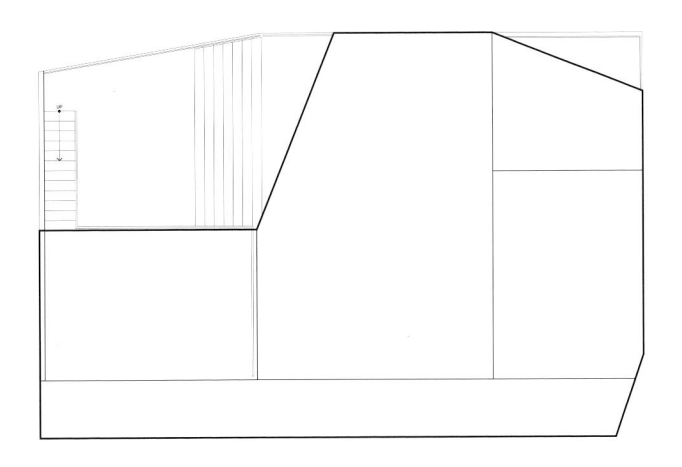

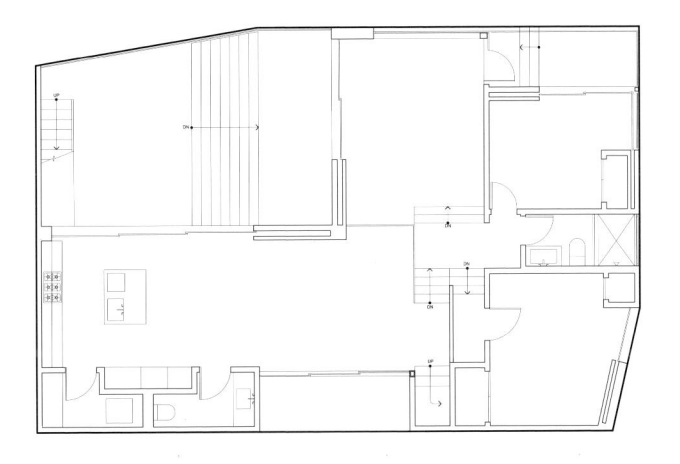

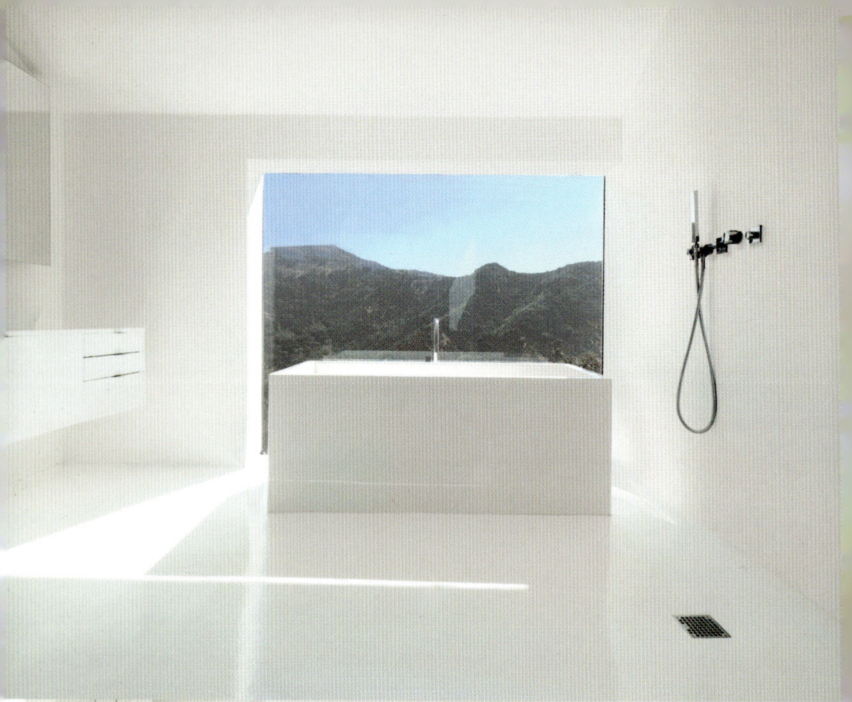

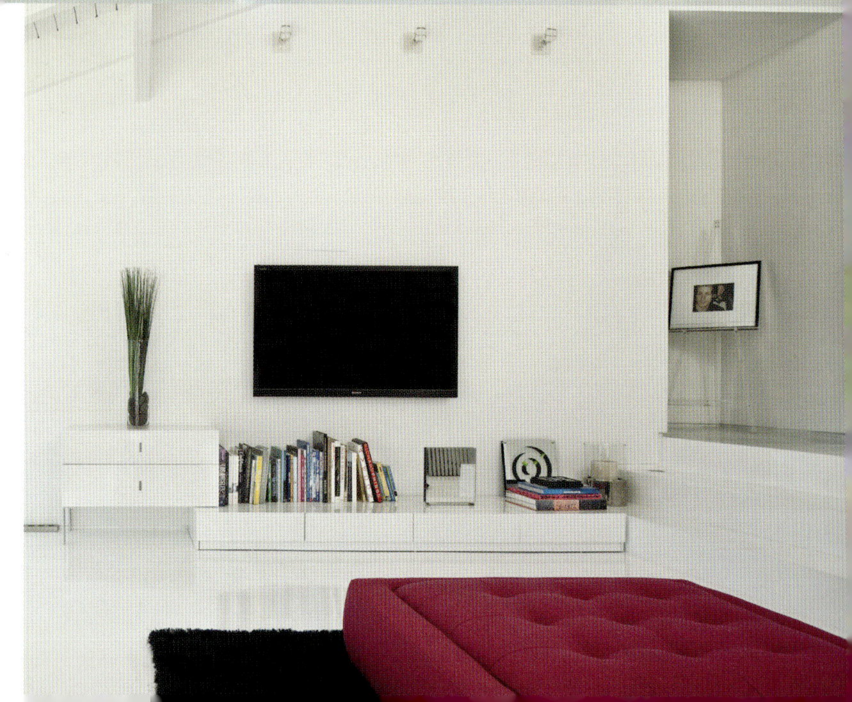

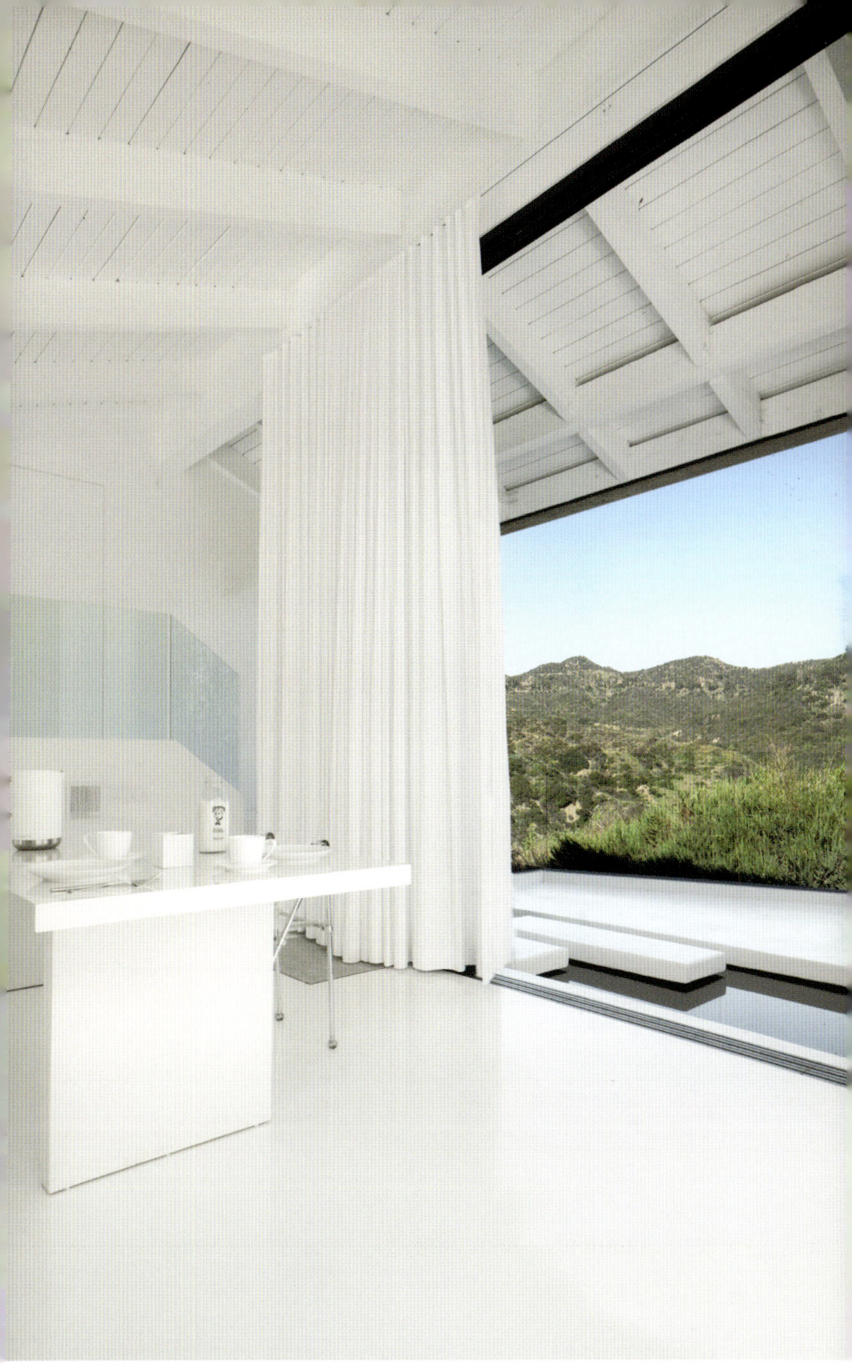

Redesigned interior to fit the needs of a family over time

Le Prado | Marseille | Padovani Maurice

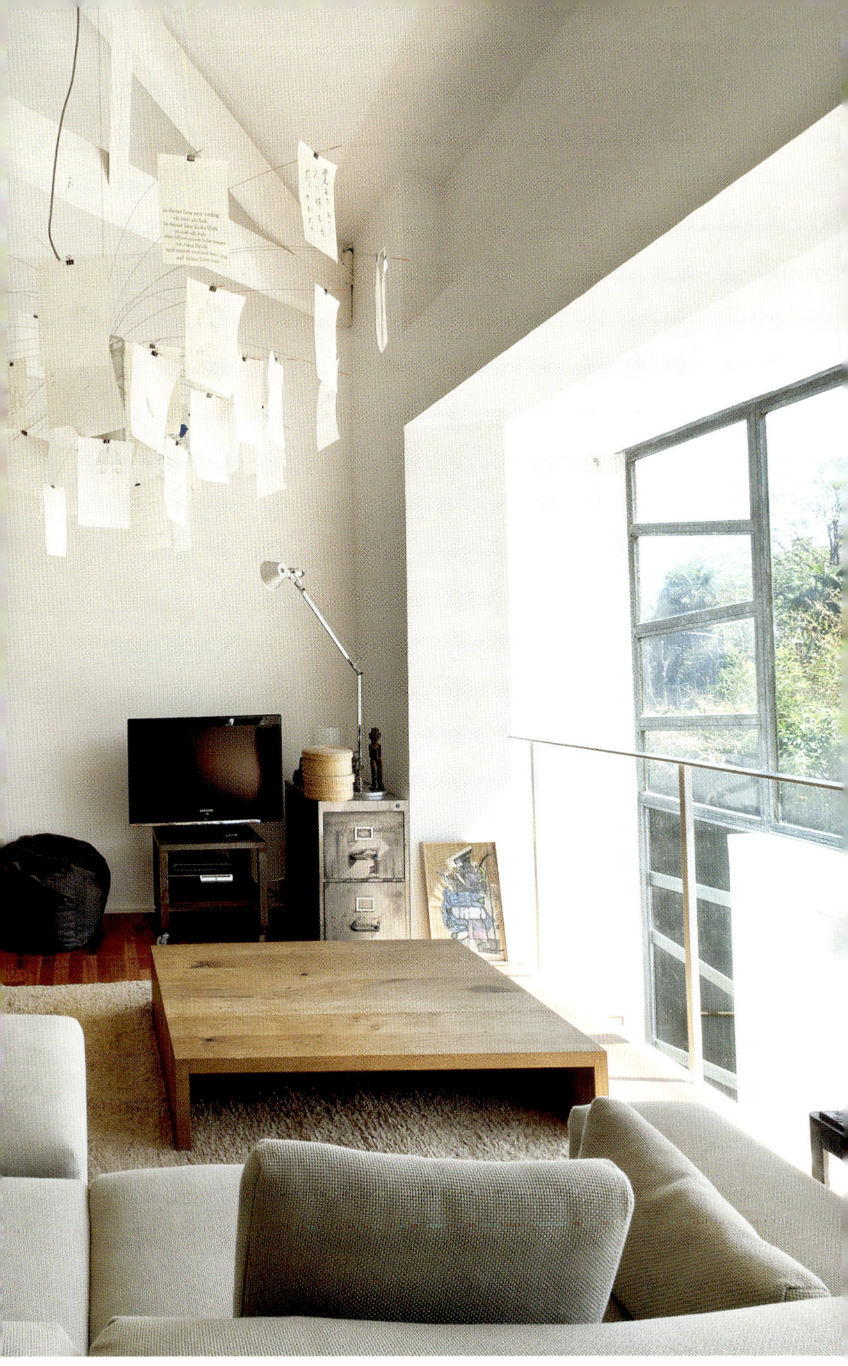

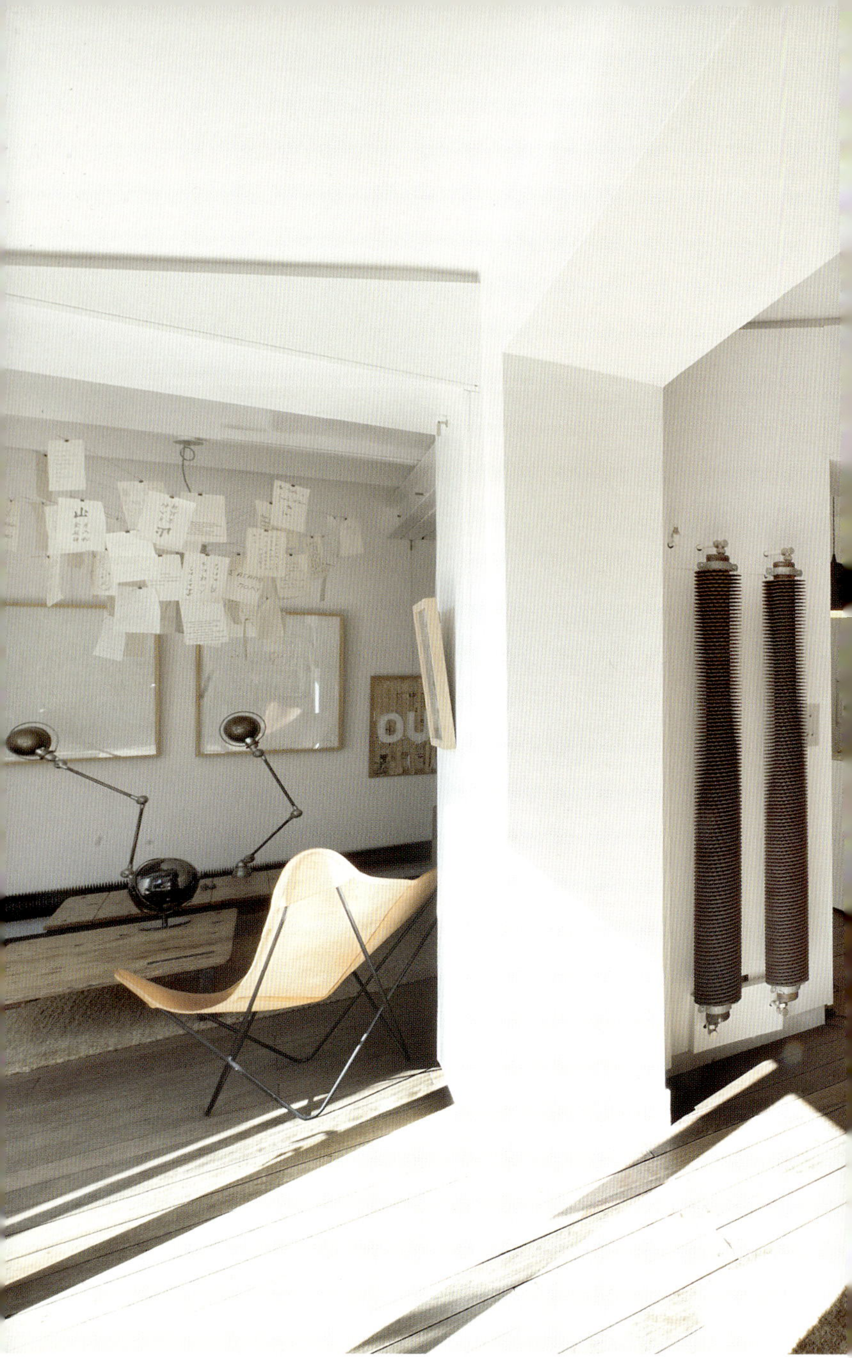

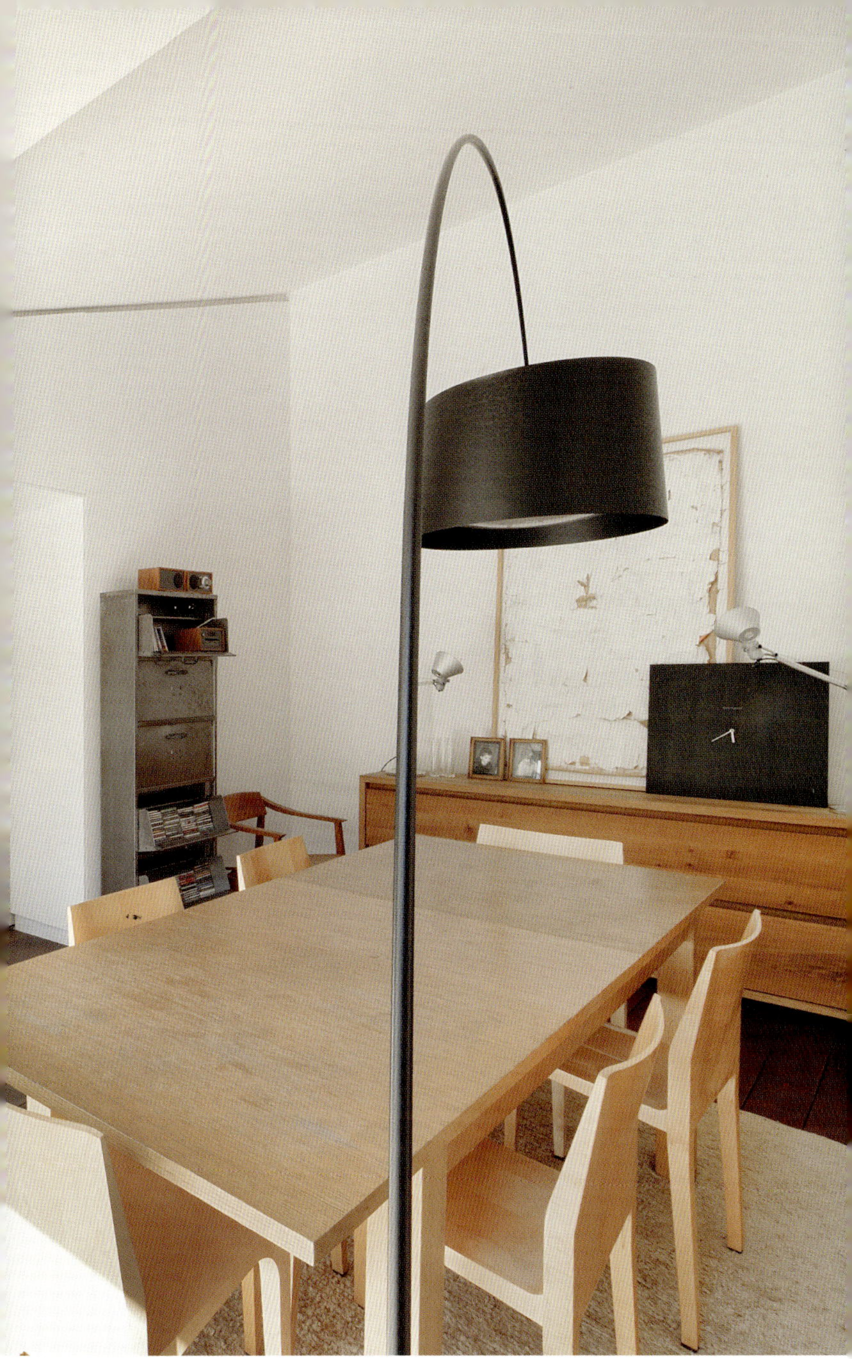

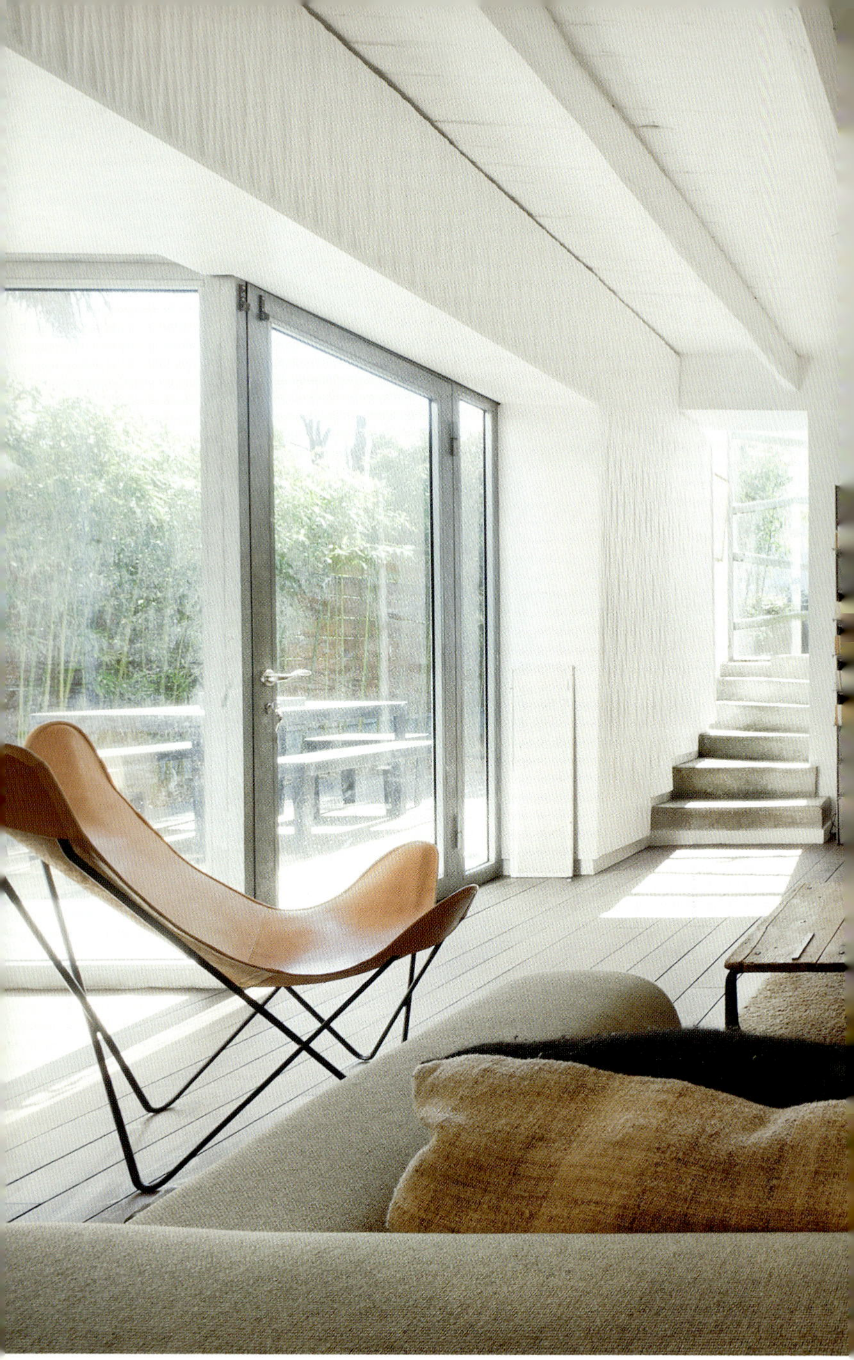

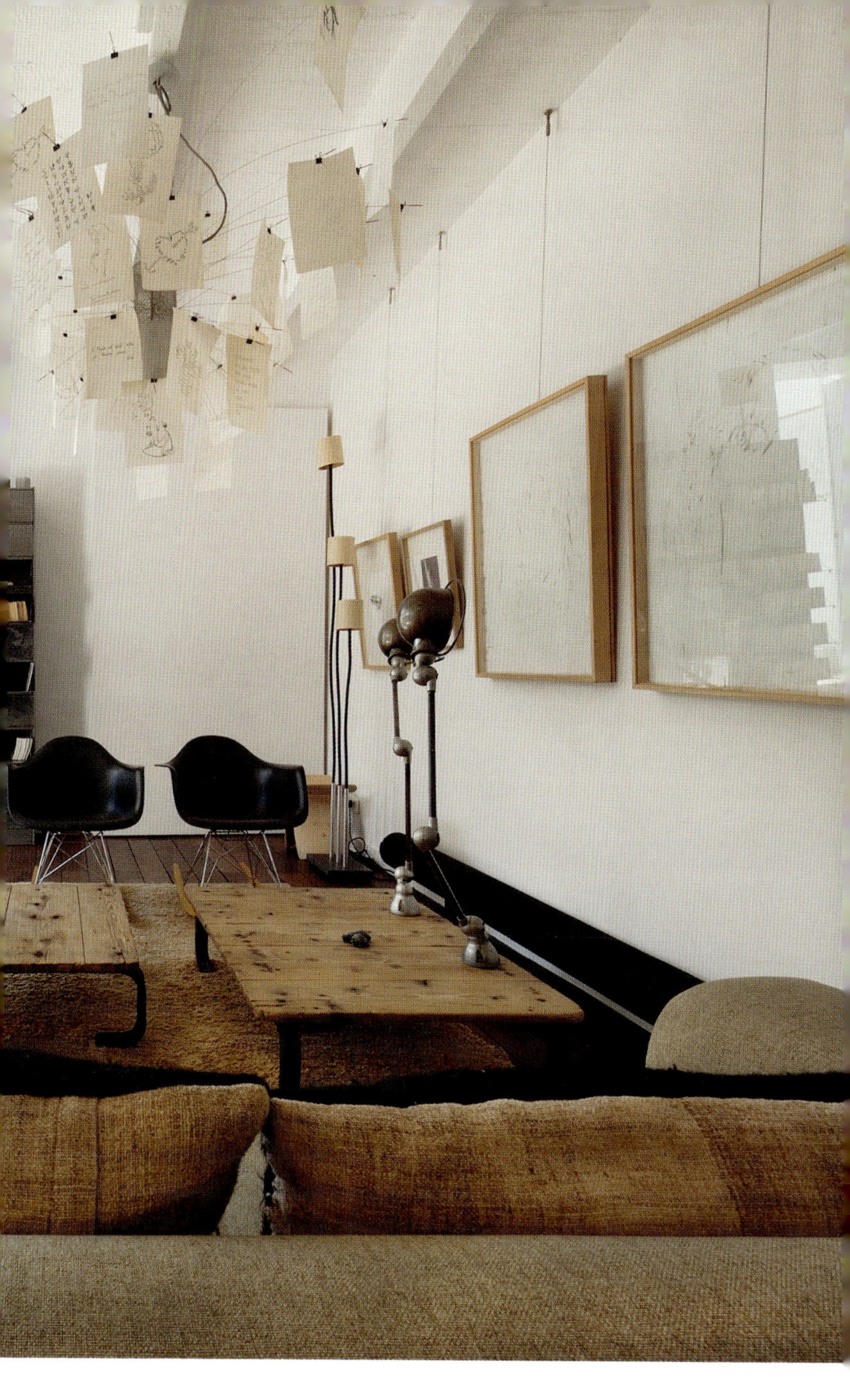

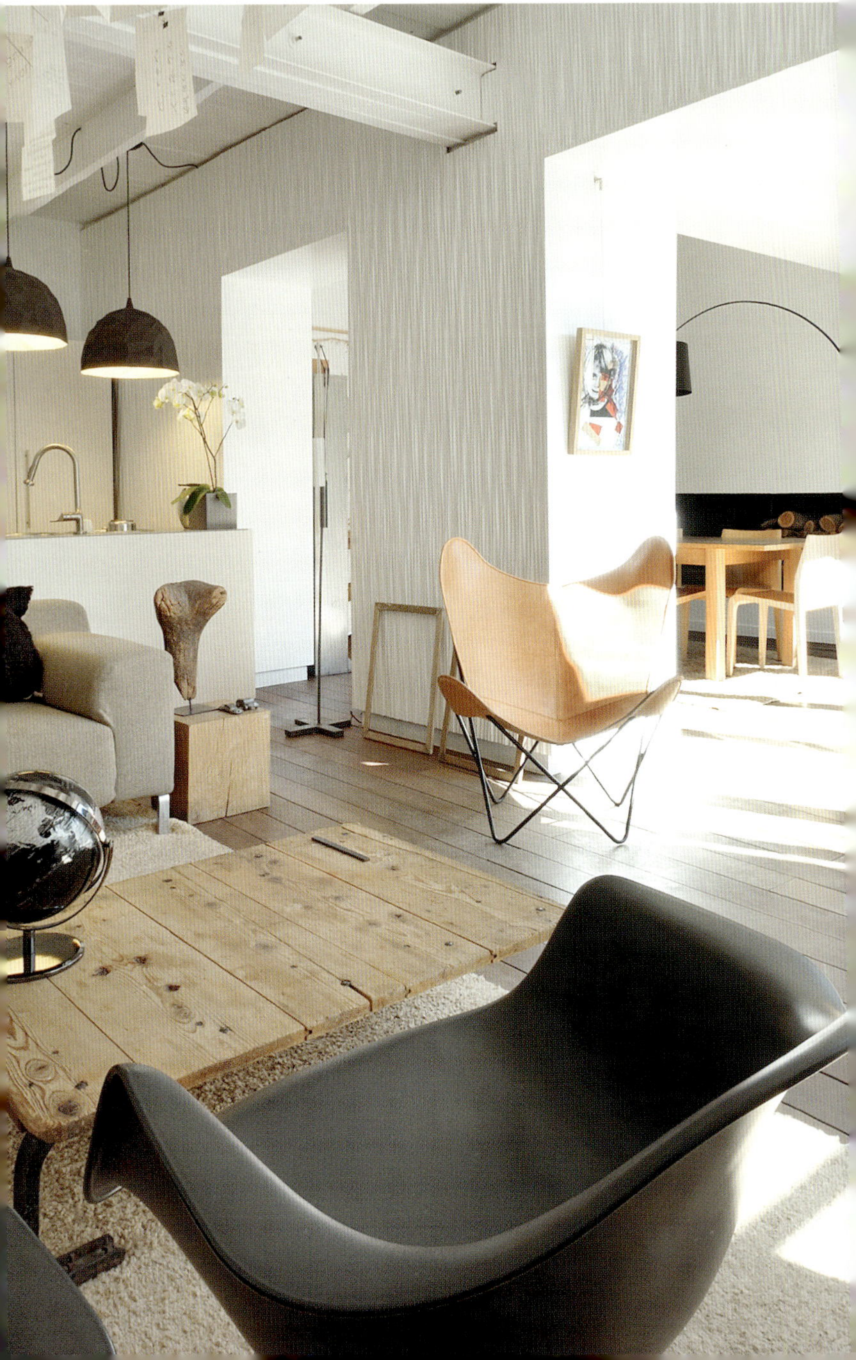

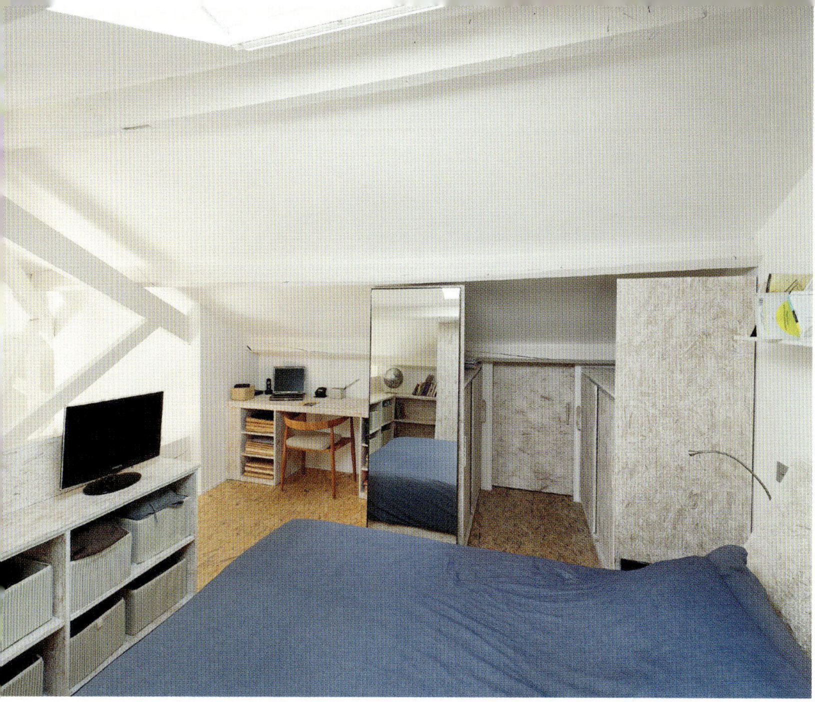

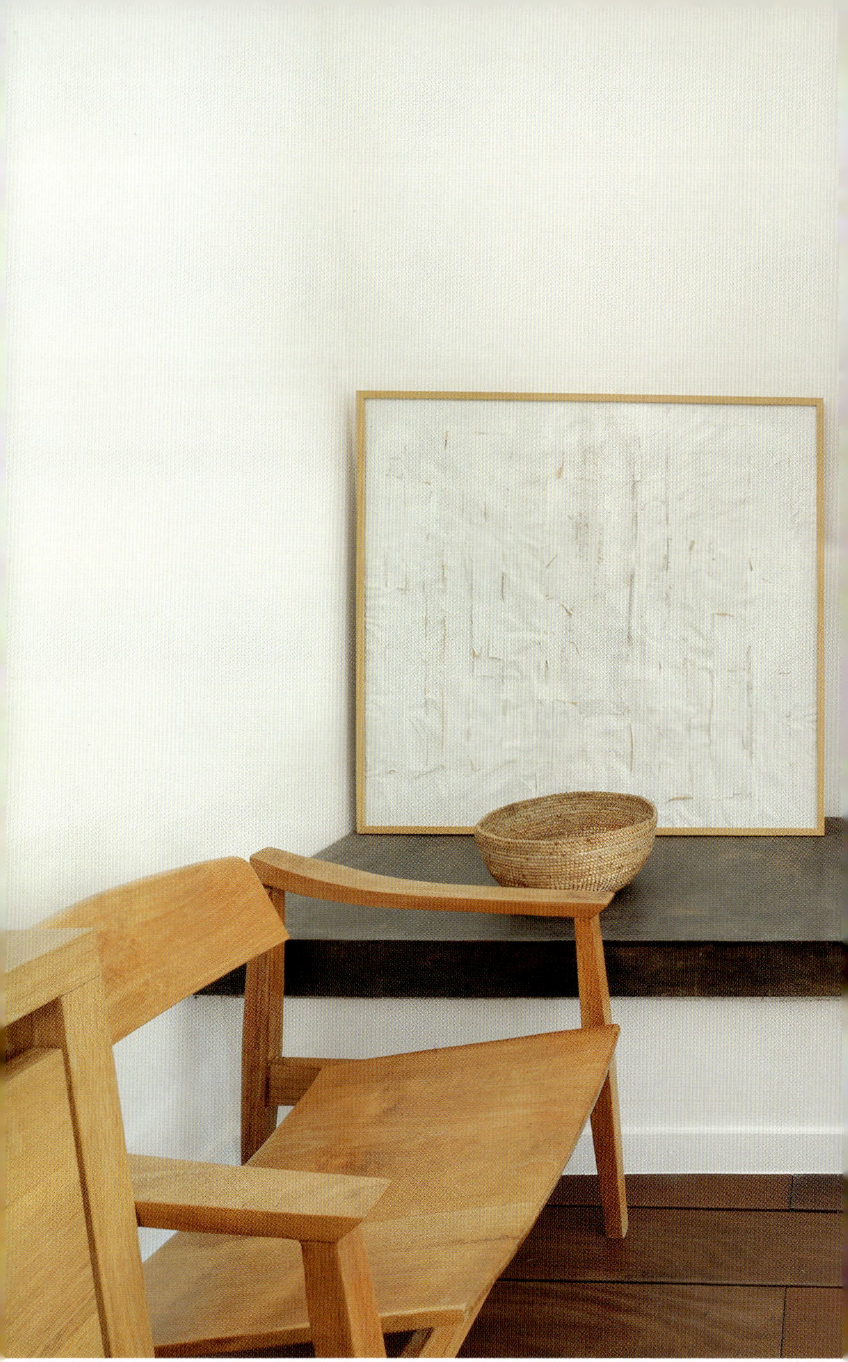

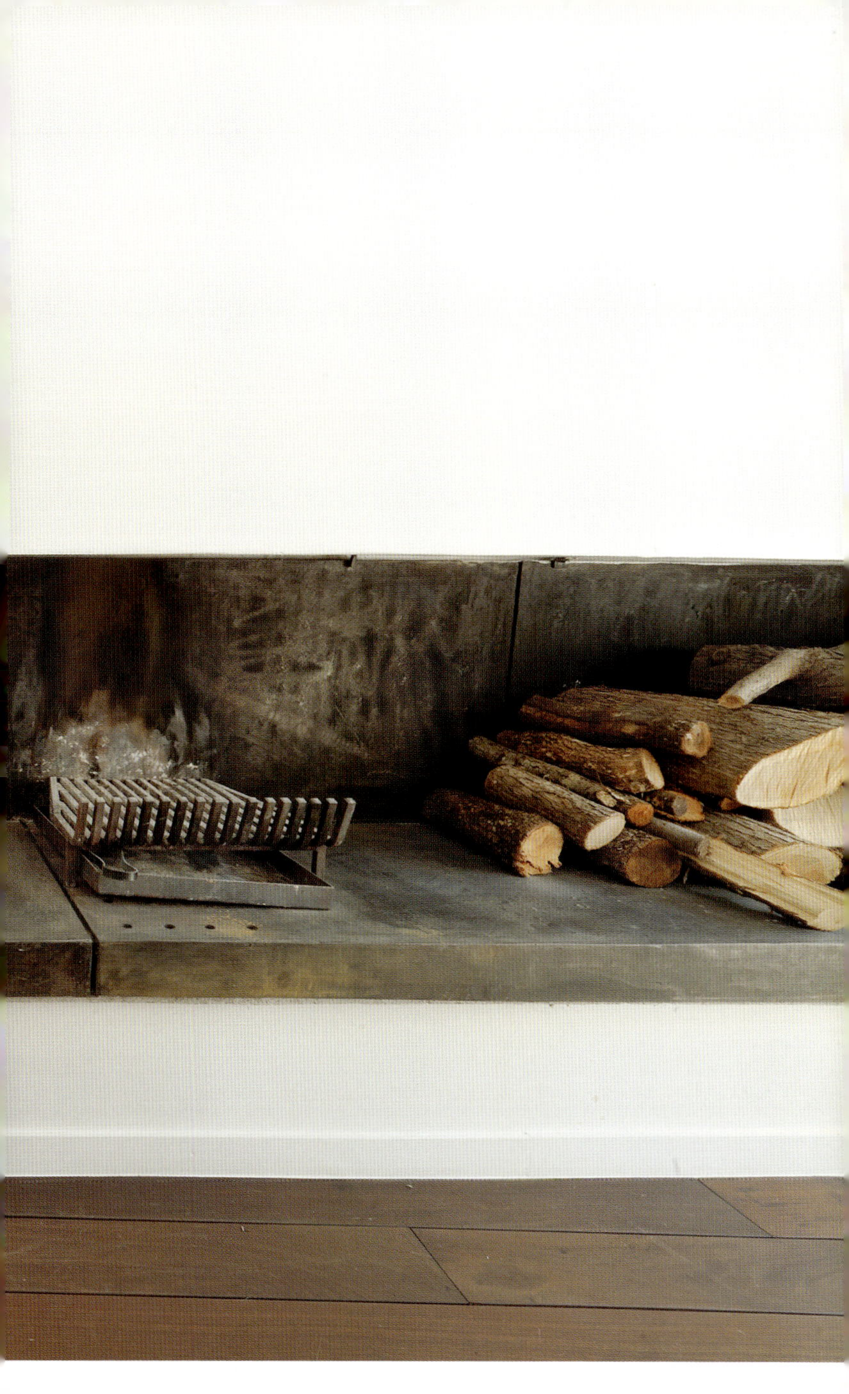

Chiavelli Residence | Monfumo | Filippo Caprioglio – Caprioglio Associati Studio di Architettura

Existing and contemporary interior merge to create an industrial minimalistic living space.

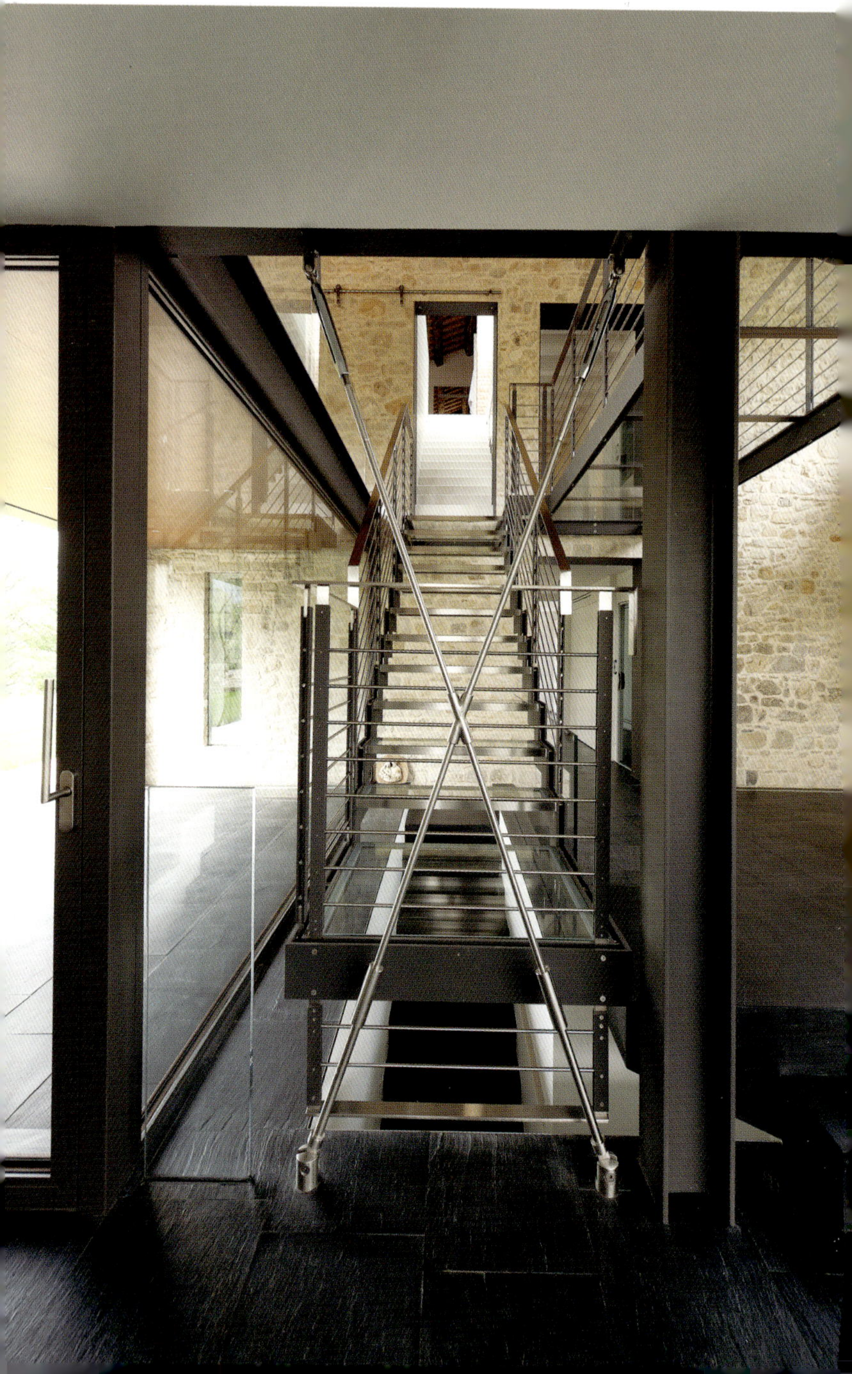

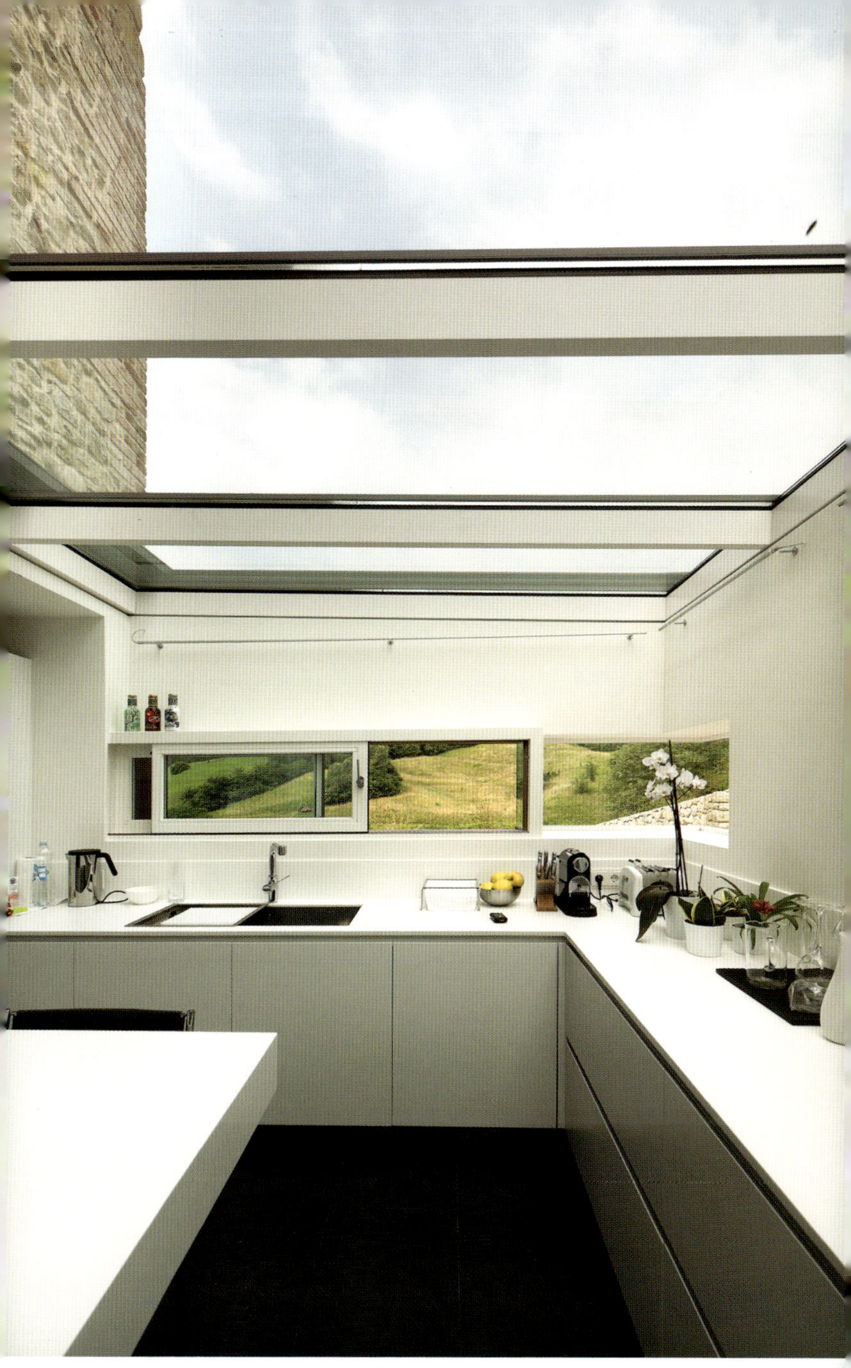

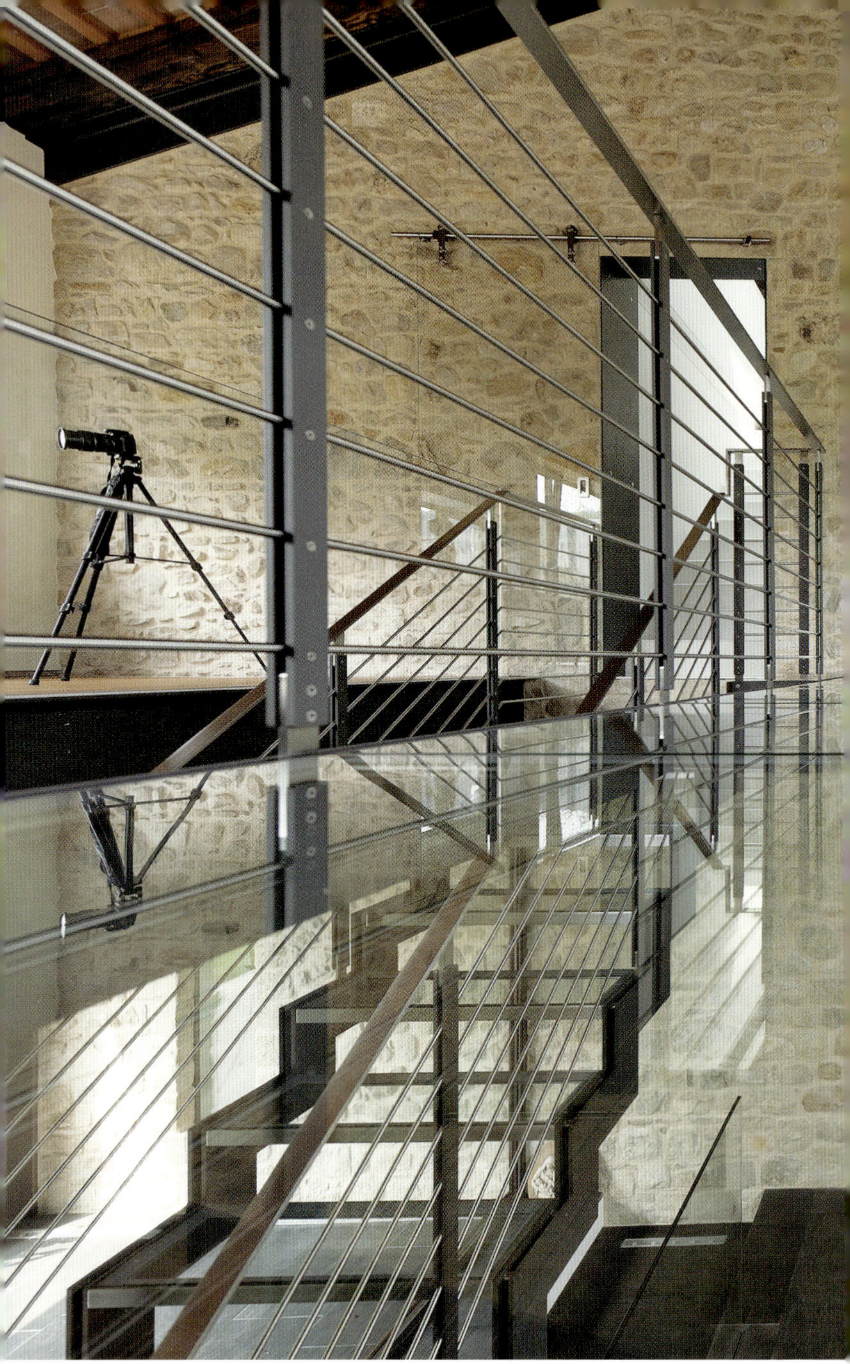

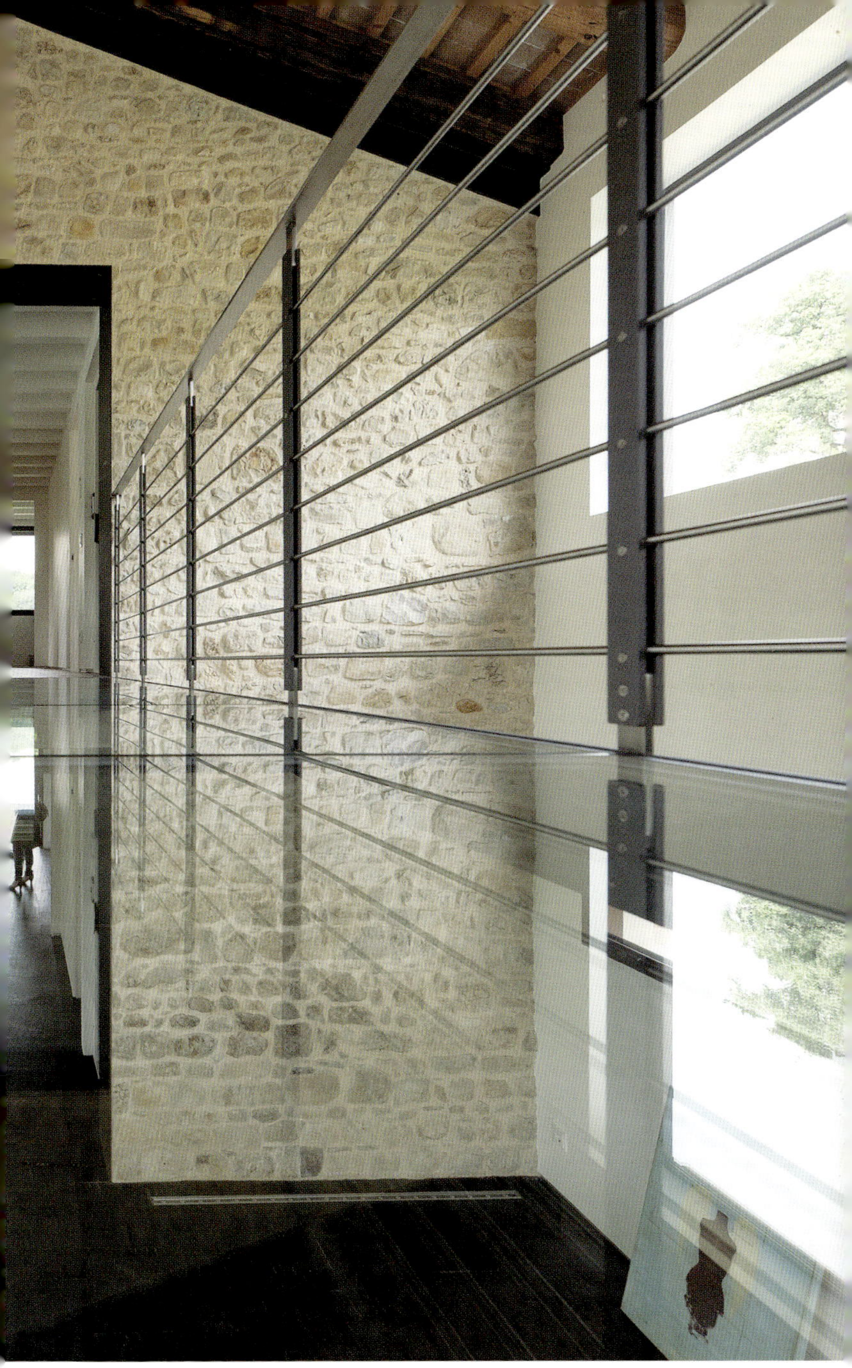

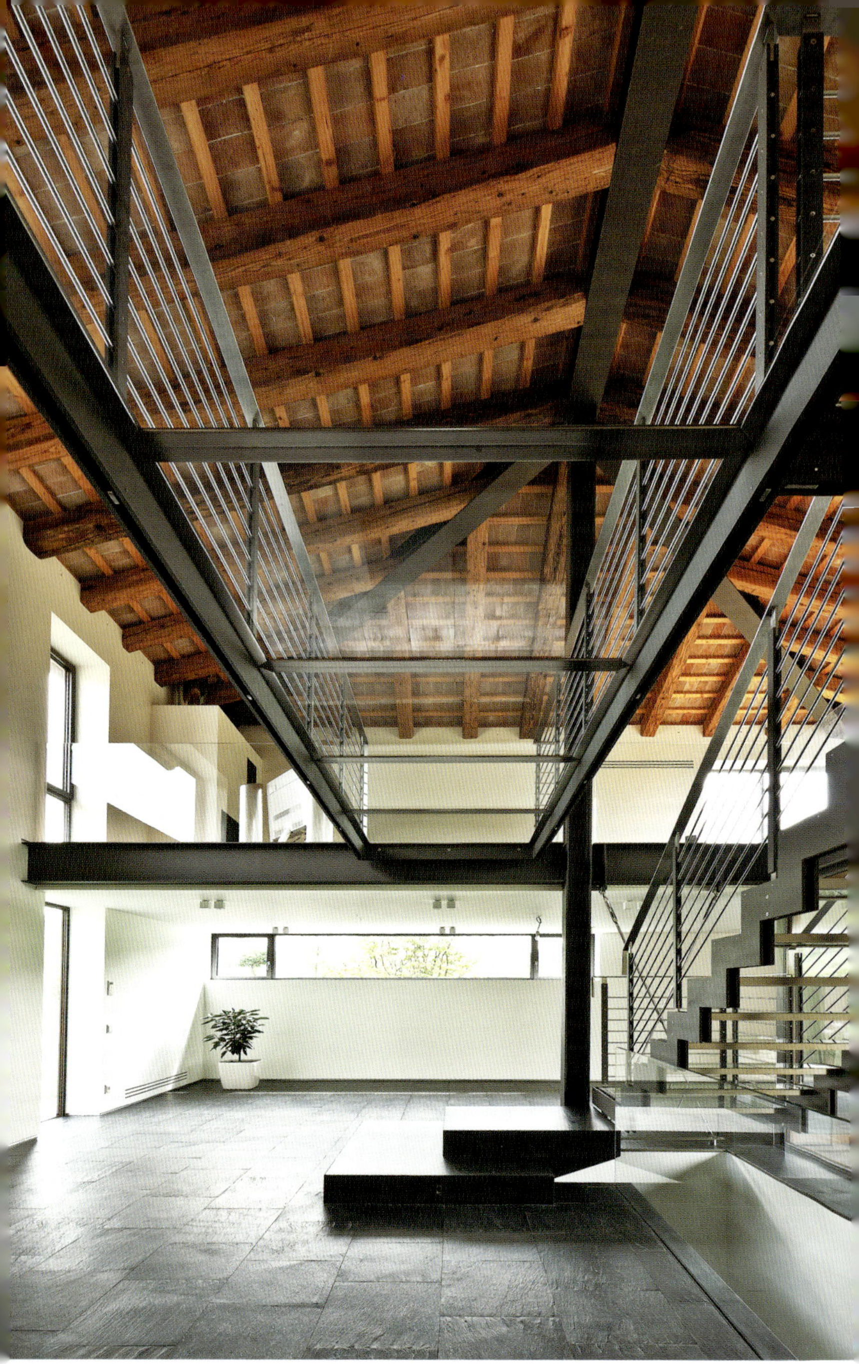

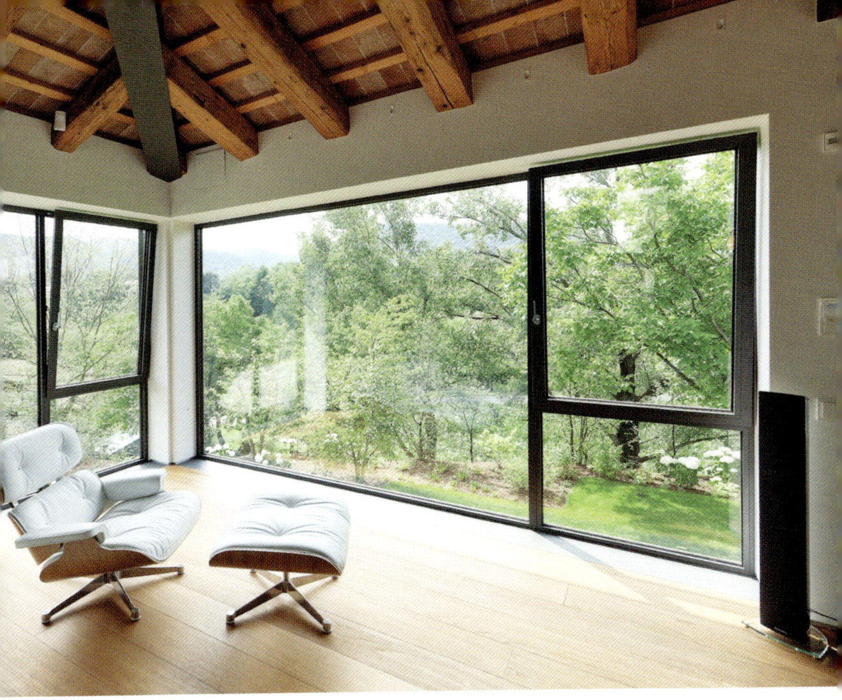

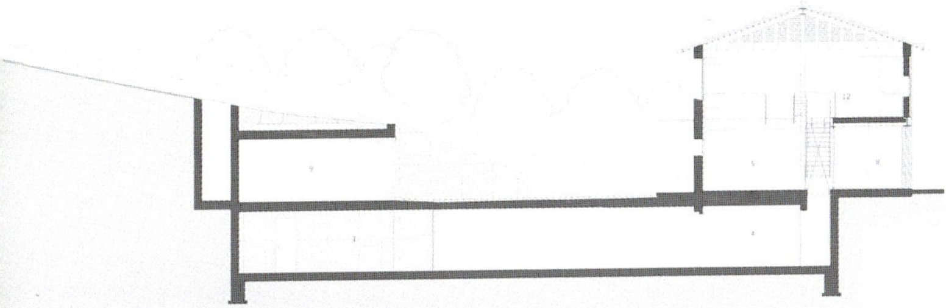

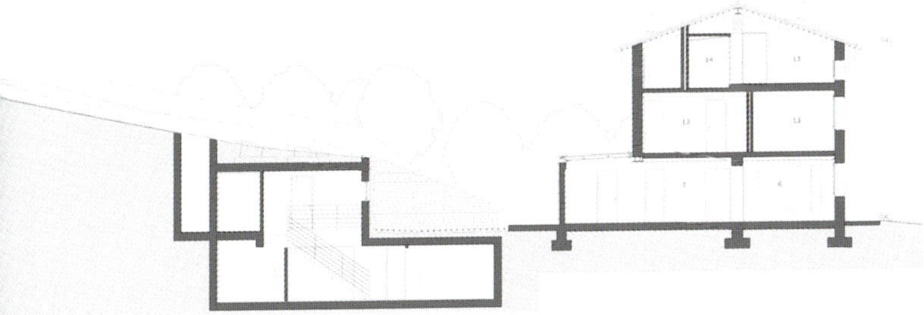

126 | **Parisien / Raymond Residence** | Montreal | Naturehumaine

This simple and modest home offers a rich spatial experience with generous and luminous spaces.

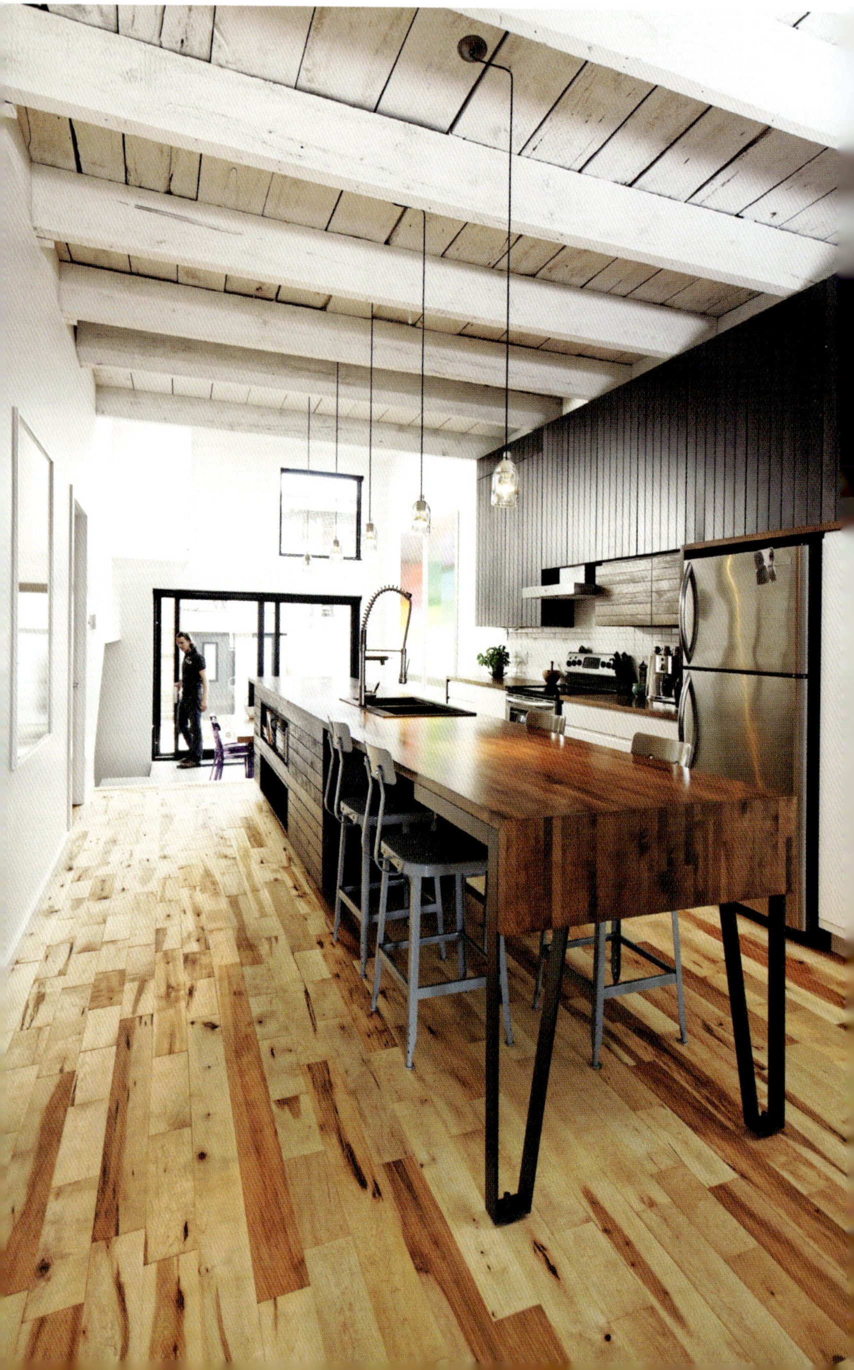

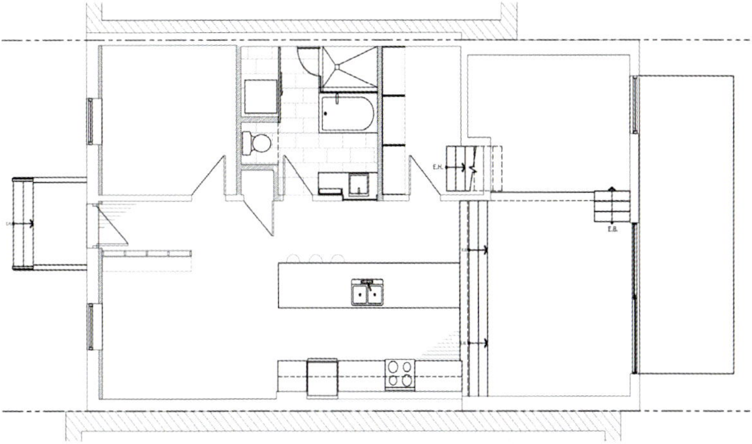
E.H.
E.B.

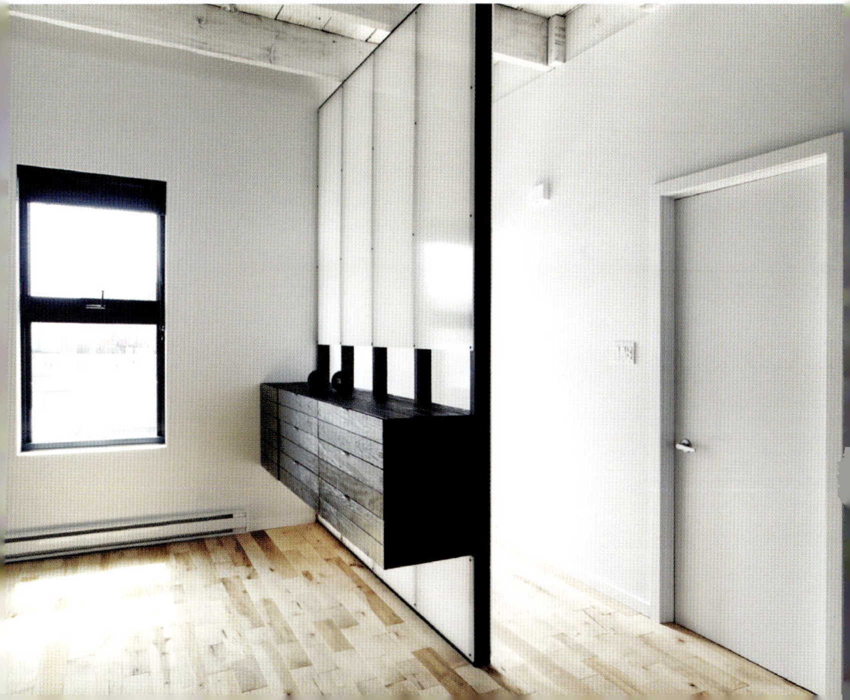

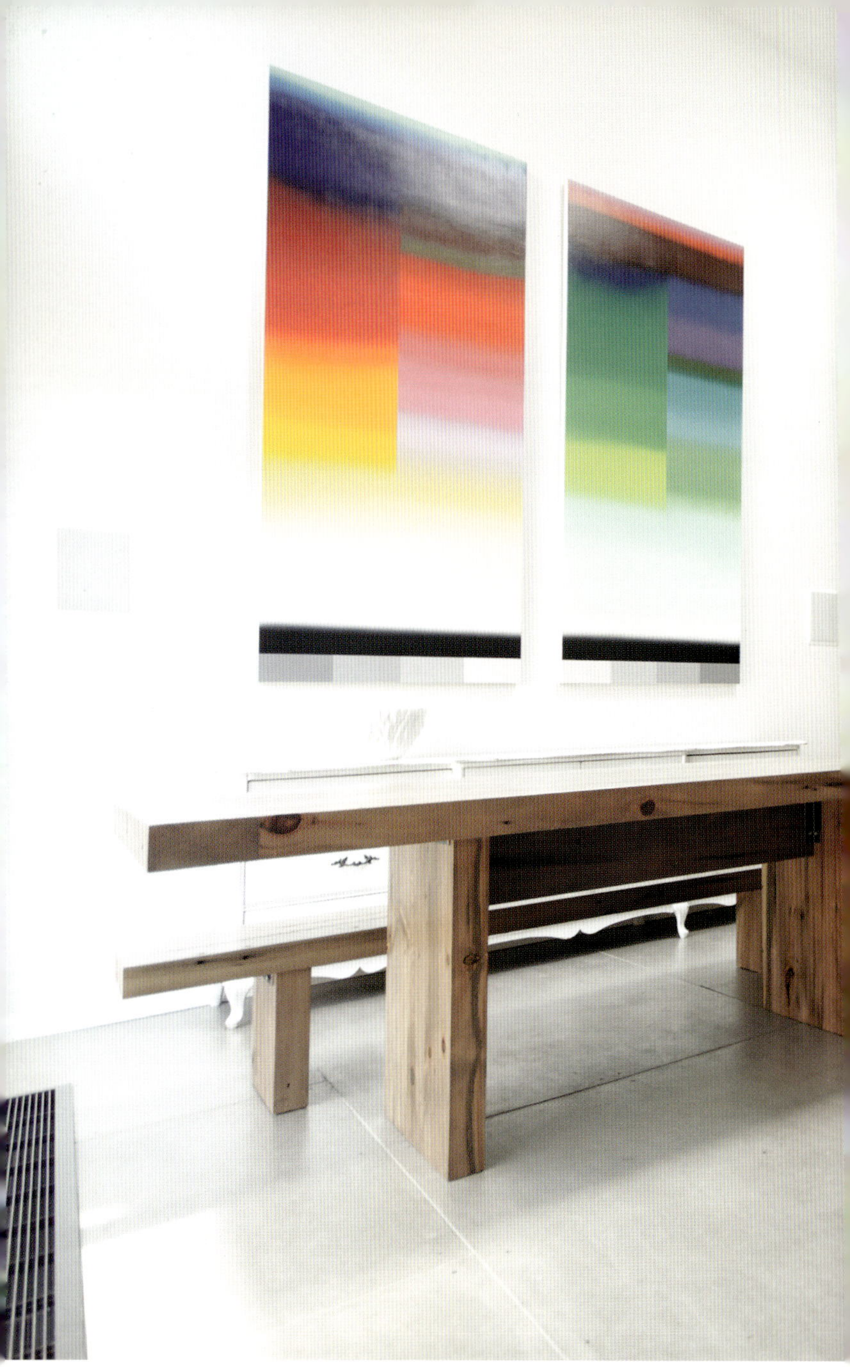

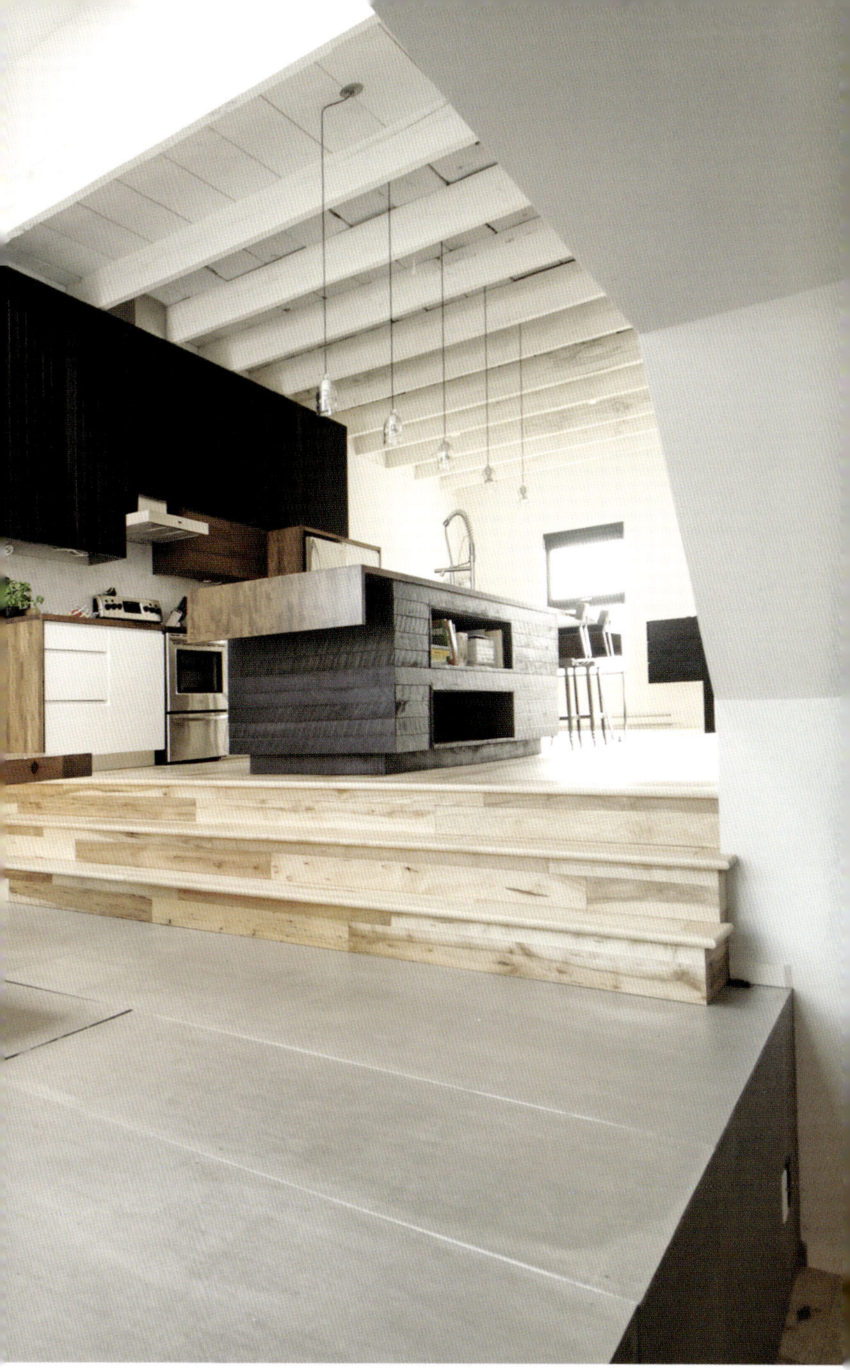

Casa Luz | Muxbal, Guatemala City | Paz arquitectura

The design maintains a close visual **relationship between each** indoor space and the **adjacent** landscape.

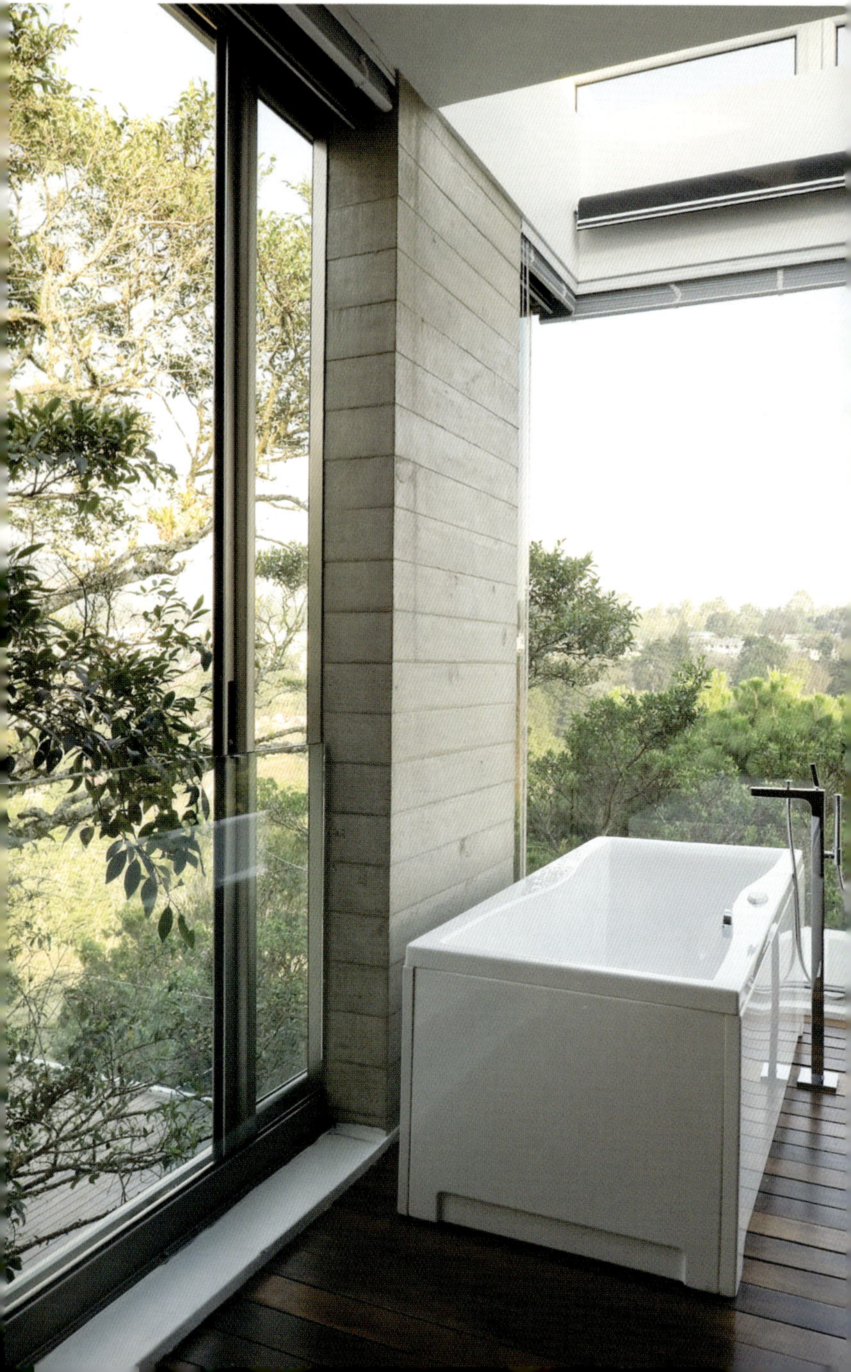

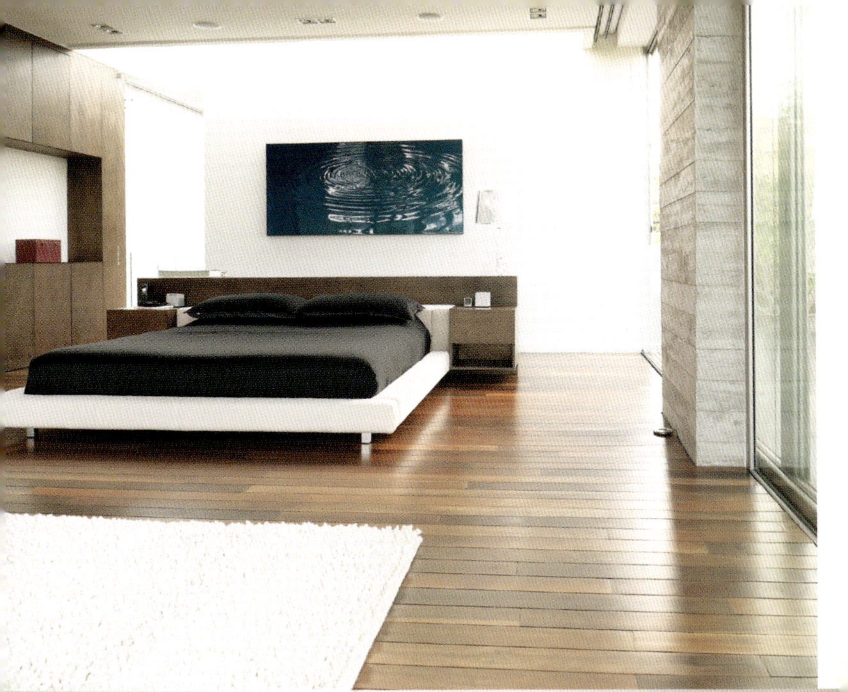
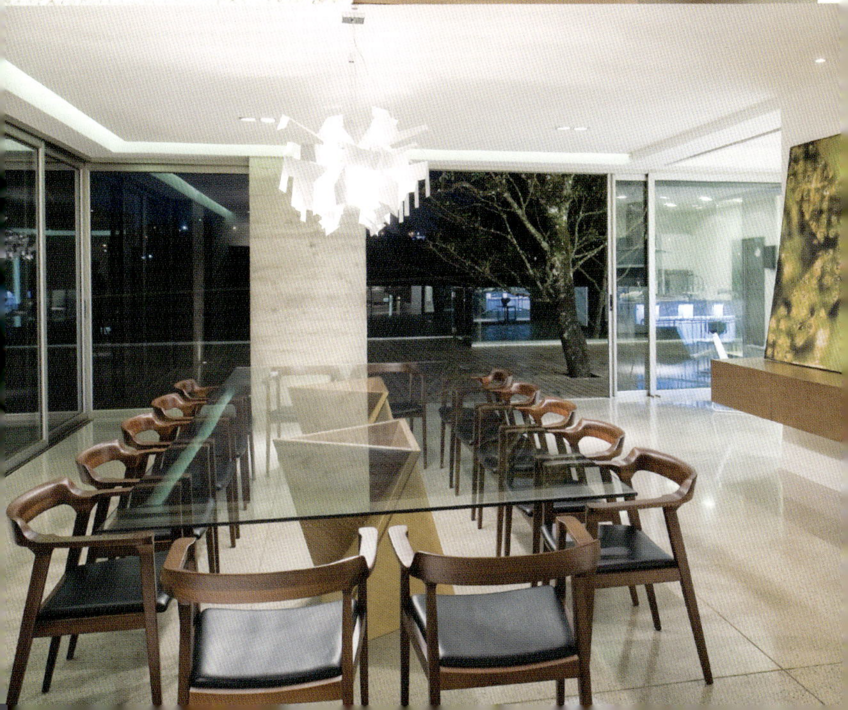

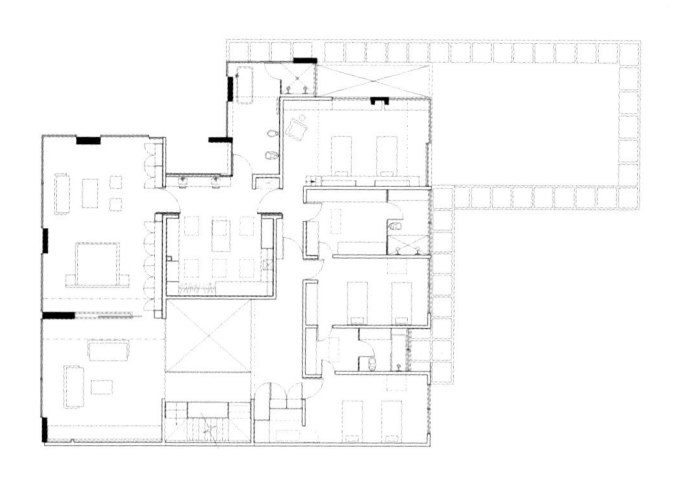

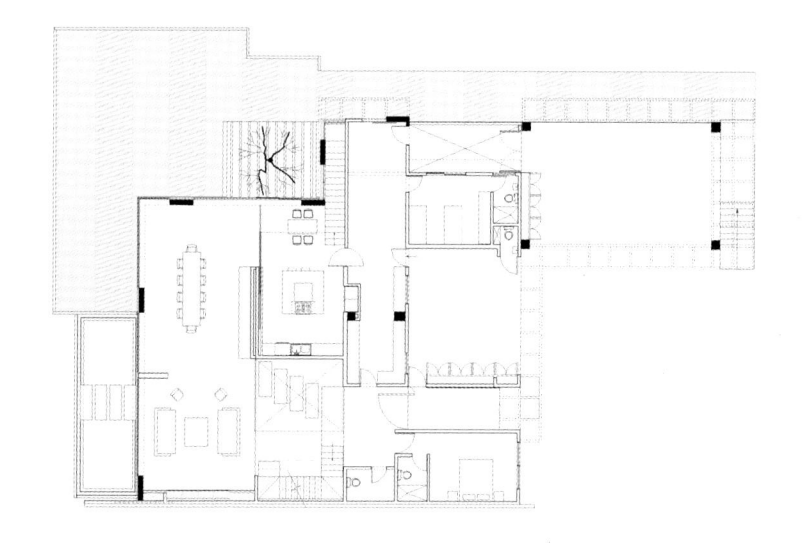

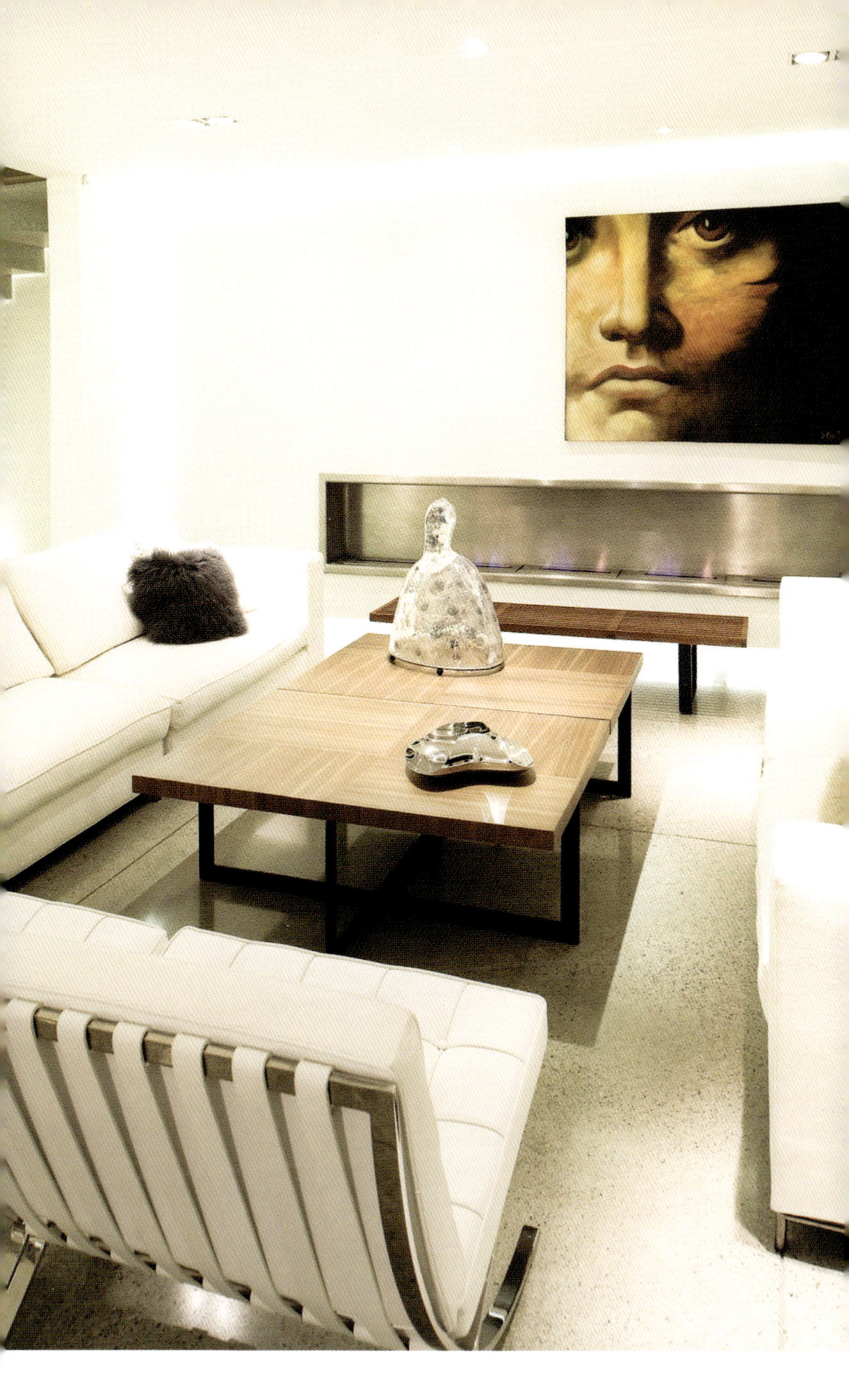

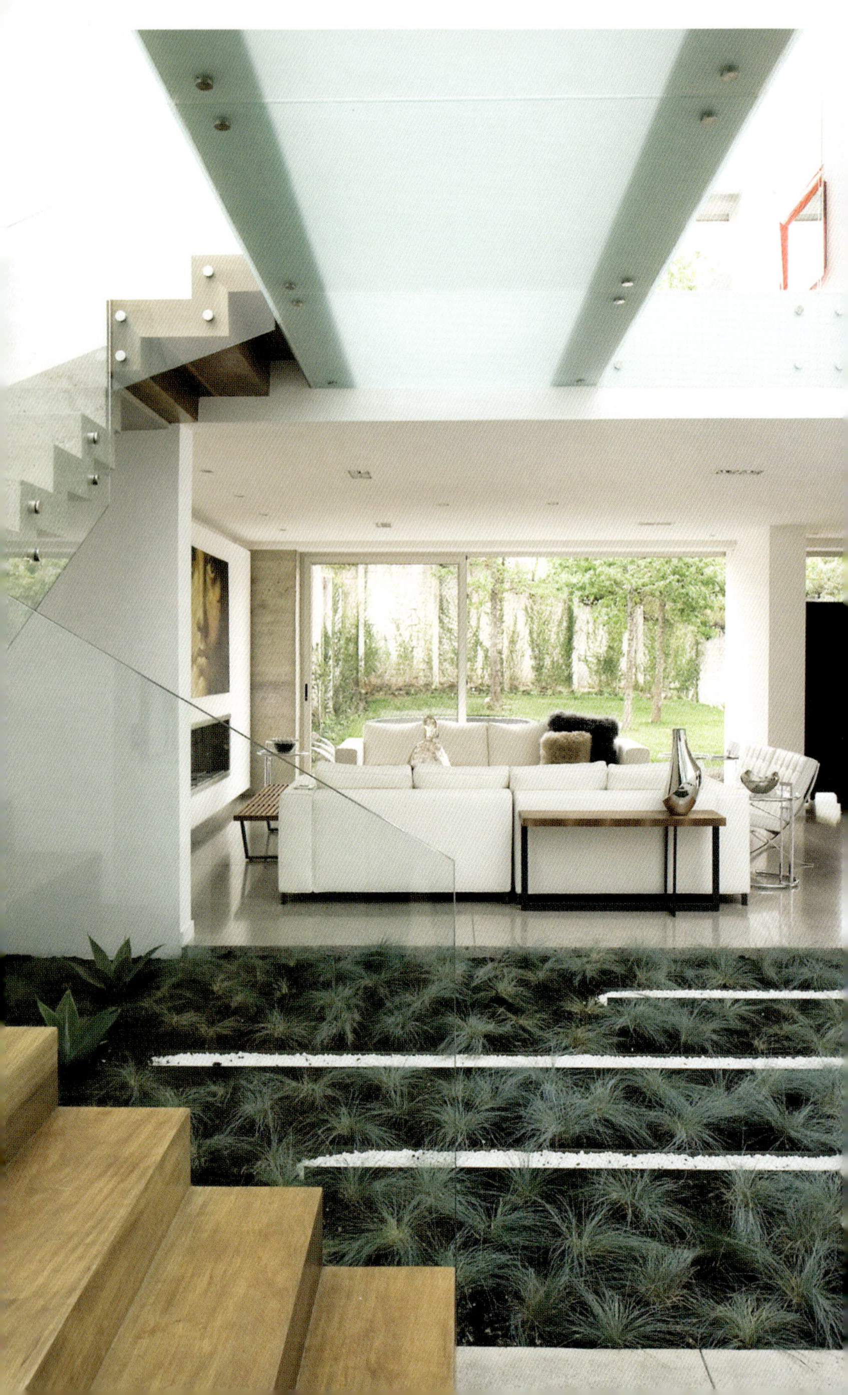

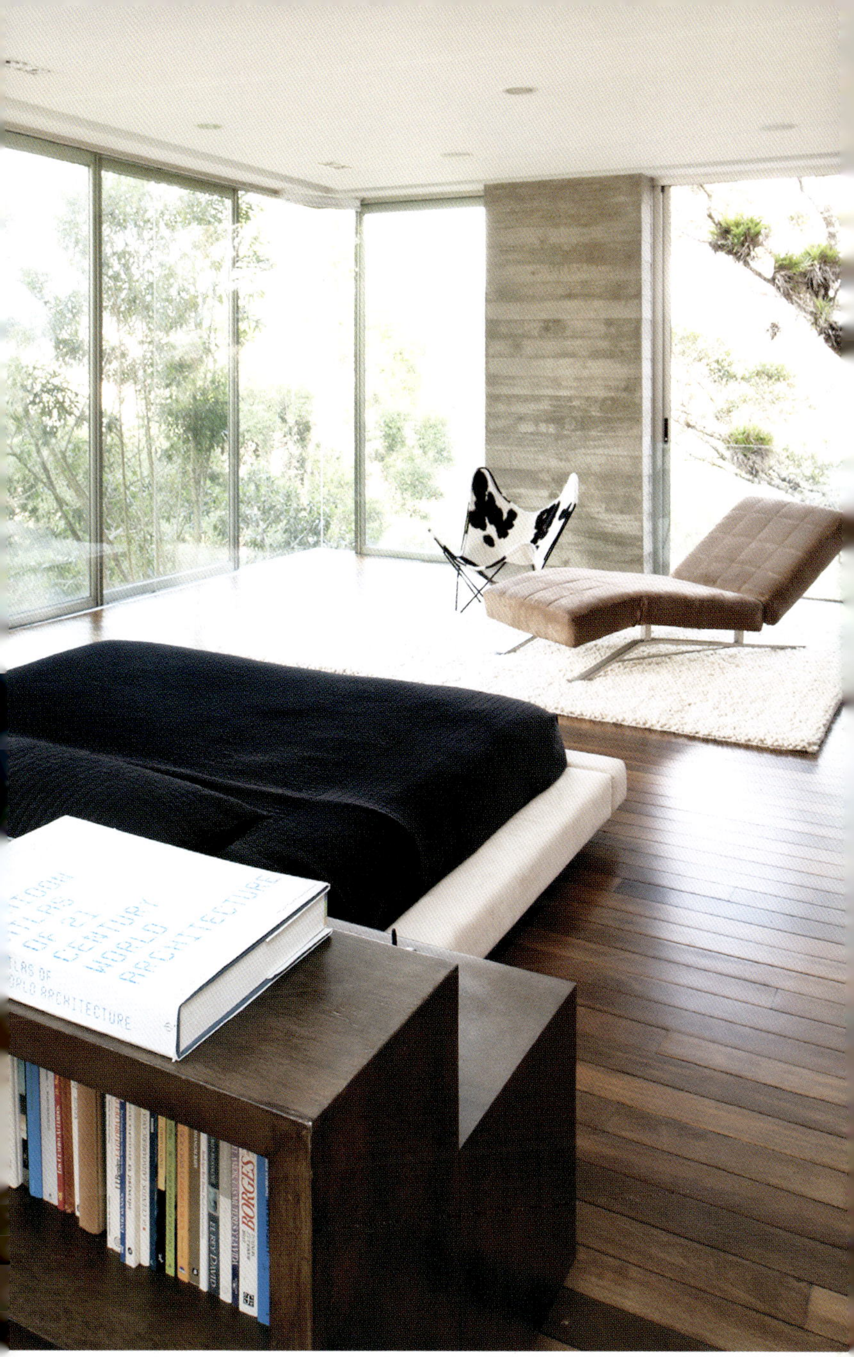
OF 21
CENTURY
WORLD
ARCHITECTURE
BORGES

140 | **Cameron Loft** | New York | SchappacherWhite

The design pulls together both sleek and rustic elements under a unified palette of black and white.

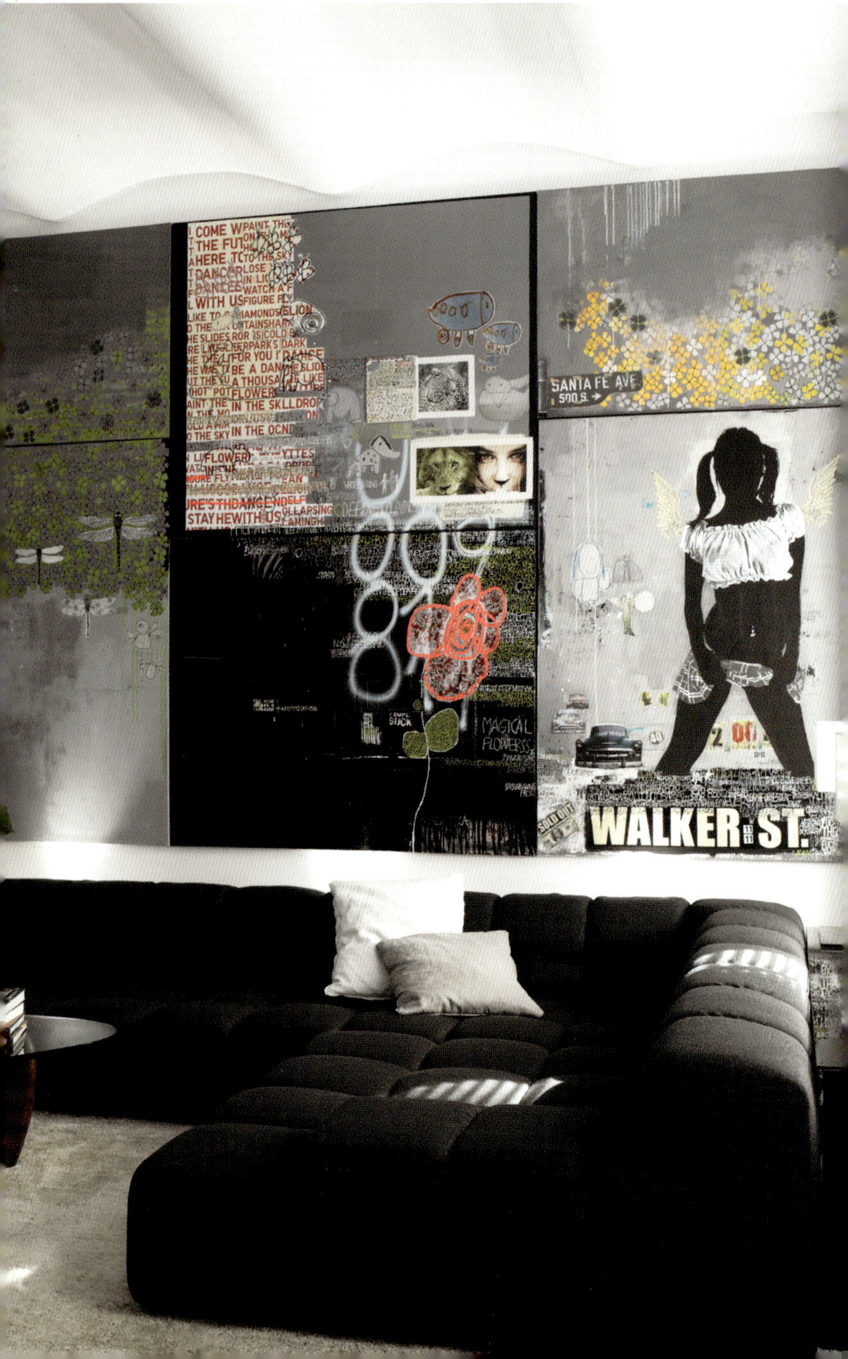
SANTA FE AVE
500 S.
WALKER ST.

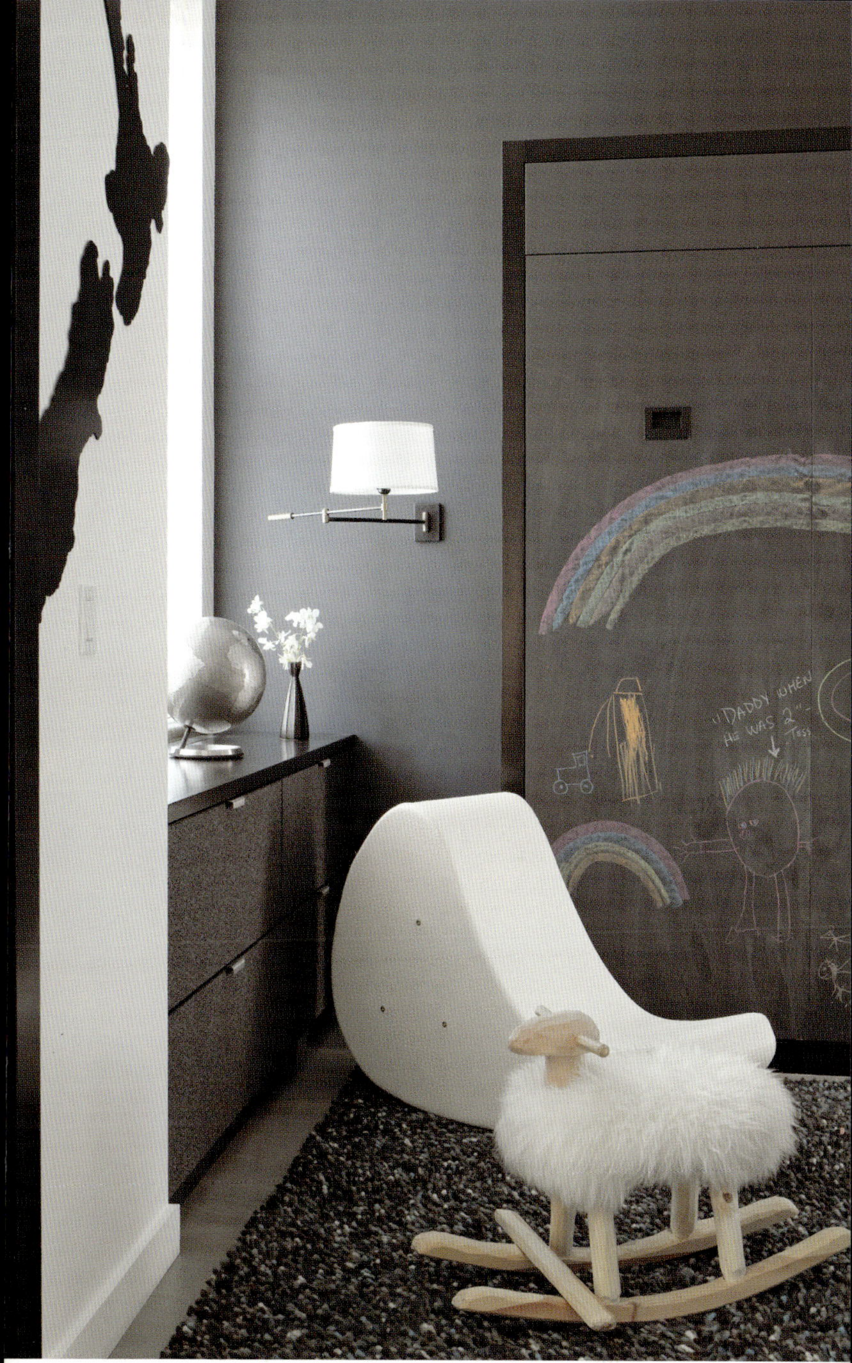
"DADDY WHEN HE WAS 2" - TESS

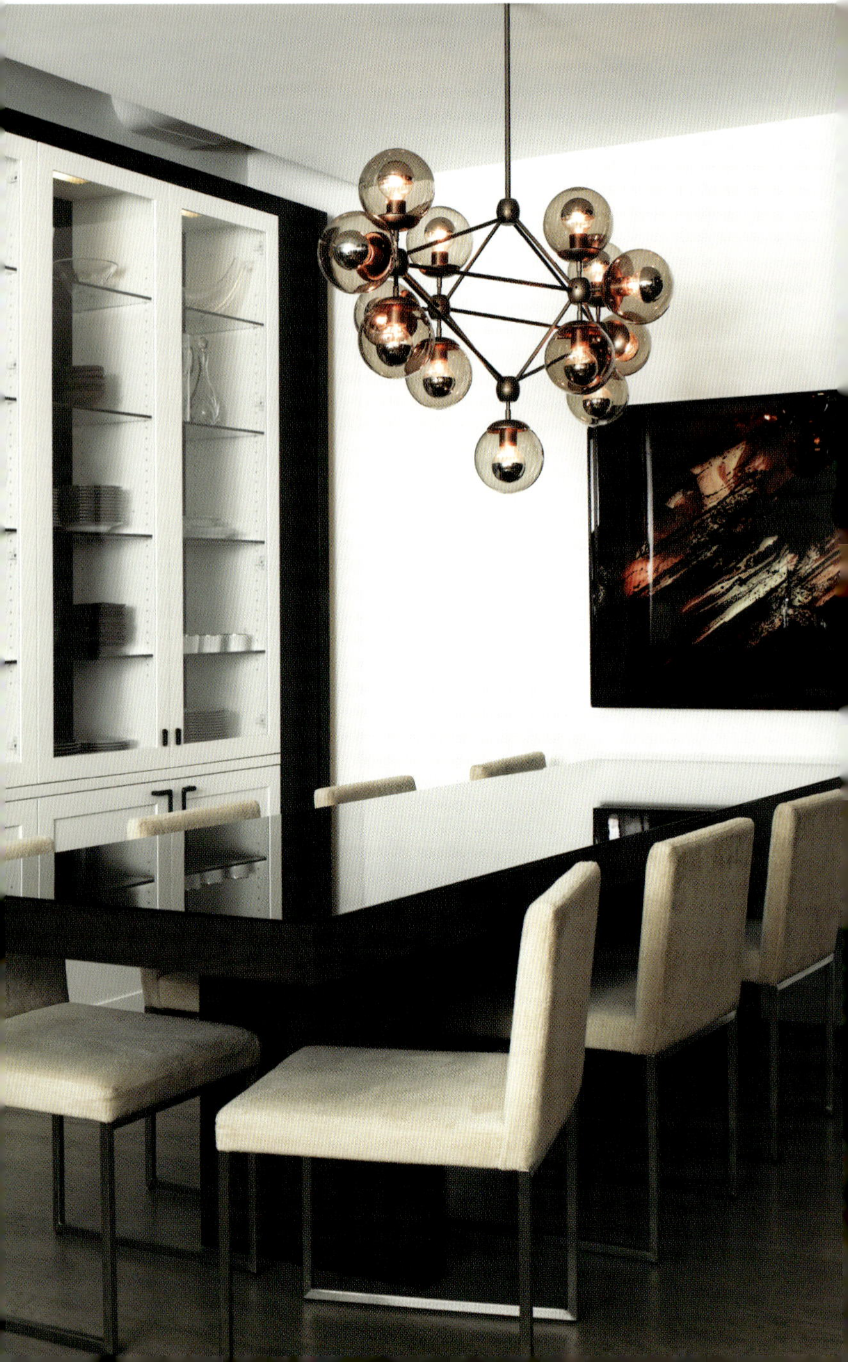

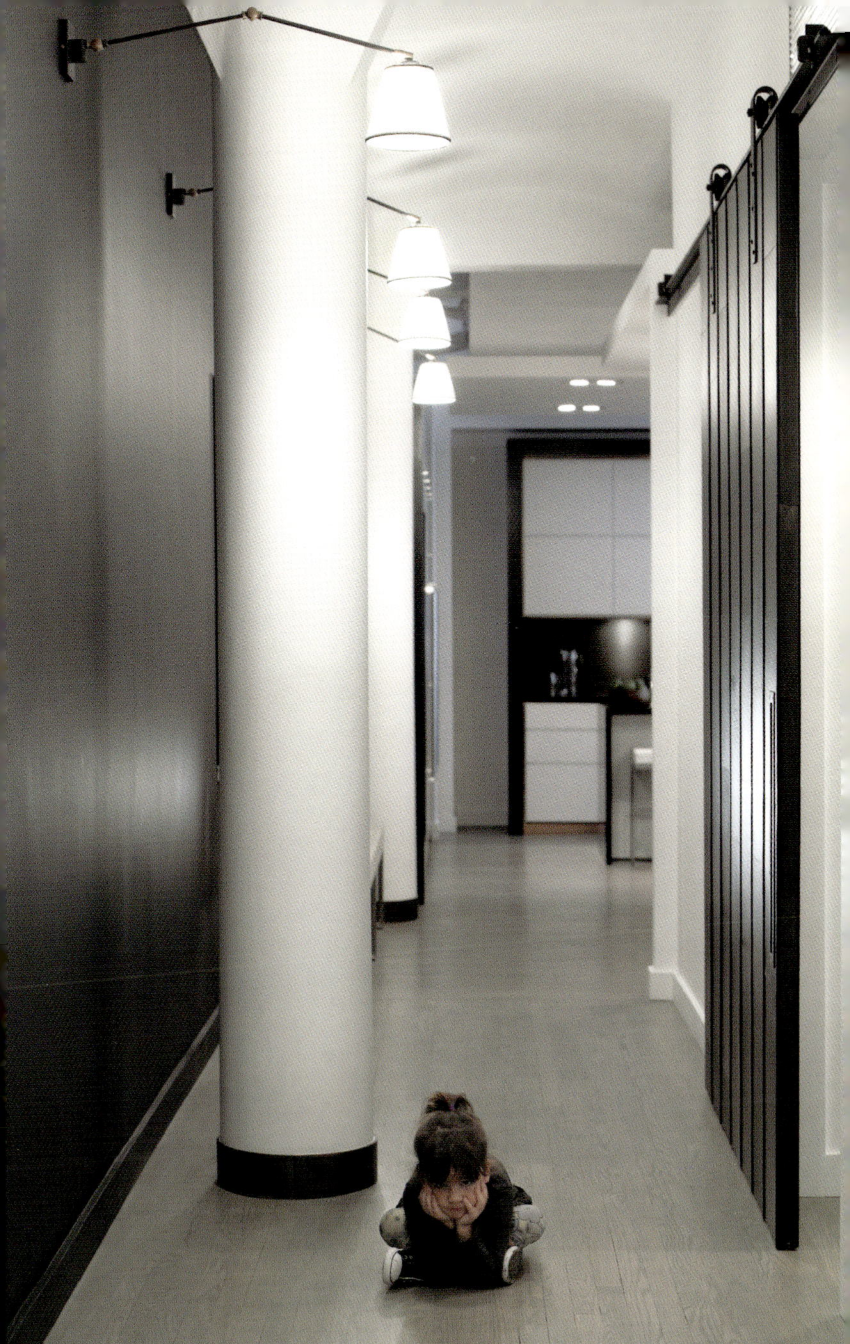

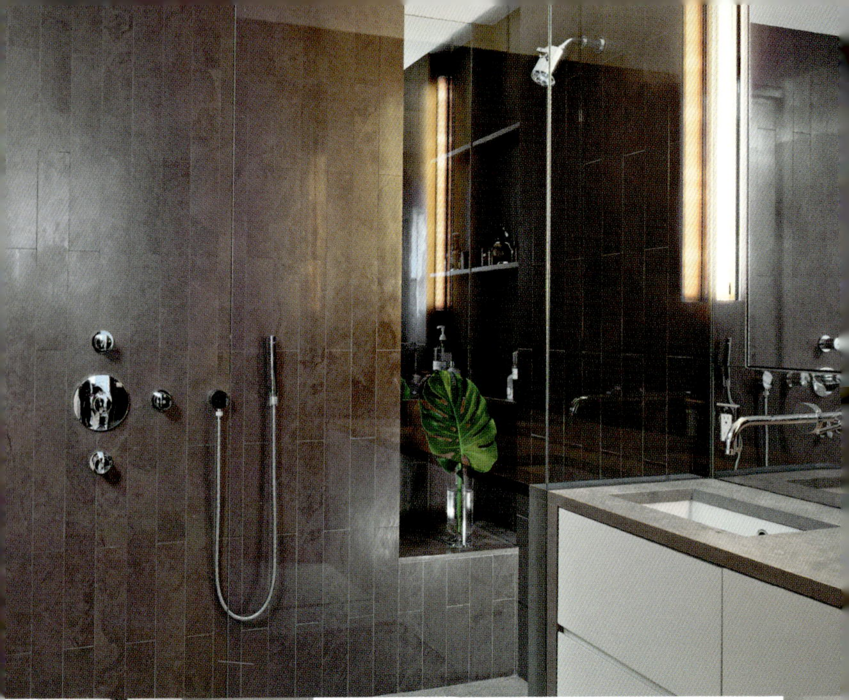
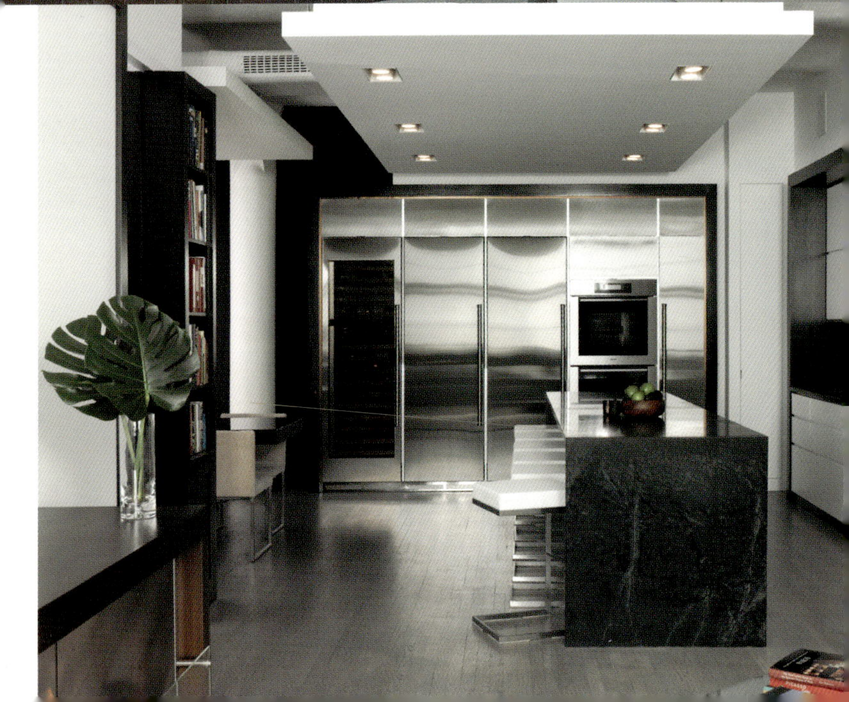

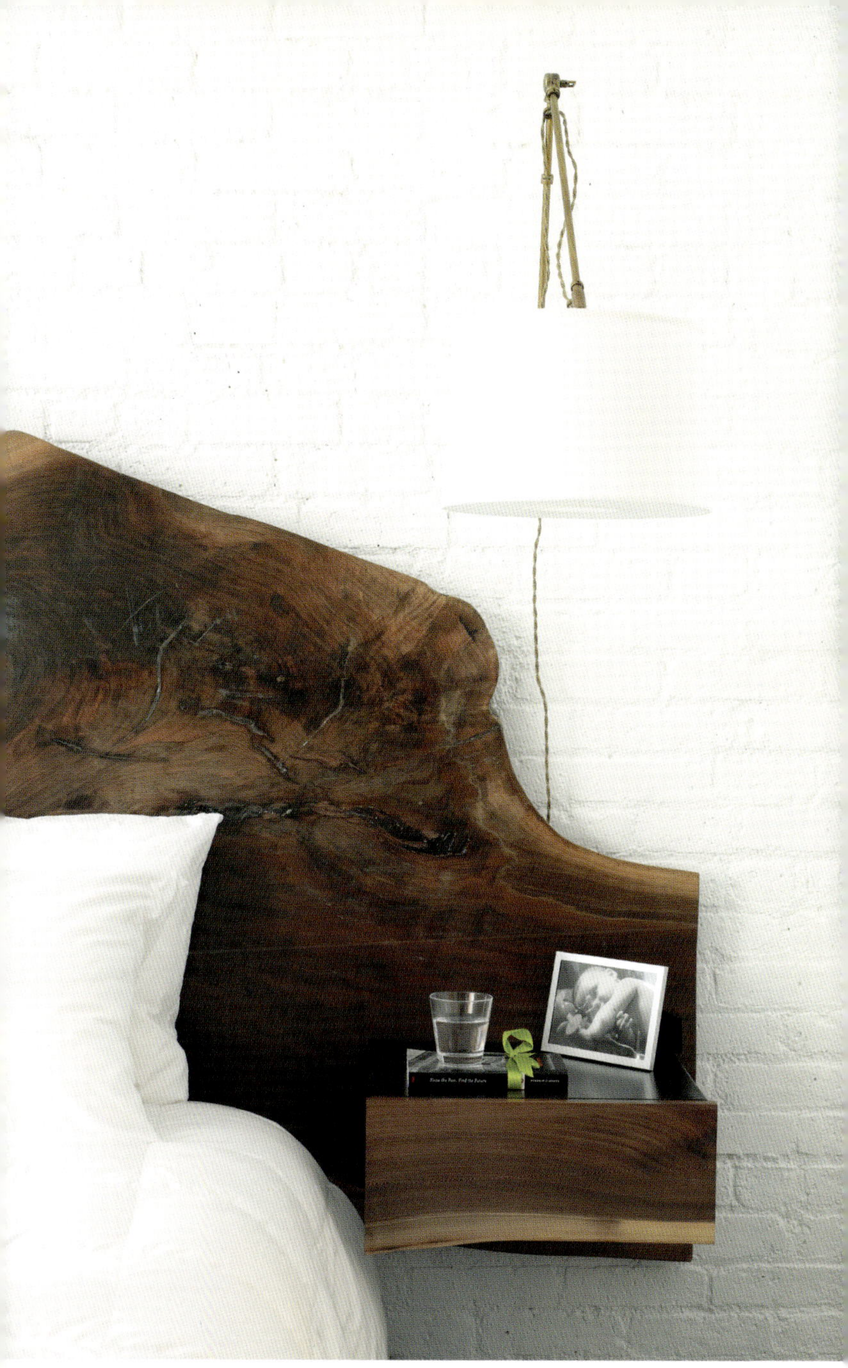

148 | **Transformer** | New York | Studio Garneau

An adaptive mini-loft where layered spaces dynamically reveal and conceal in response to different uses

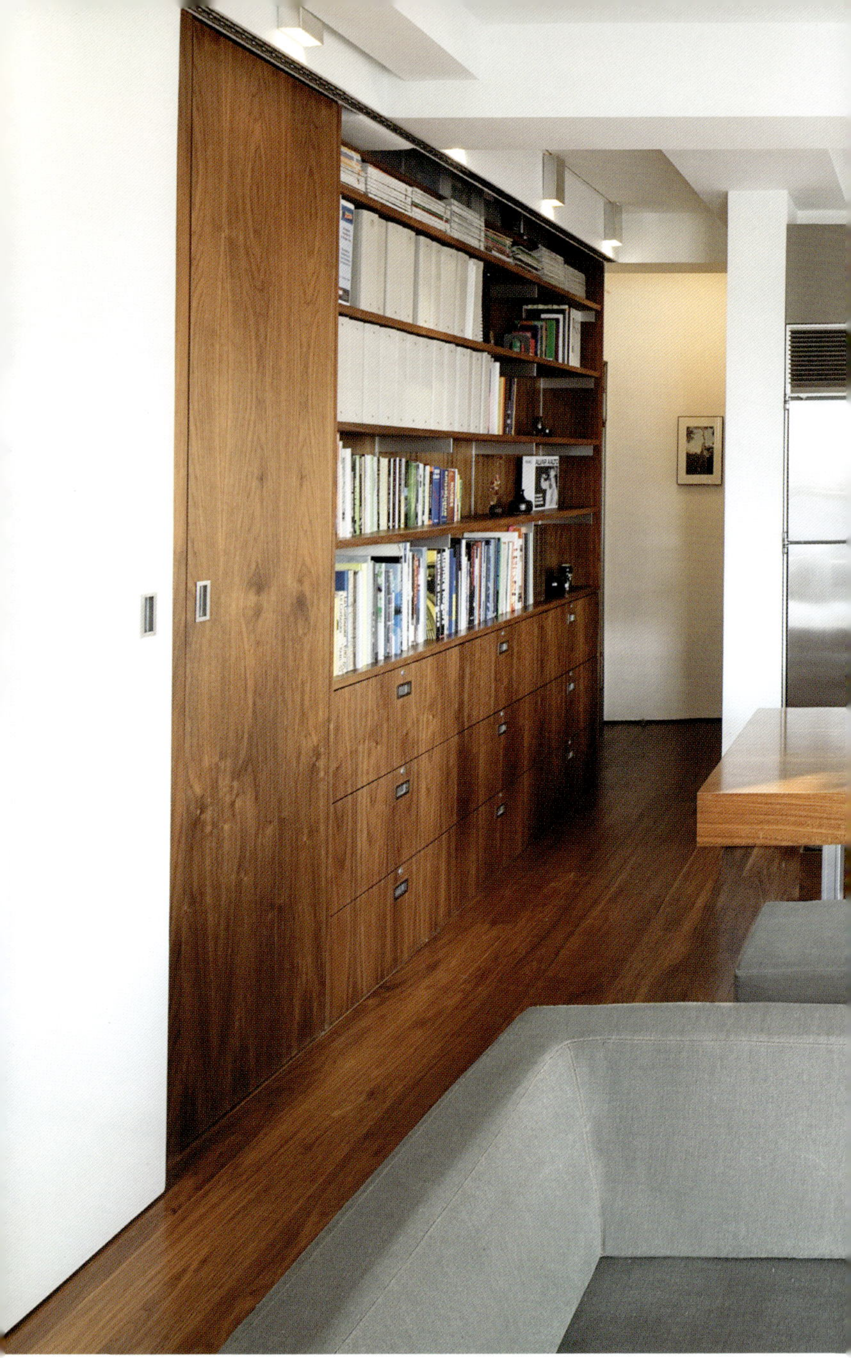

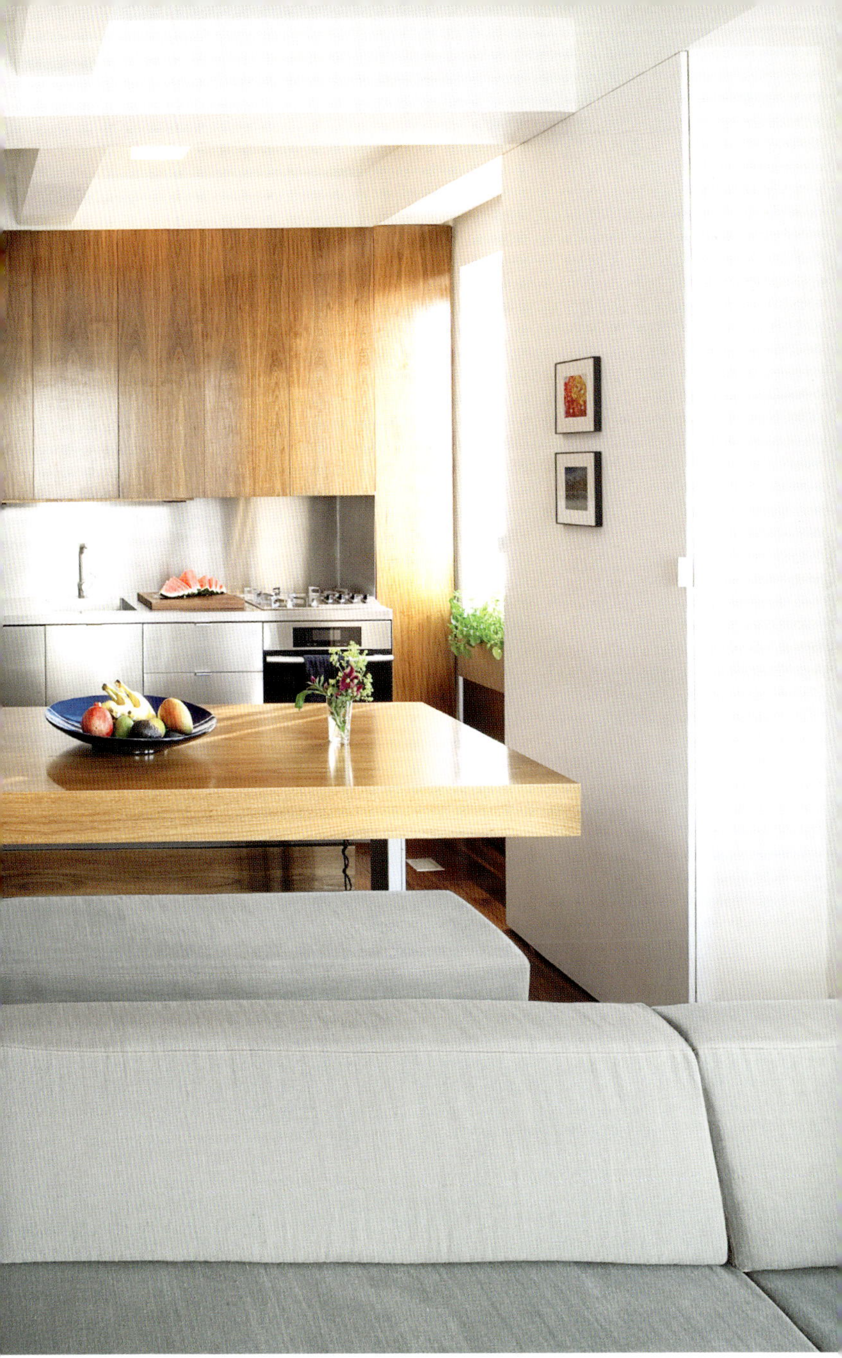

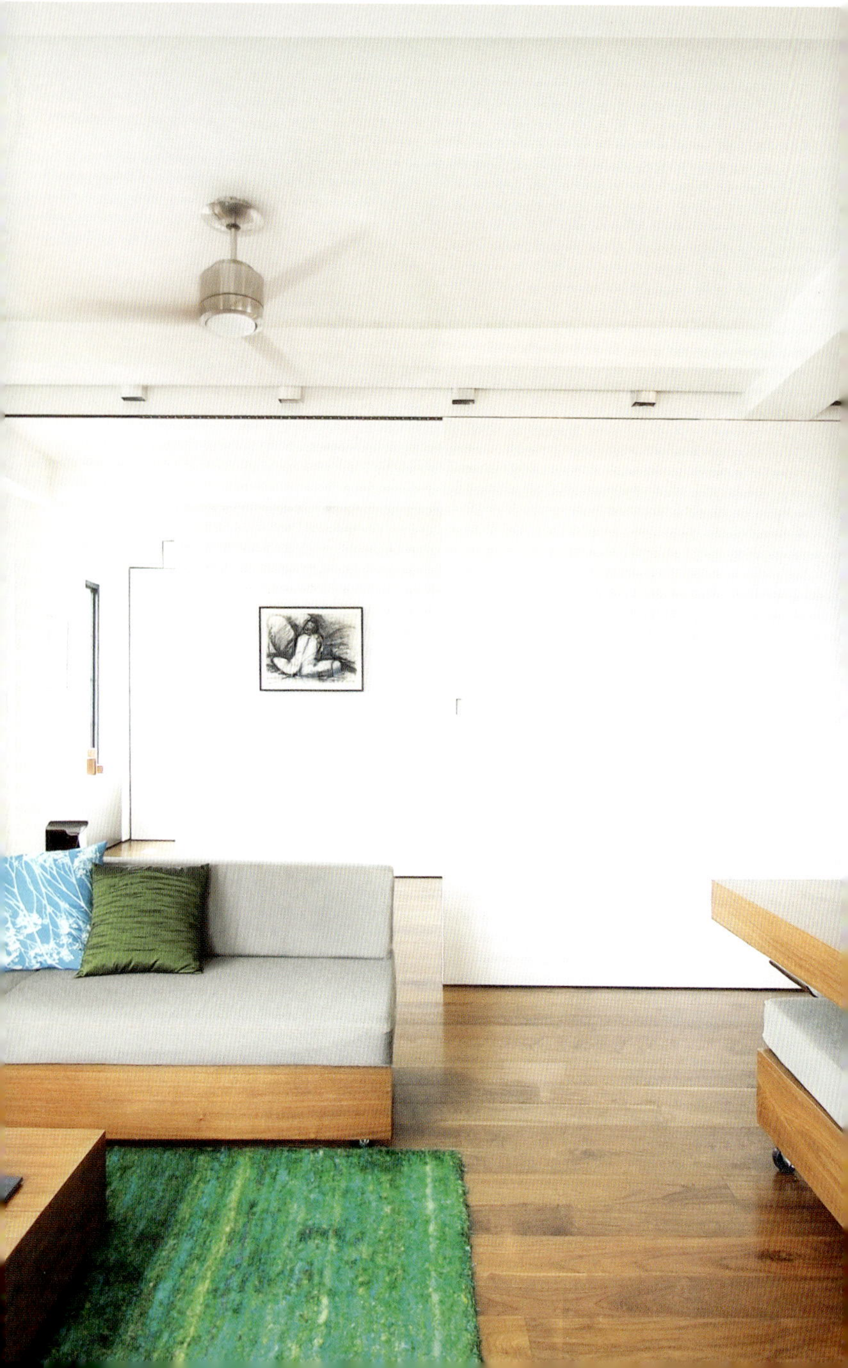

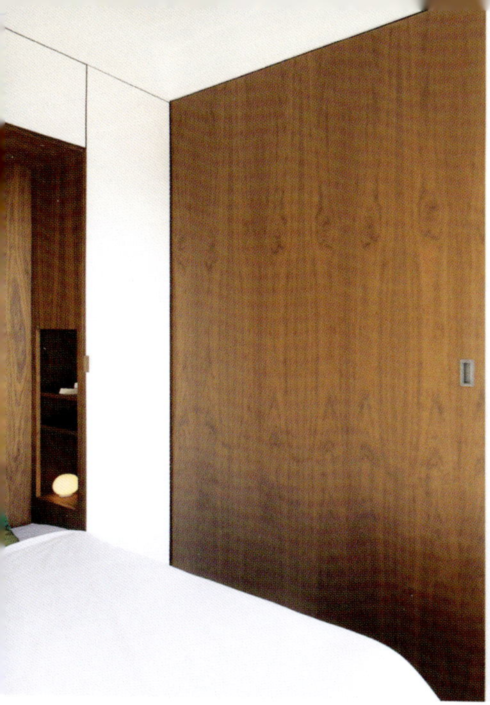

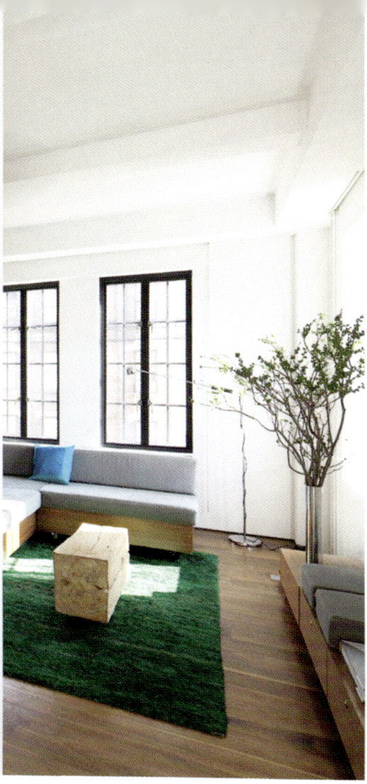

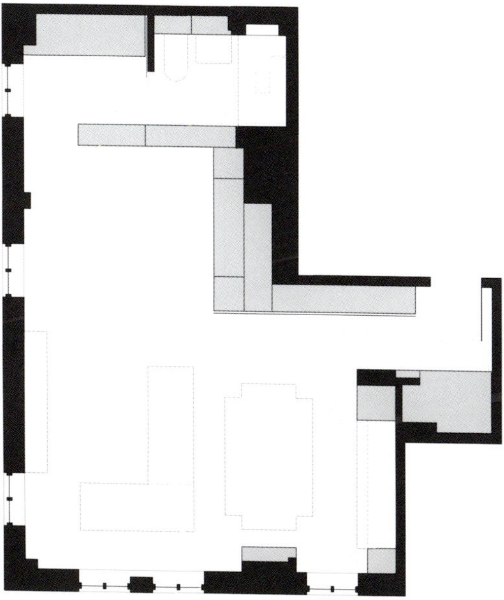

A dynamic, multipurpose design element **generates spatial** continuity and programmatic **efficiency** in this **one-bedroom** apartment.

Krastev/Nikolova Residence | New York | su11 architecture + design

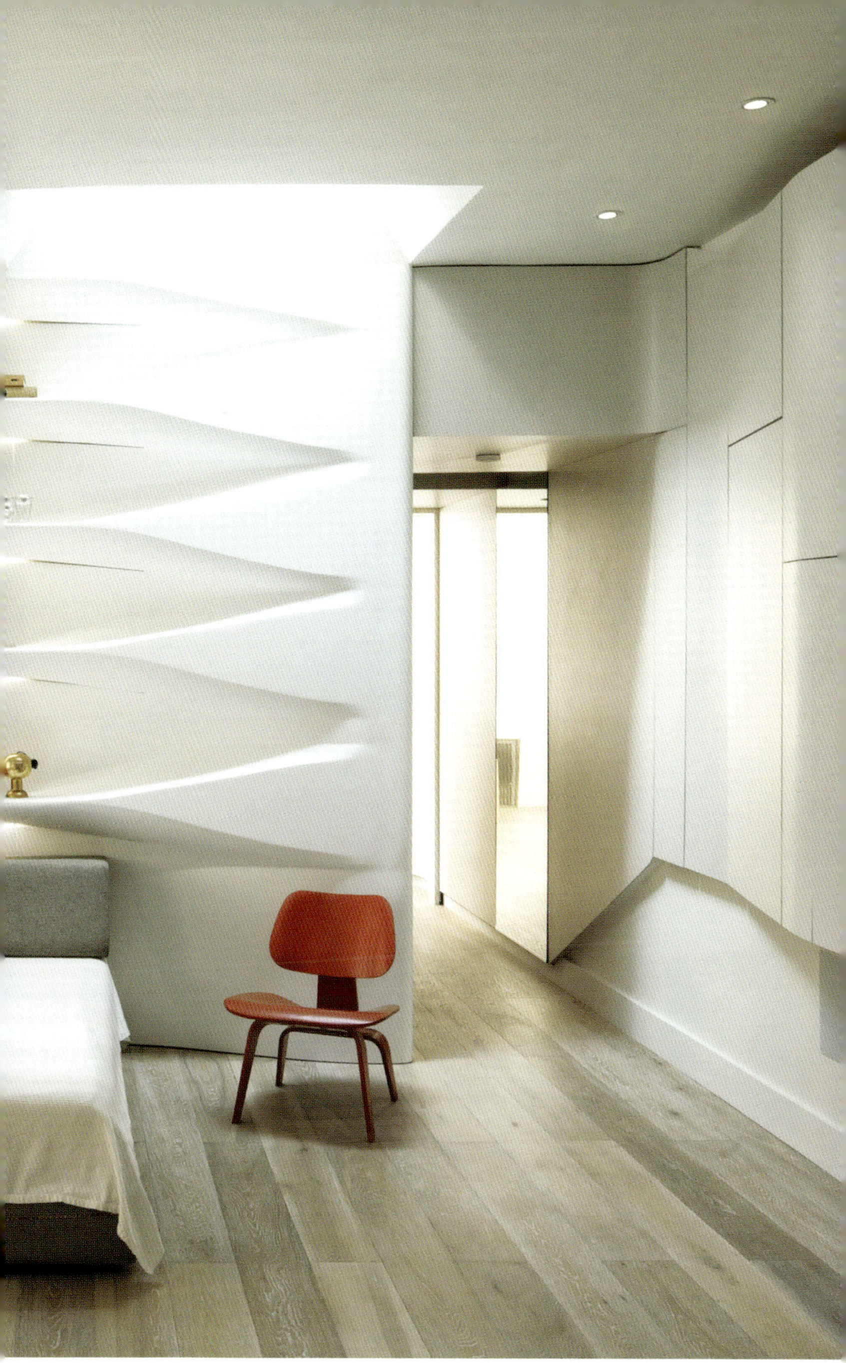

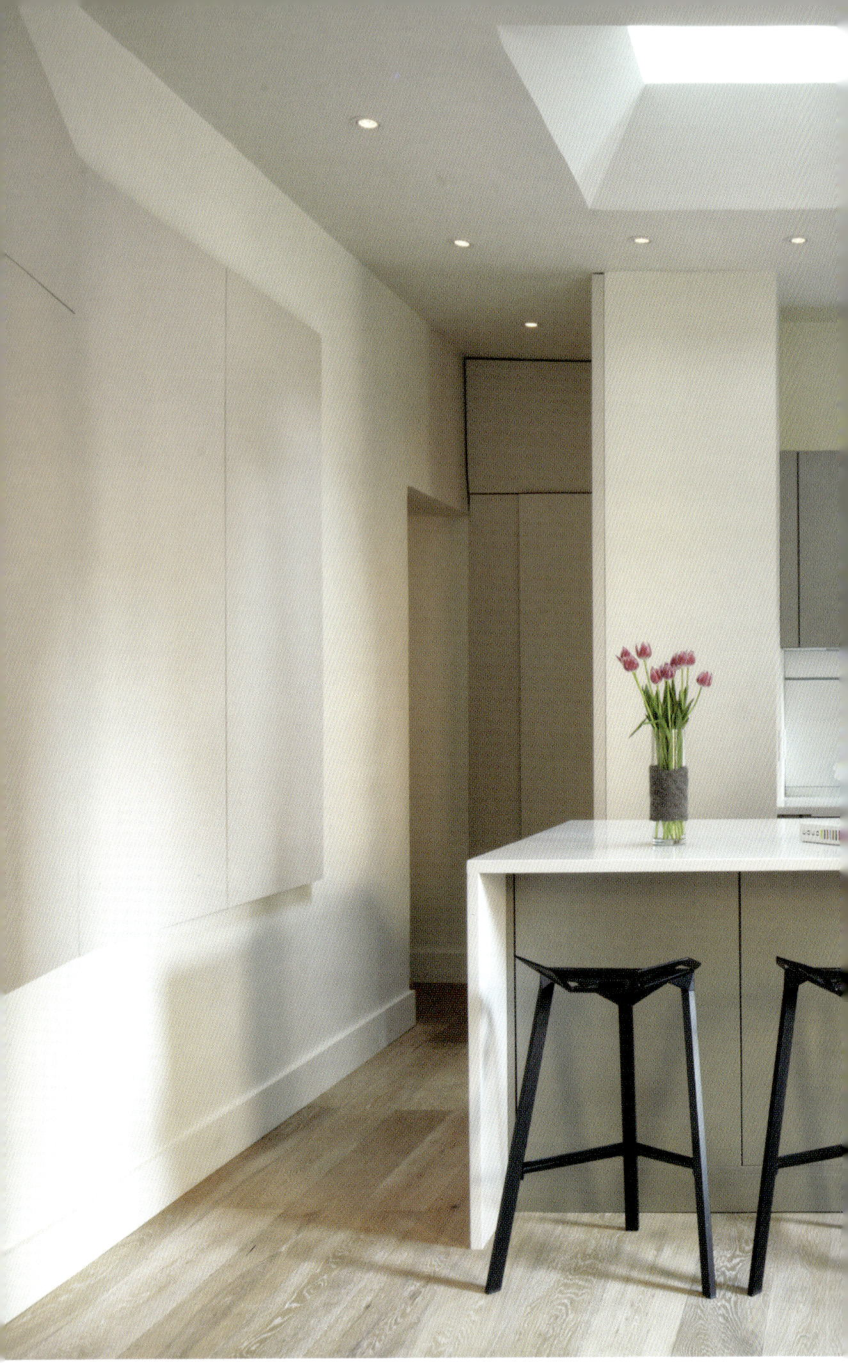

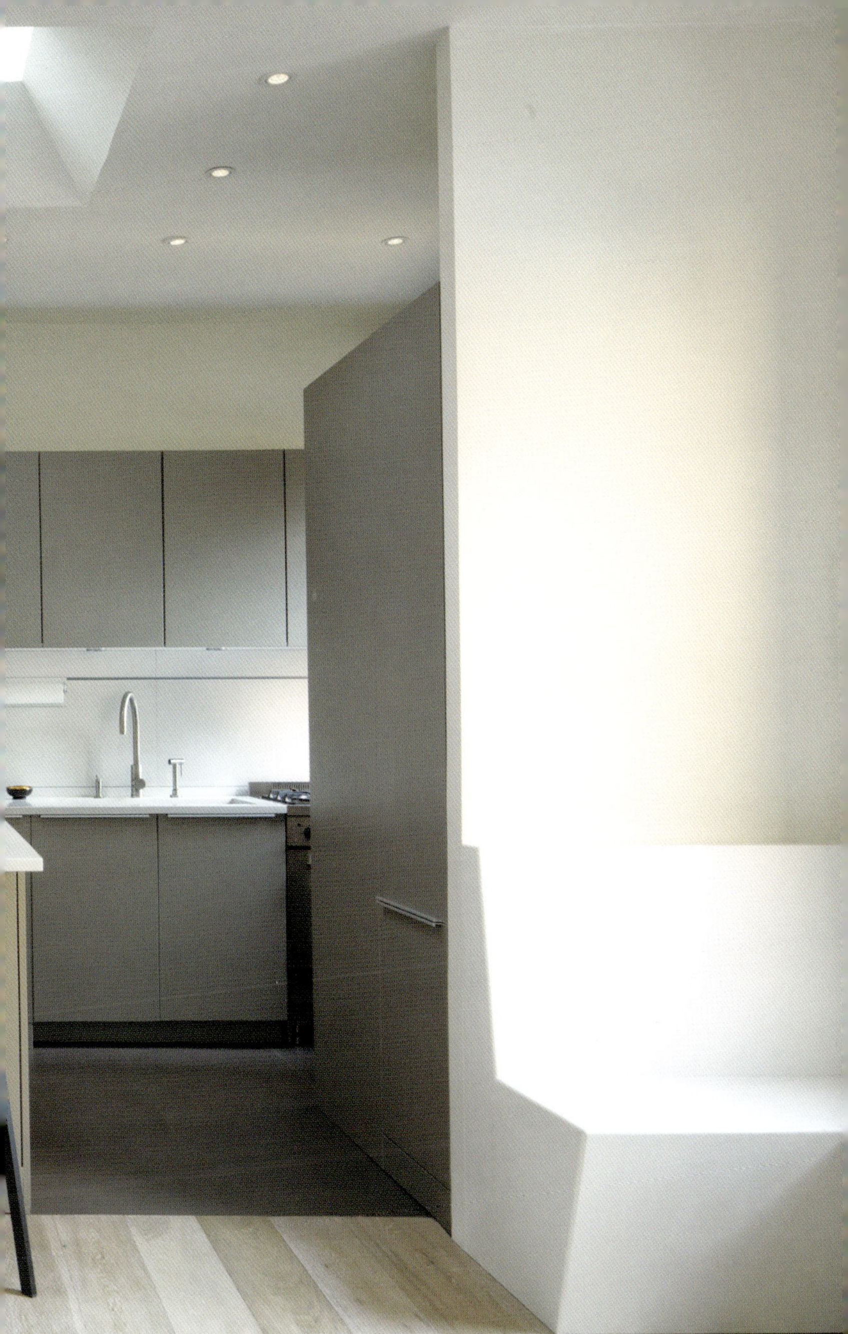

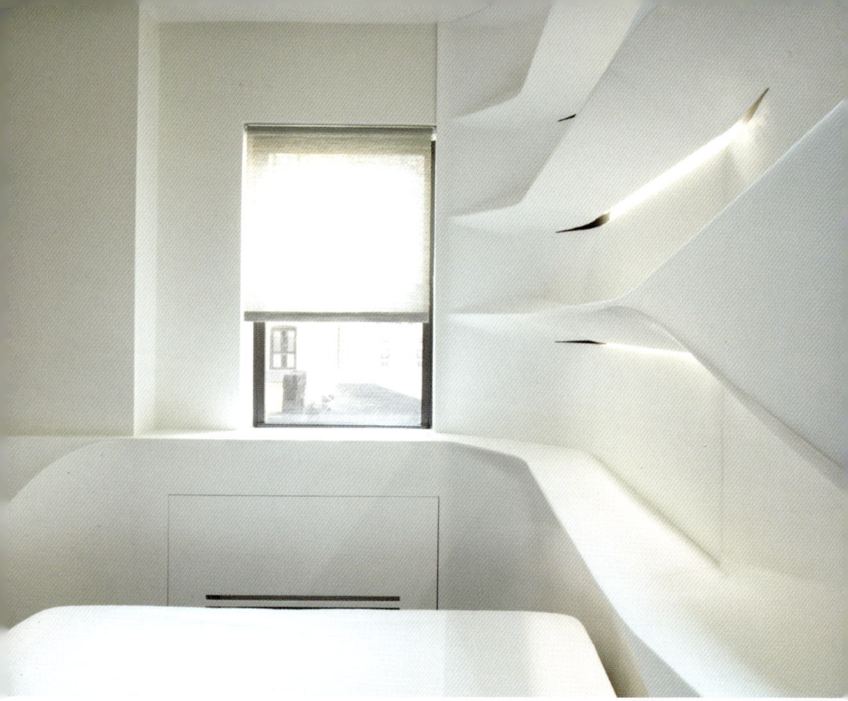

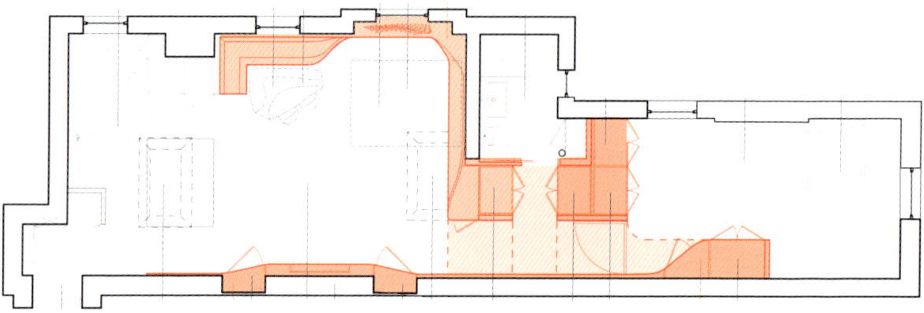

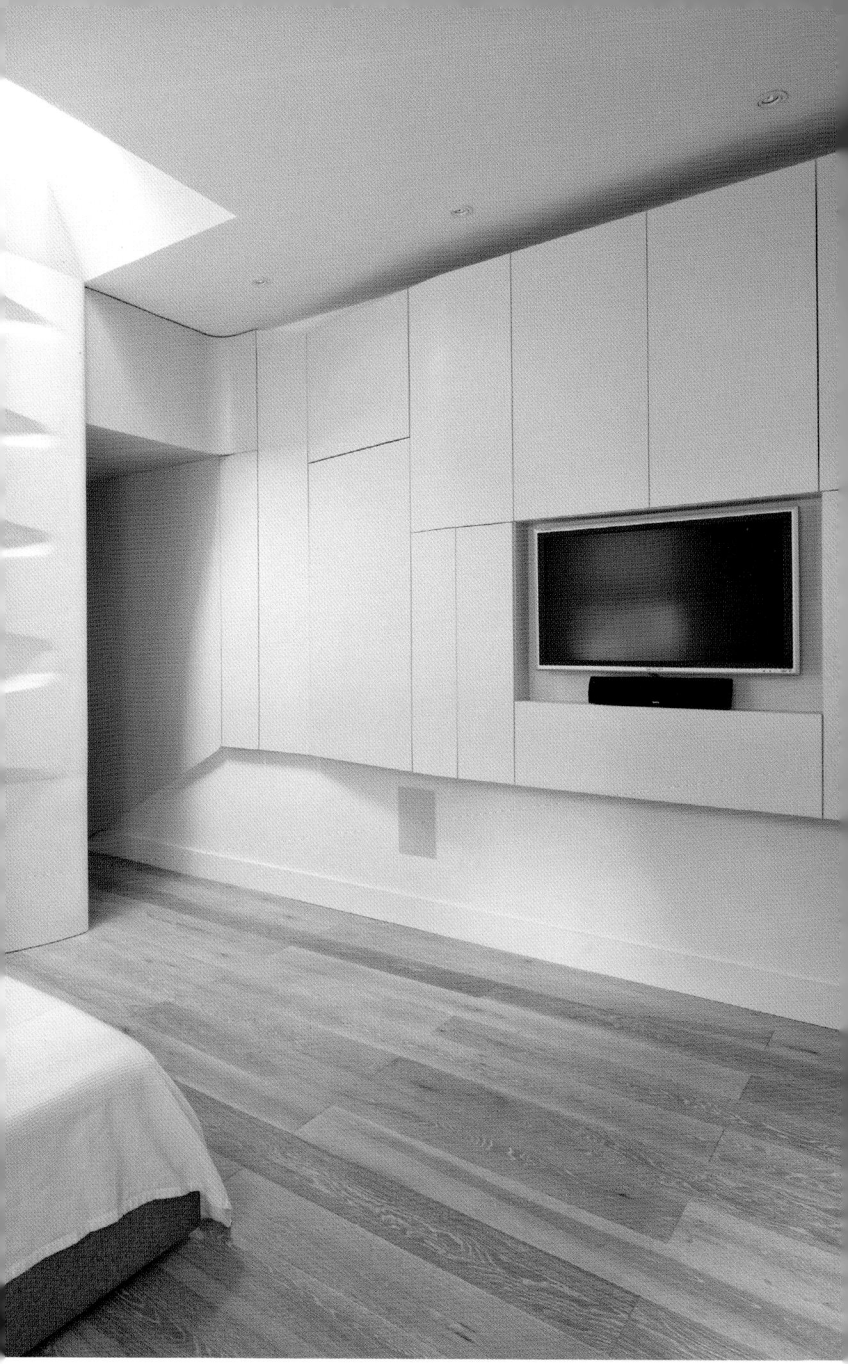

Fragments of a 19th-century **stable block are incorporated** into a bold contemporary **house.**

Stable Acre | Norfolk | David Kohn

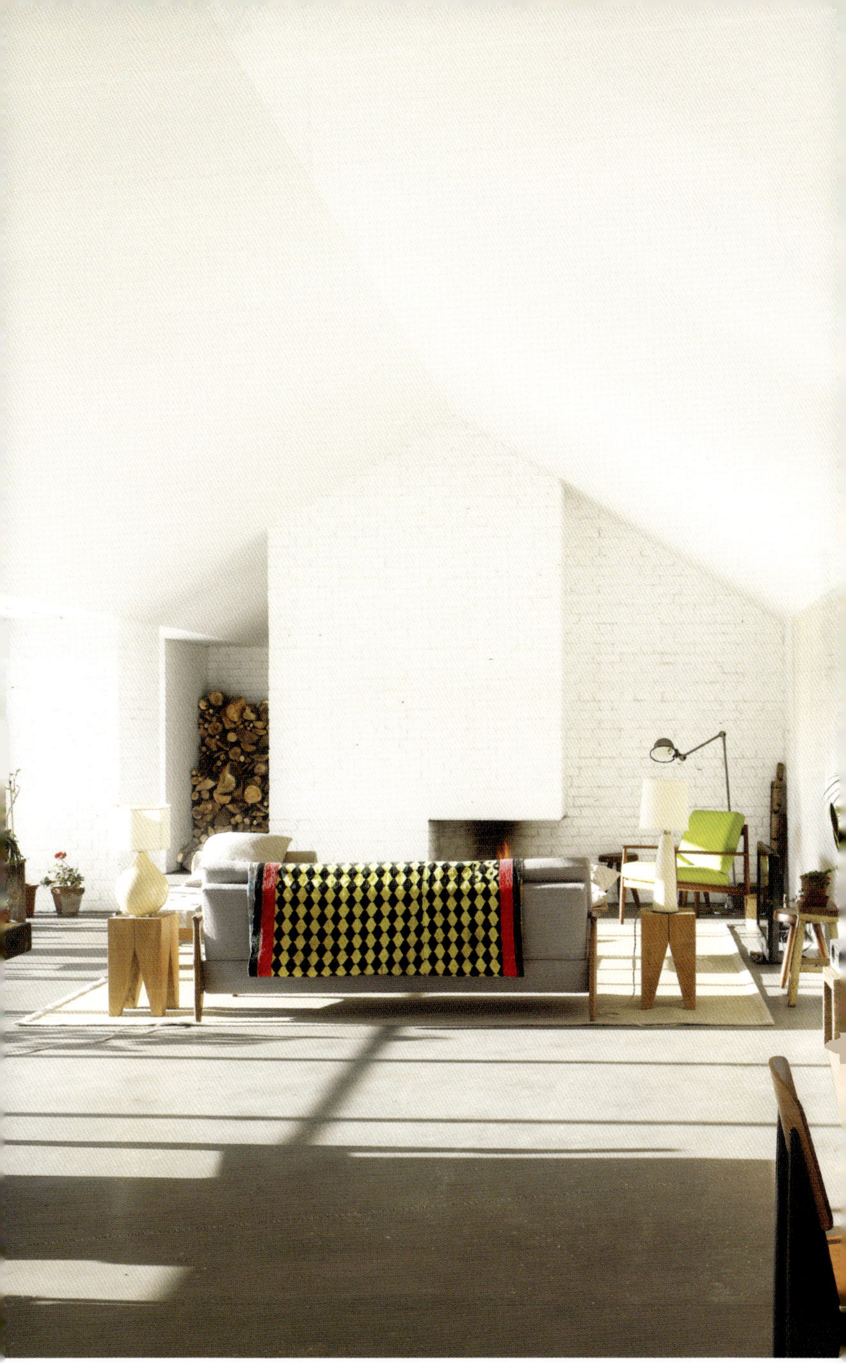

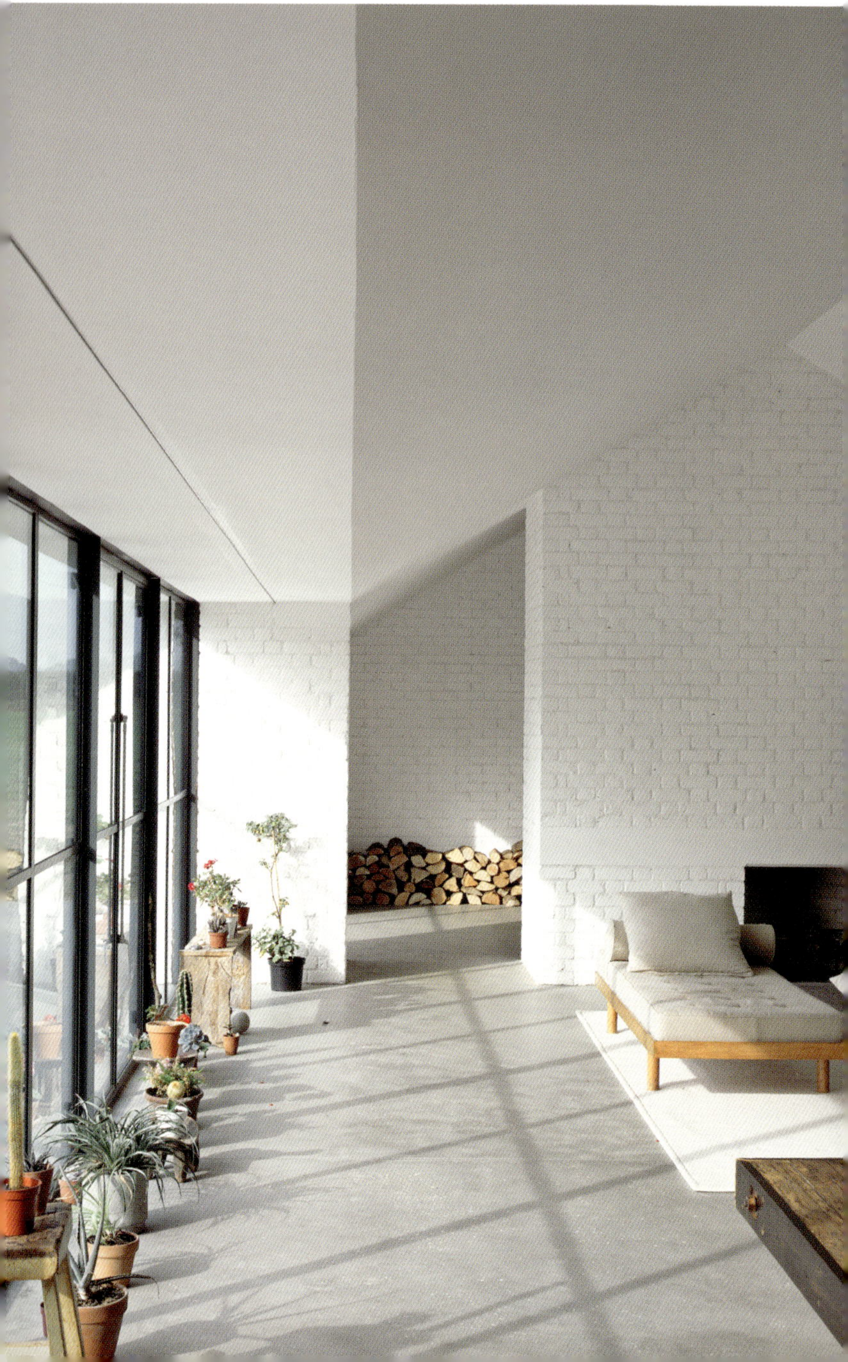

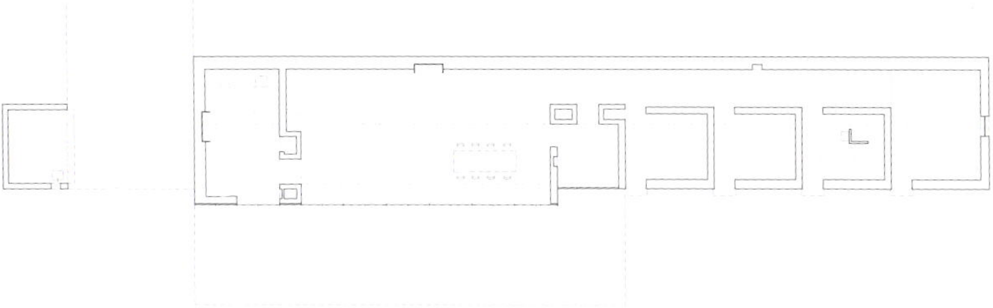

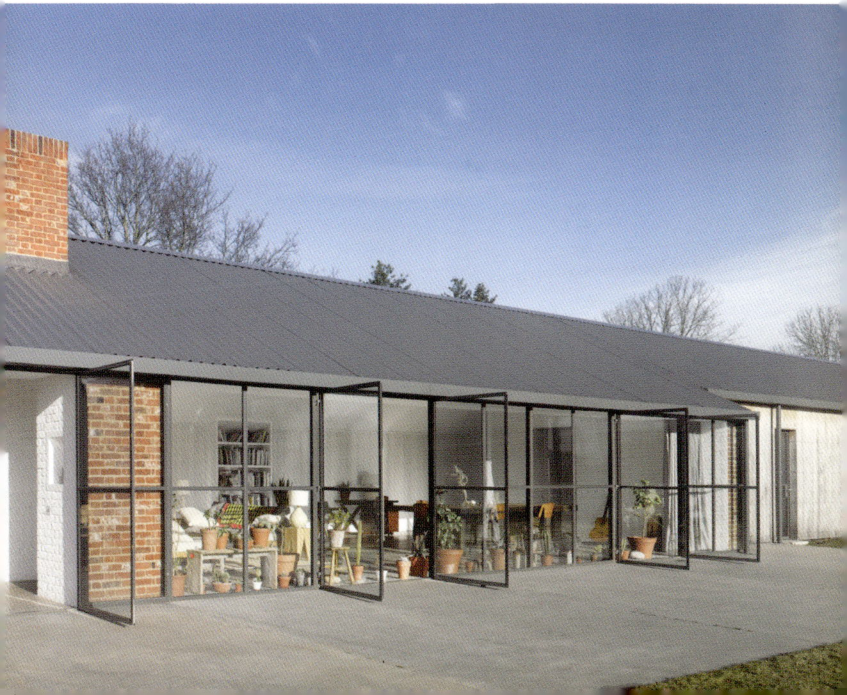

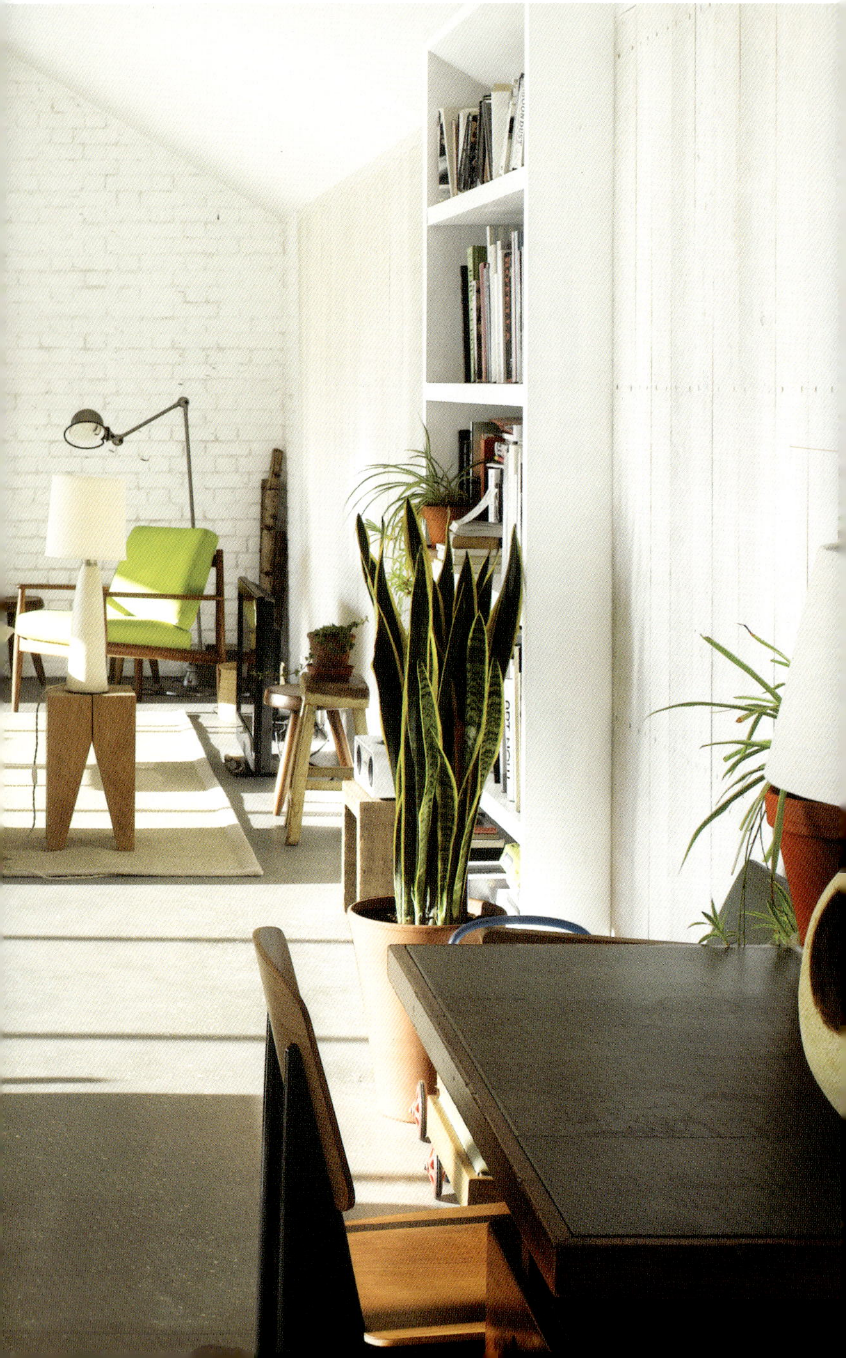

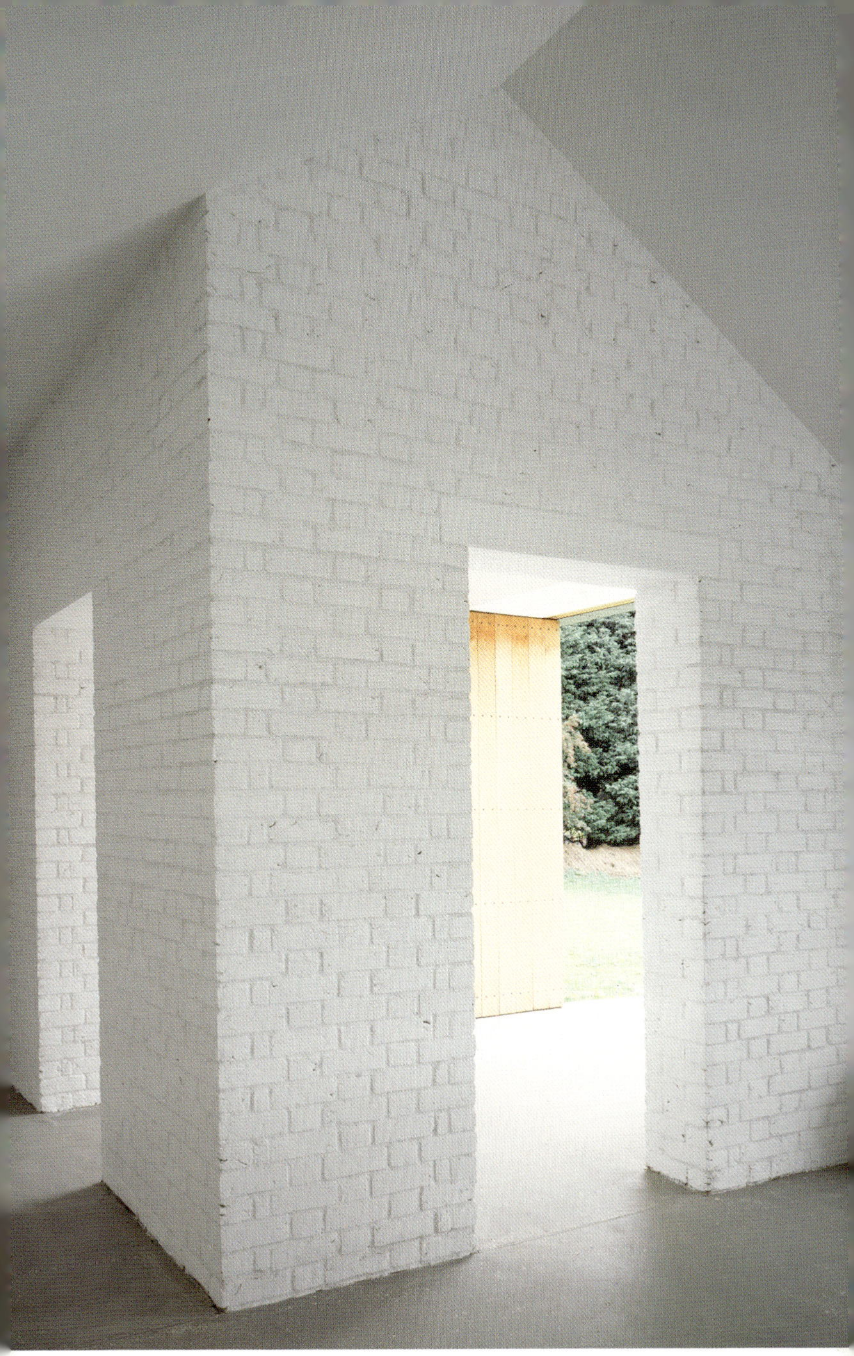

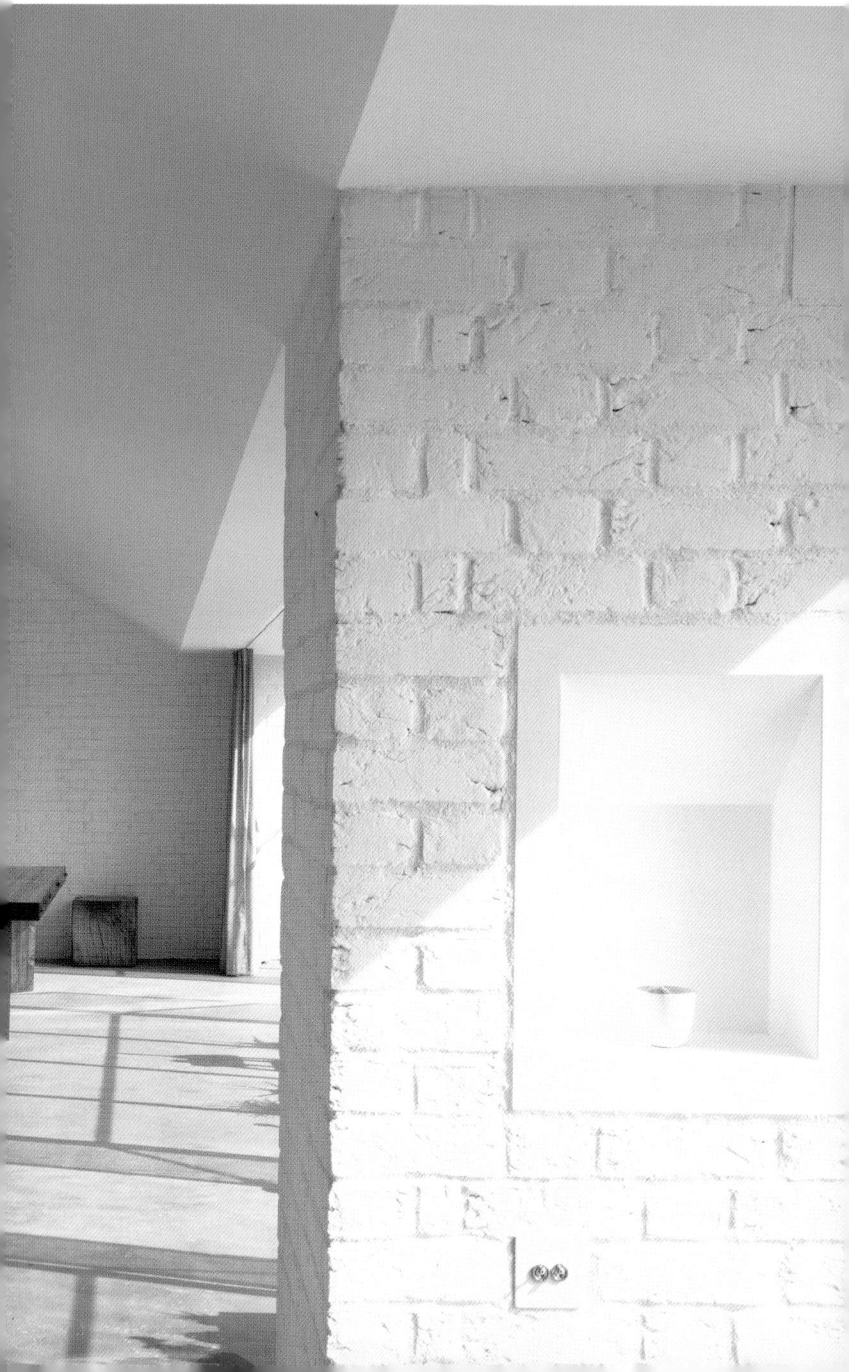

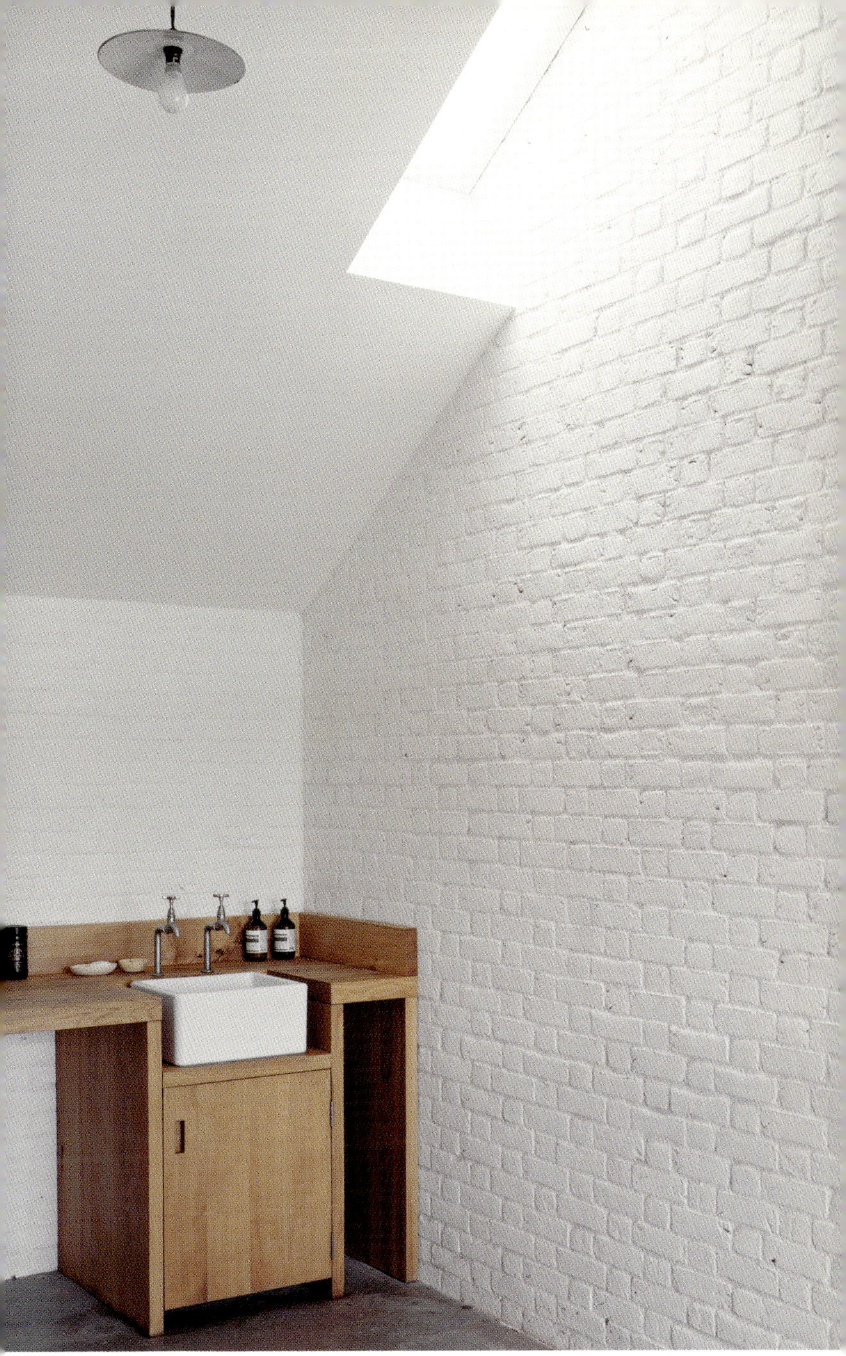

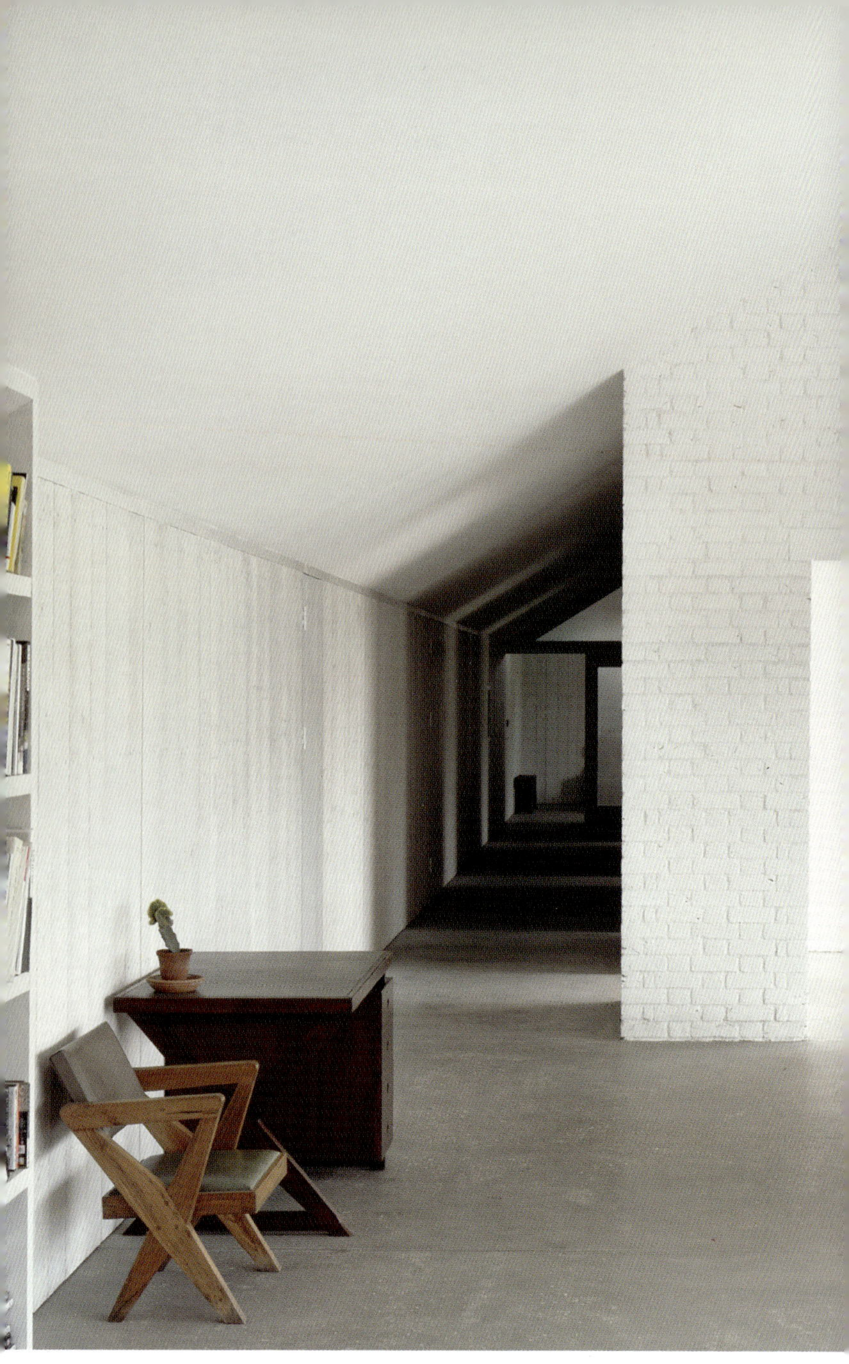

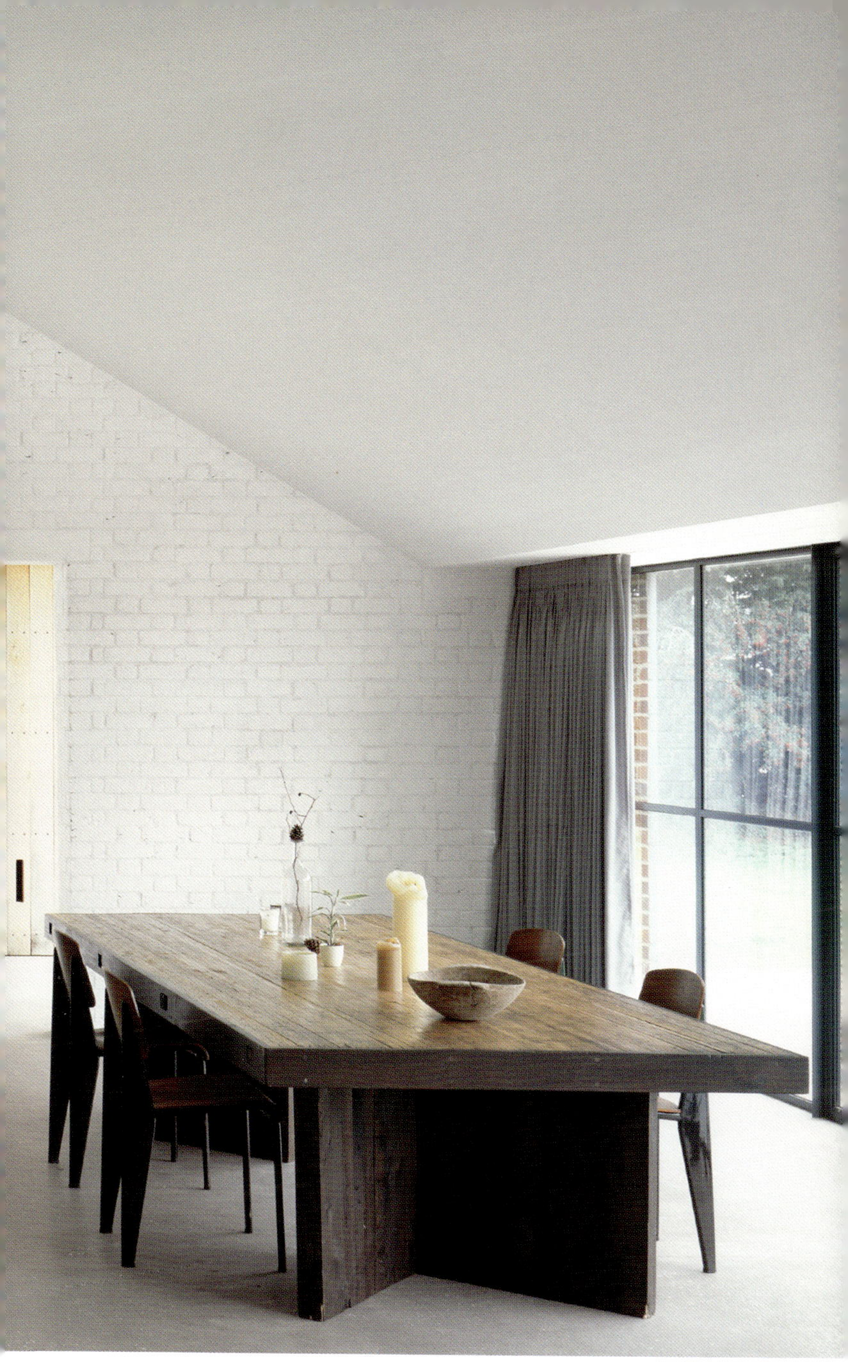

House in Uenoshiba | Osaka | Fujiwaramuro Architects

A trail of plants splits the building into **two, ensuring** that adequate **light enters** the **interior.**

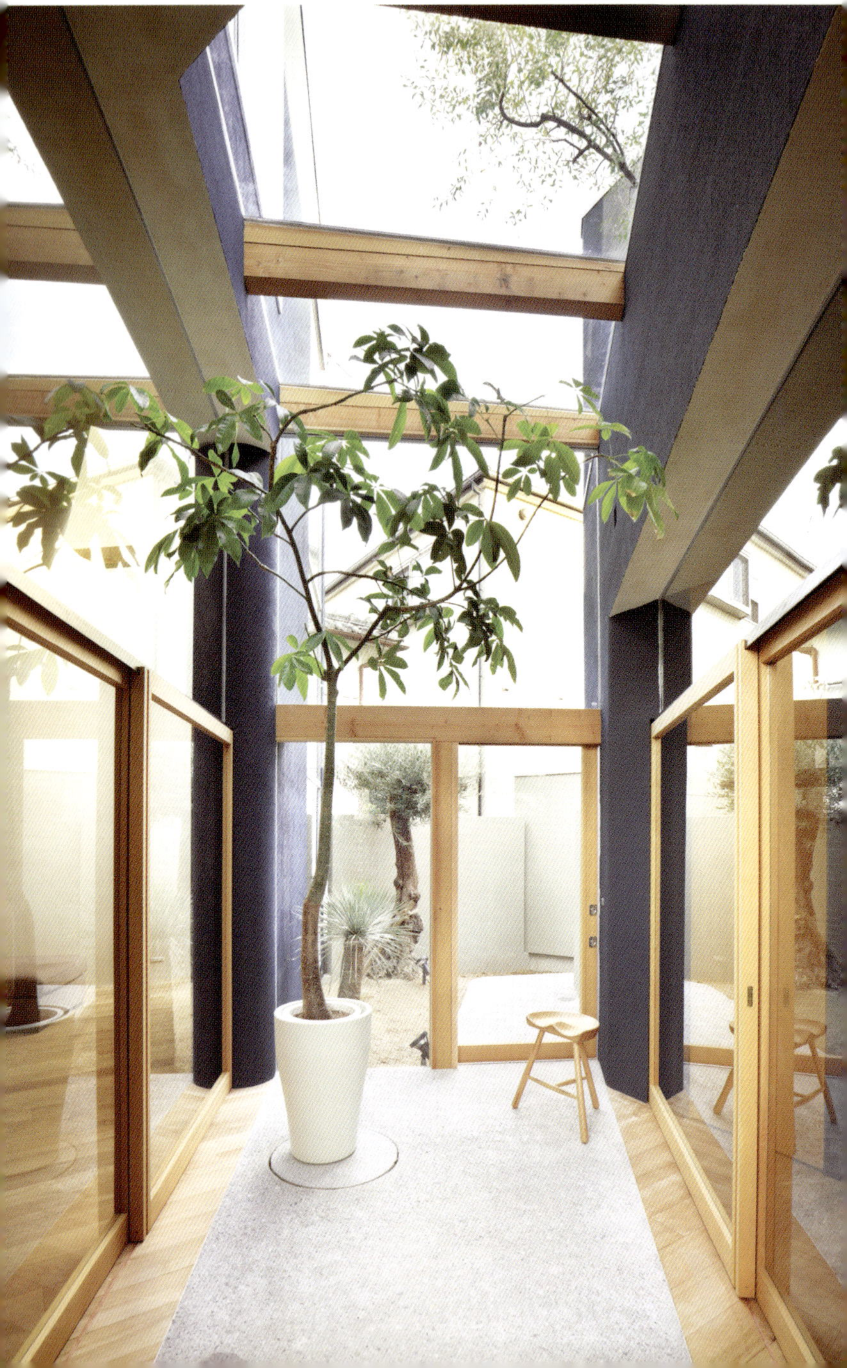

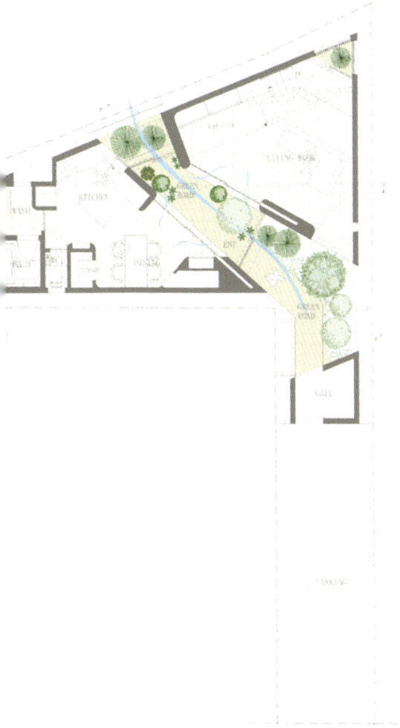

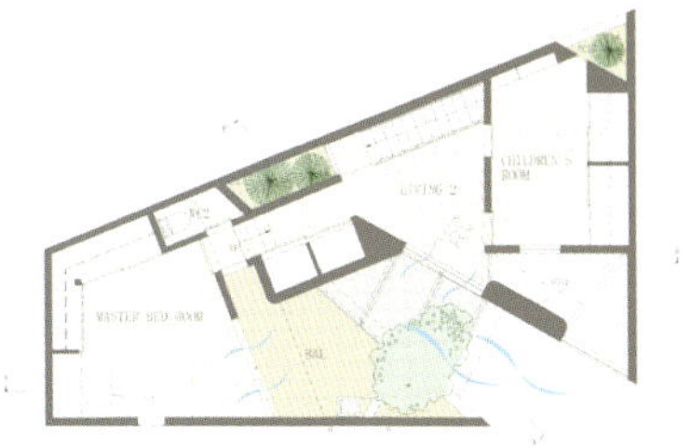

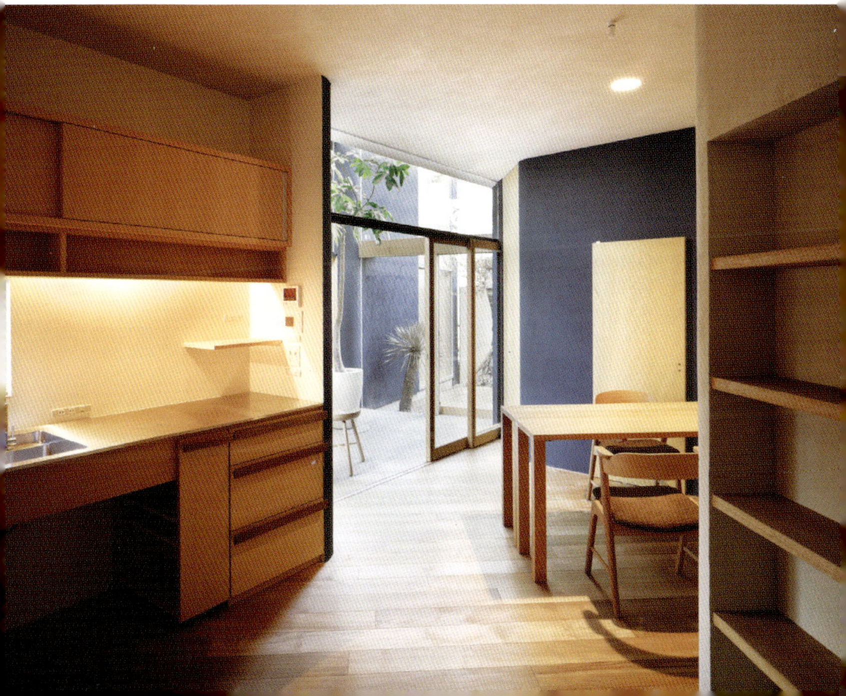

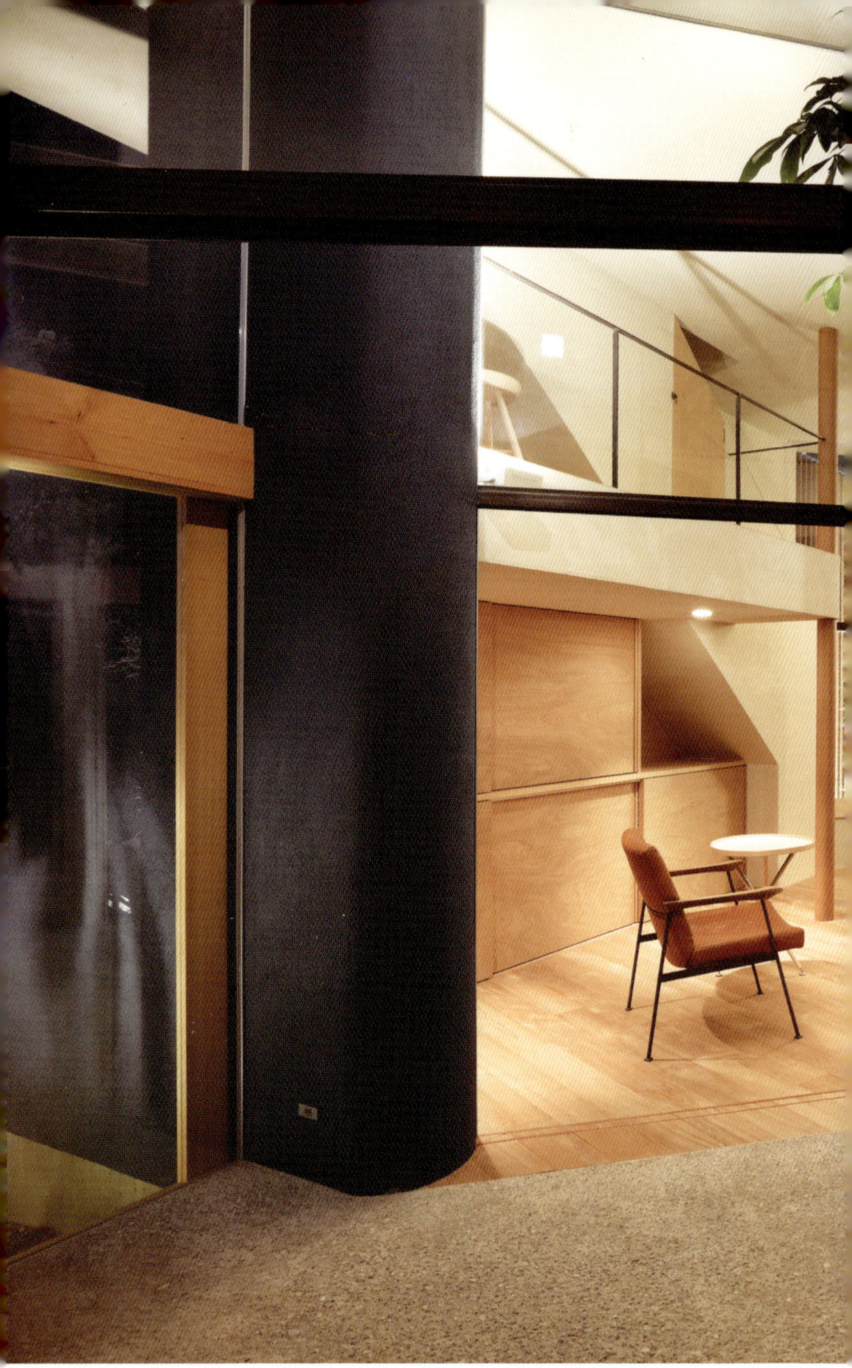

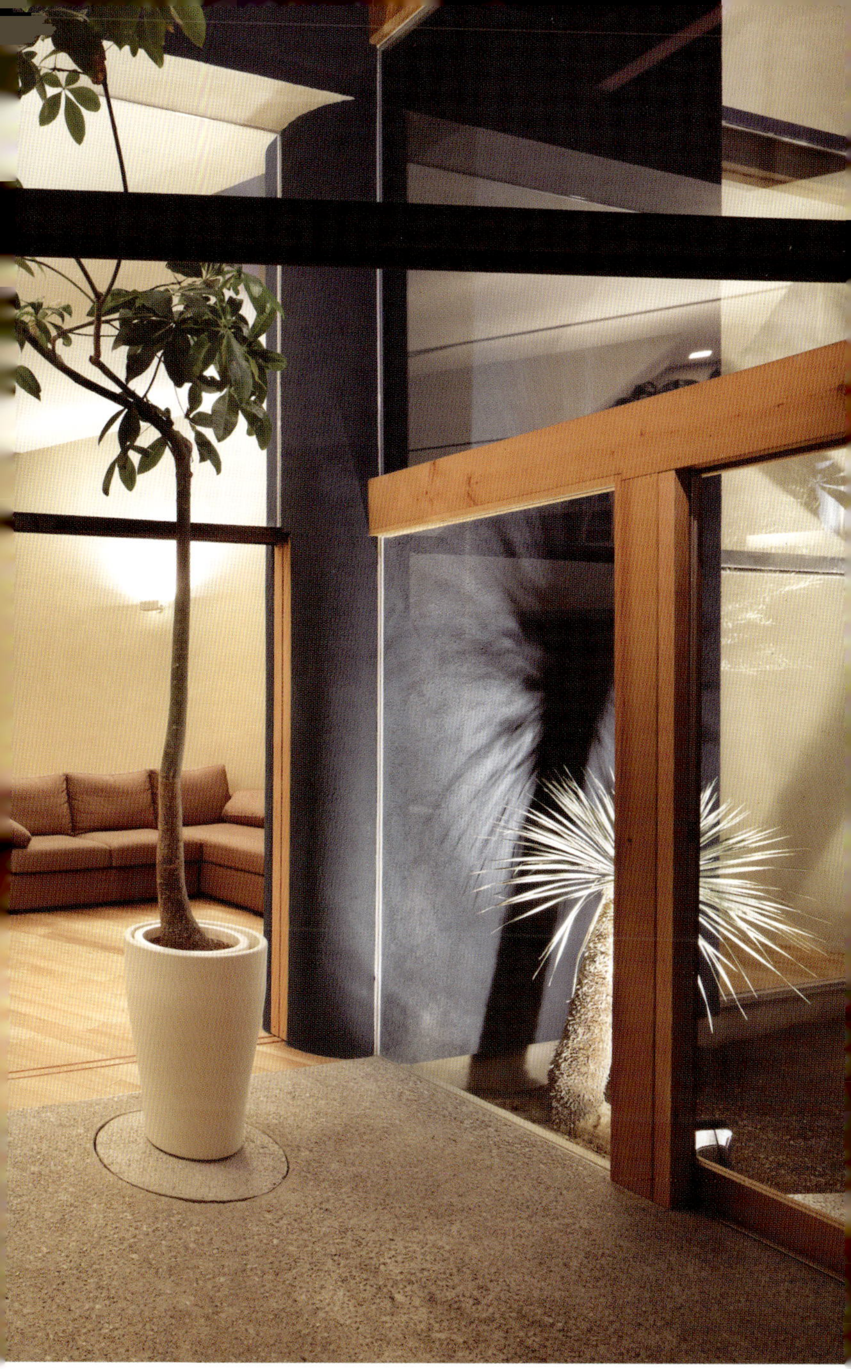

176 | **Summerhouse Skåne** | Österlen | LASC Studio

An unpretentious summerhouse that brings the direct relation to nature and splashes of bright colors

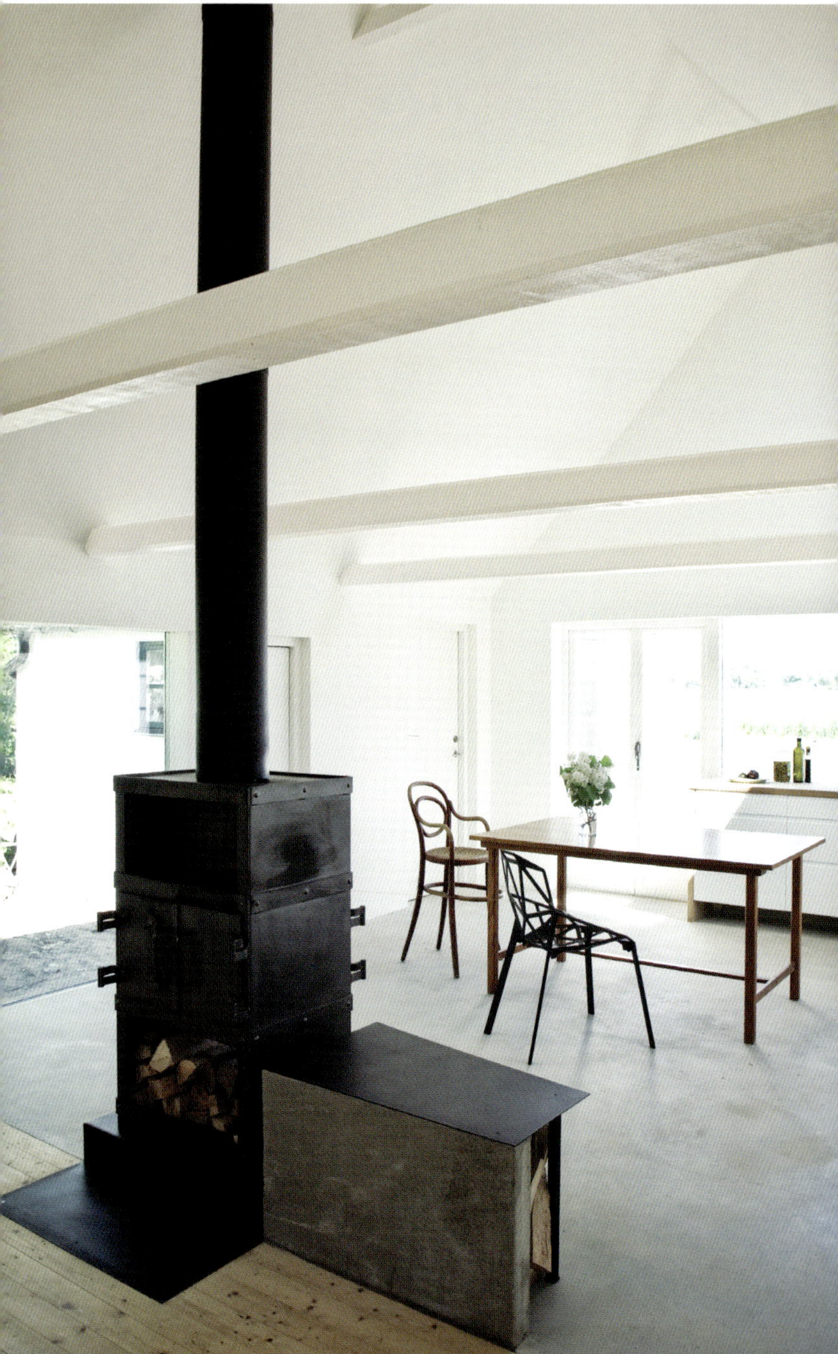

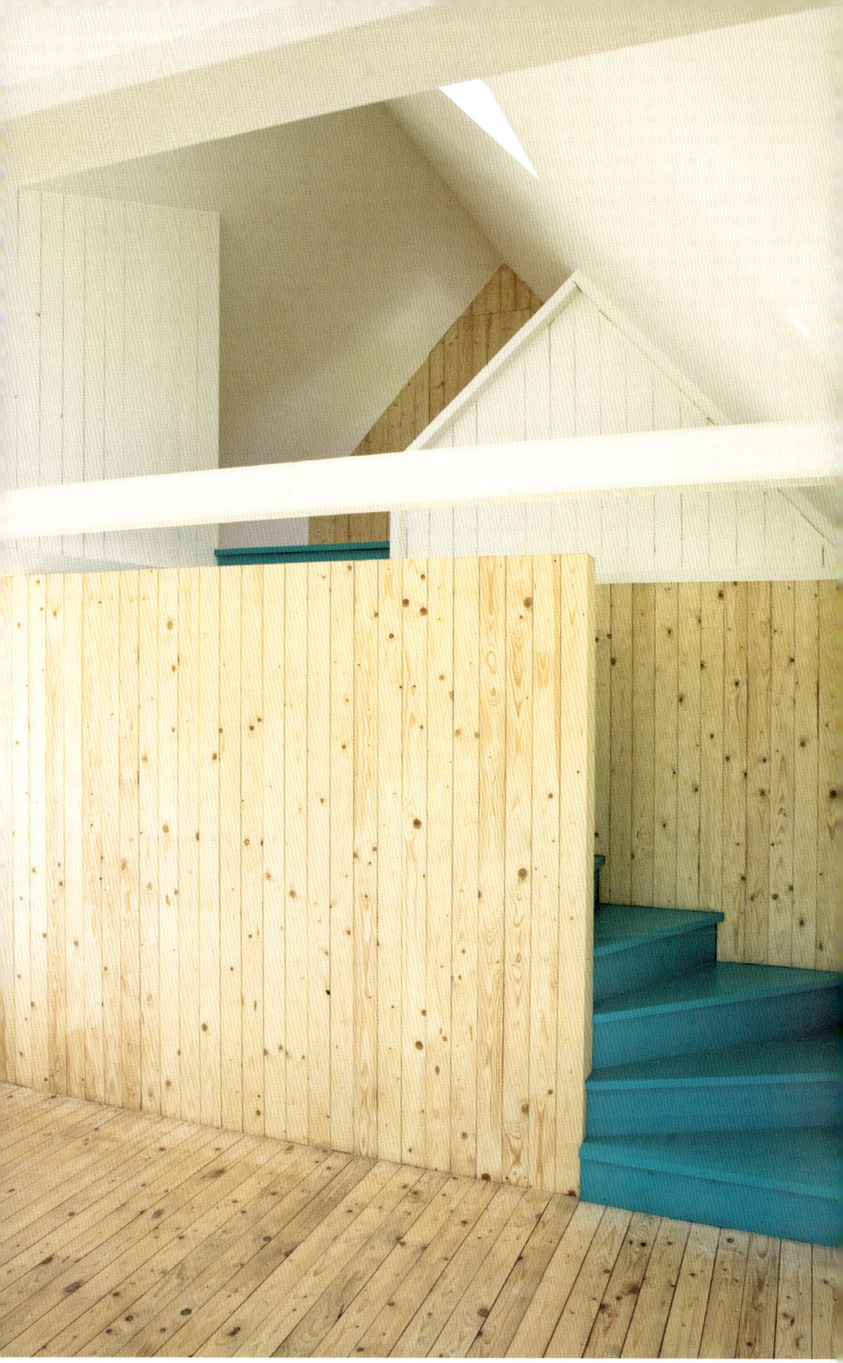

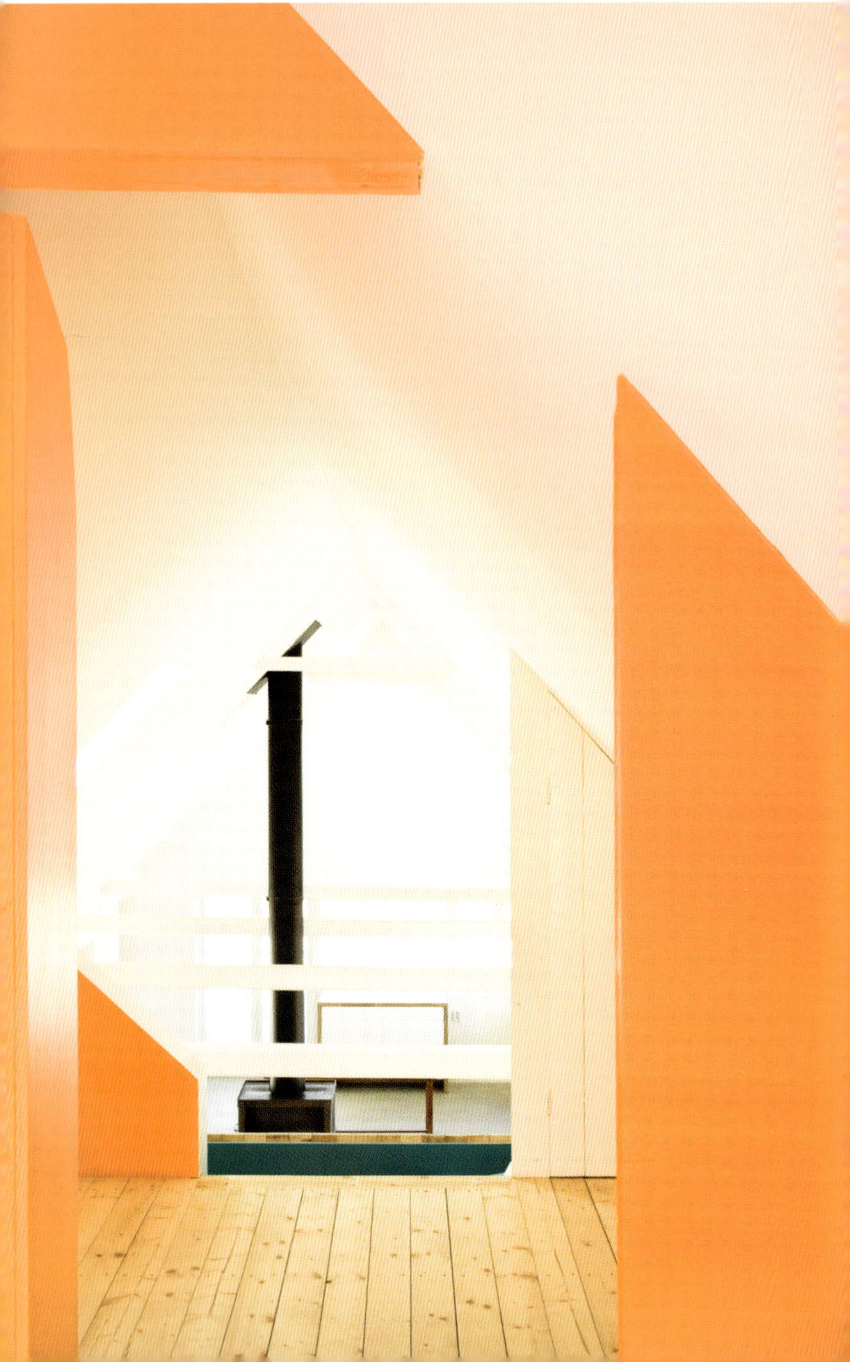

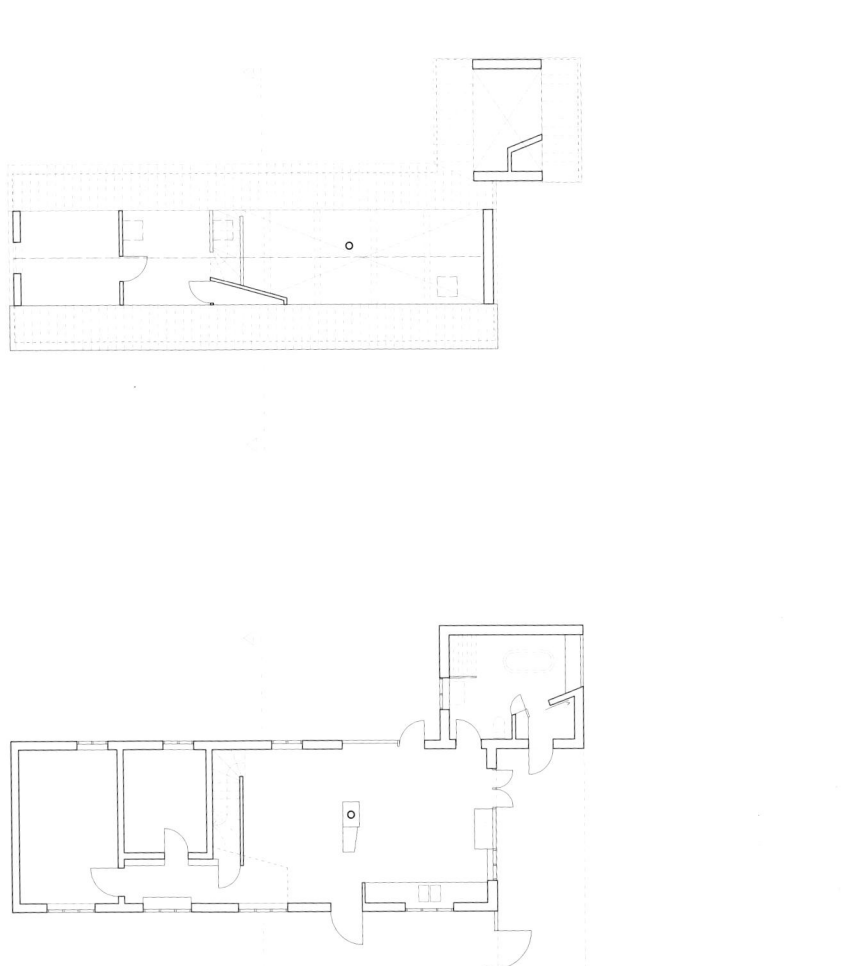

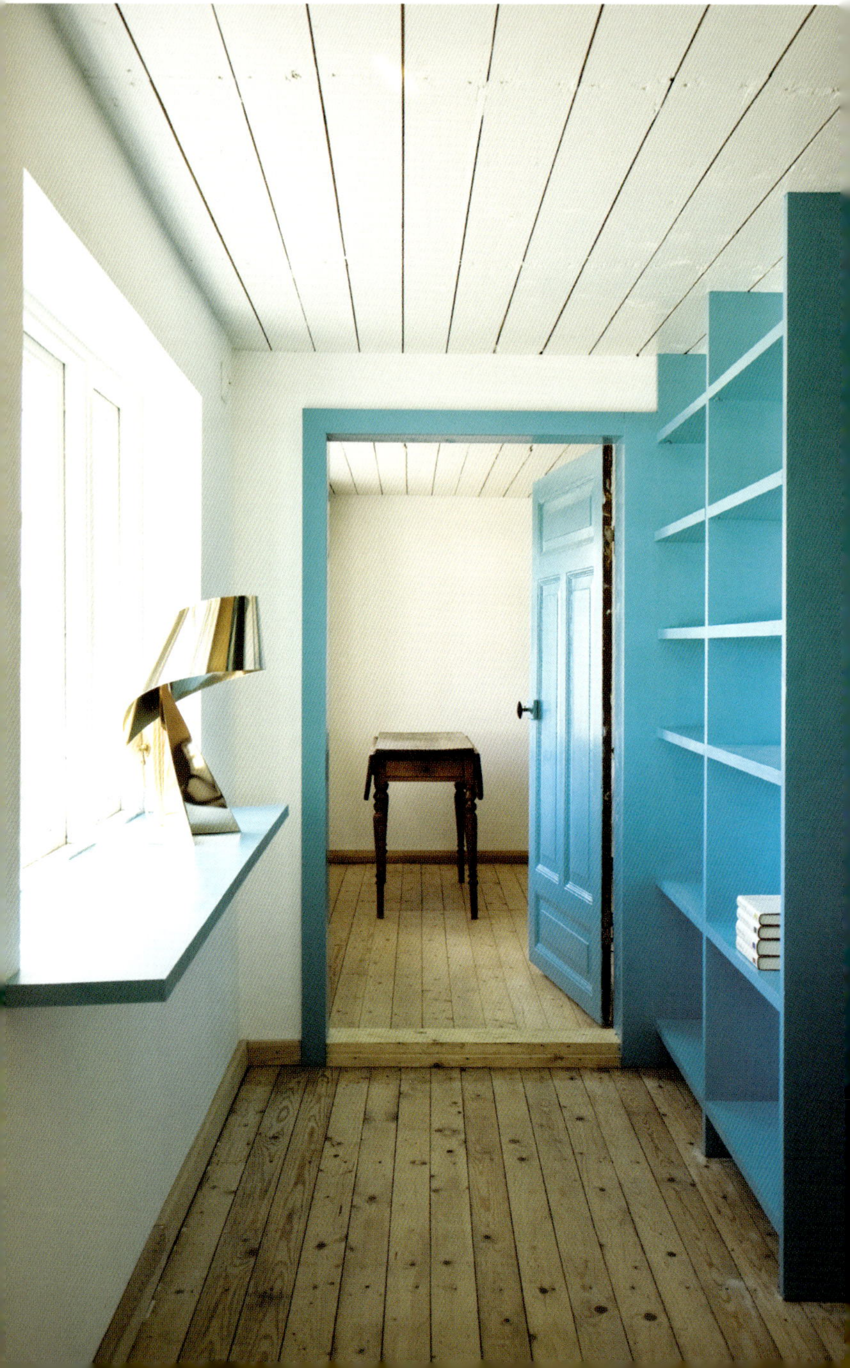

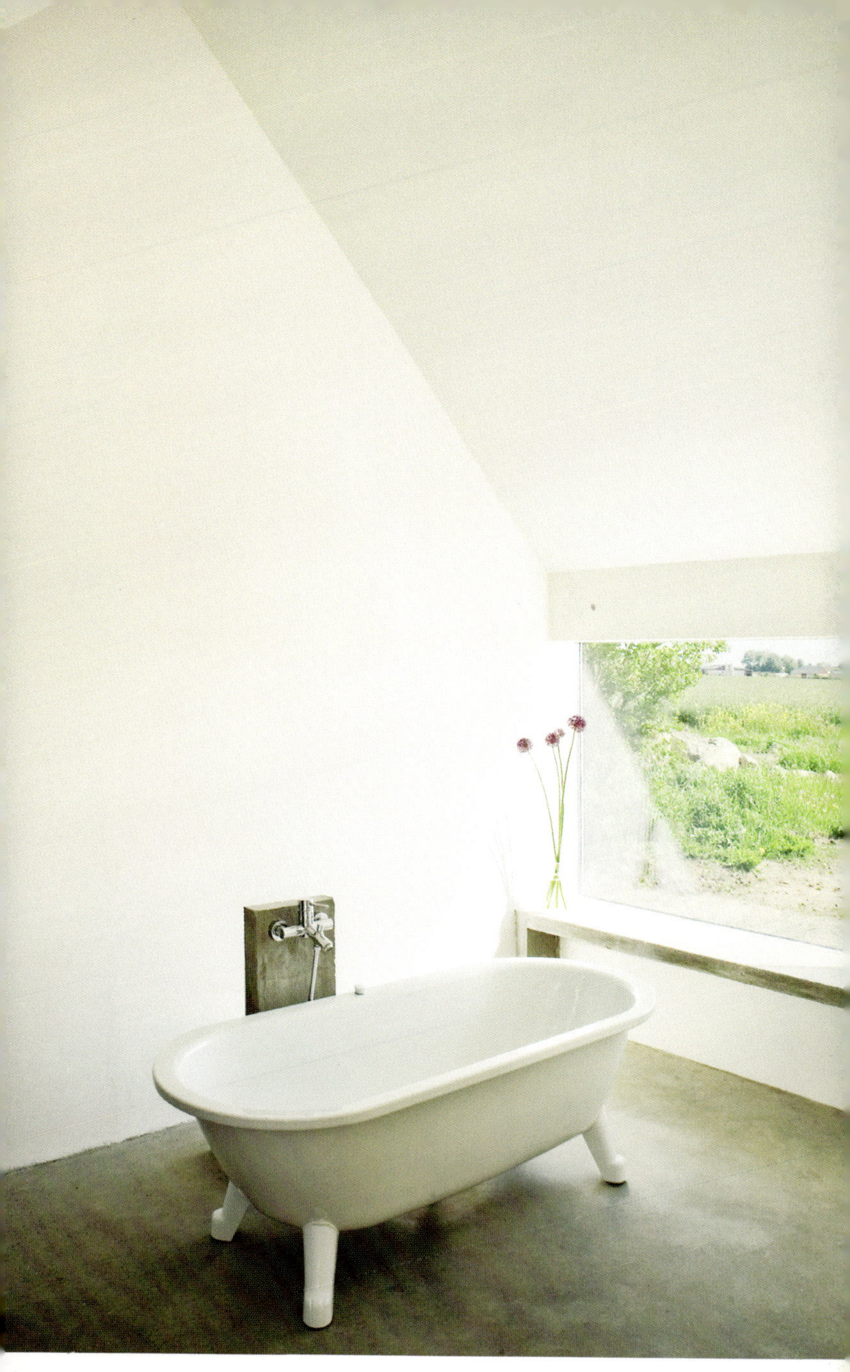

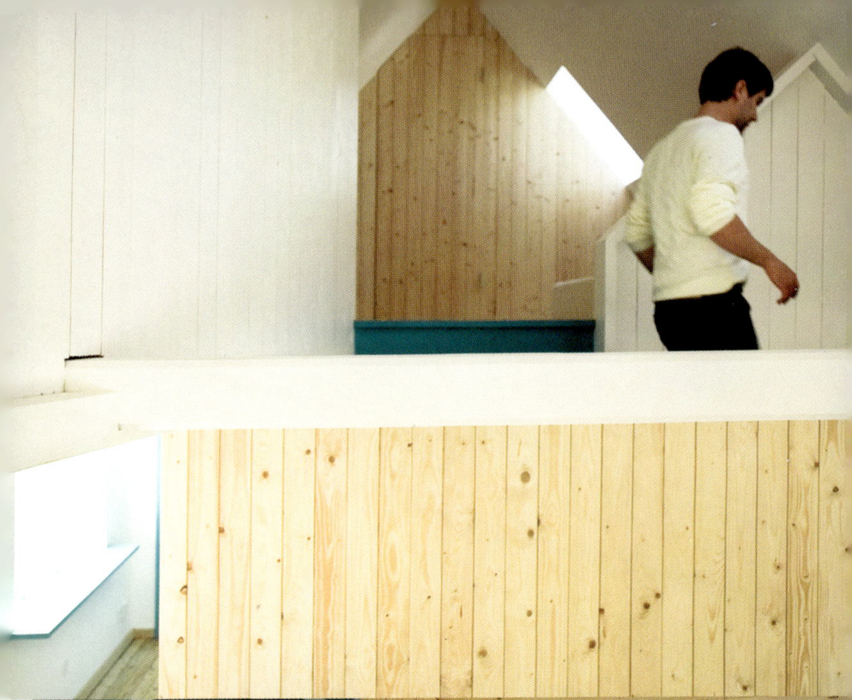

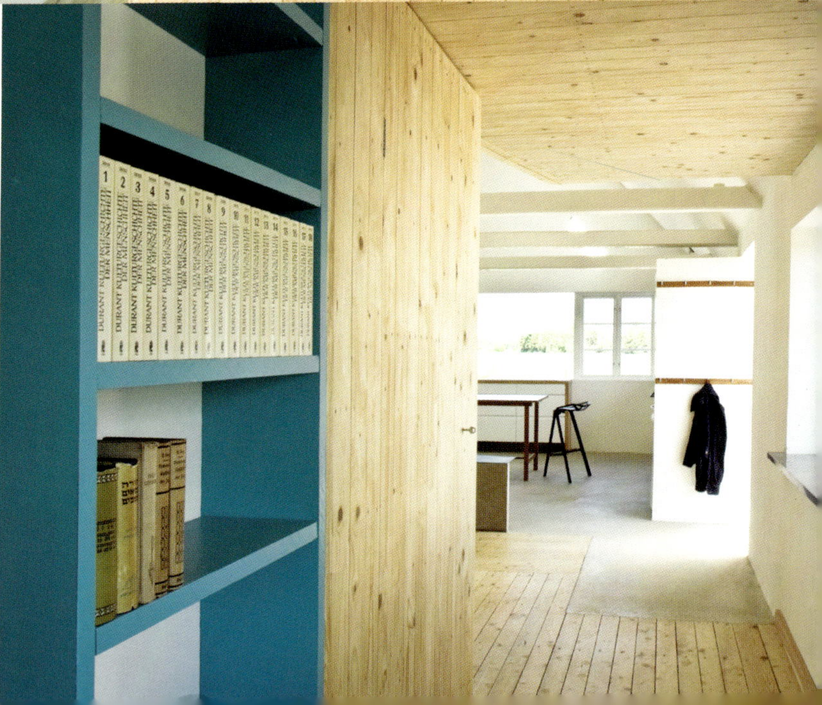

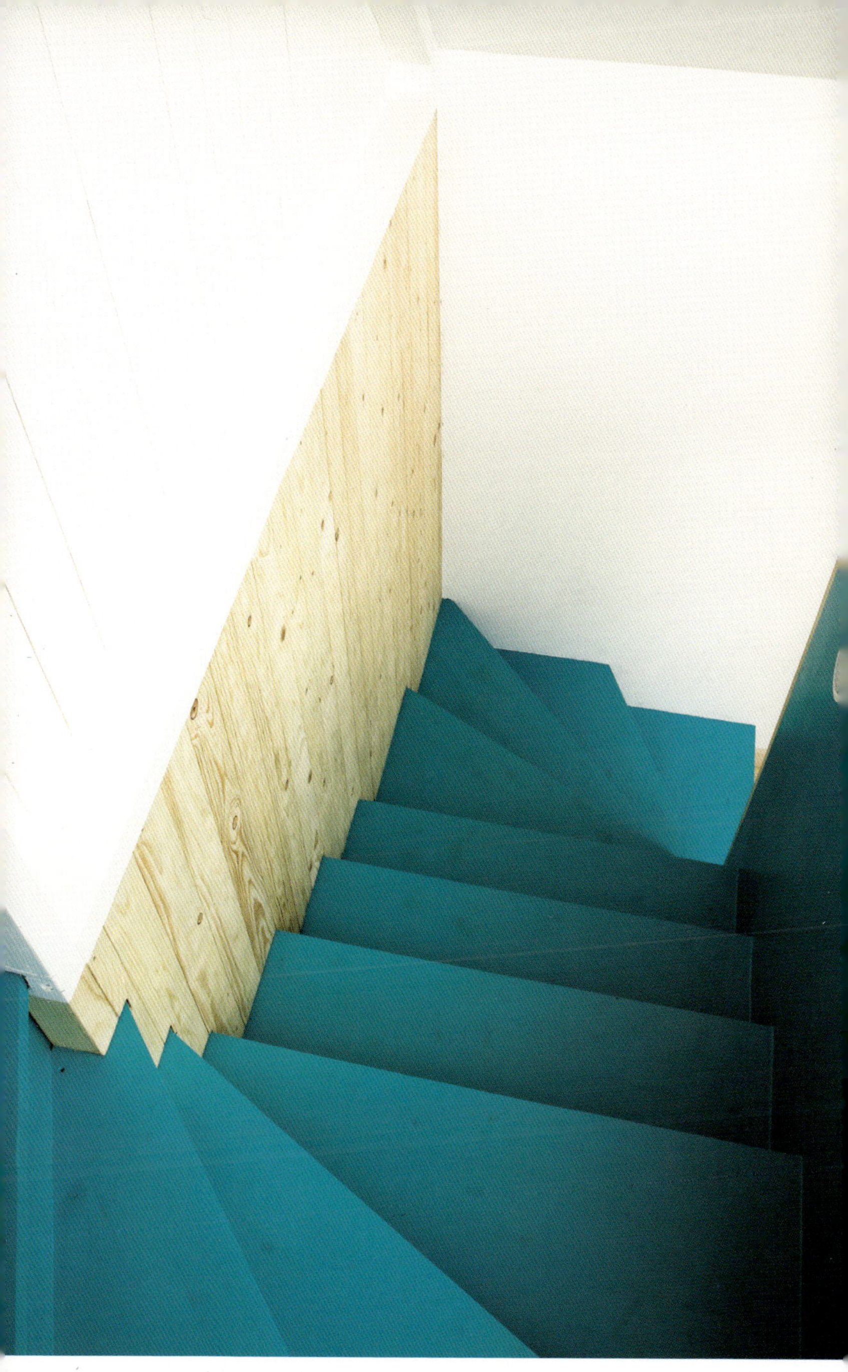

Villa Fabrica | Pyrgos Kallistis, Santorini Island | Palimpsest | Architects + Engineers office

A factory transformed: creating a sleek and minimal loft-style vacation retreat

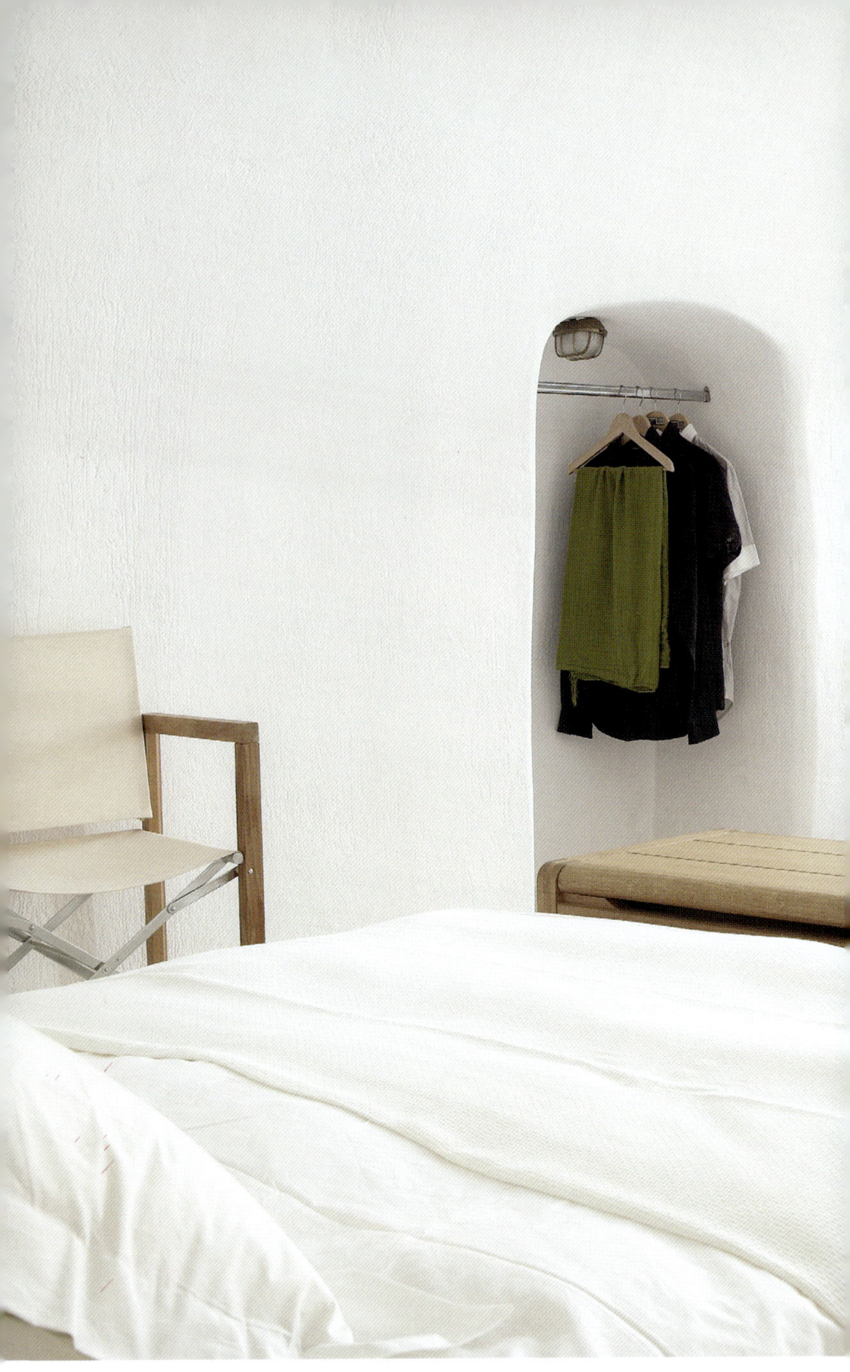

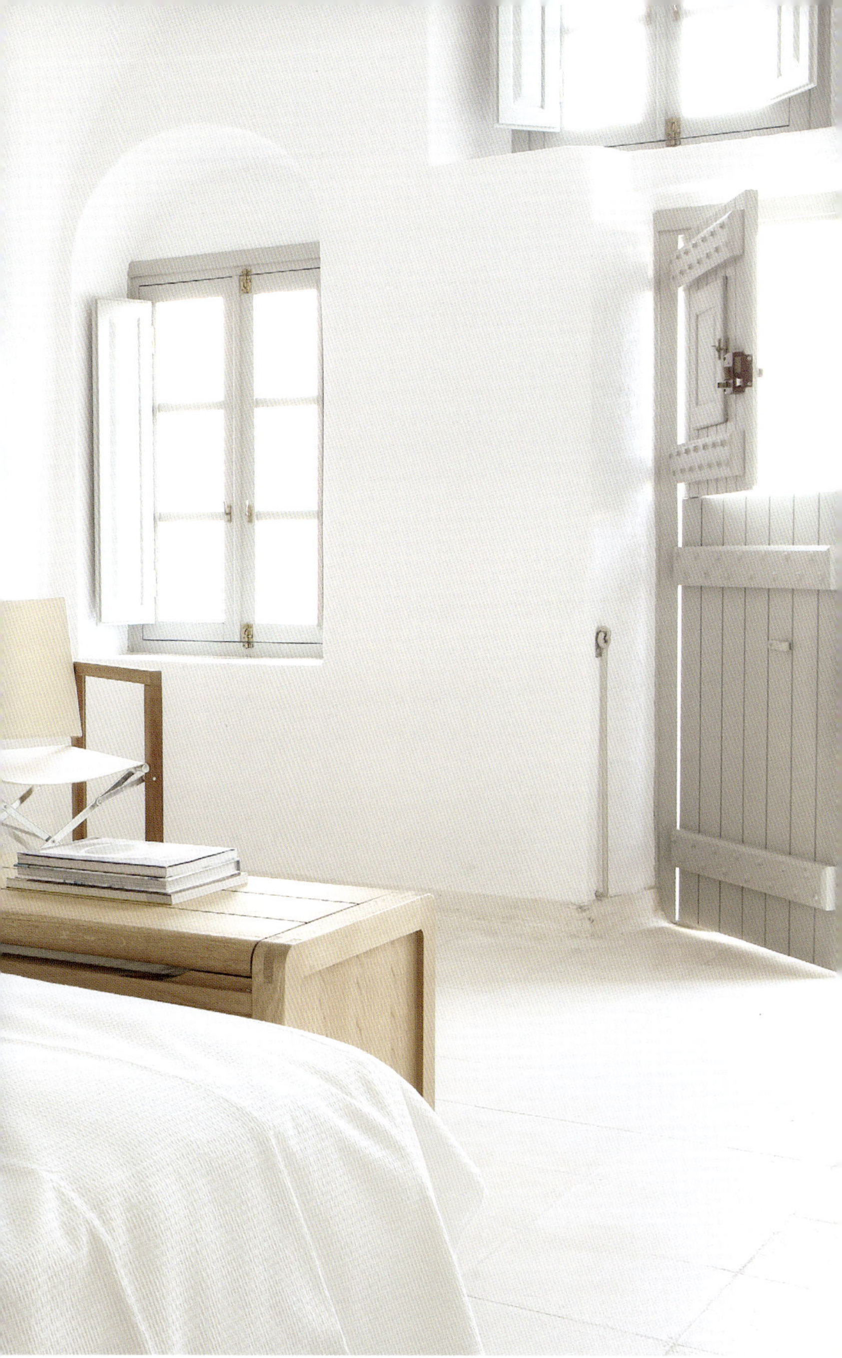

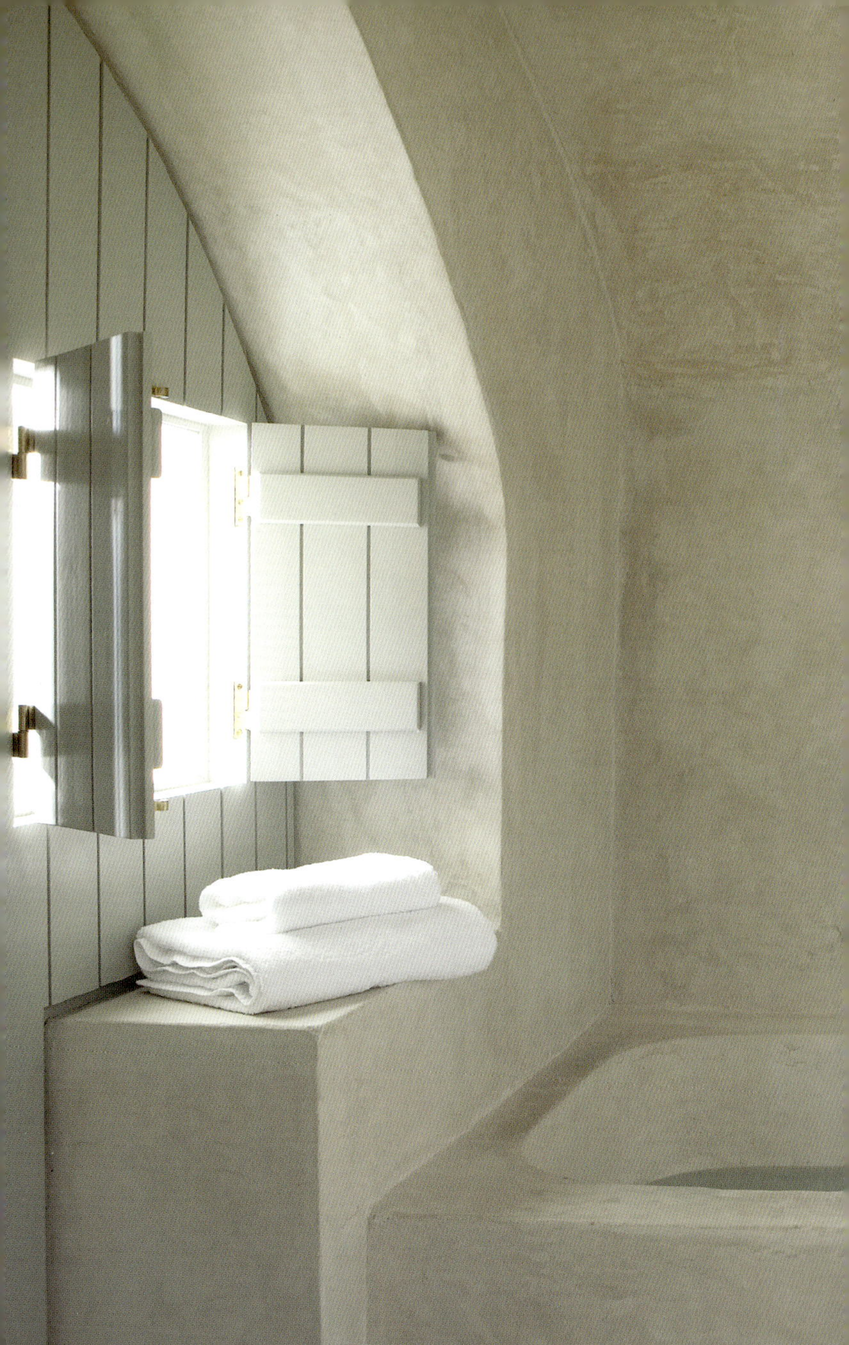

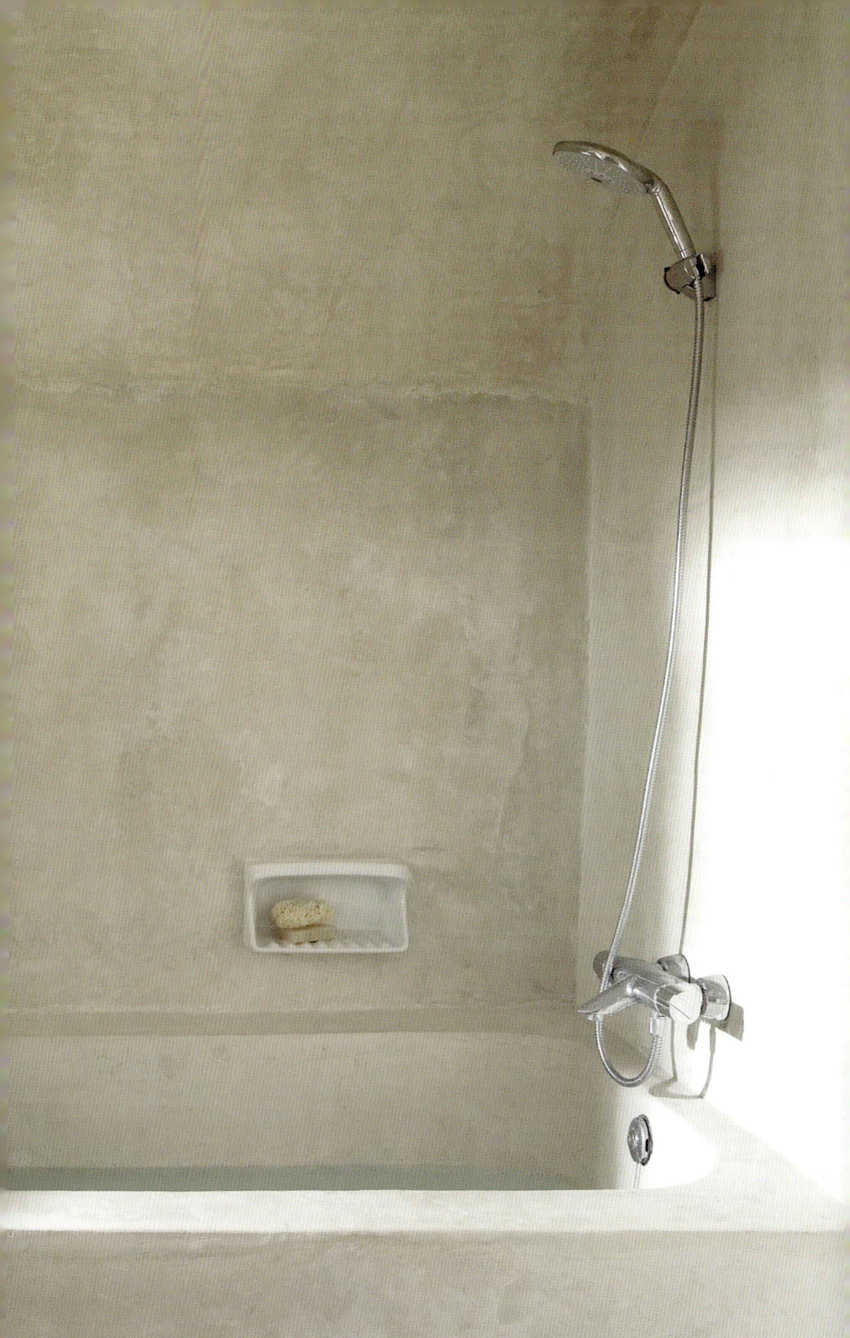

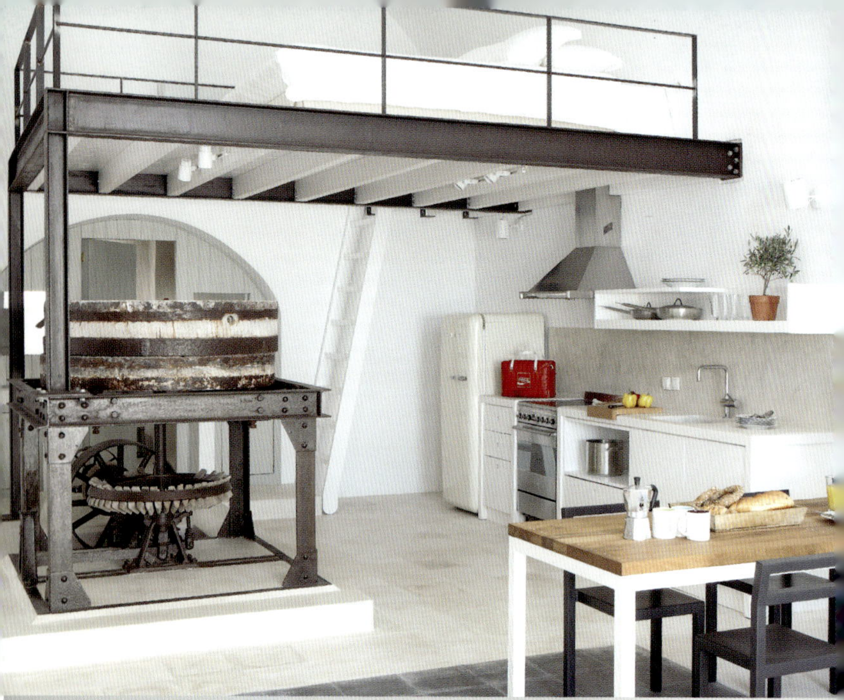

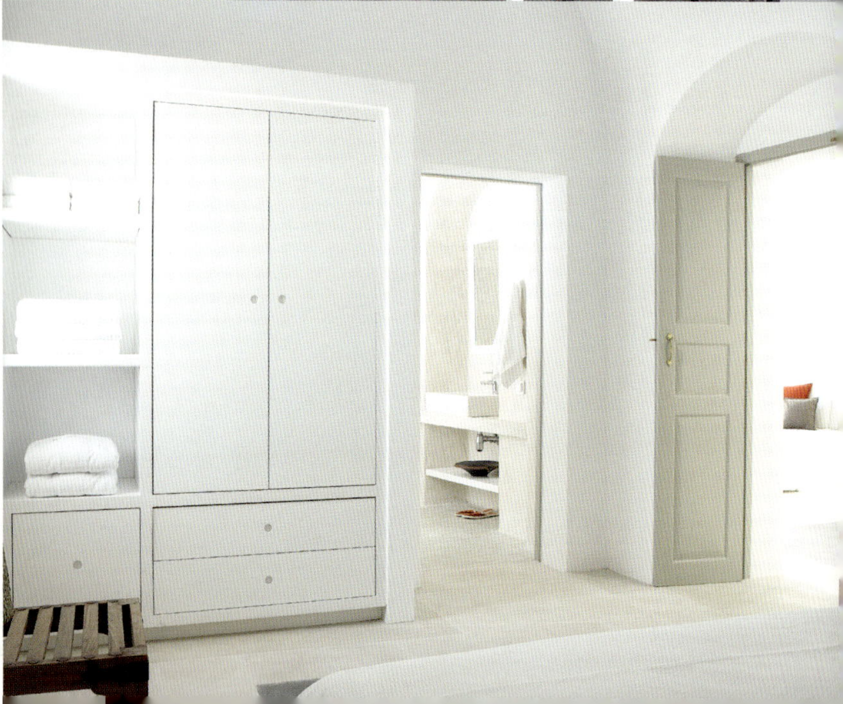

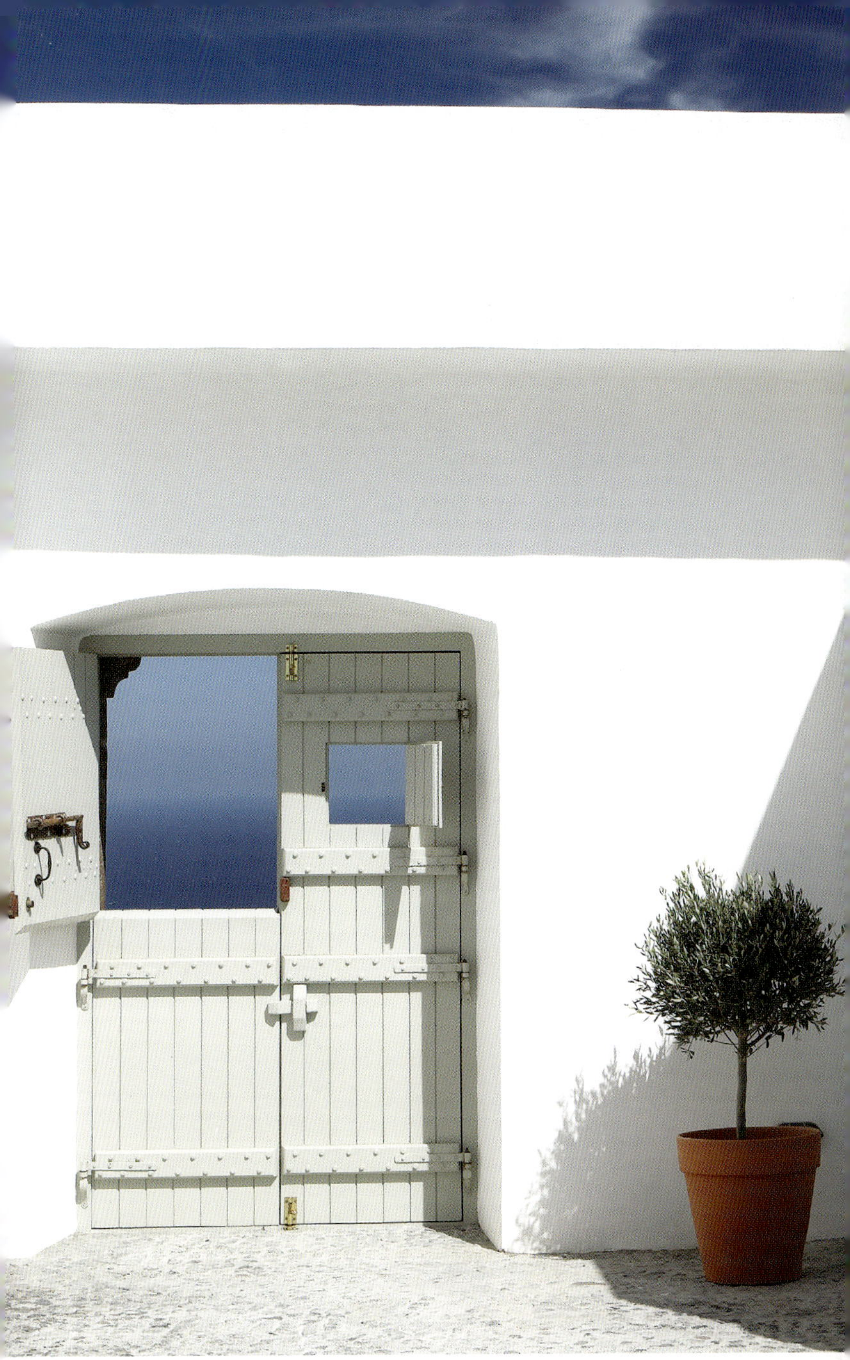

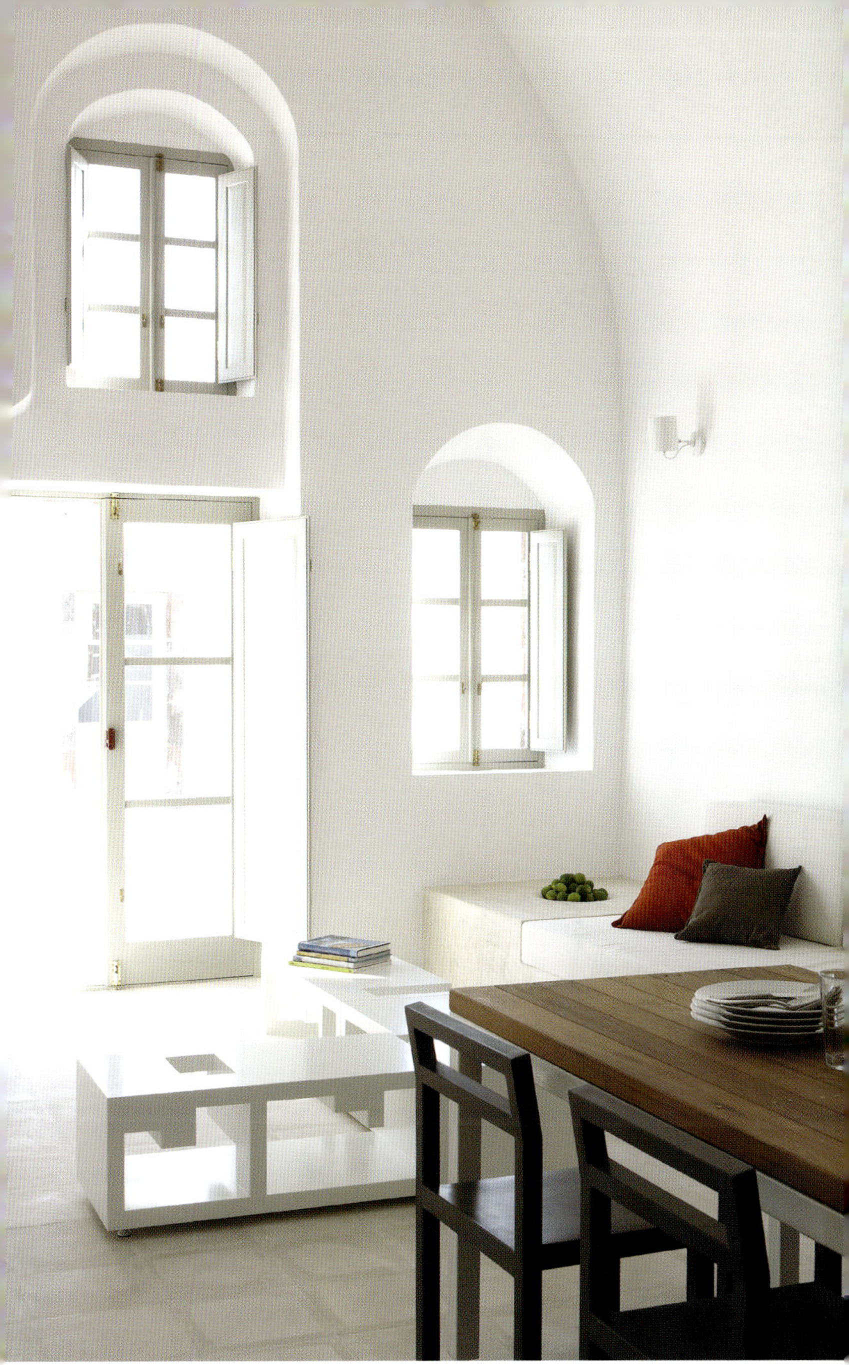

Living today with a taste of the past

196 | **San Sebastián Apartment** | San Sebastián | Mikel Irastorza

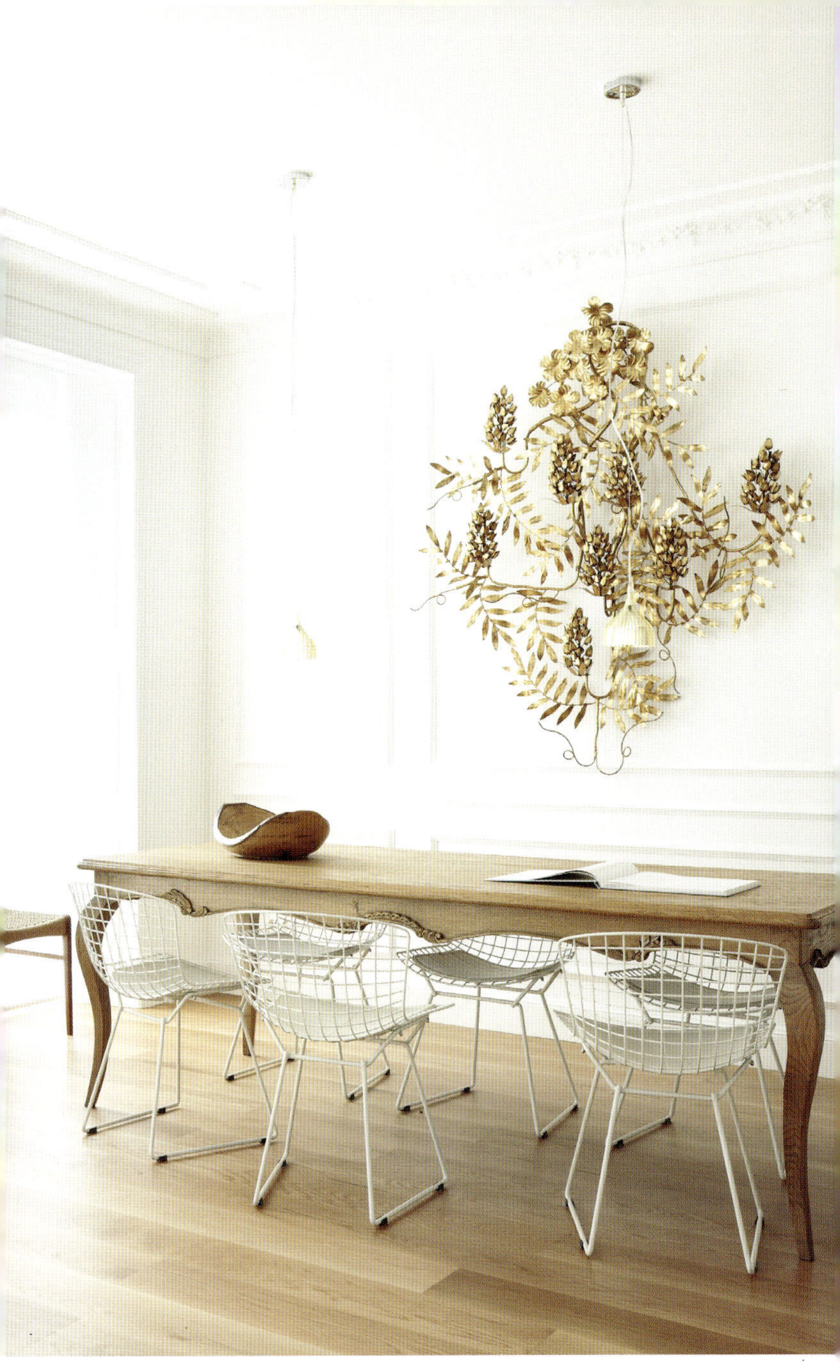

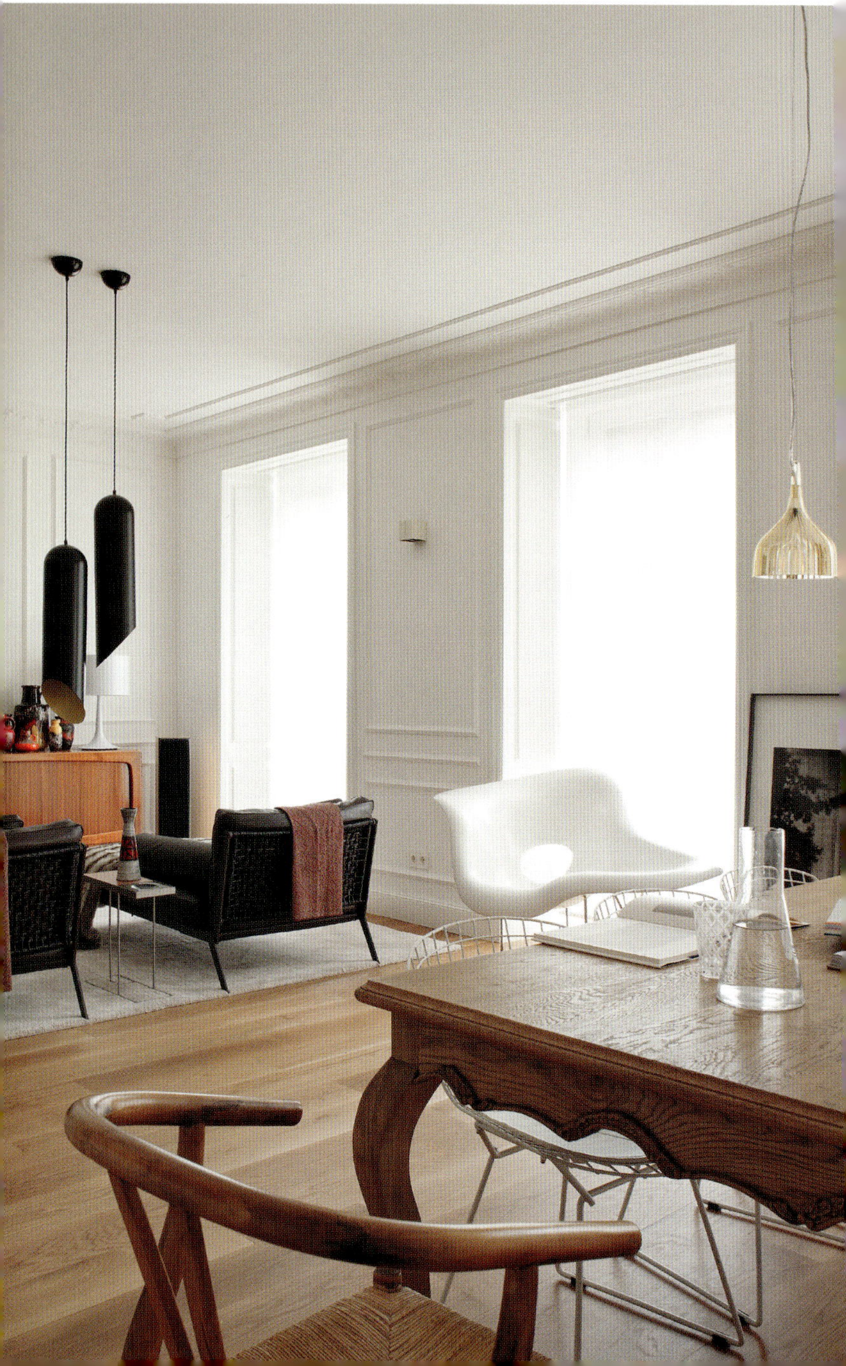

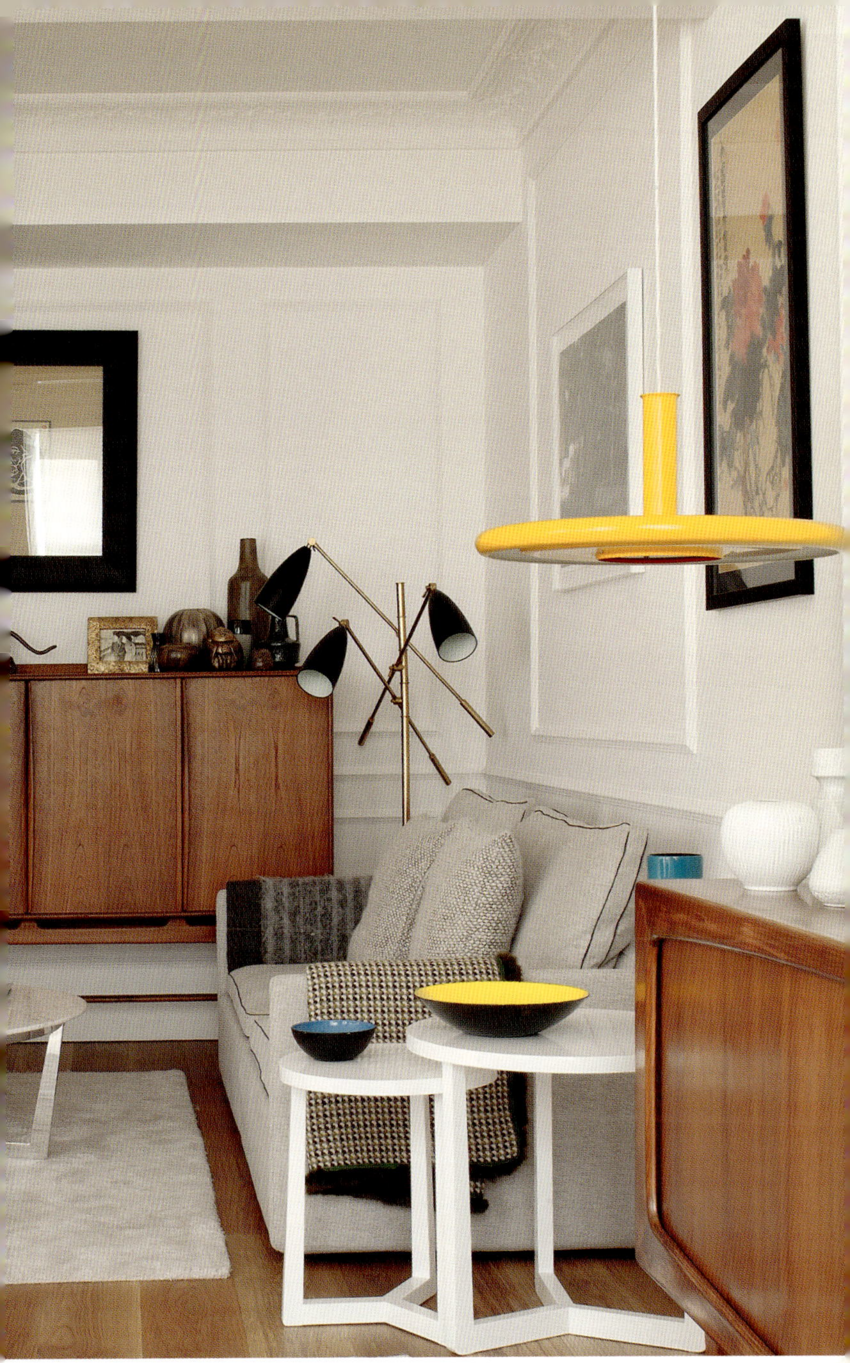

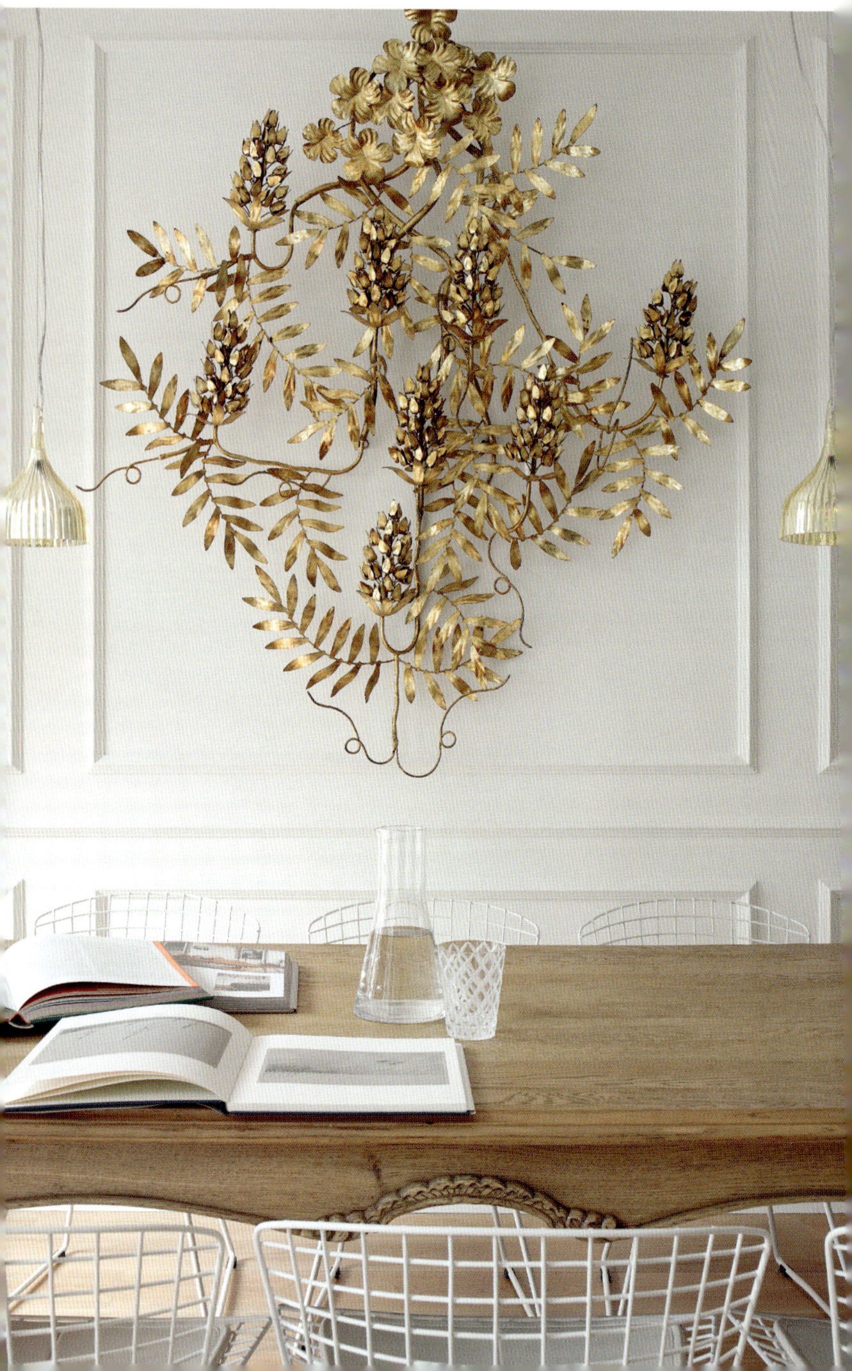

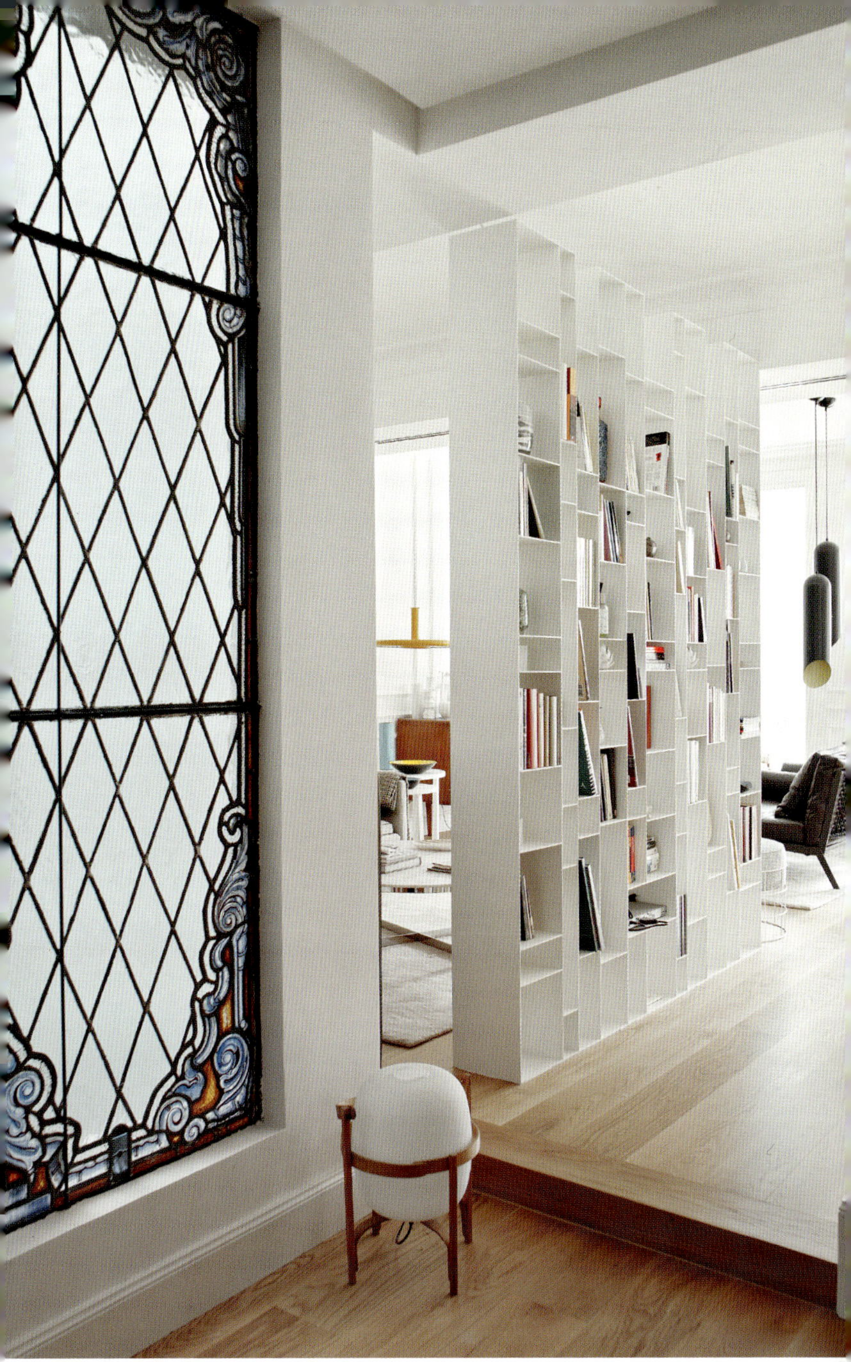

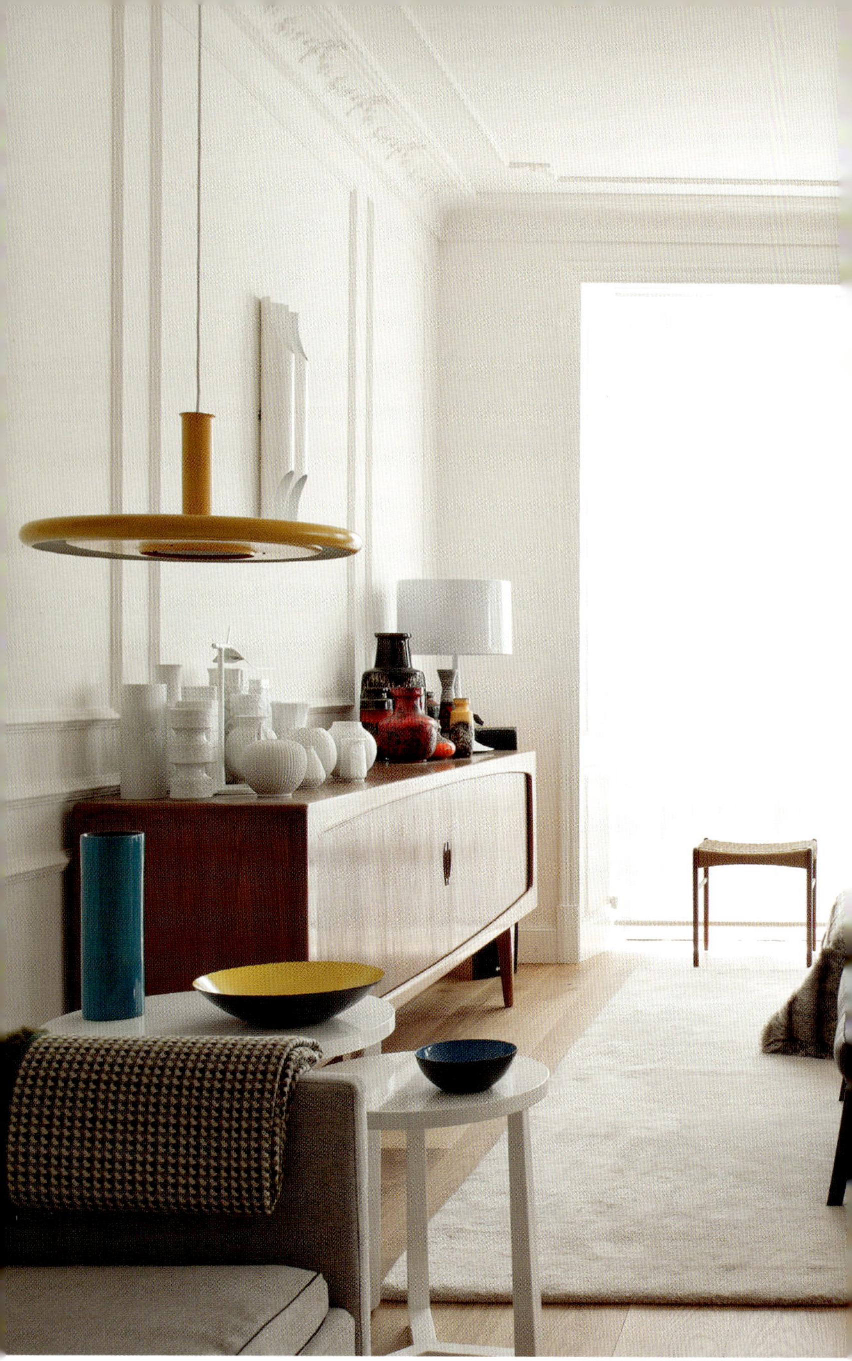

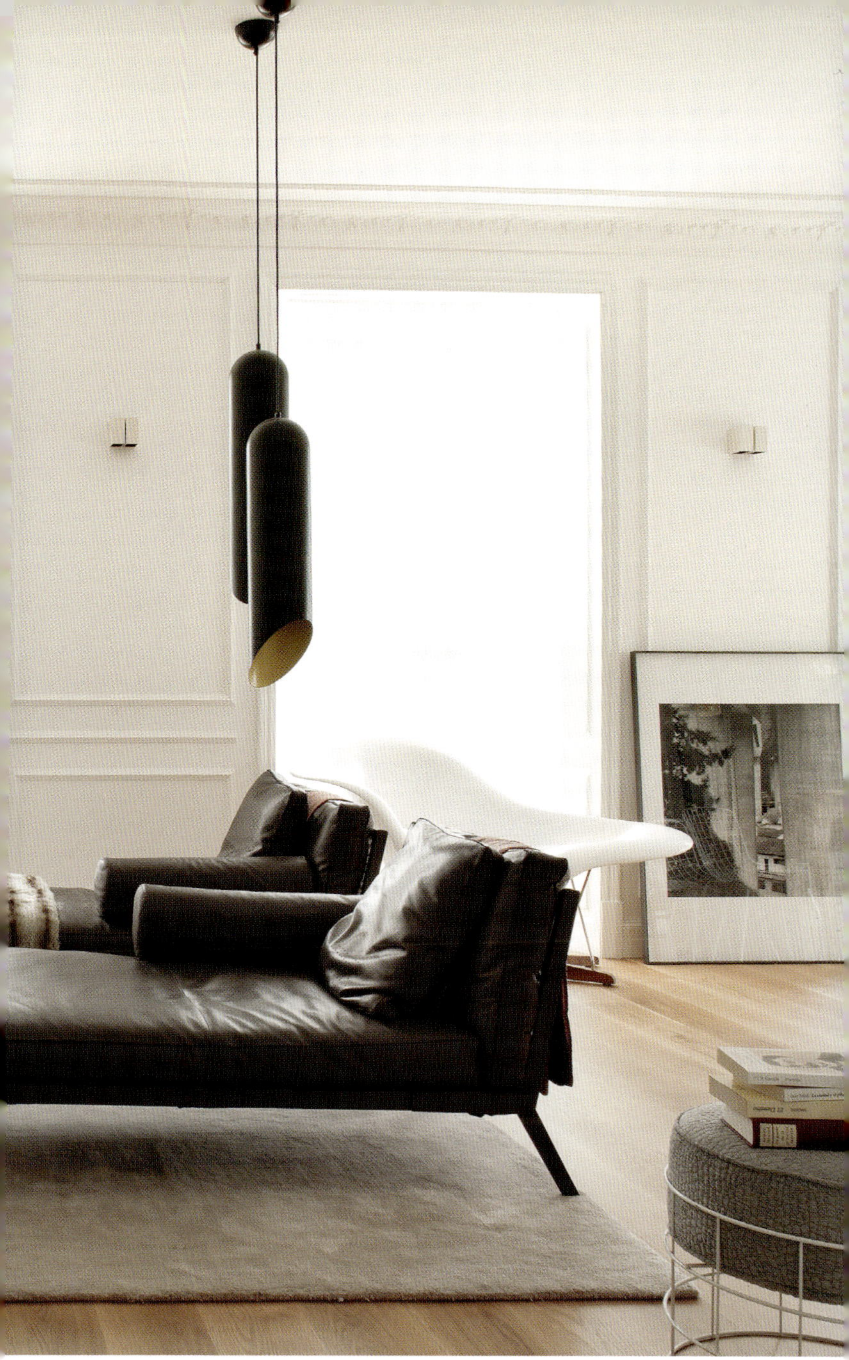

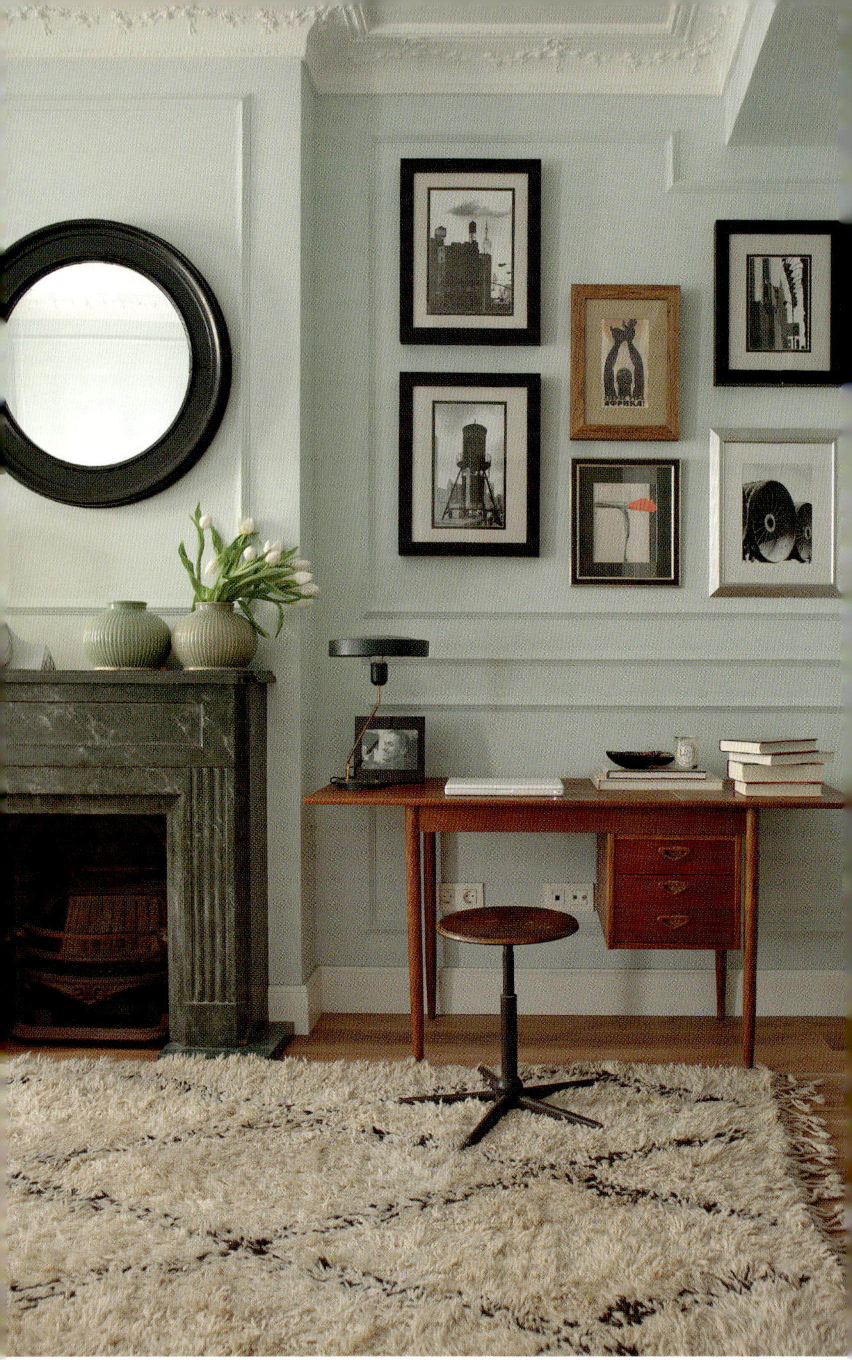
АФРИКА!

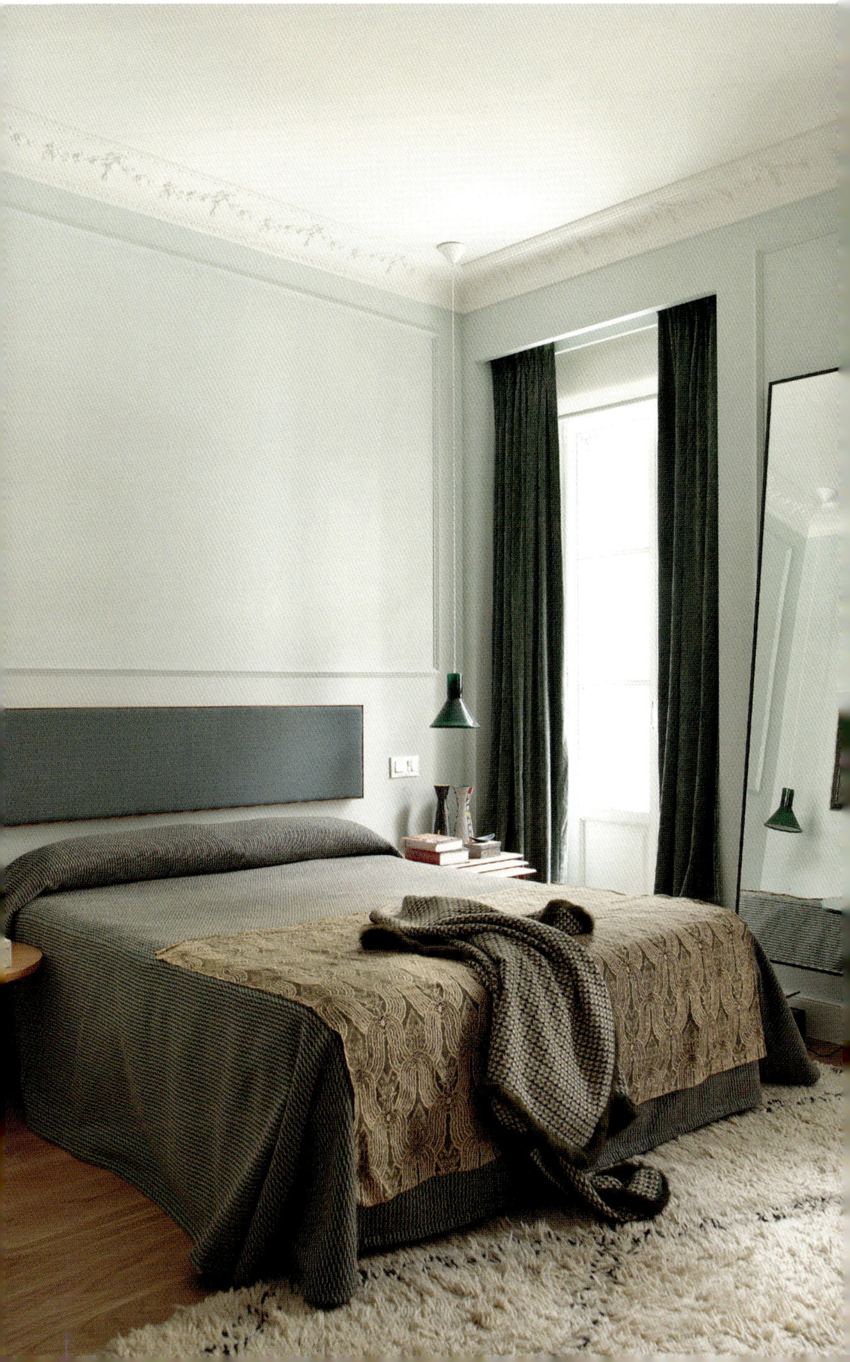

Fidalga 727 | São Paulo | Sub Estúdio

This cozy duplex apartment features **modular pieces** that uncover **new rooms,** and **allow** smaller spaces to open up **more freely.**

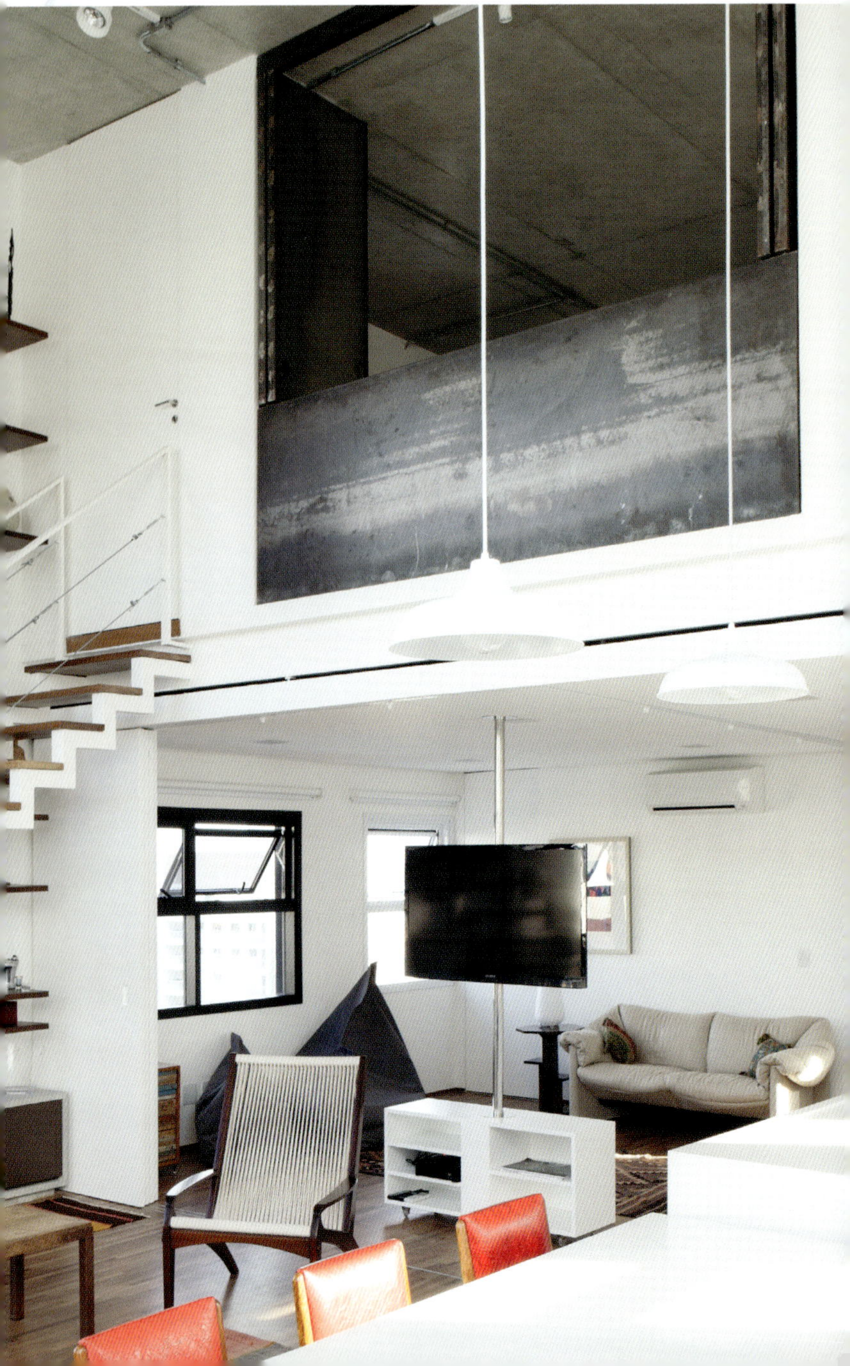

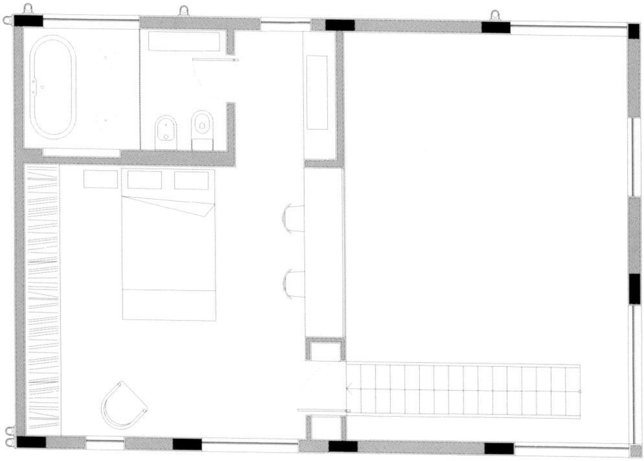

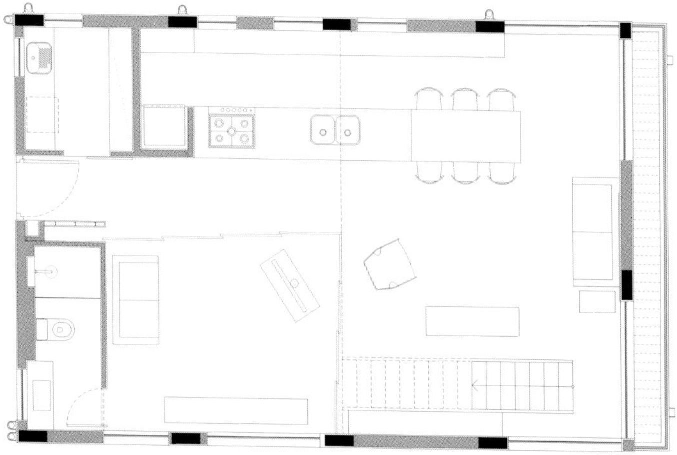

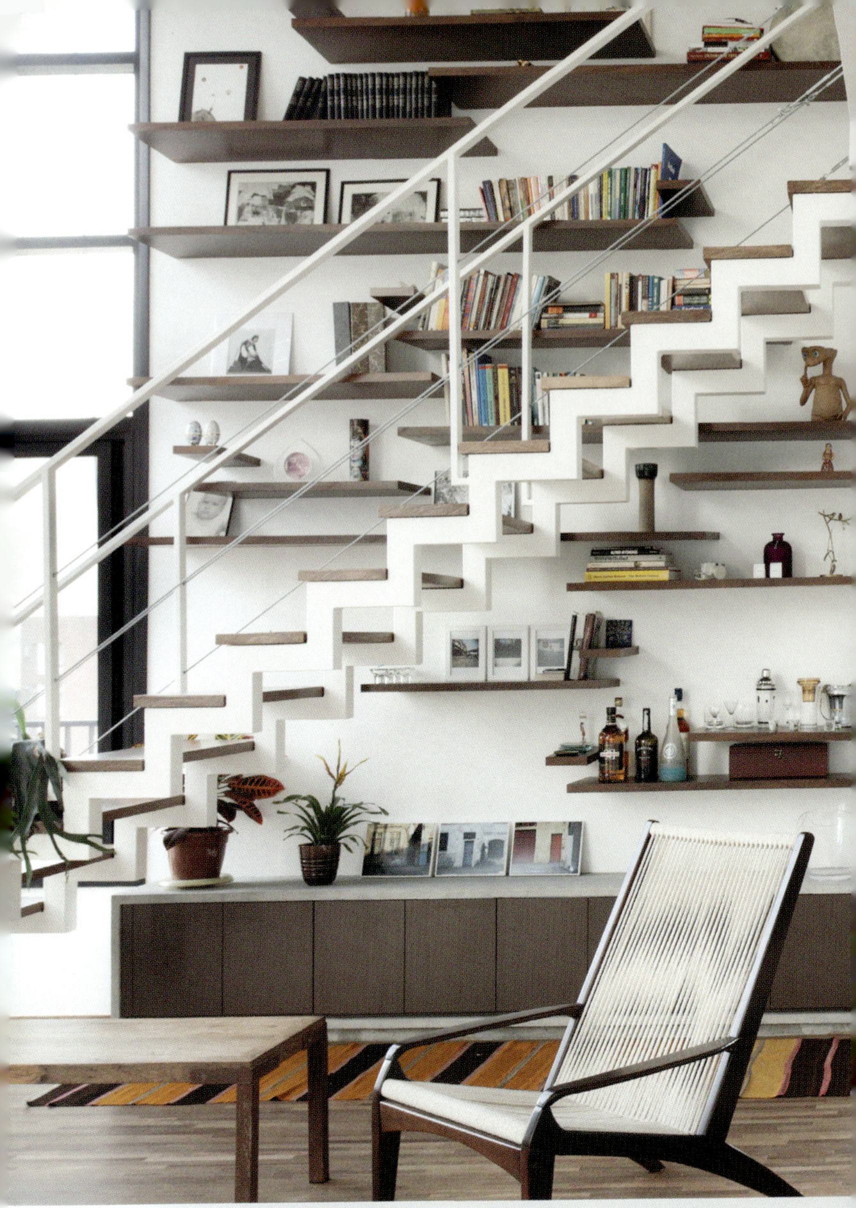

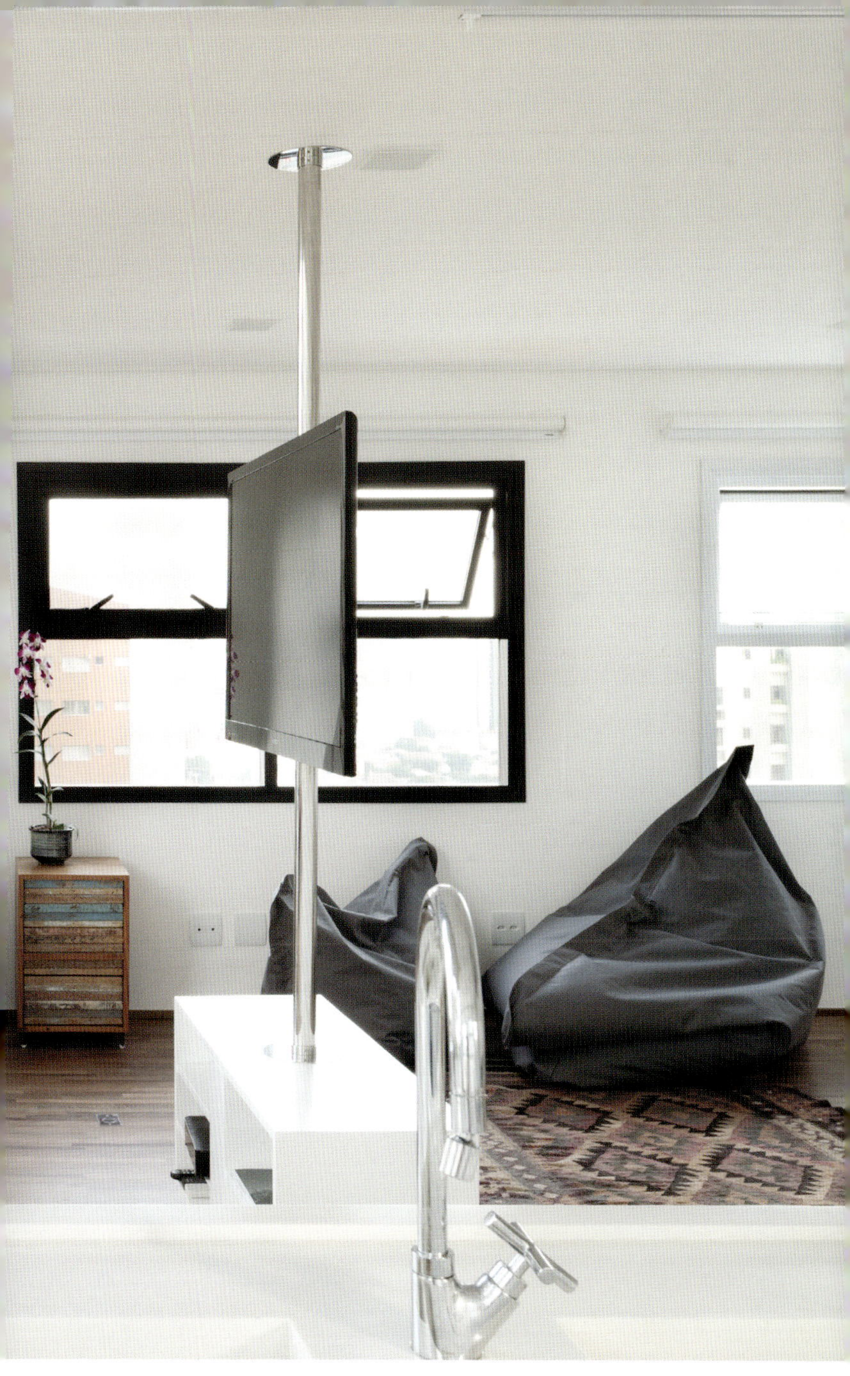

212 | **Apartment on Oscar Freire Street** | São Paulo | Felipe Hess

The materials, art works & furniture provide calmness & comfort to this urban home.

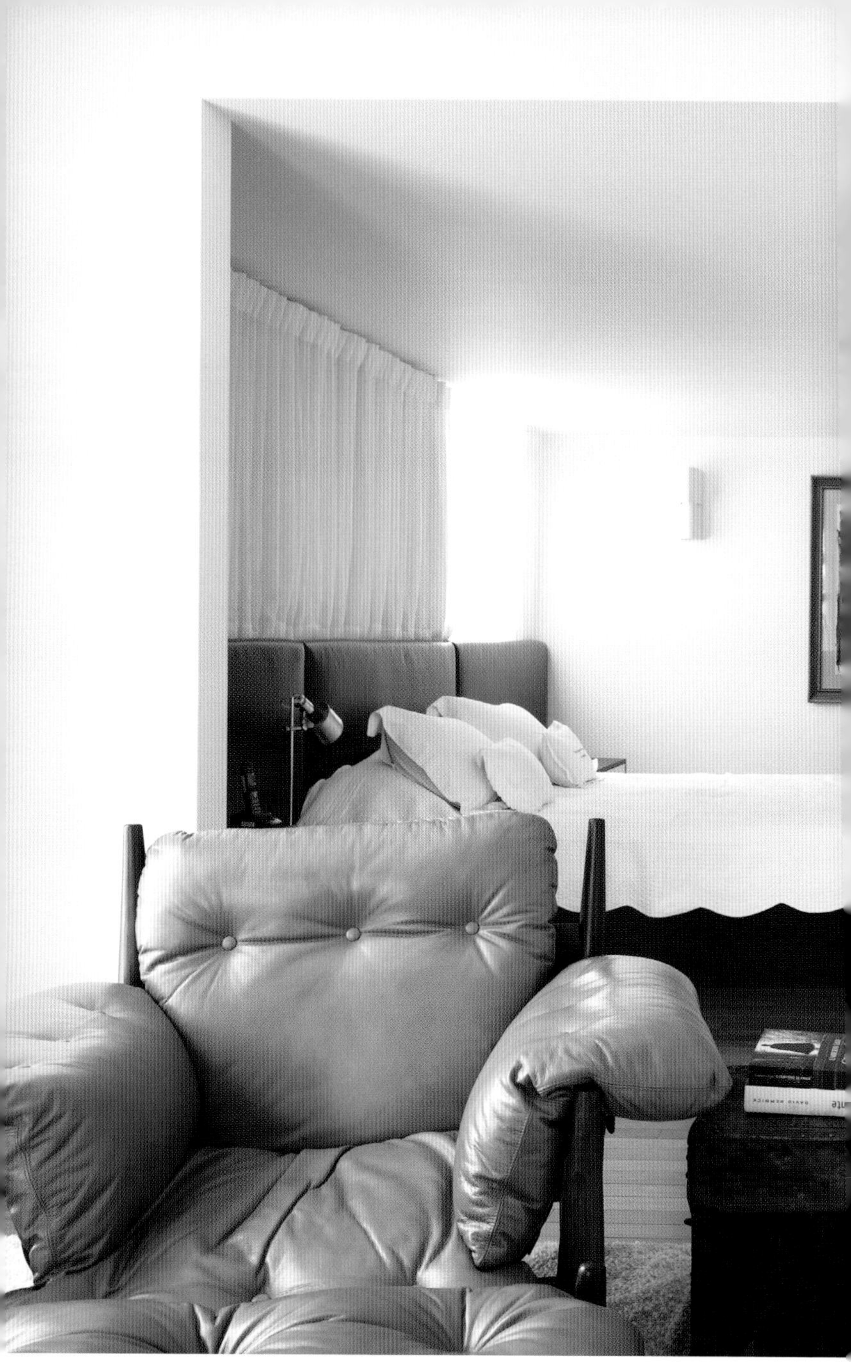

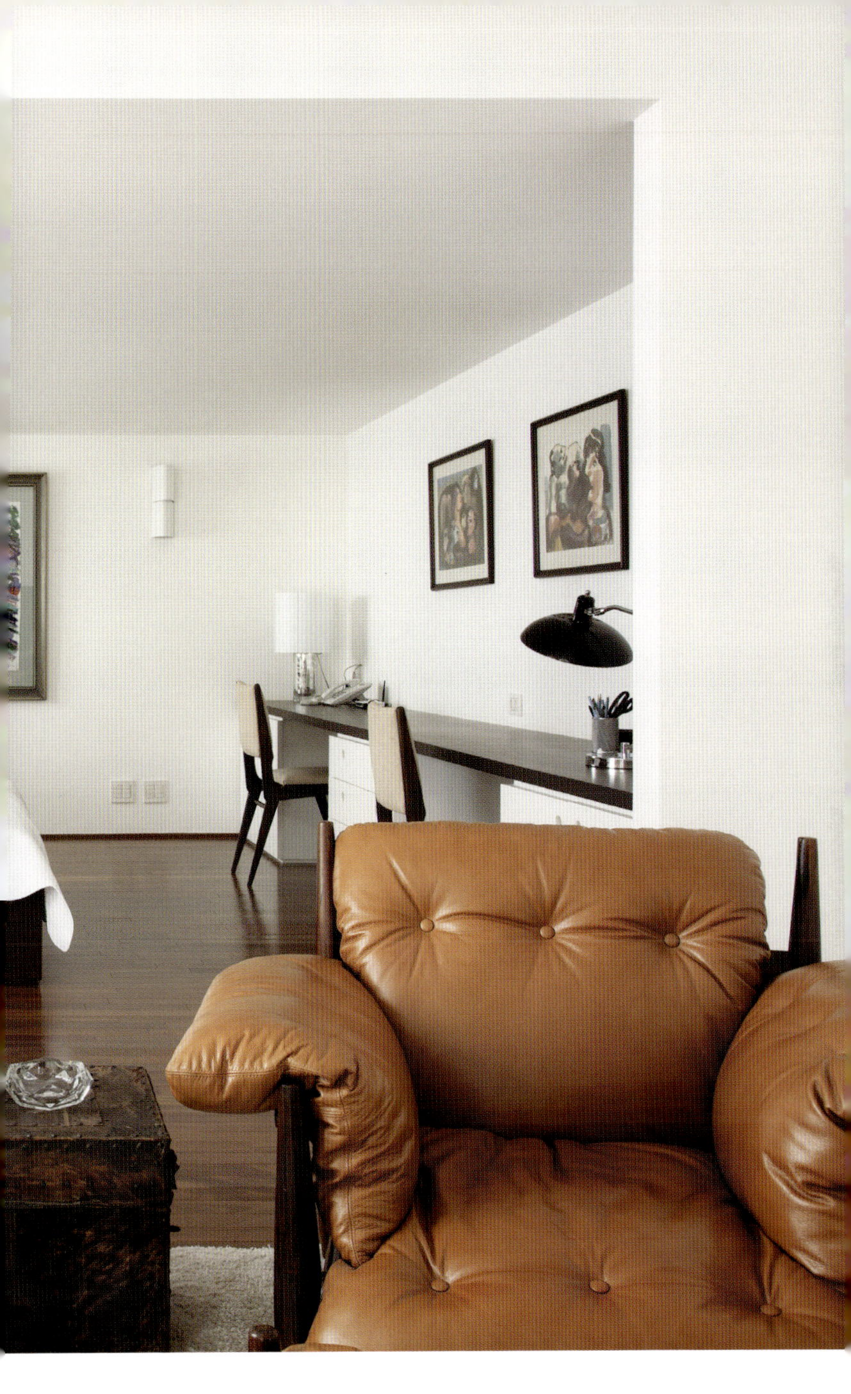

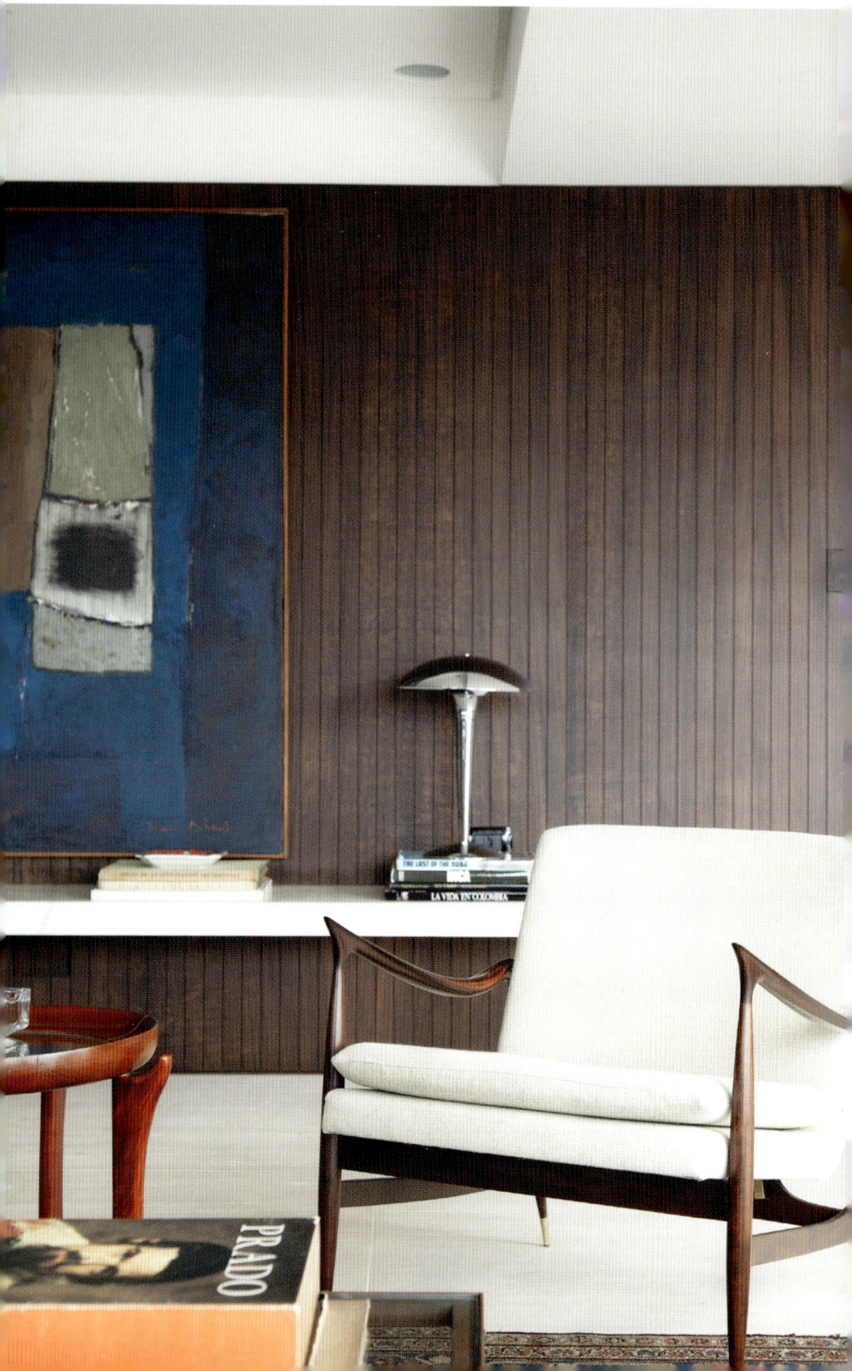
LA VIDA EN COLOMBIA
PRADO

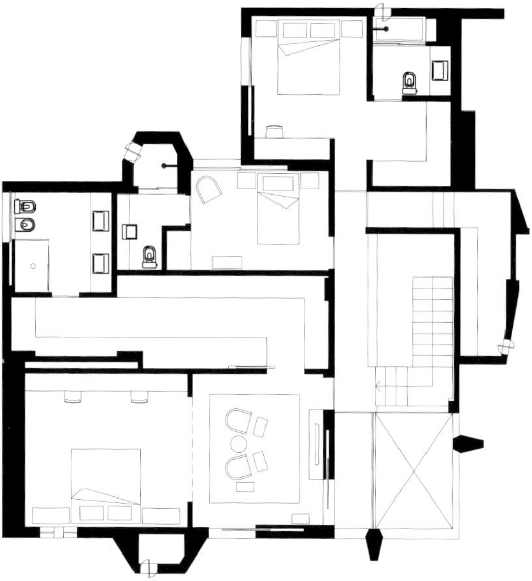

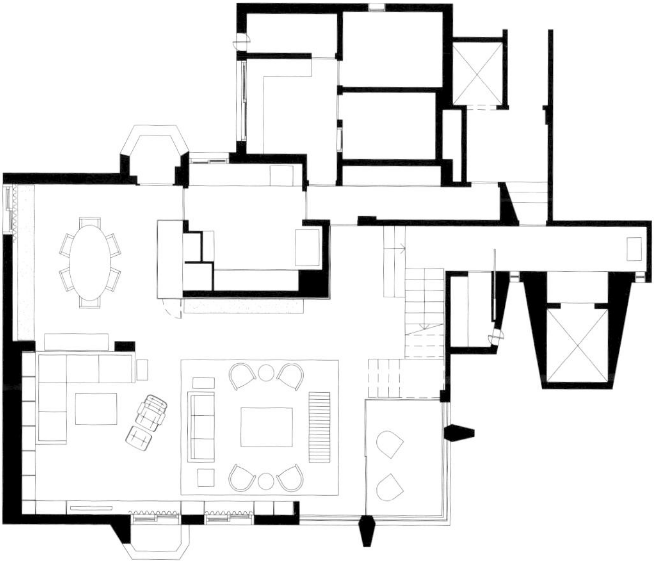

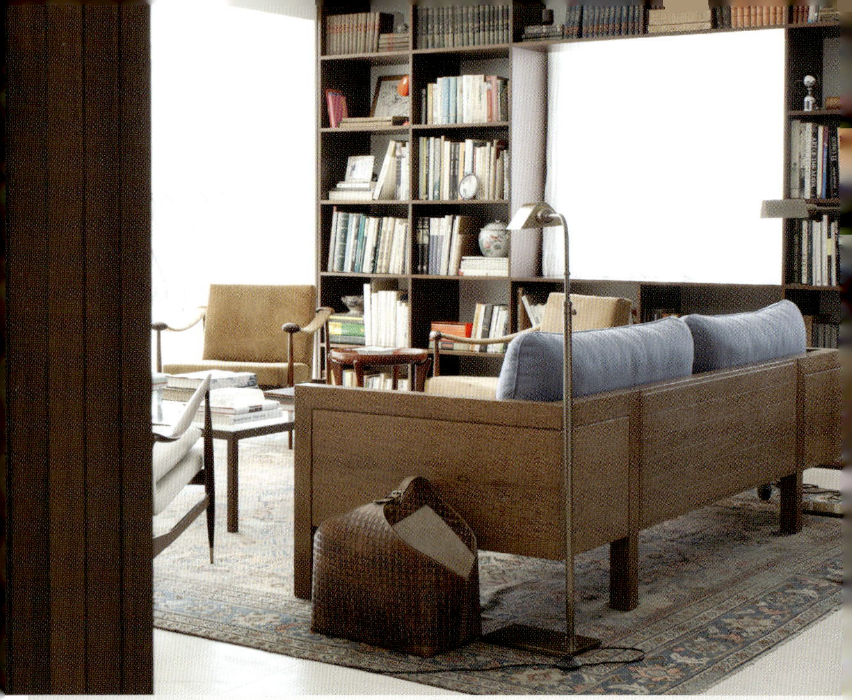
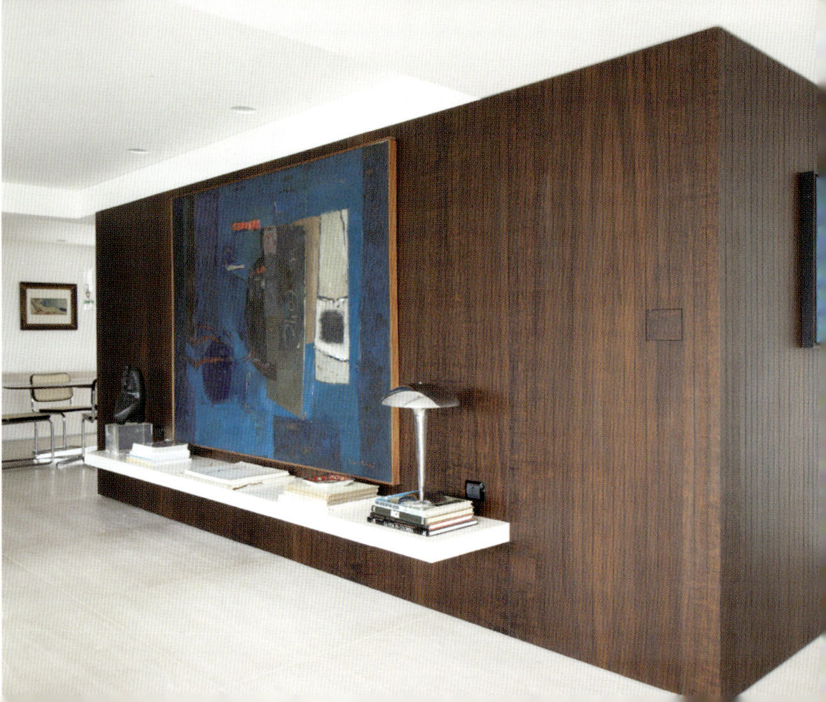

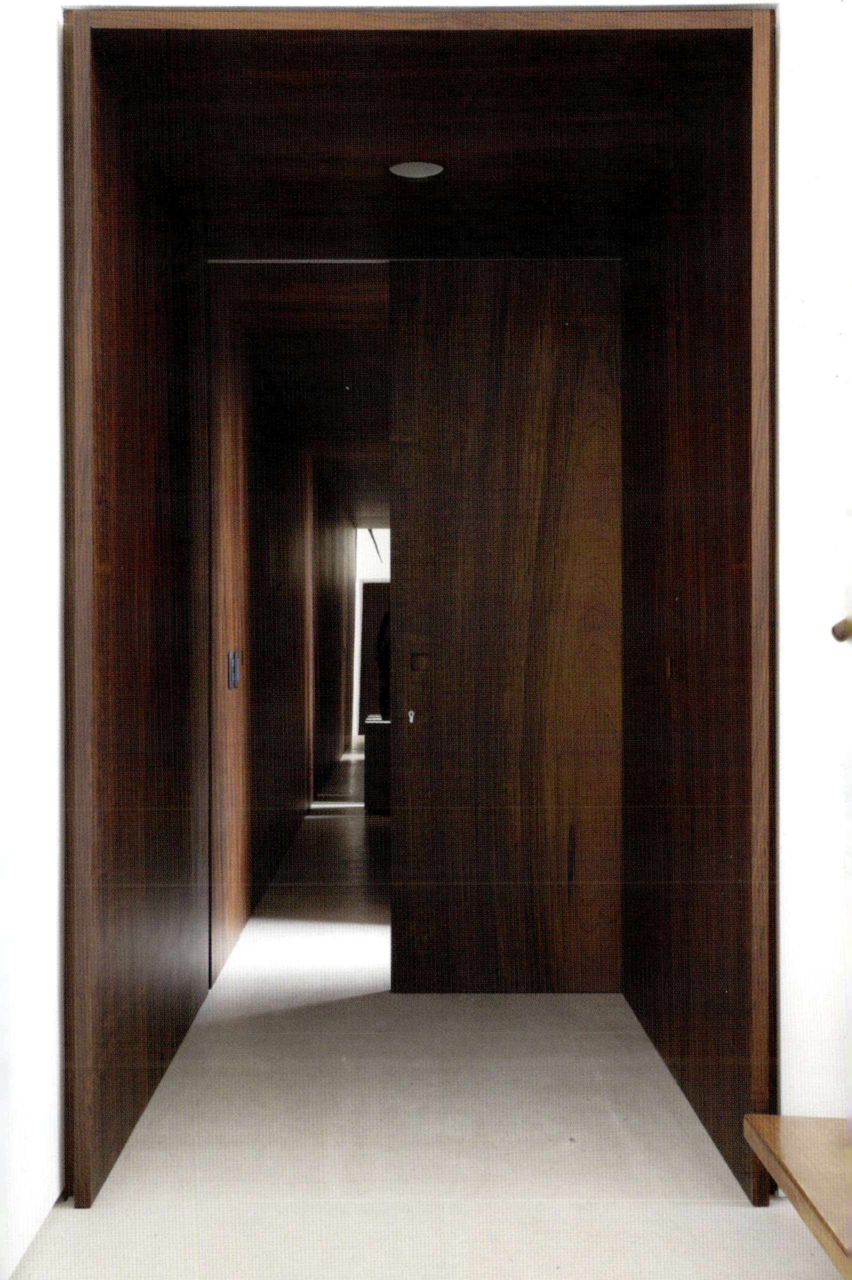

Timeless retro interior featuring graphic wallpapers & designer pieces

Abbade Apartment | São Paulo | WHYDESIGN / Guto Requena, Maurício Arruda and Tatiana Sakurai

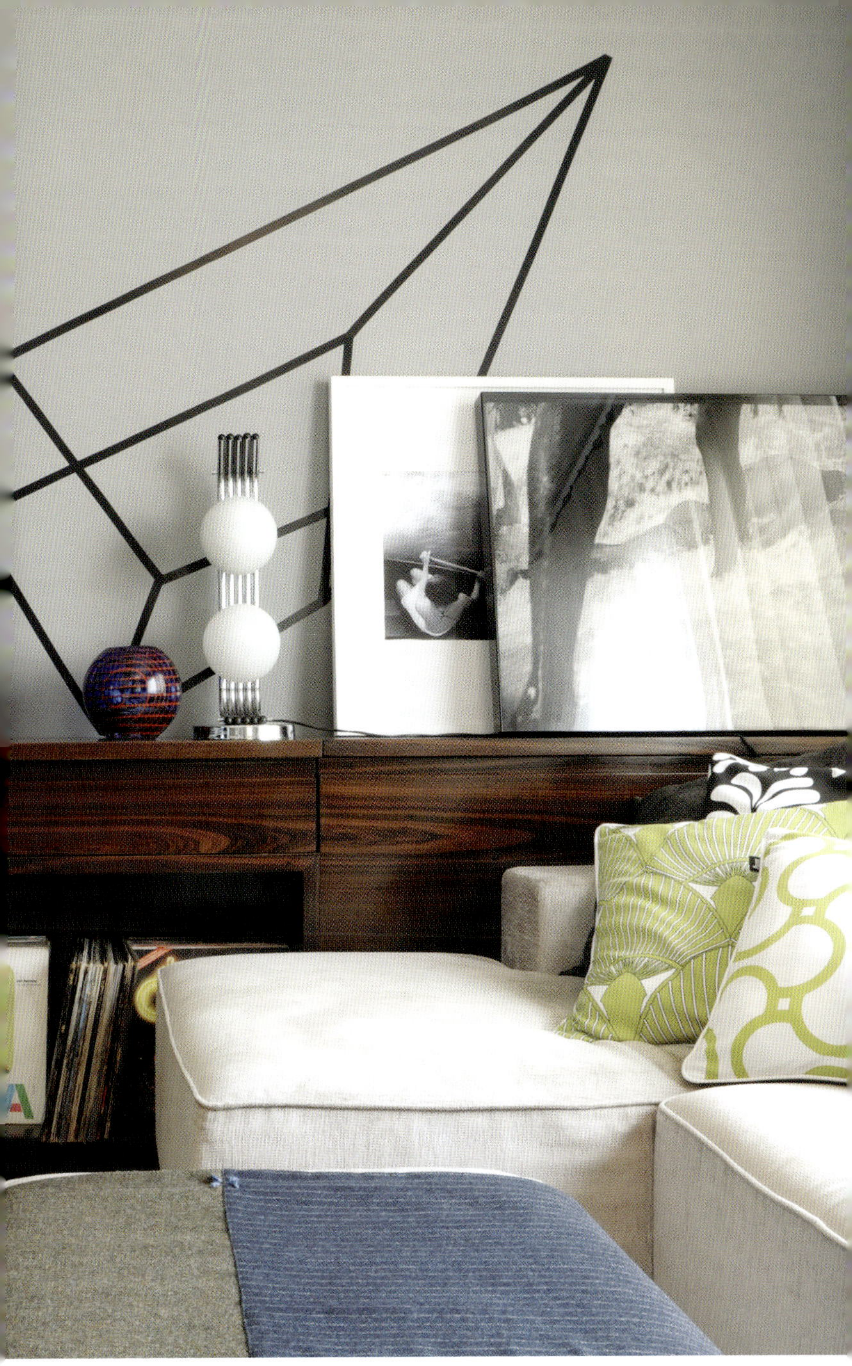

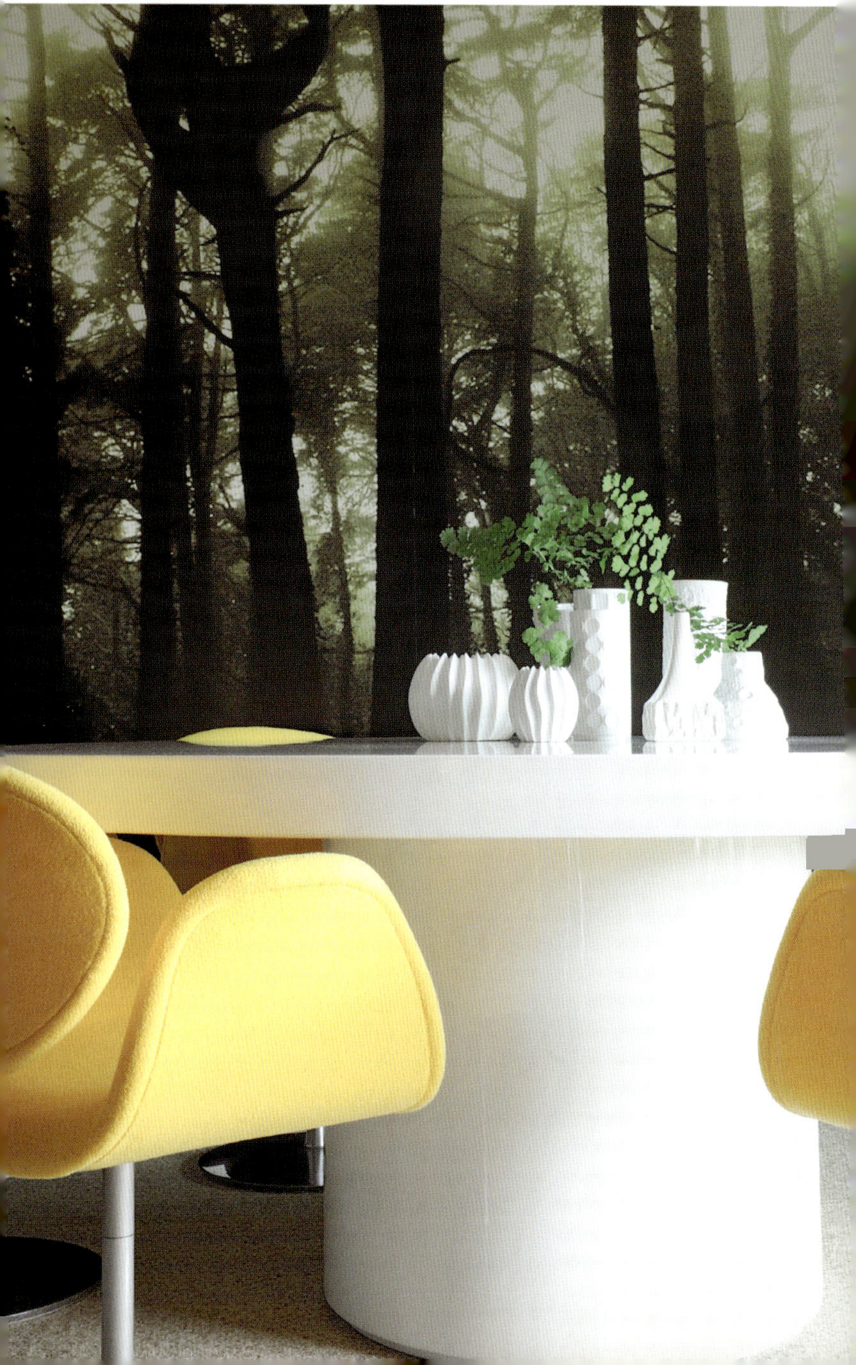

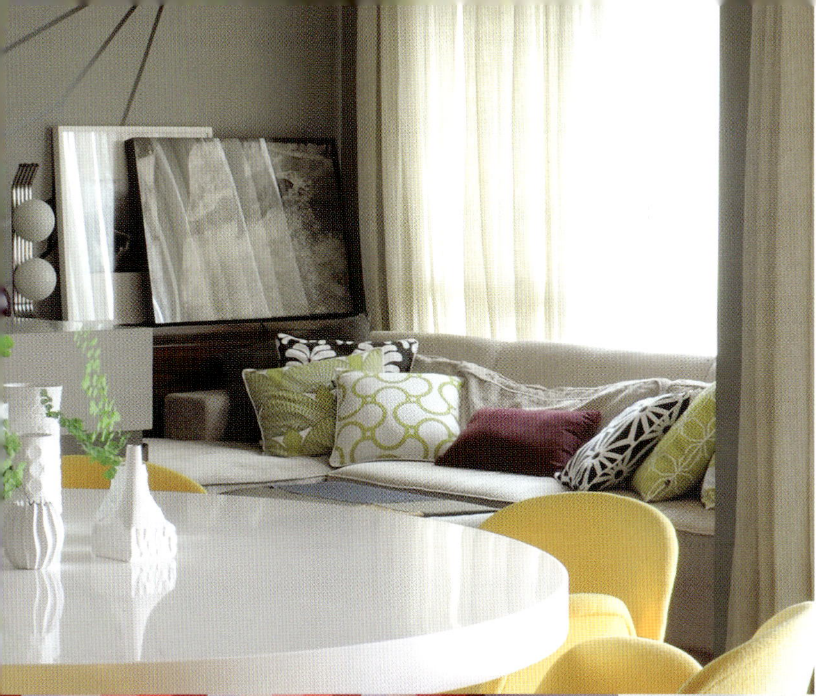

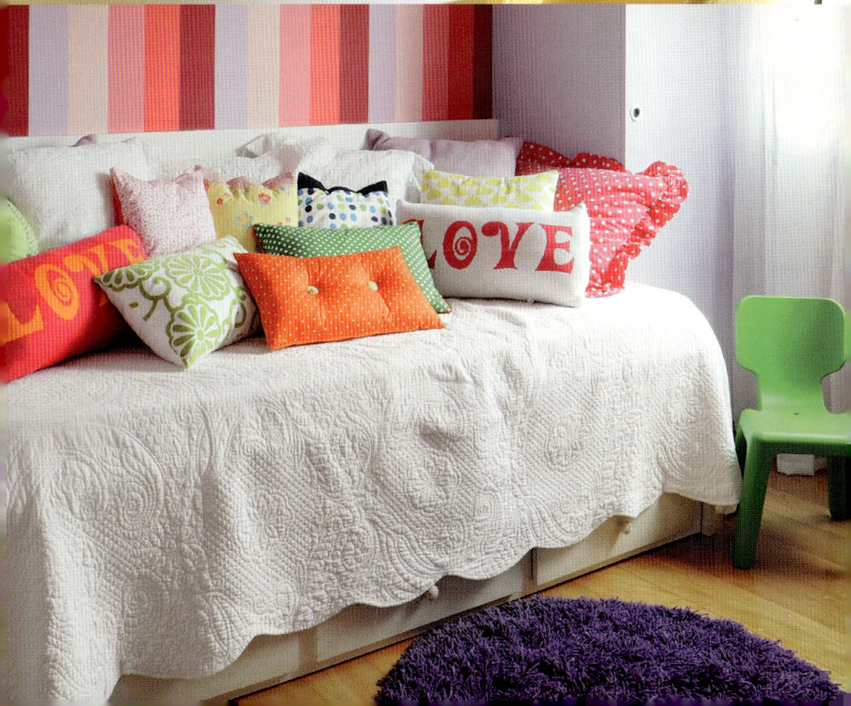
LOVE

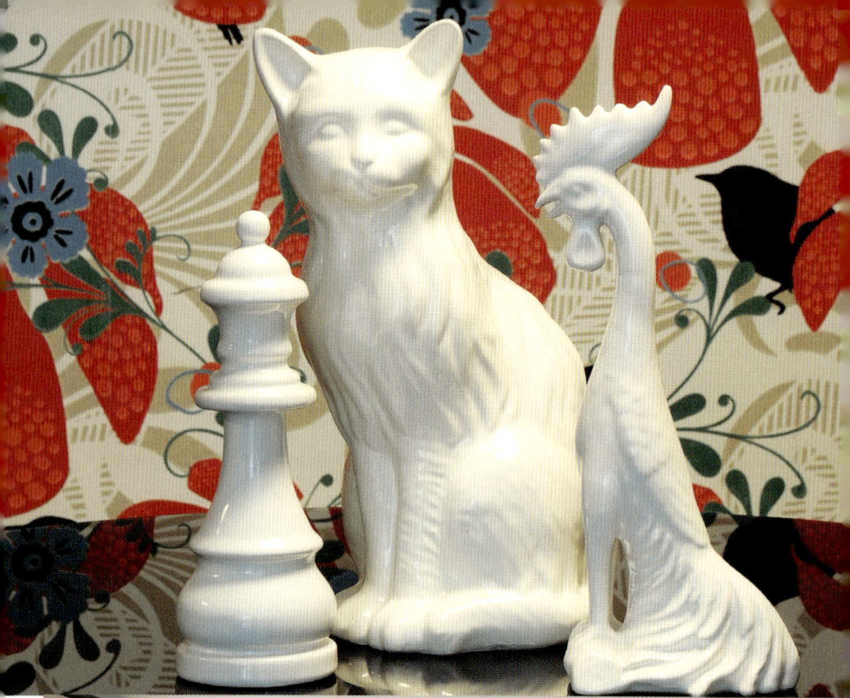

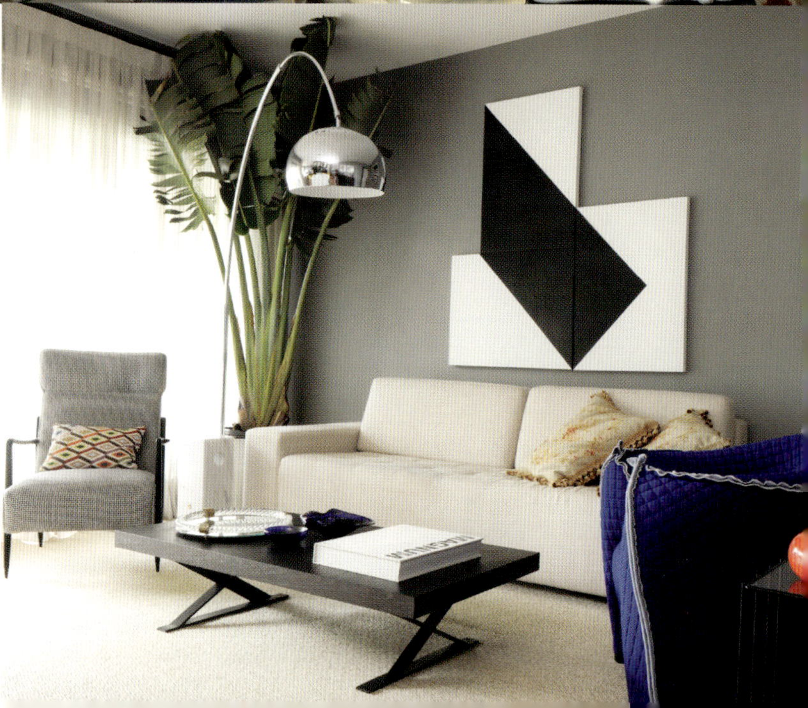

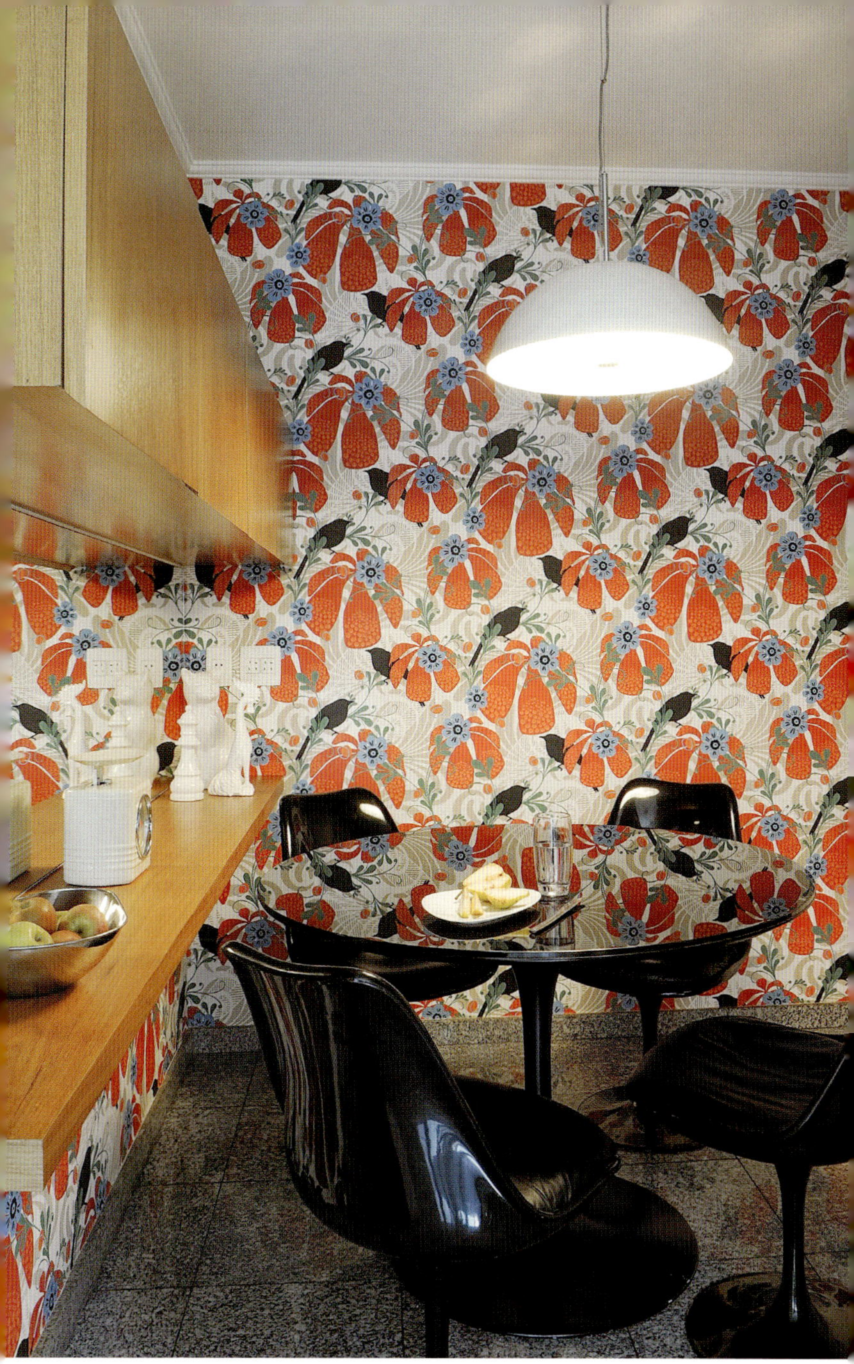

226 | **Harmonia Apartment** | São Paulo | WHYDESIGN / Guto Requena, Maurício Arruda and Tatiana Sakurai

A hip, relaxed yet highly stylish sort of interior – gritty and glamorous design all at once

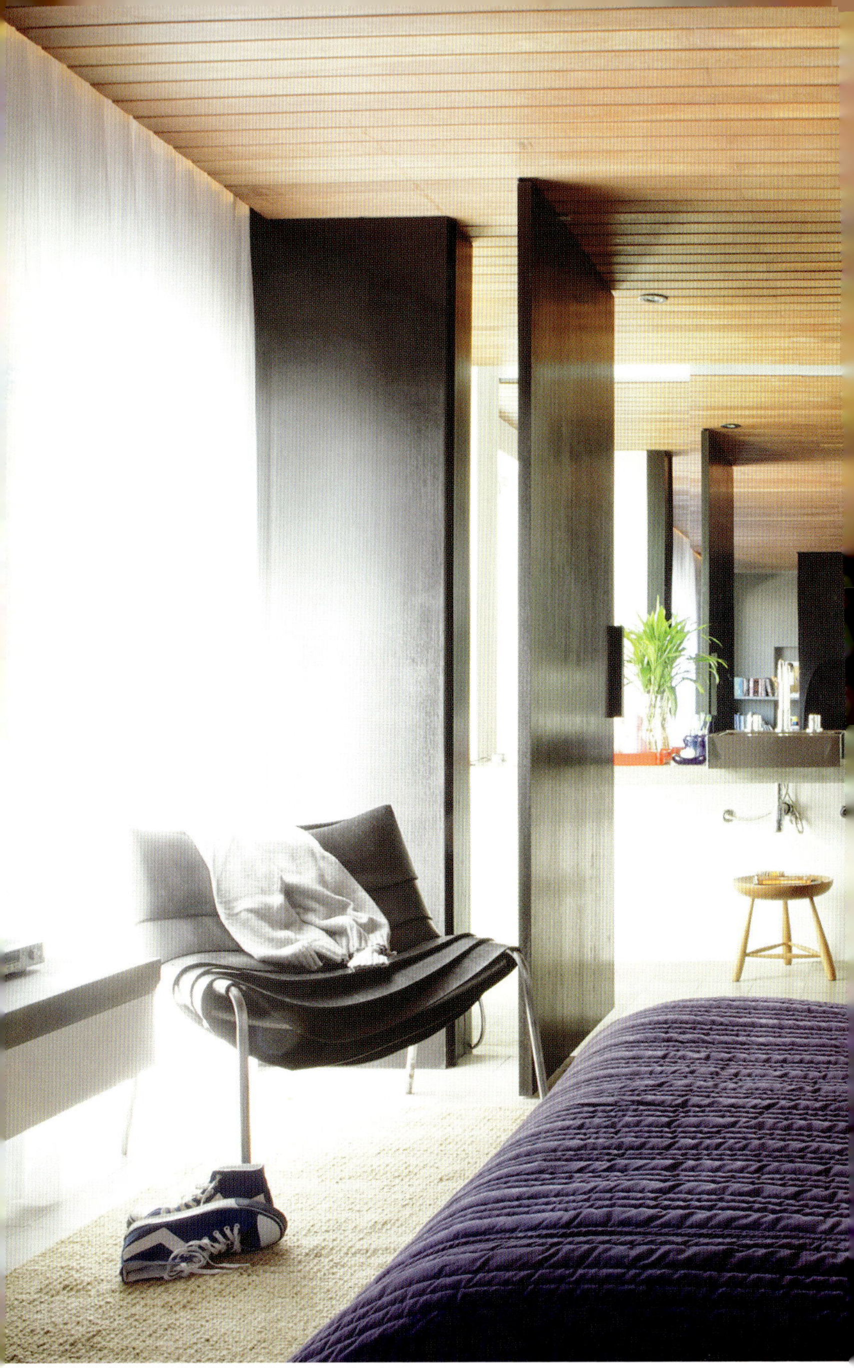

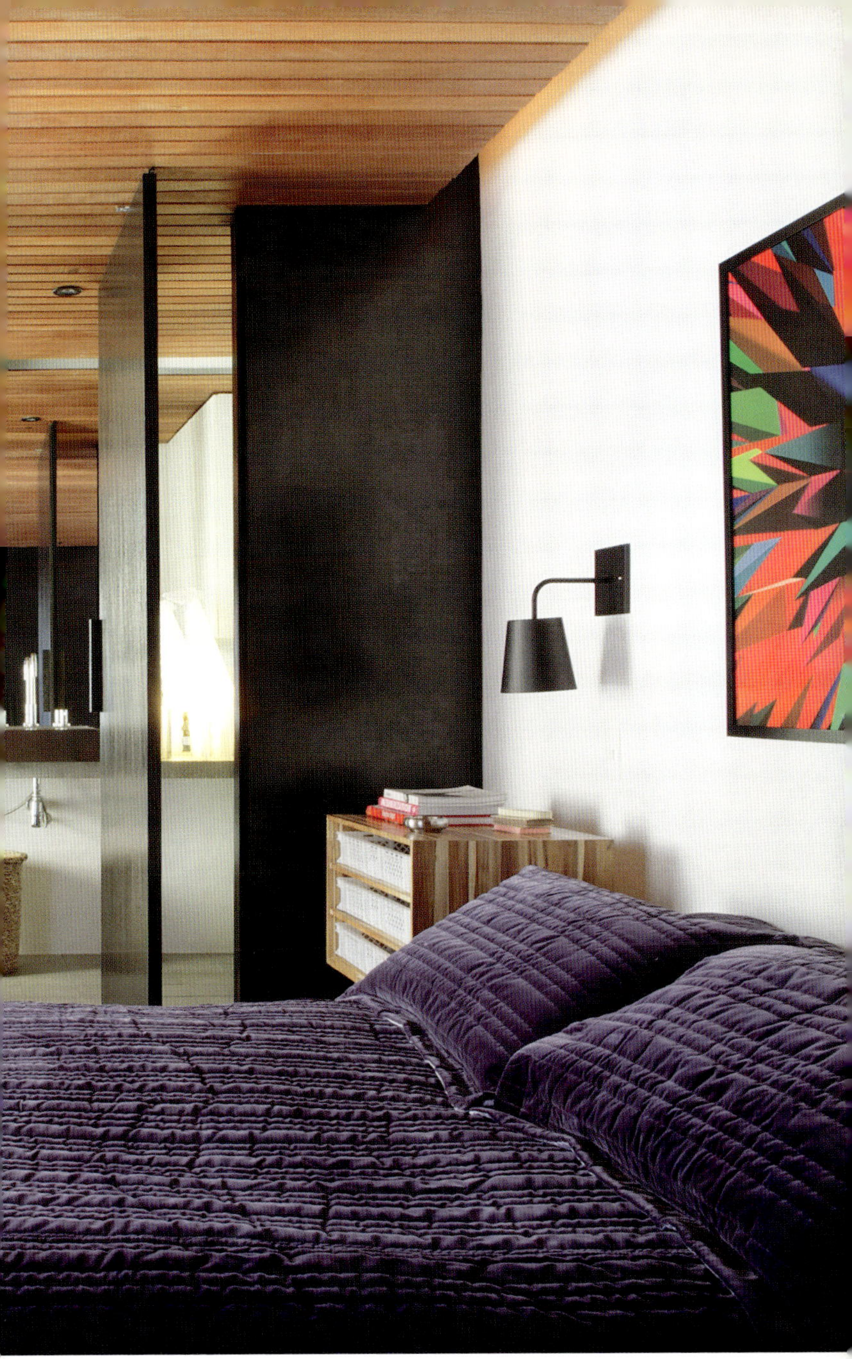

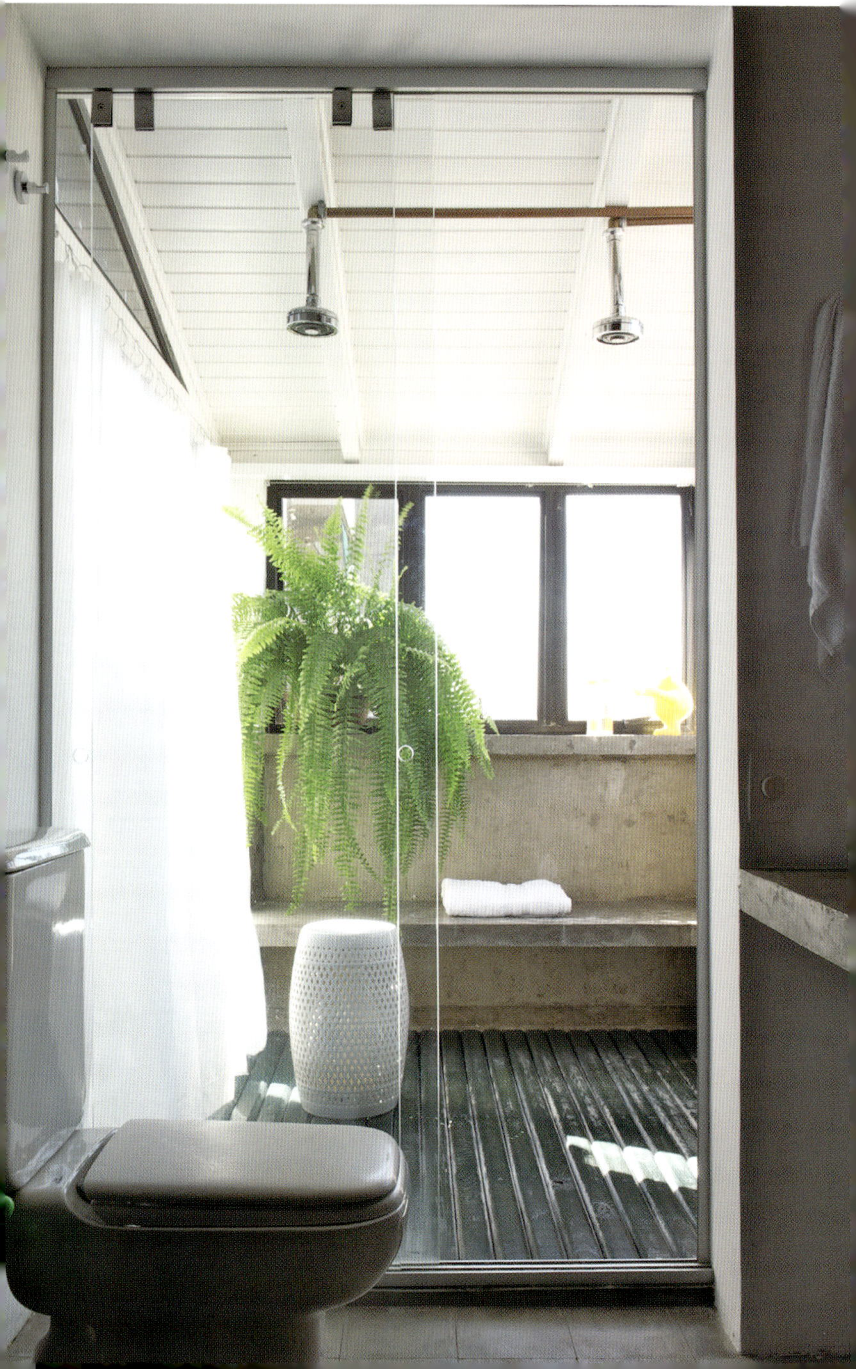

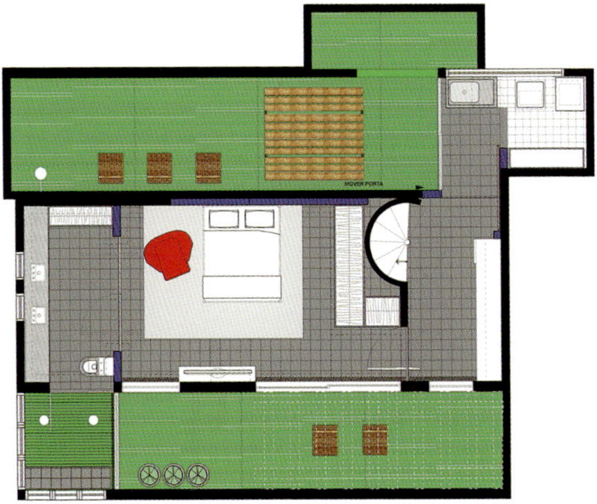
MOVER PORTA

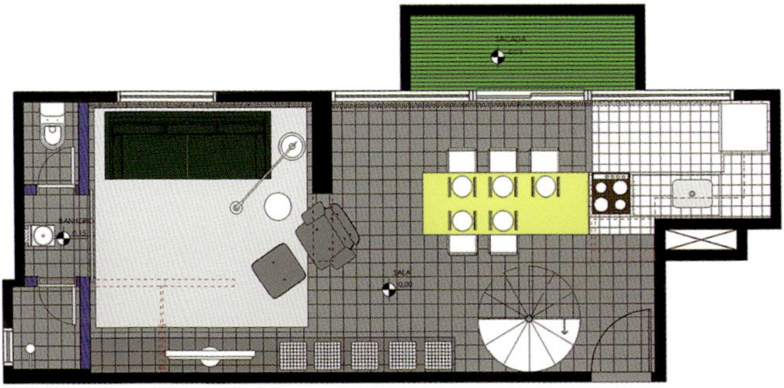
SALA

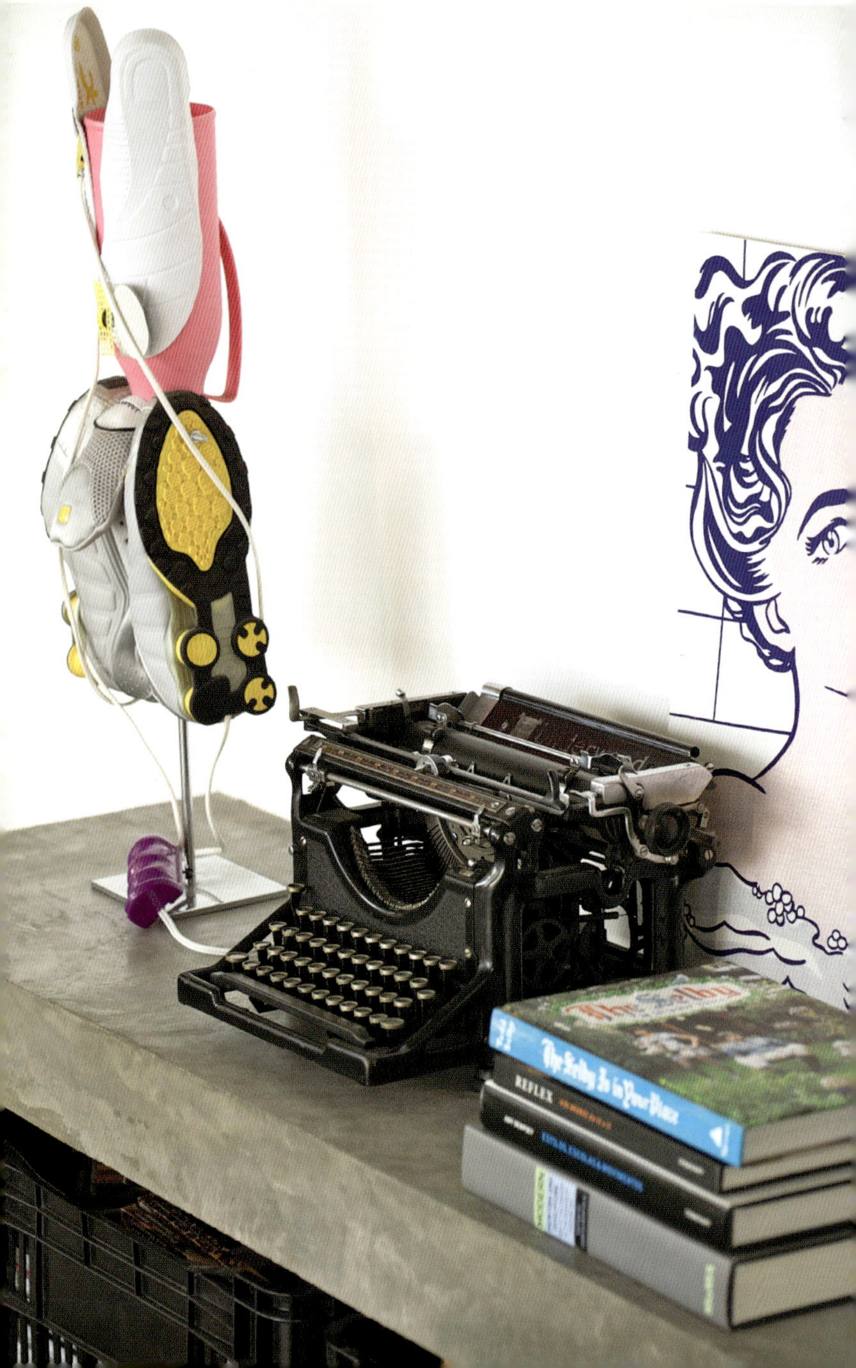
The Selby Is in Your Place
REFLEX

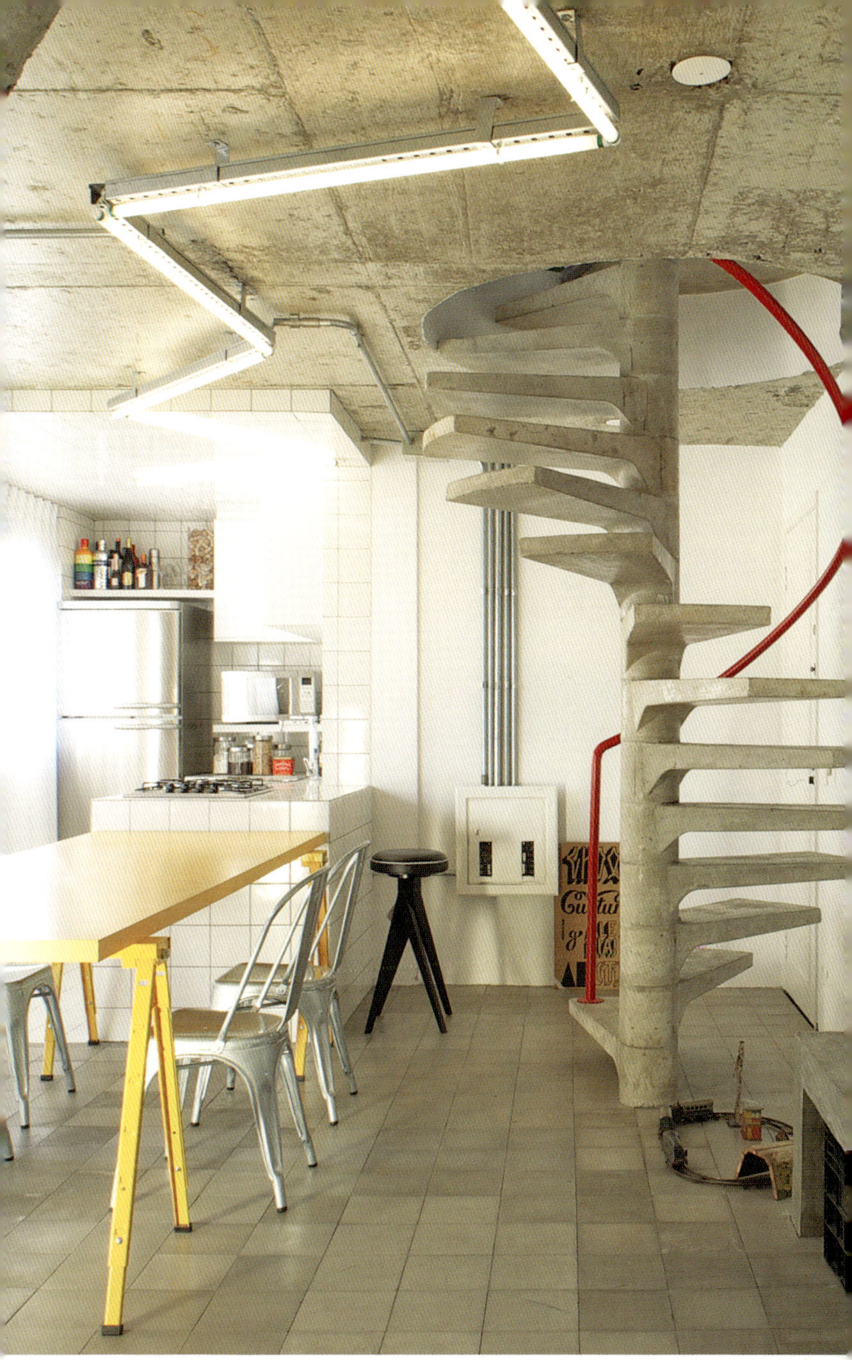

Luxury living with timeless chic taste

House of the Tree | Shenzhen | Kokaistudios

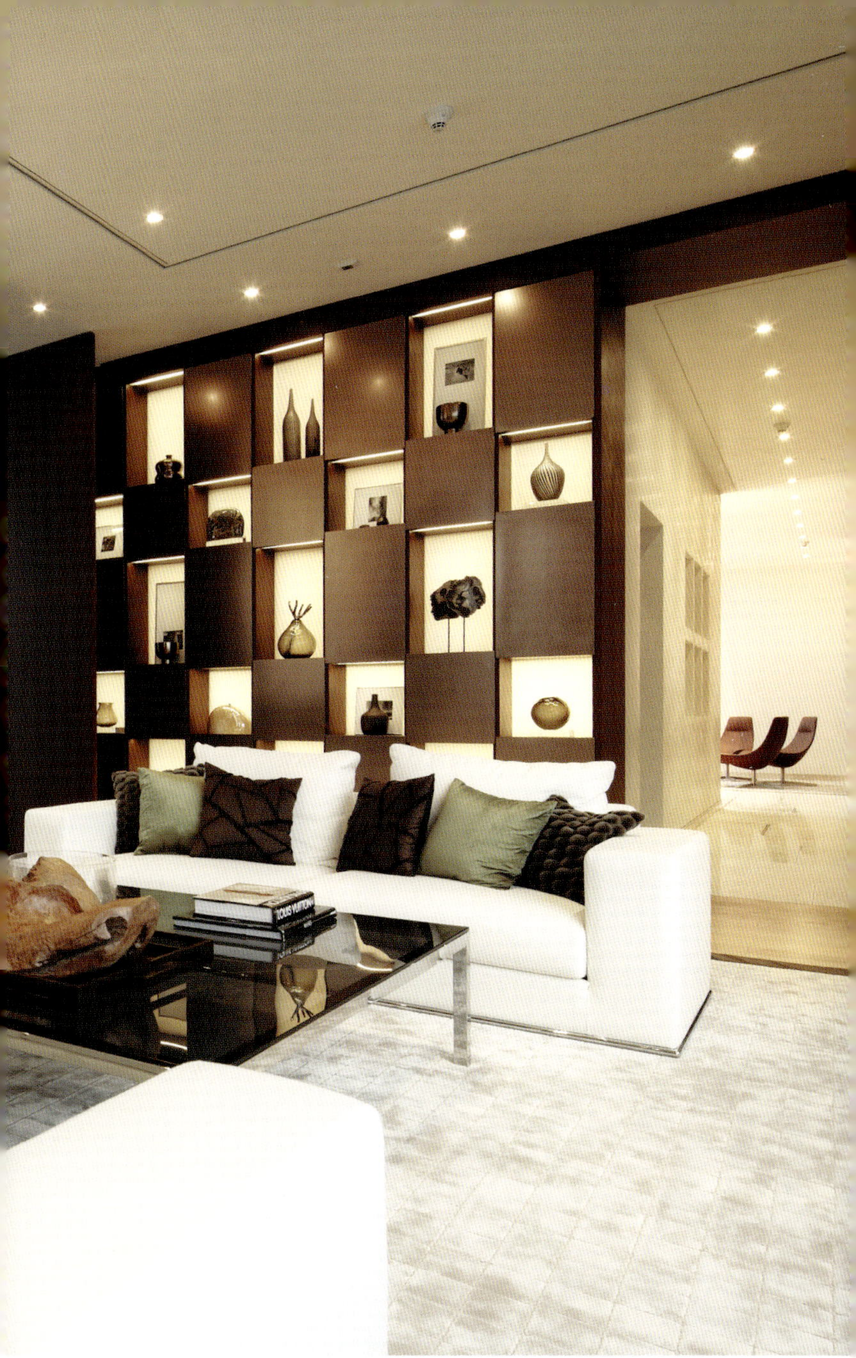
LOUIS VUITTON

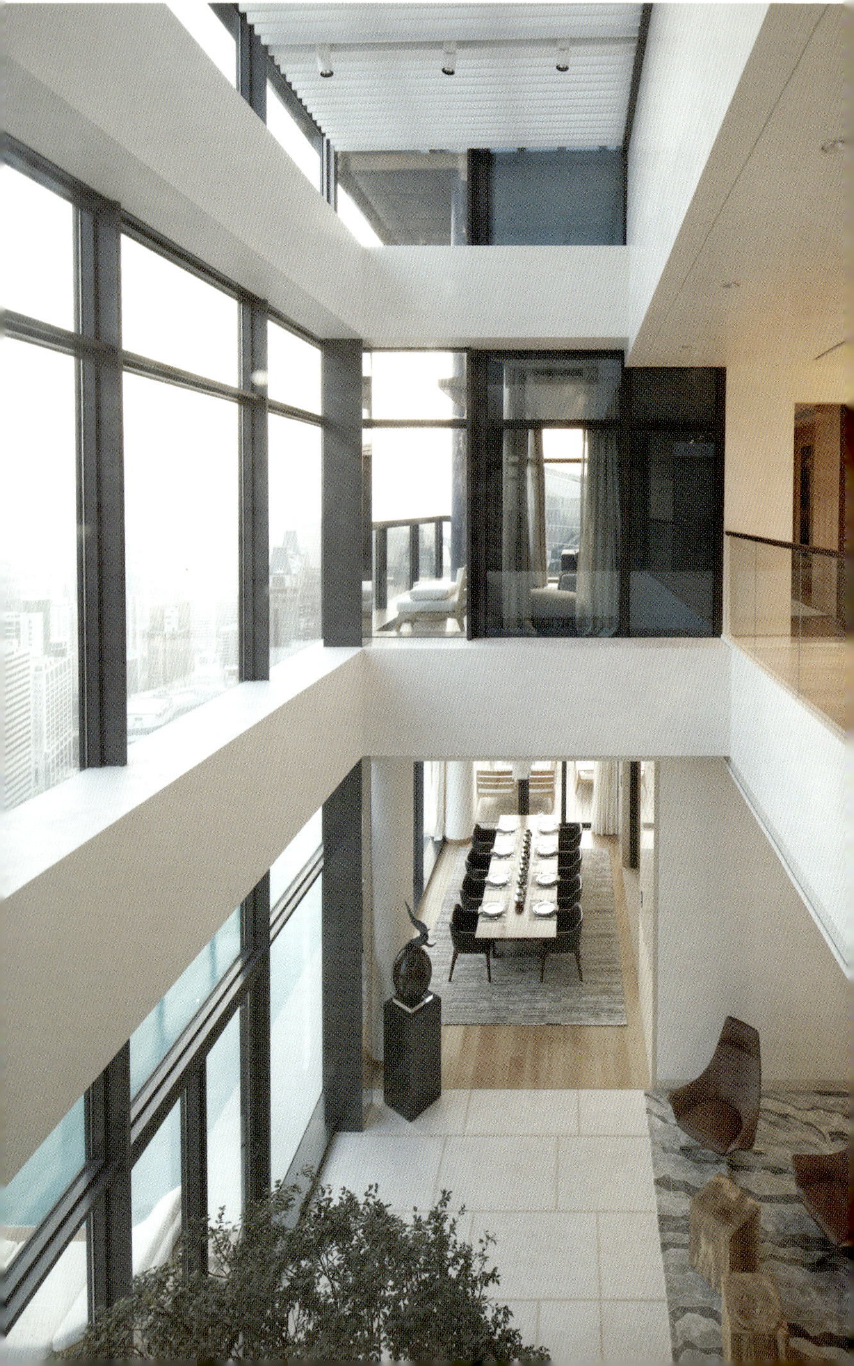

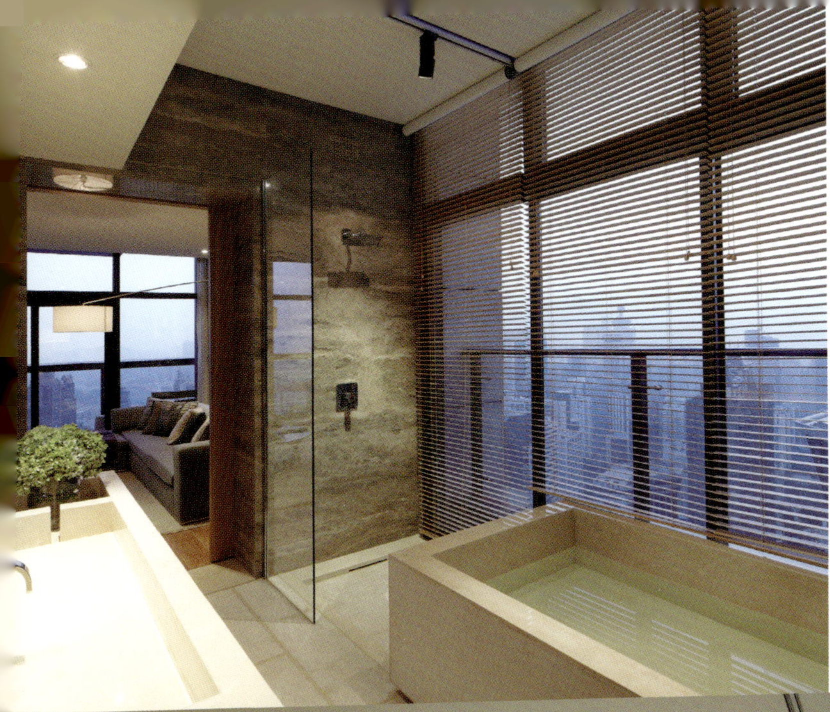

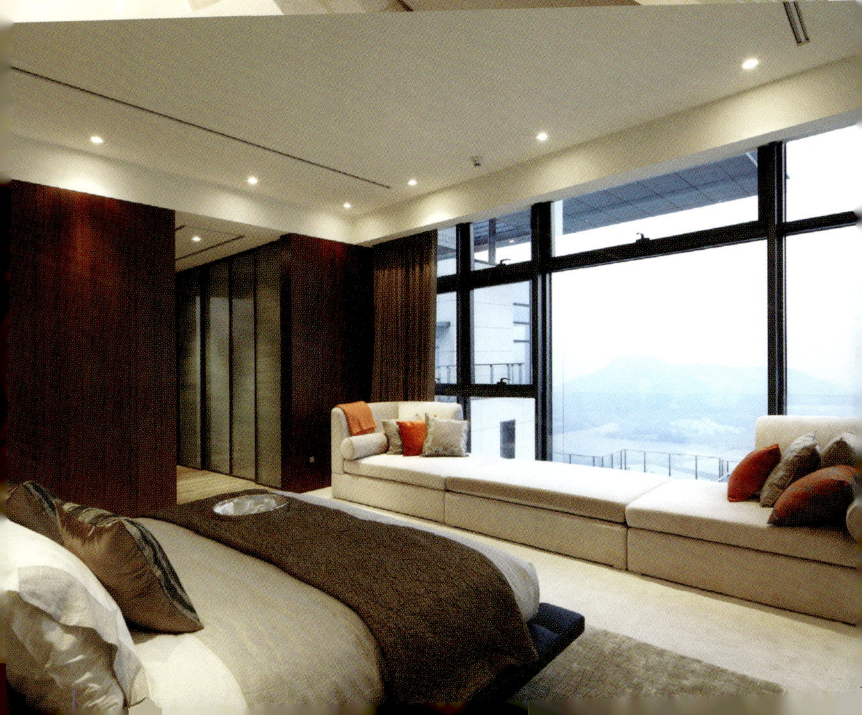

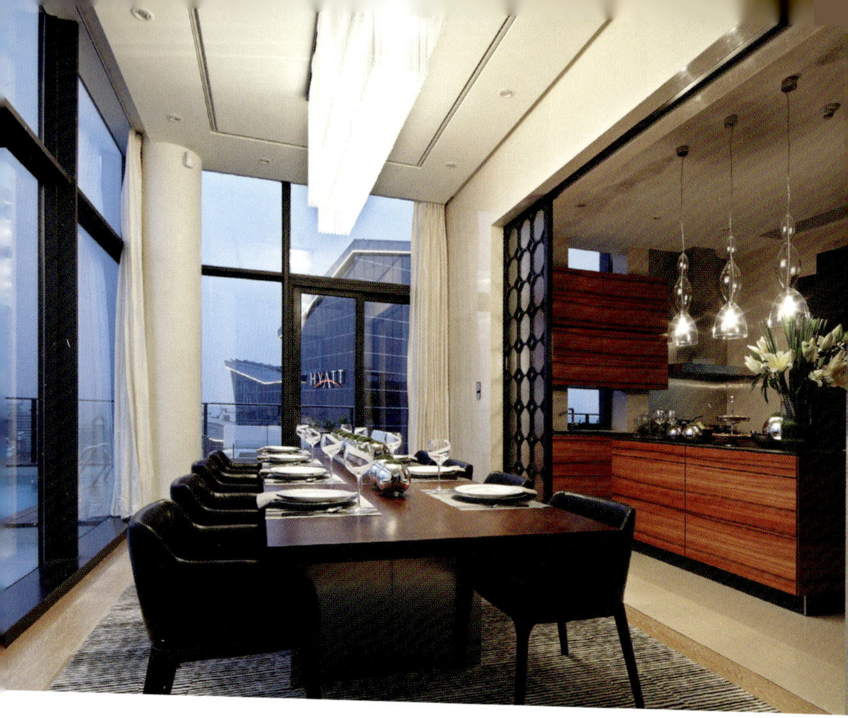

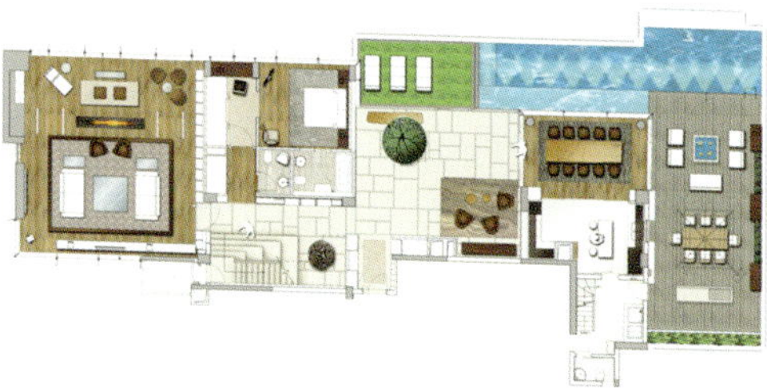

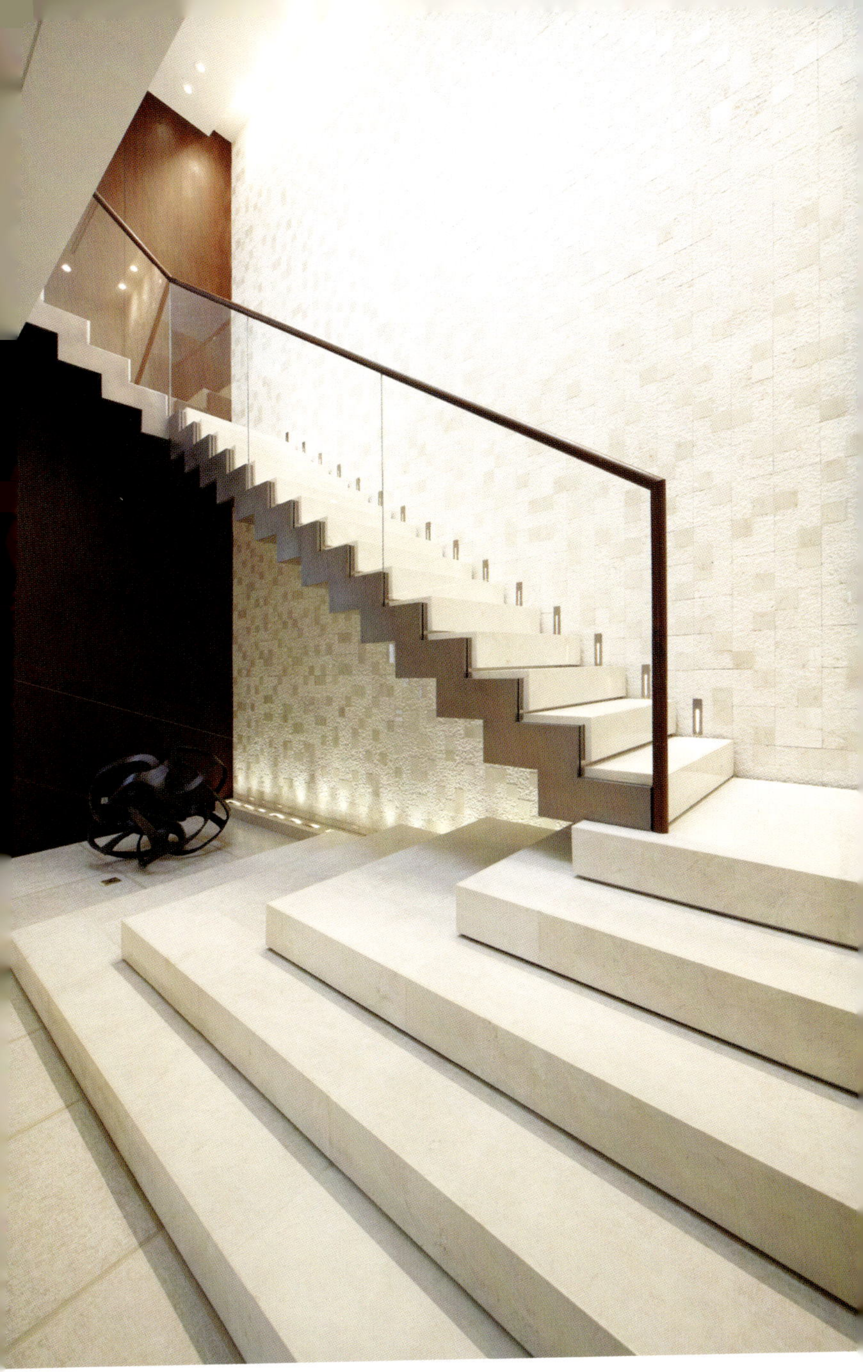

House Strauss | Stuttgart | Alexander Brenner Architekten

Fresh looking multi-generational home in one volume

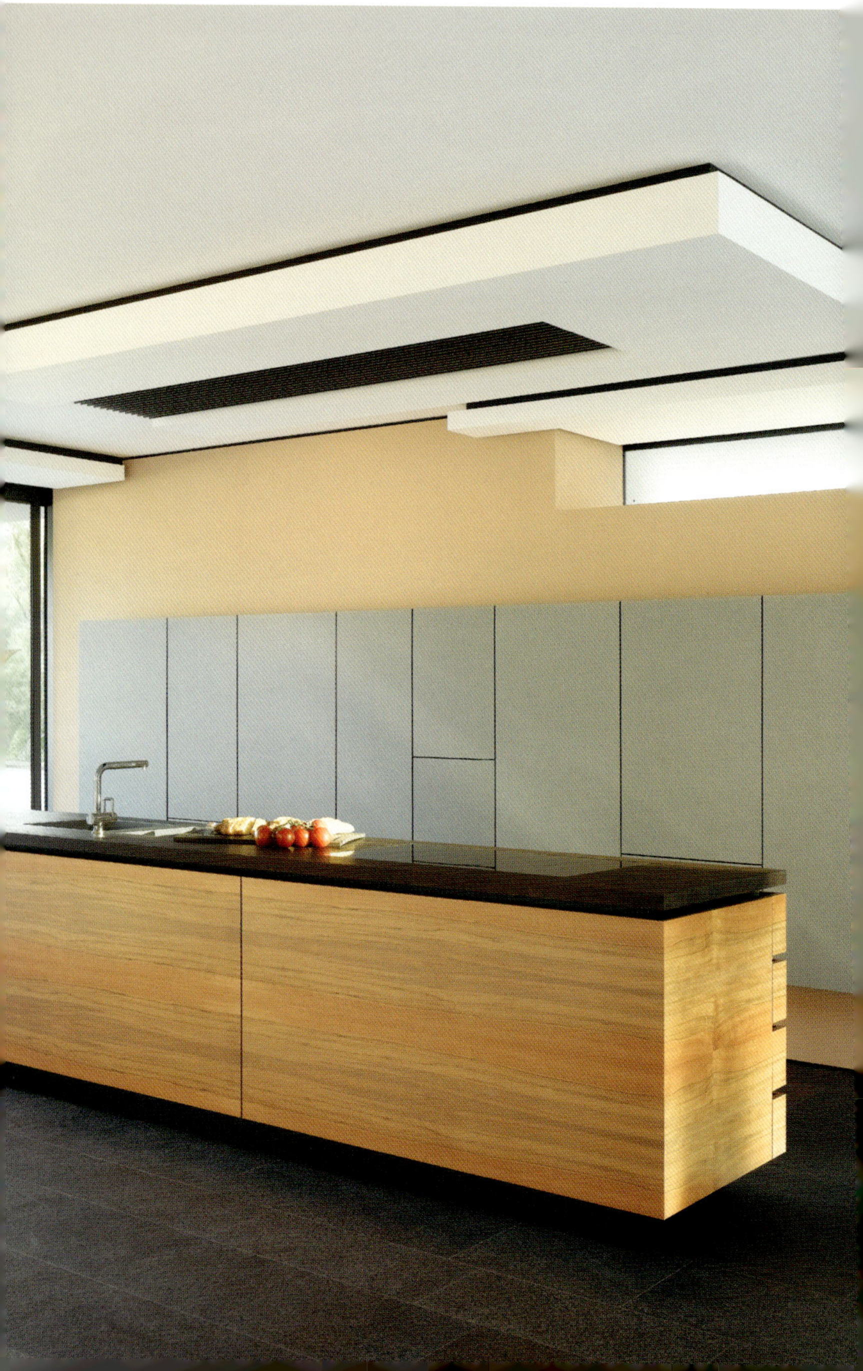

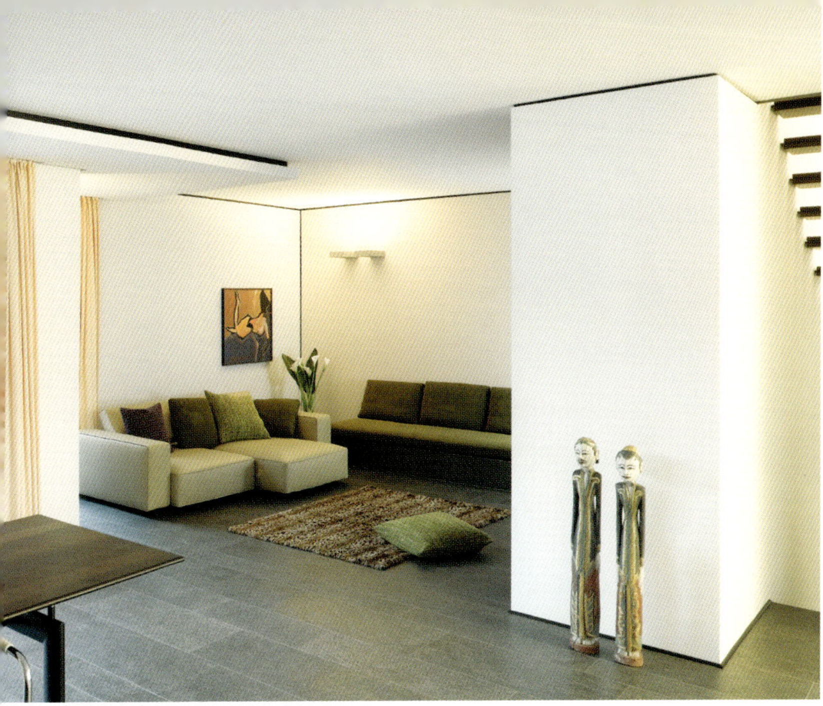

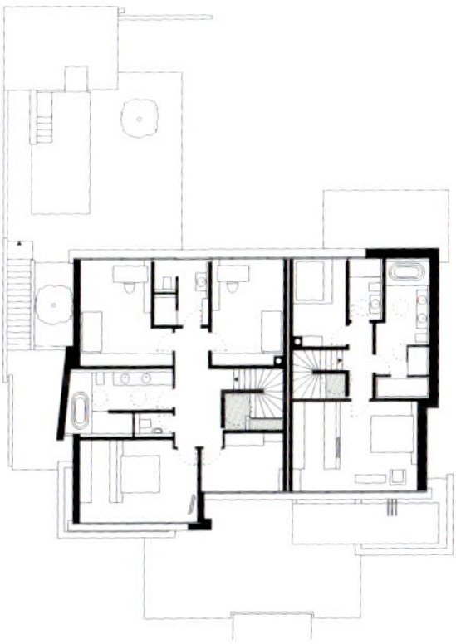

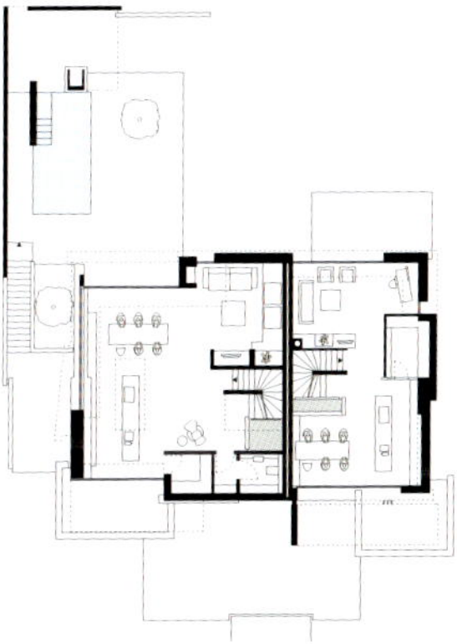

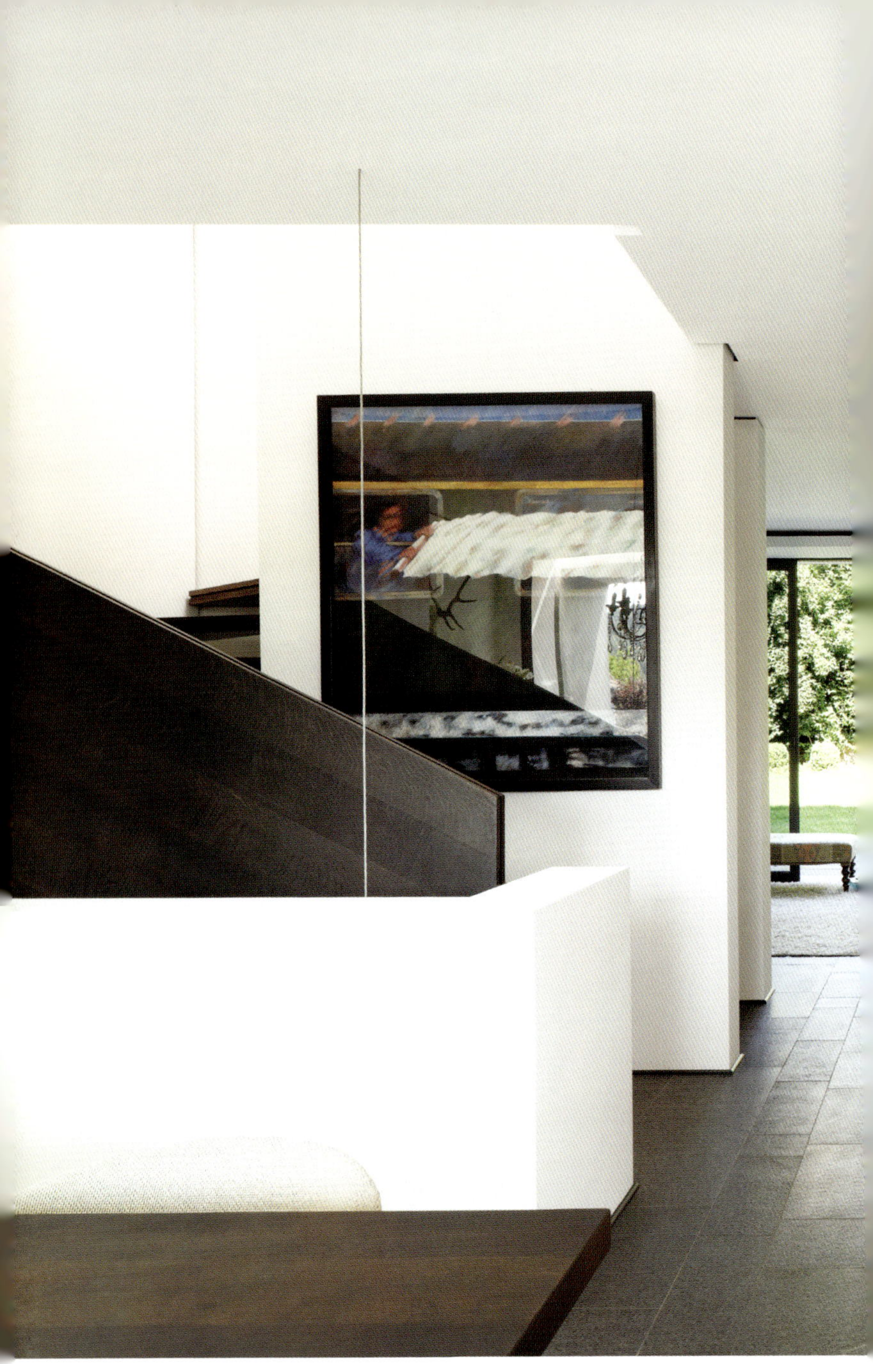

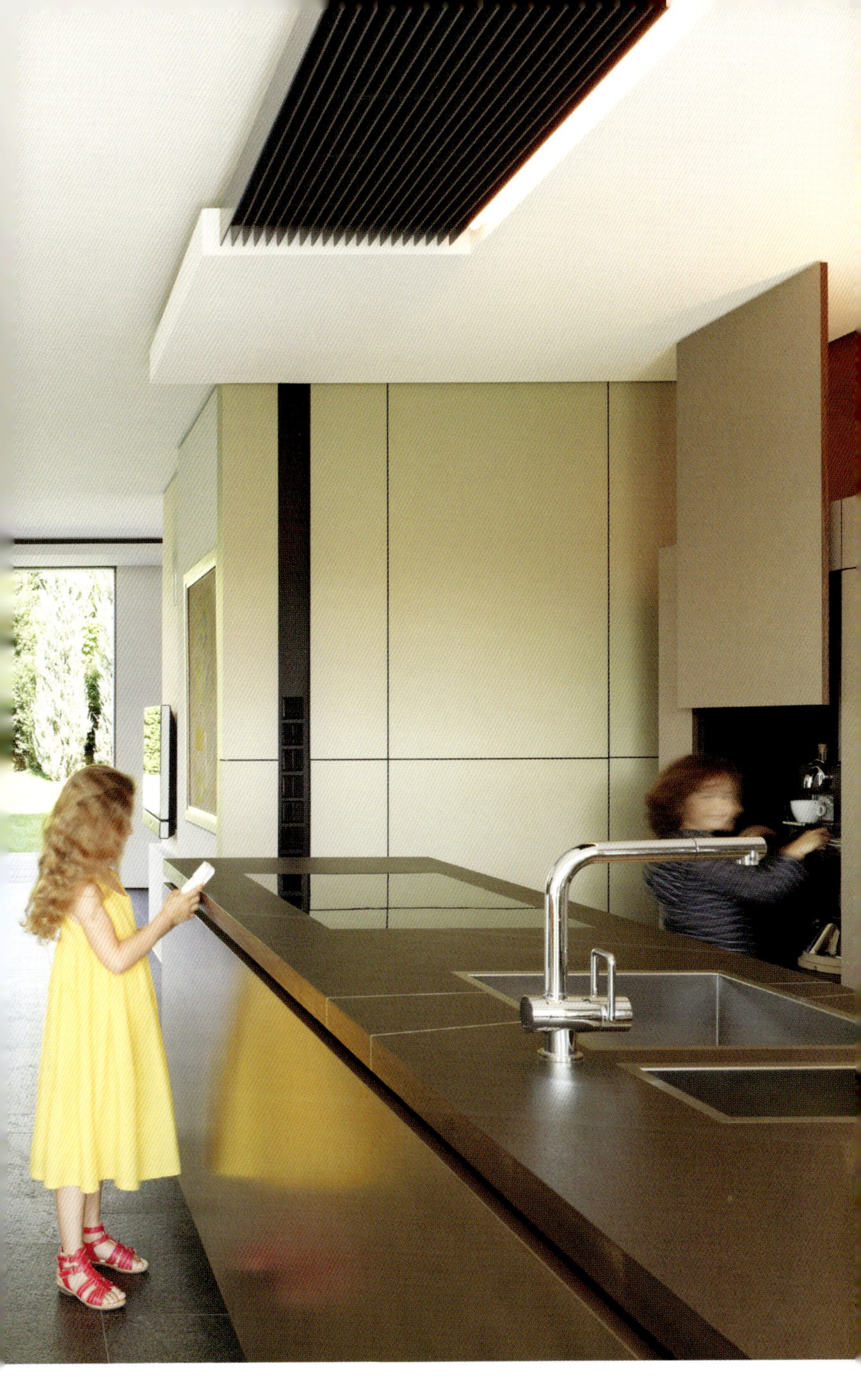

Designer pieces com
.the **straightfo**r
seaside home.

Casa del Mar | Tijuana | graciastudio

rd

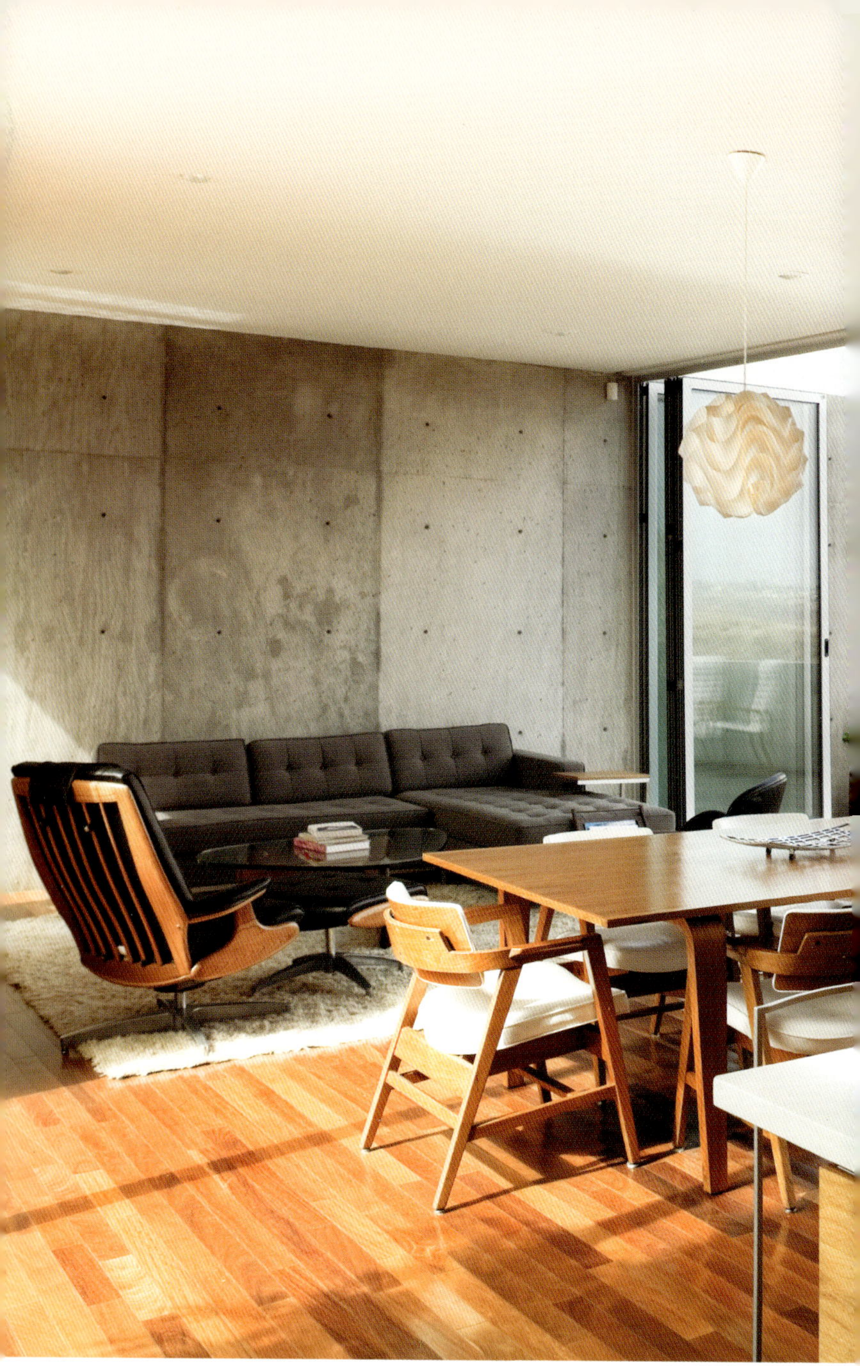

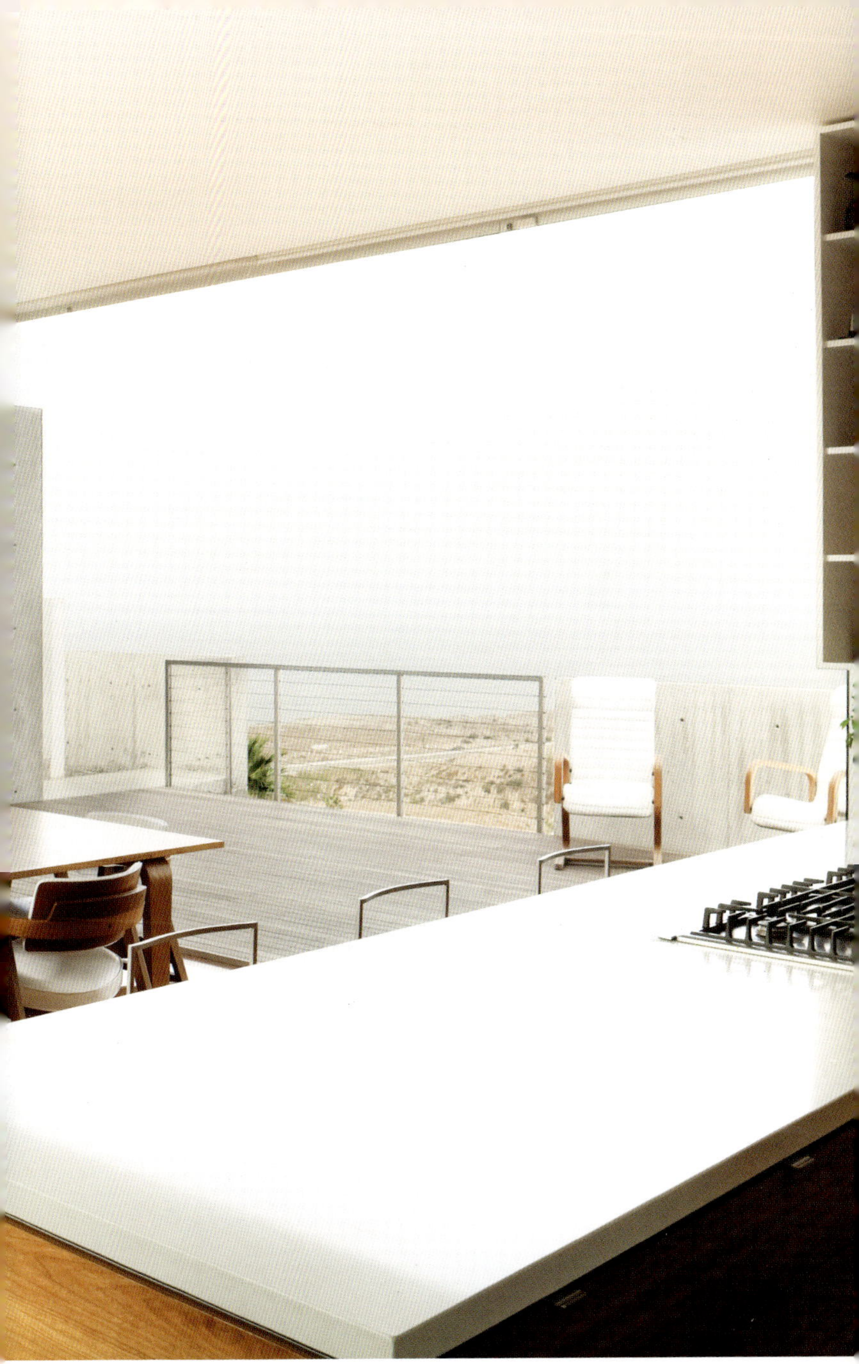

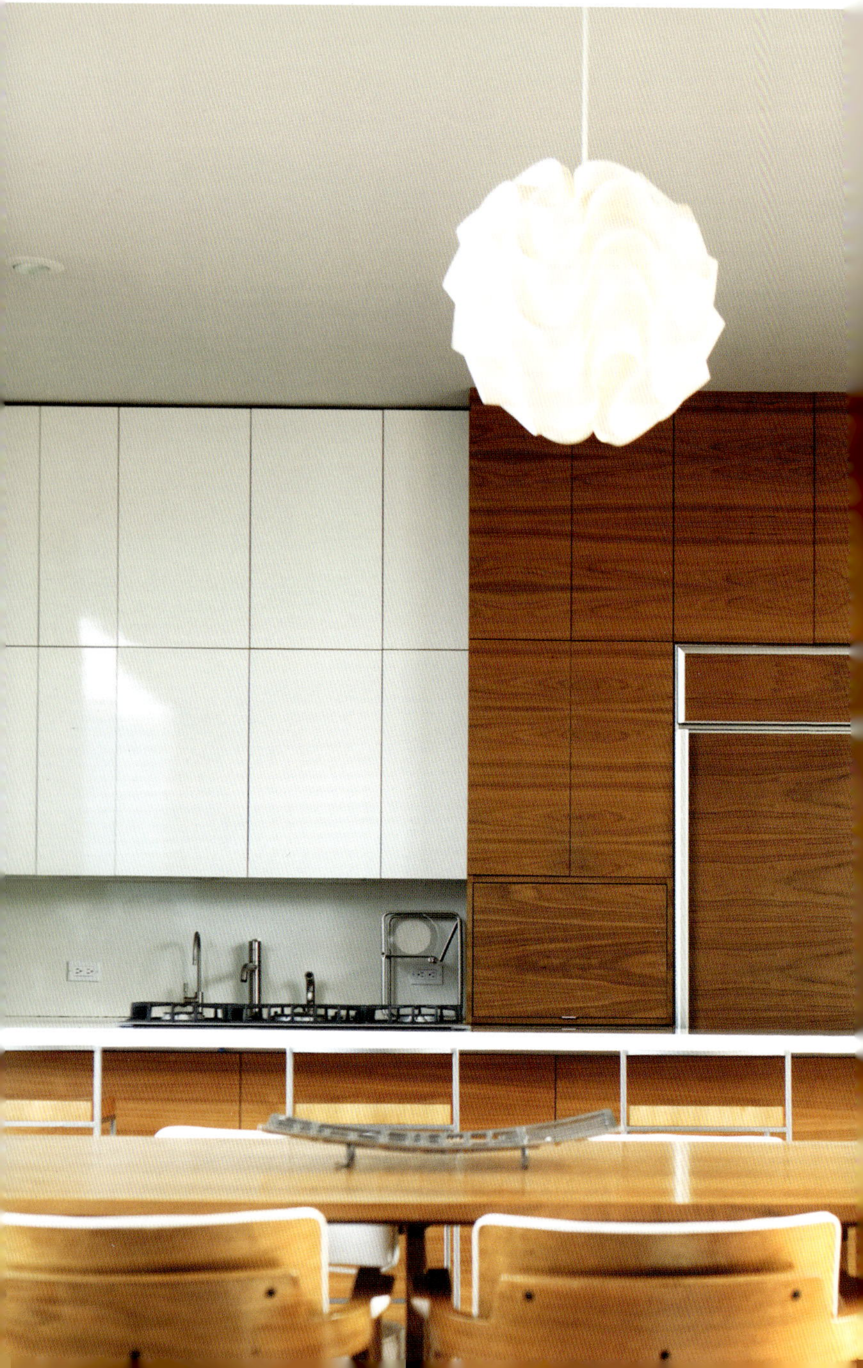

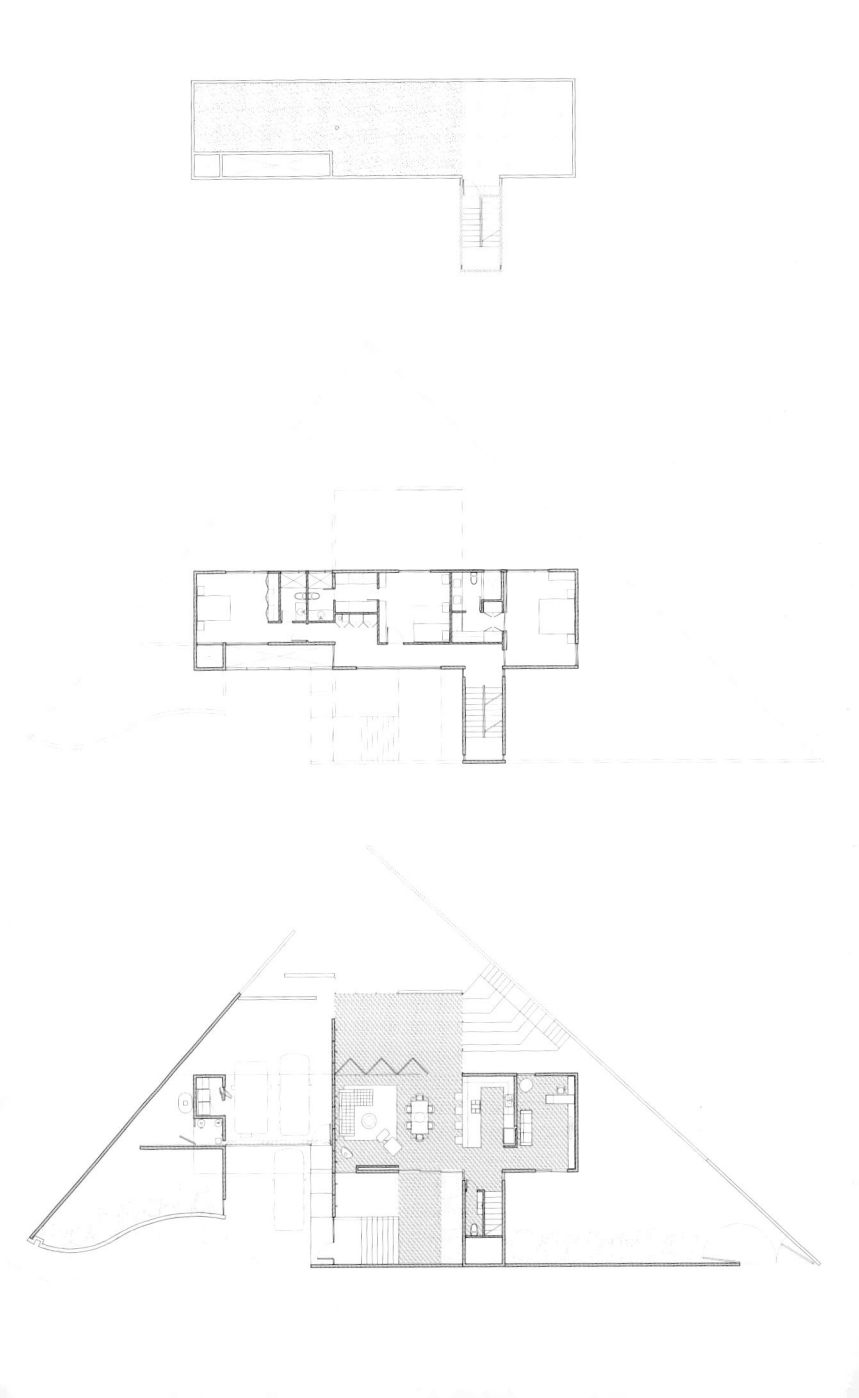

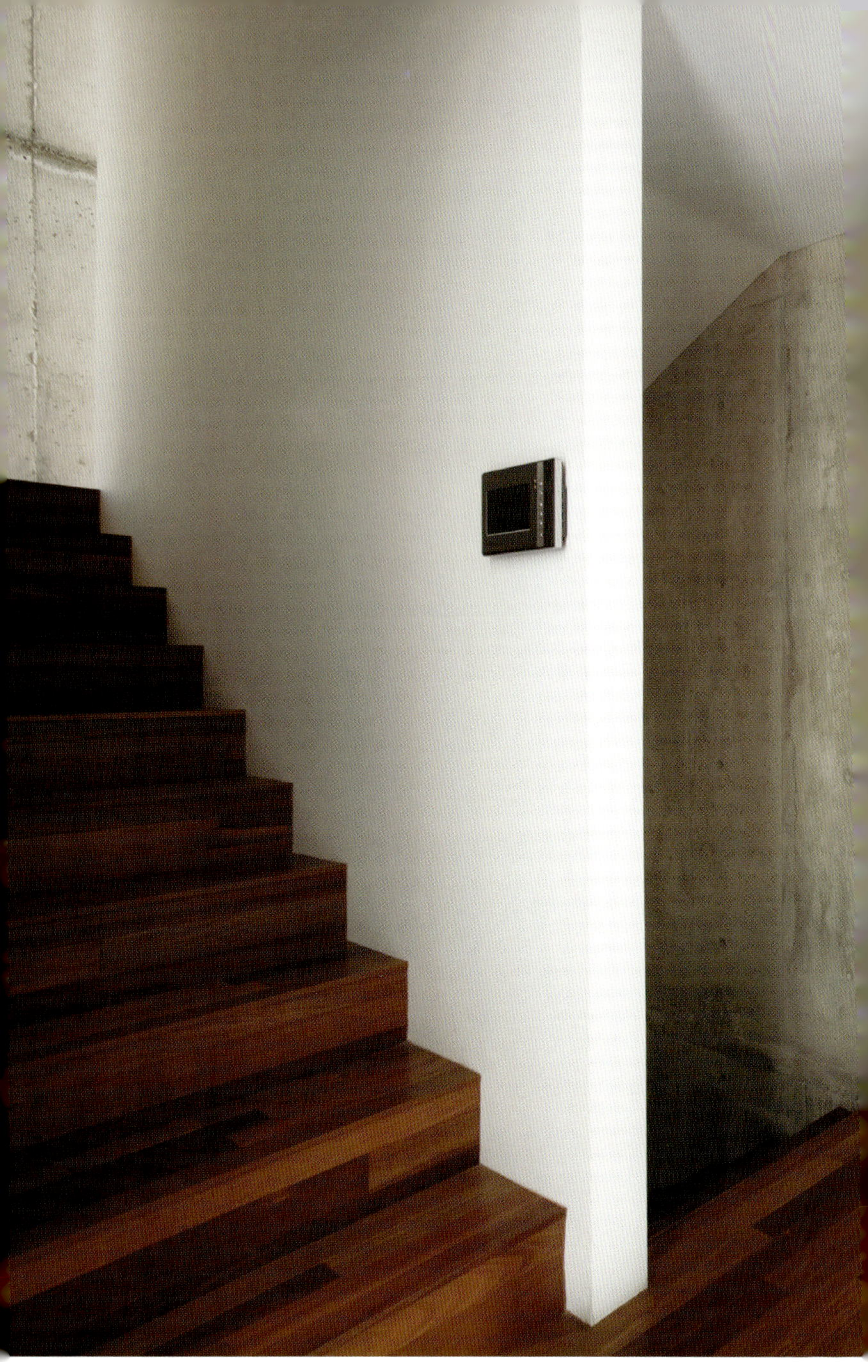

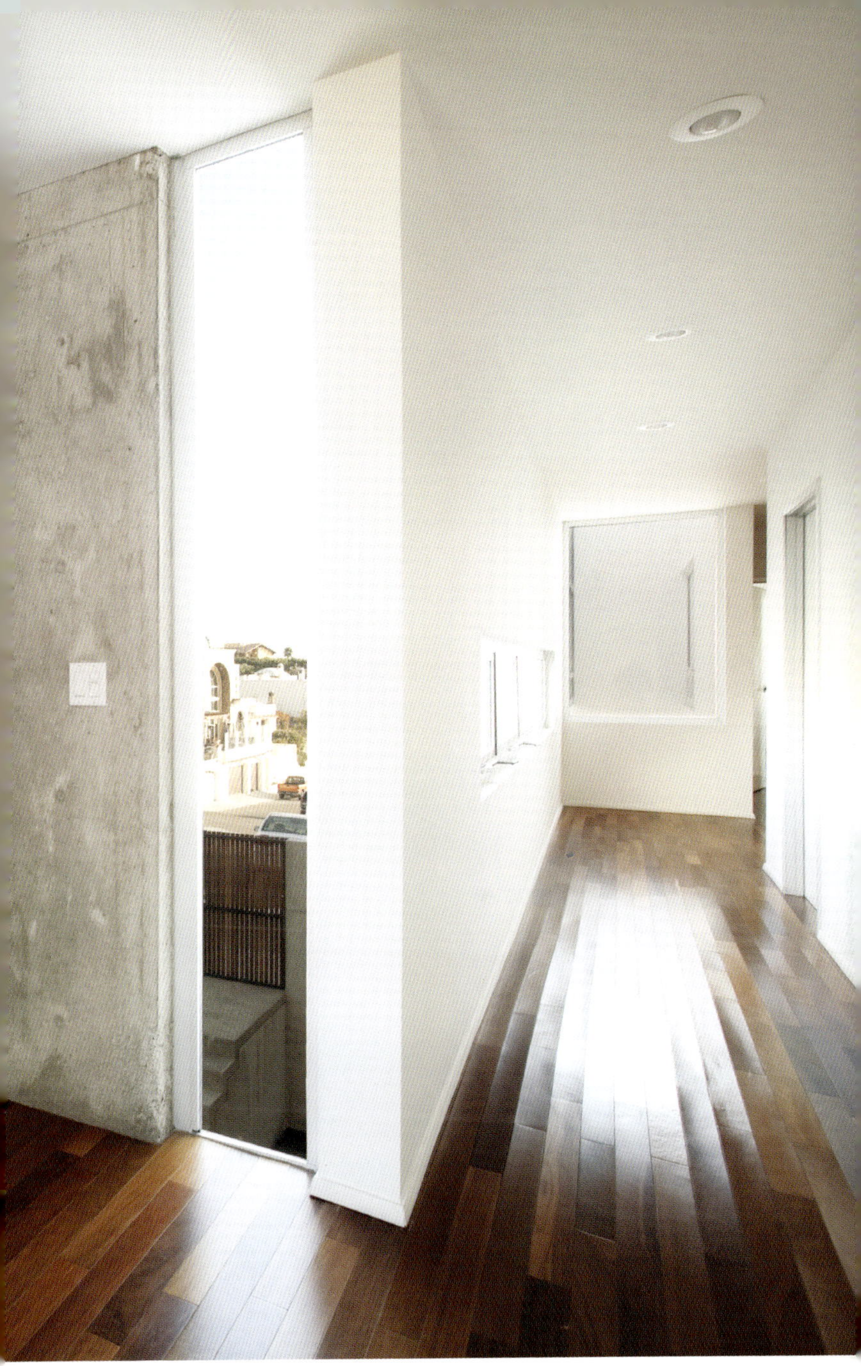

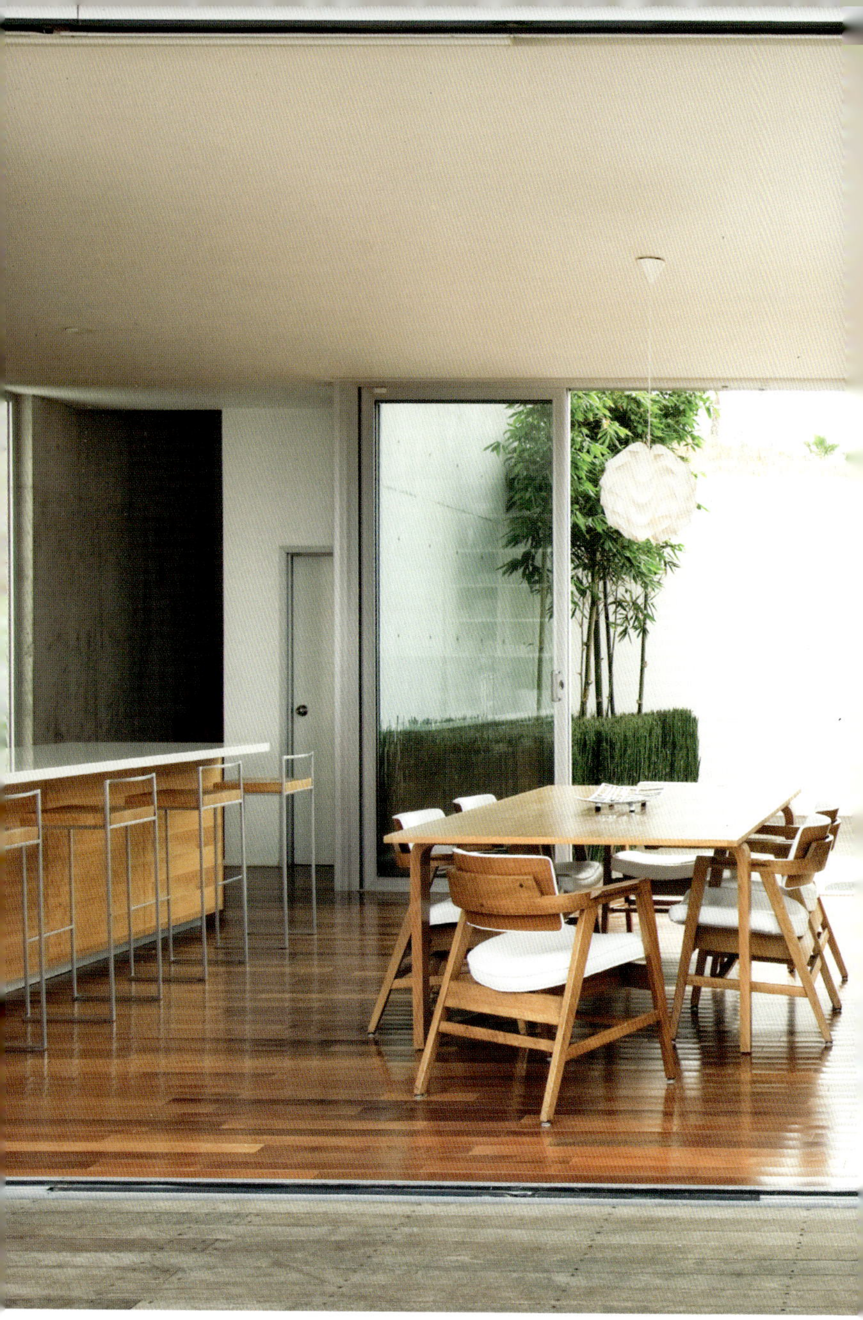

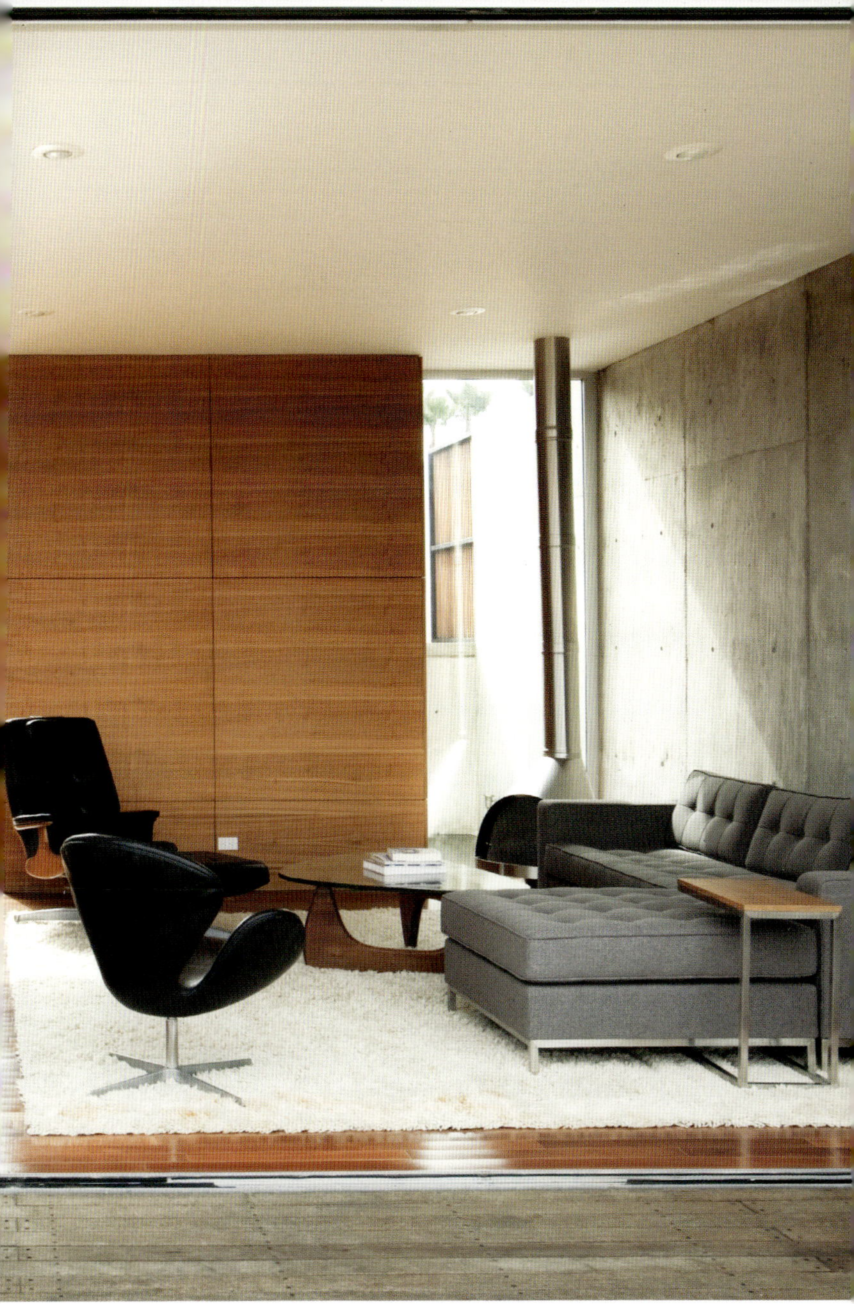

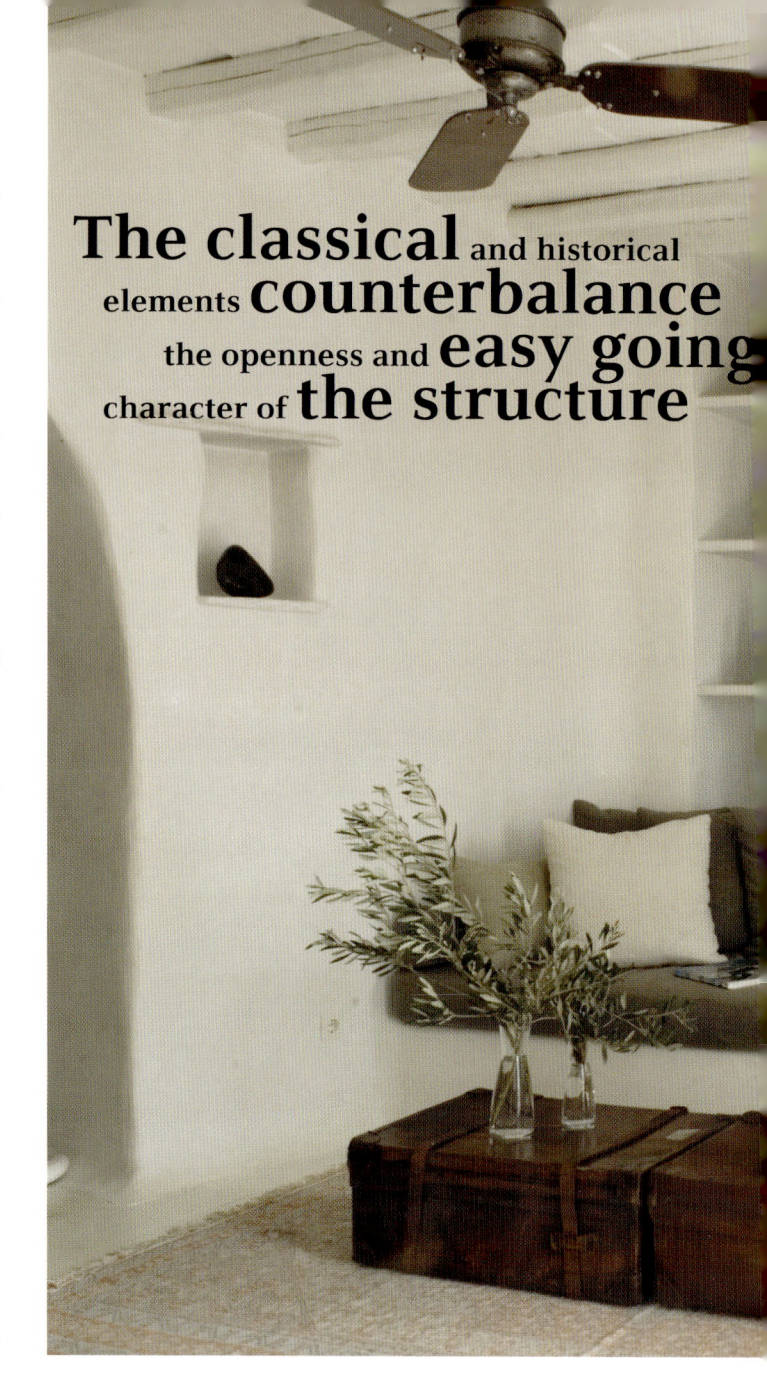

The classical and historical elements **counterbalance** the openness and **easy going** character of **the structure**

Vacation House in Tinos | Tinos Island, Cyclades | Zege architects / Marilyn Katsaris (interiors)

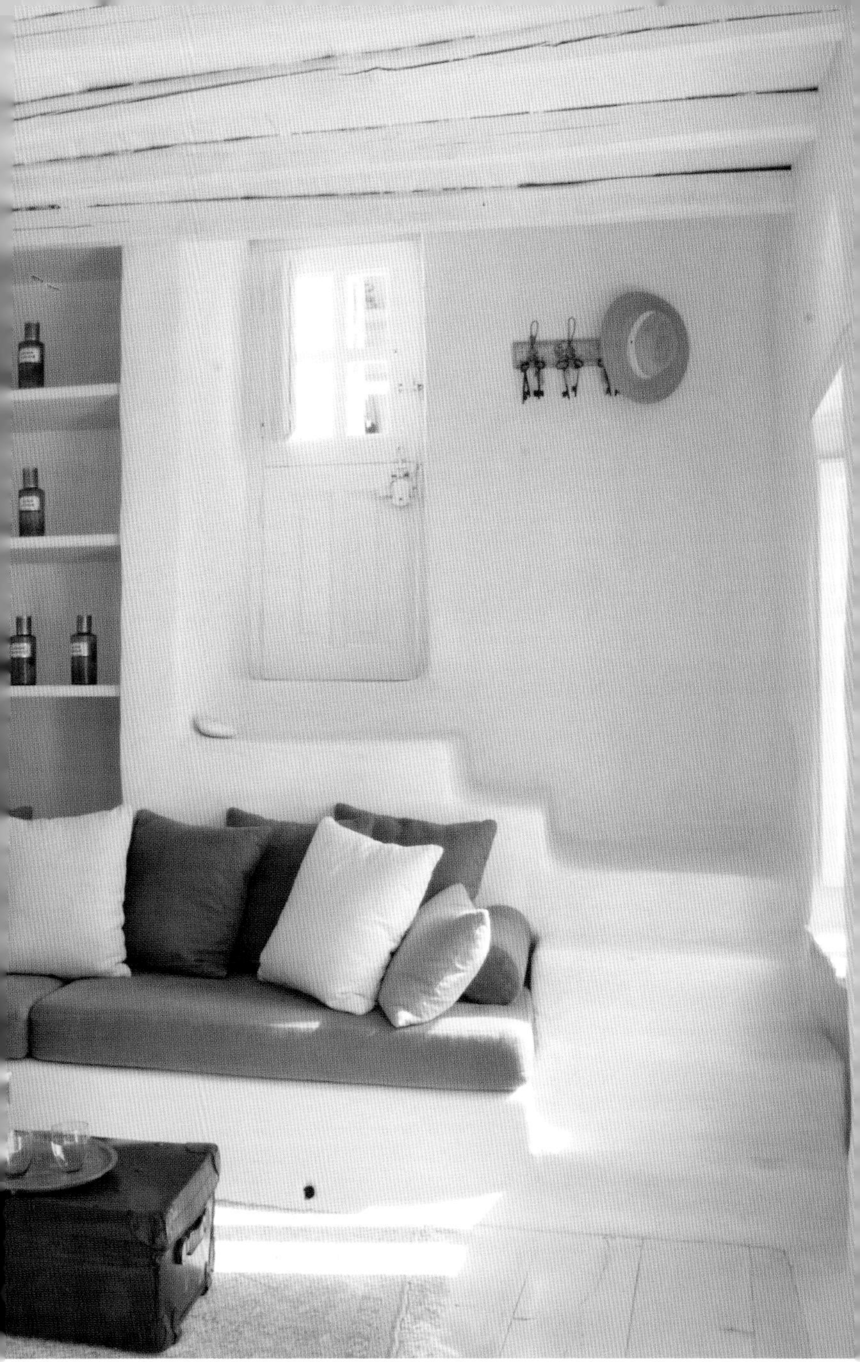

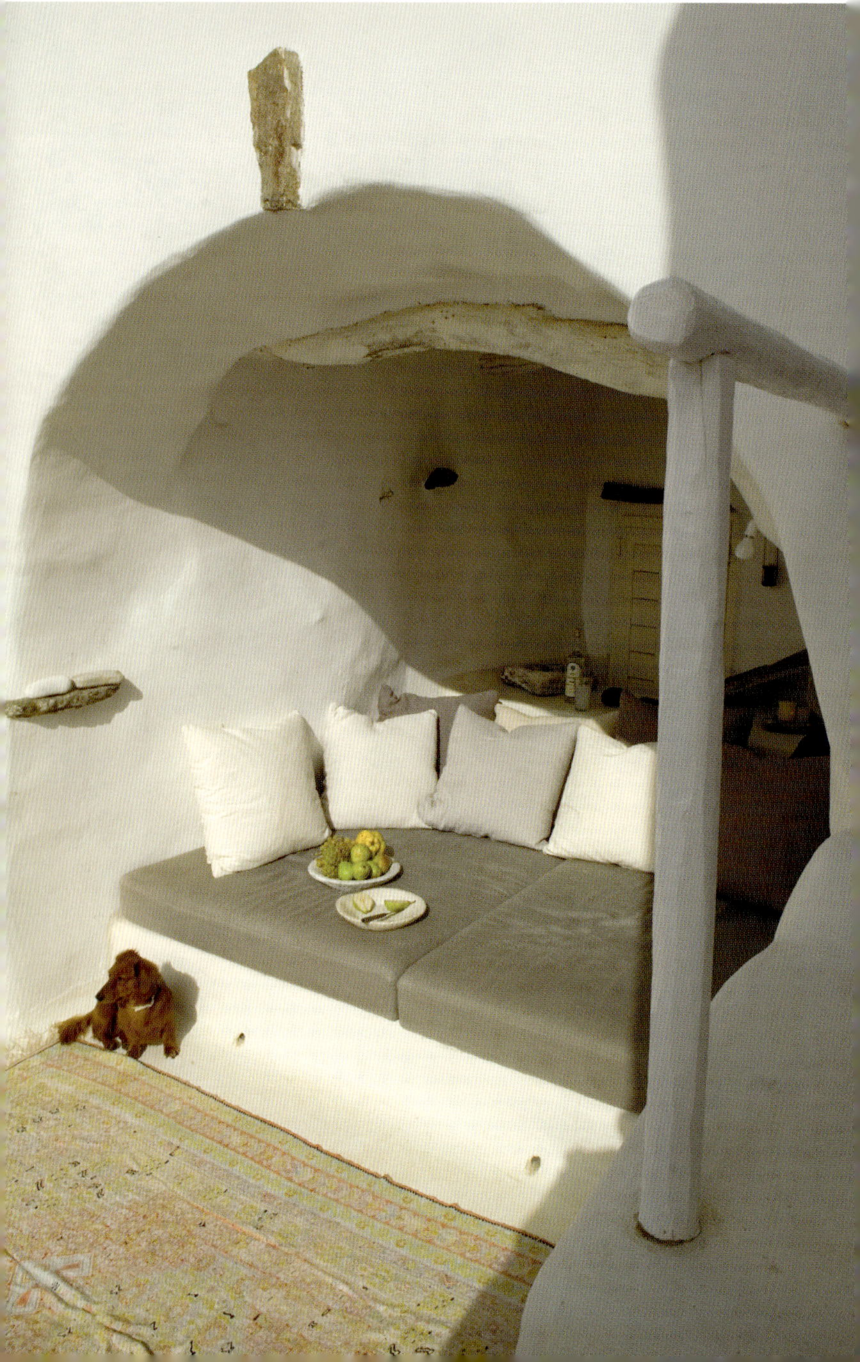

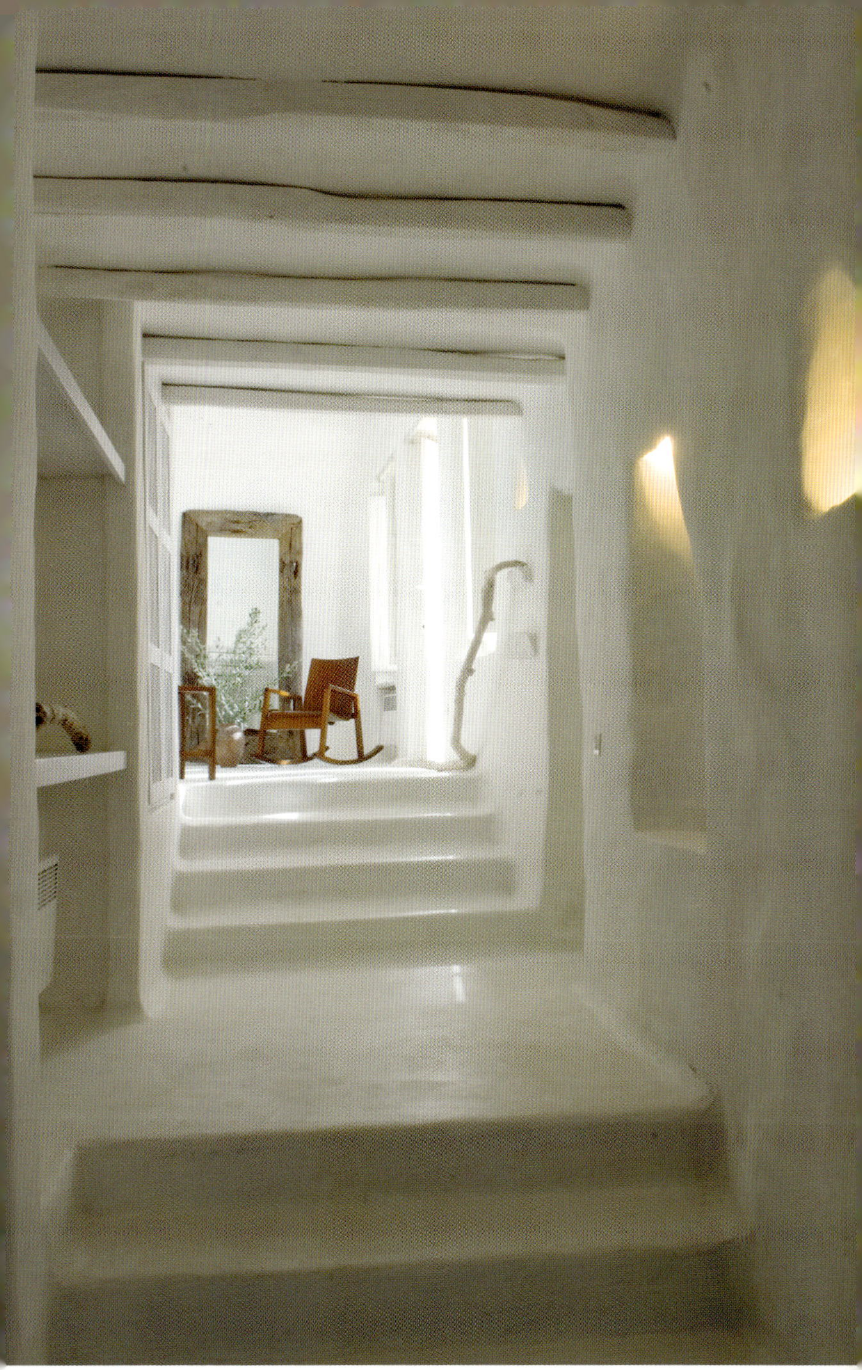

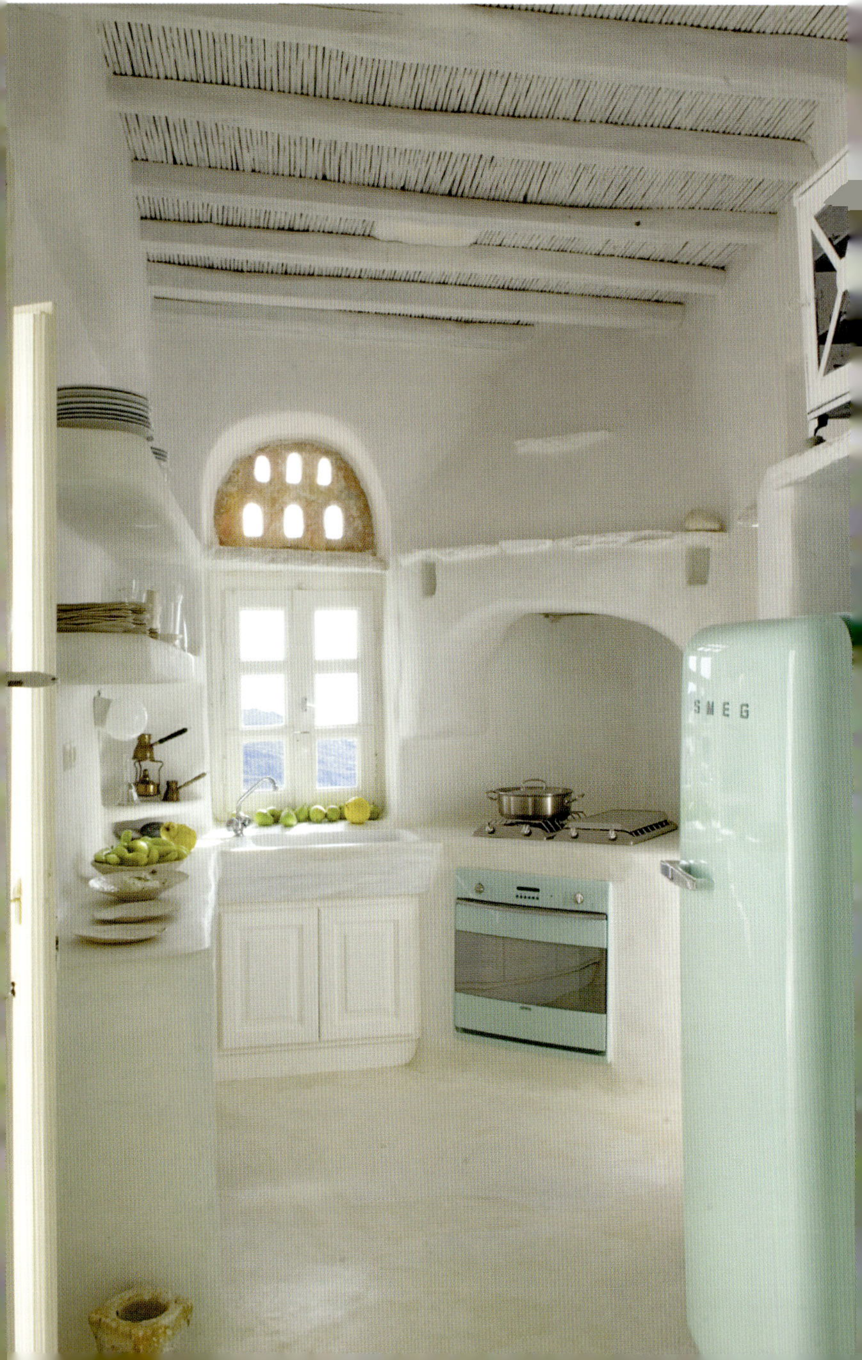
SMEG

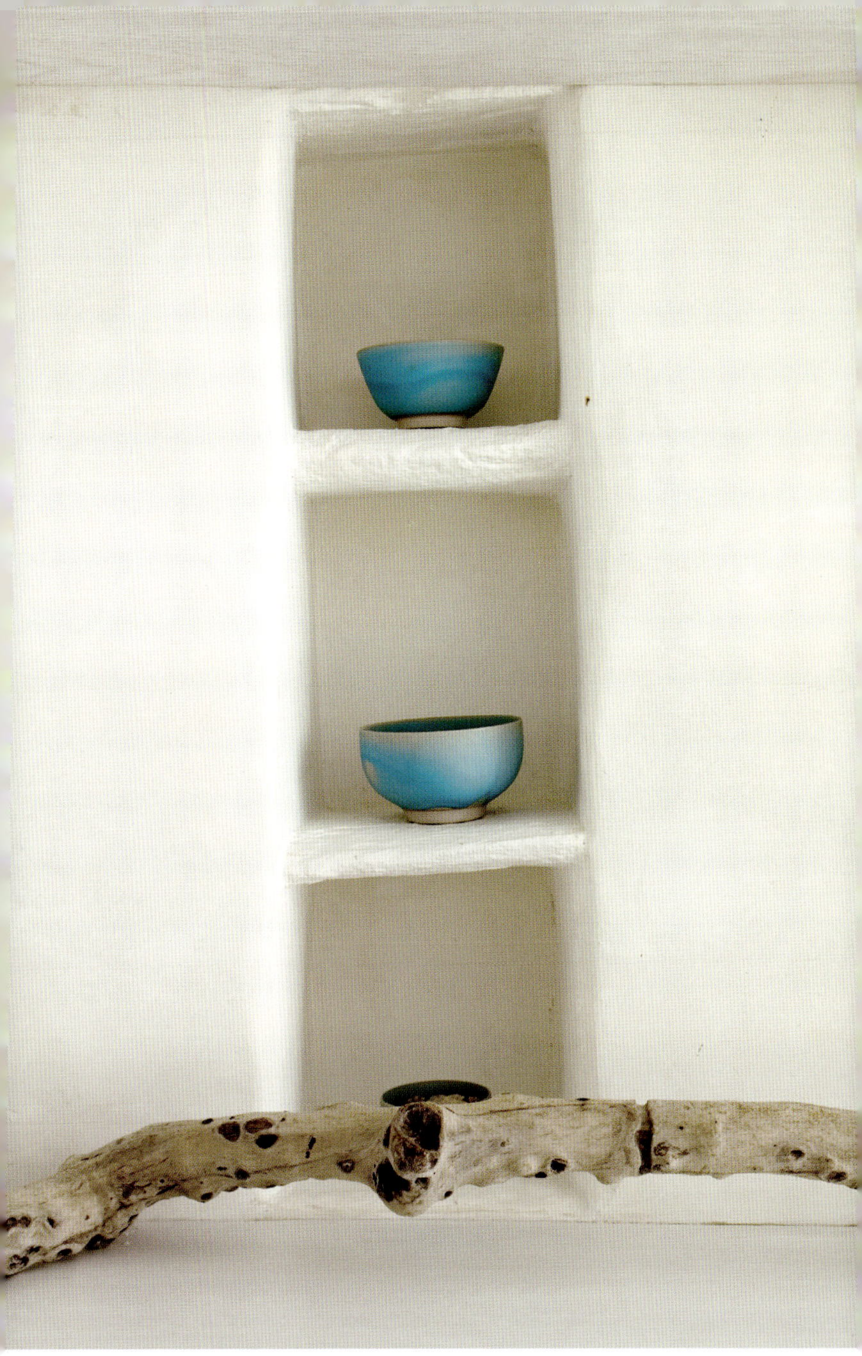

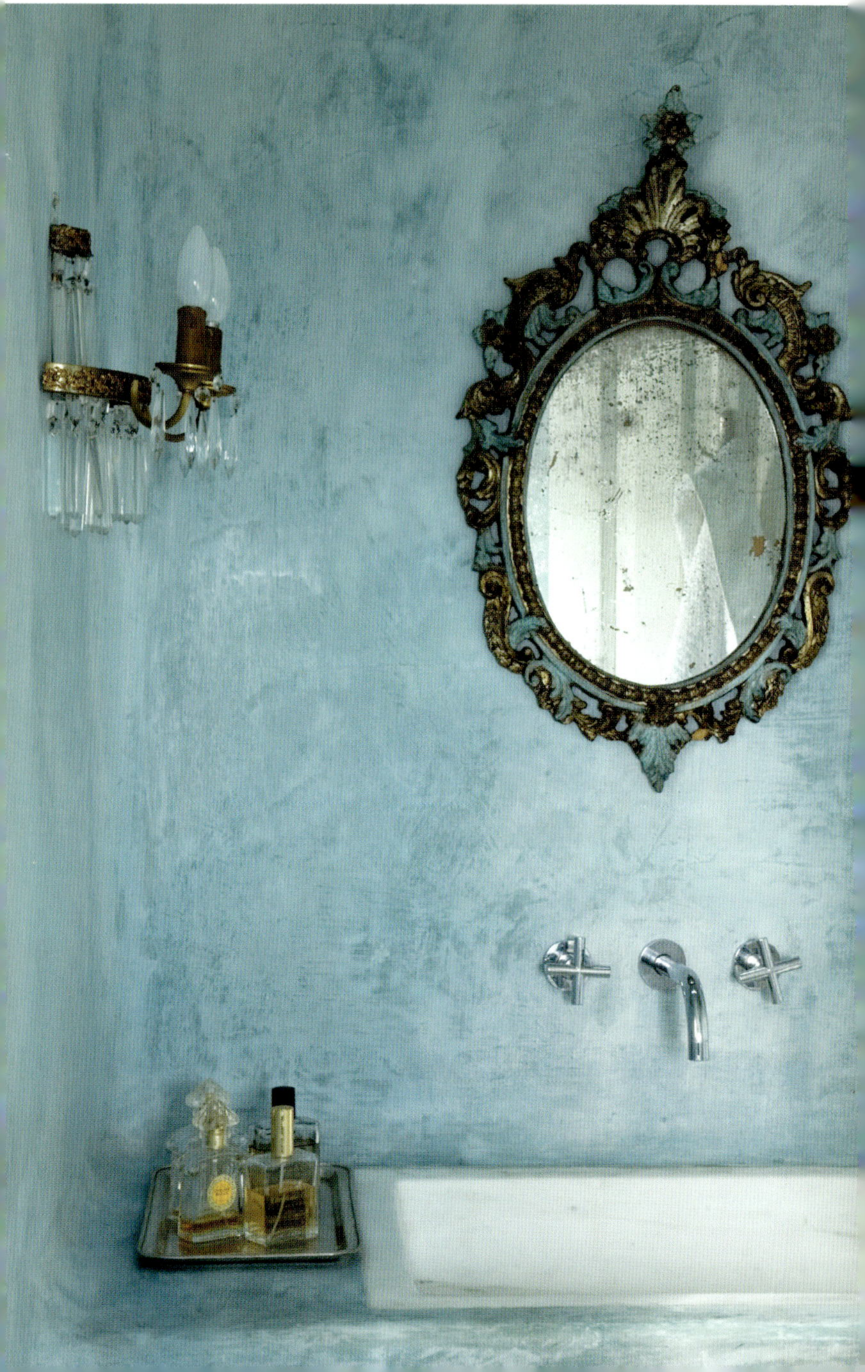

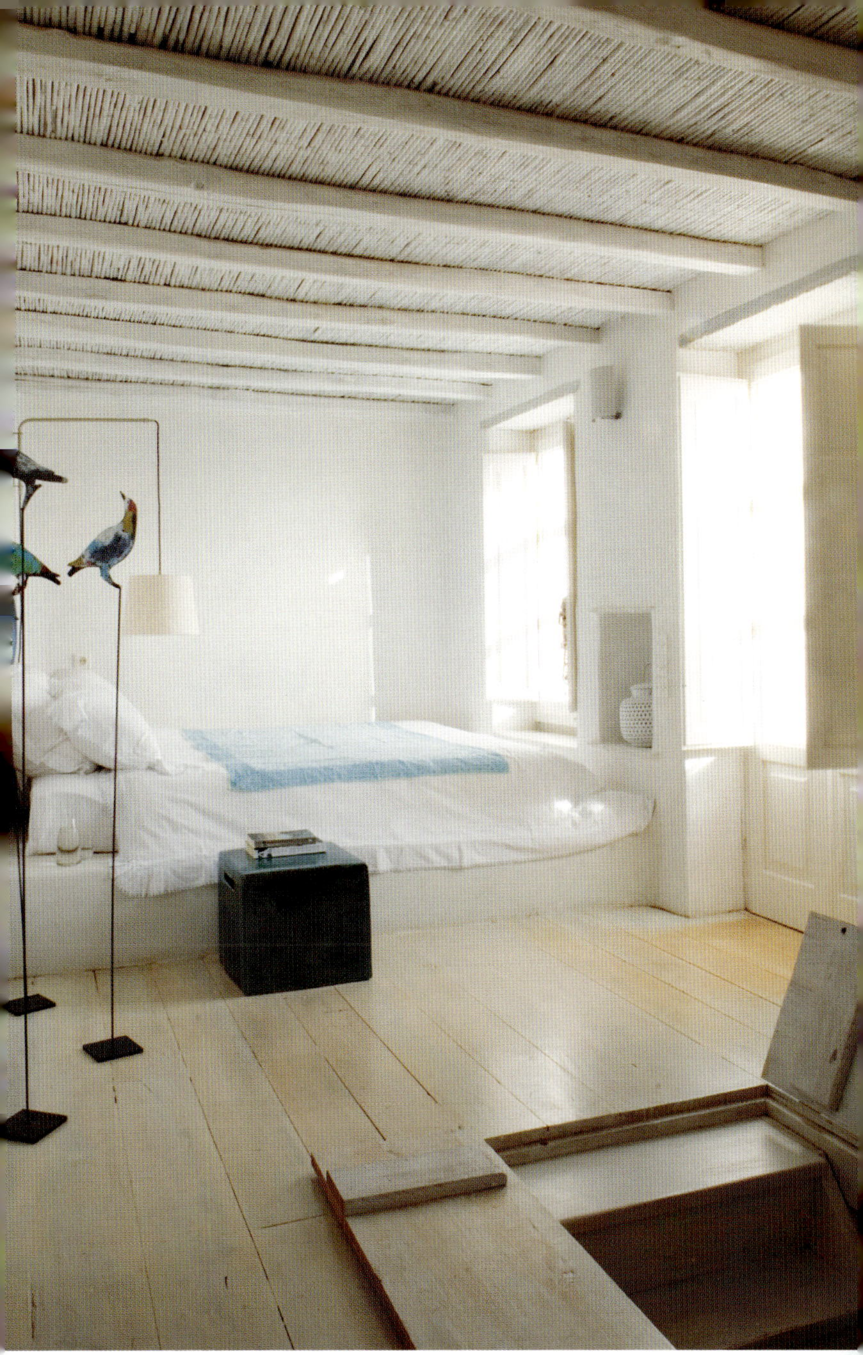

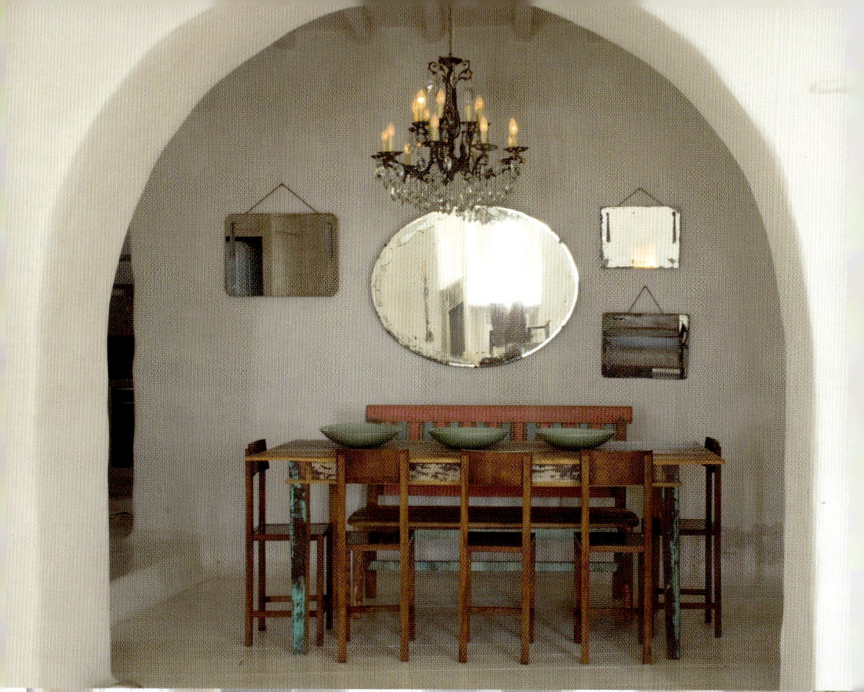

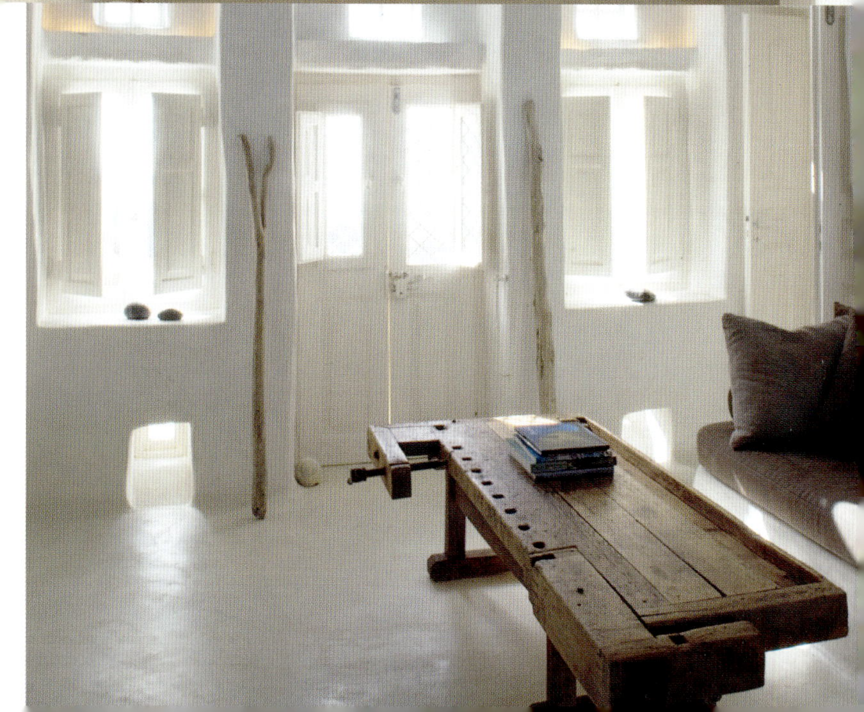

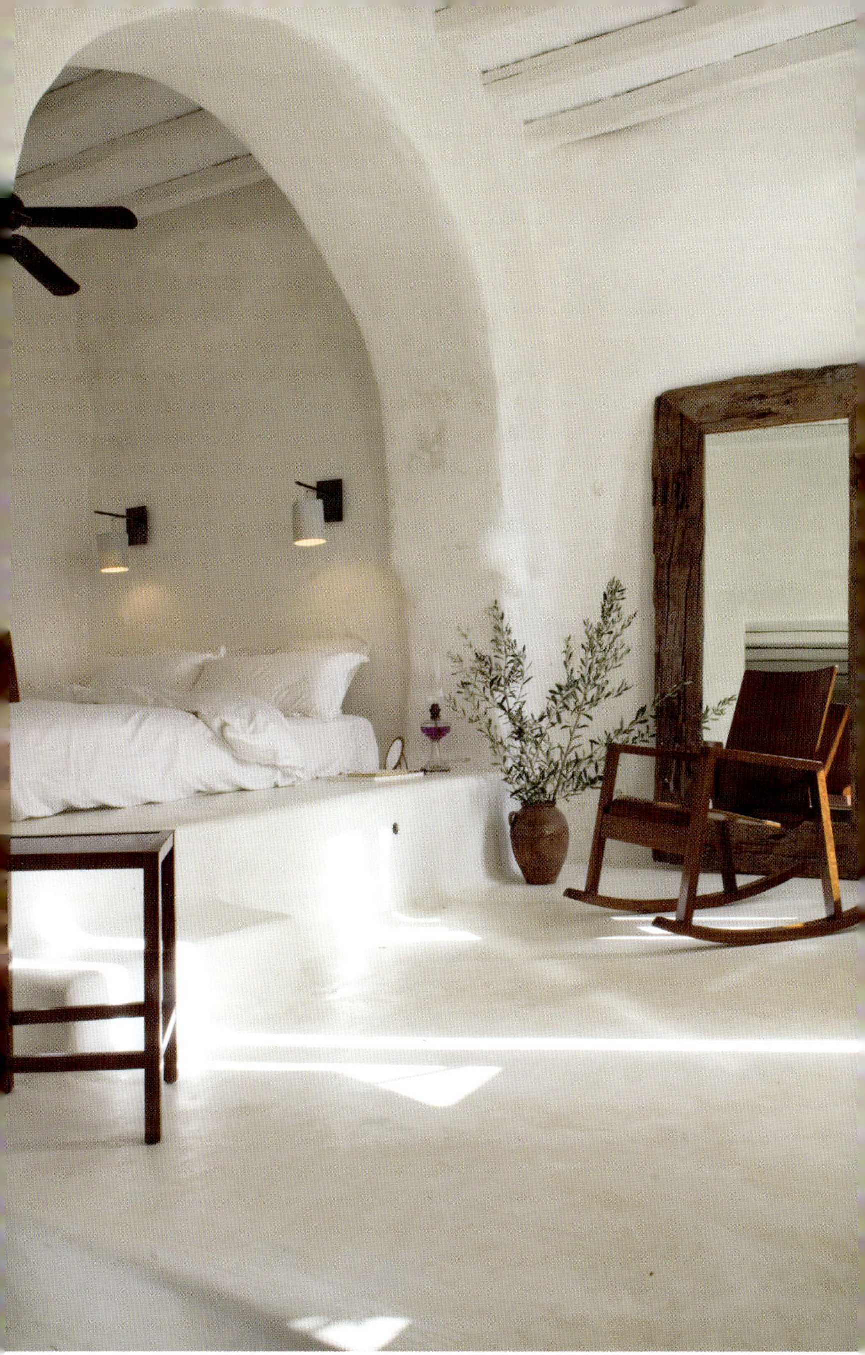

Block Townhouse | Toronto | Cecconi Simone

Simplicity belying its essential complexity

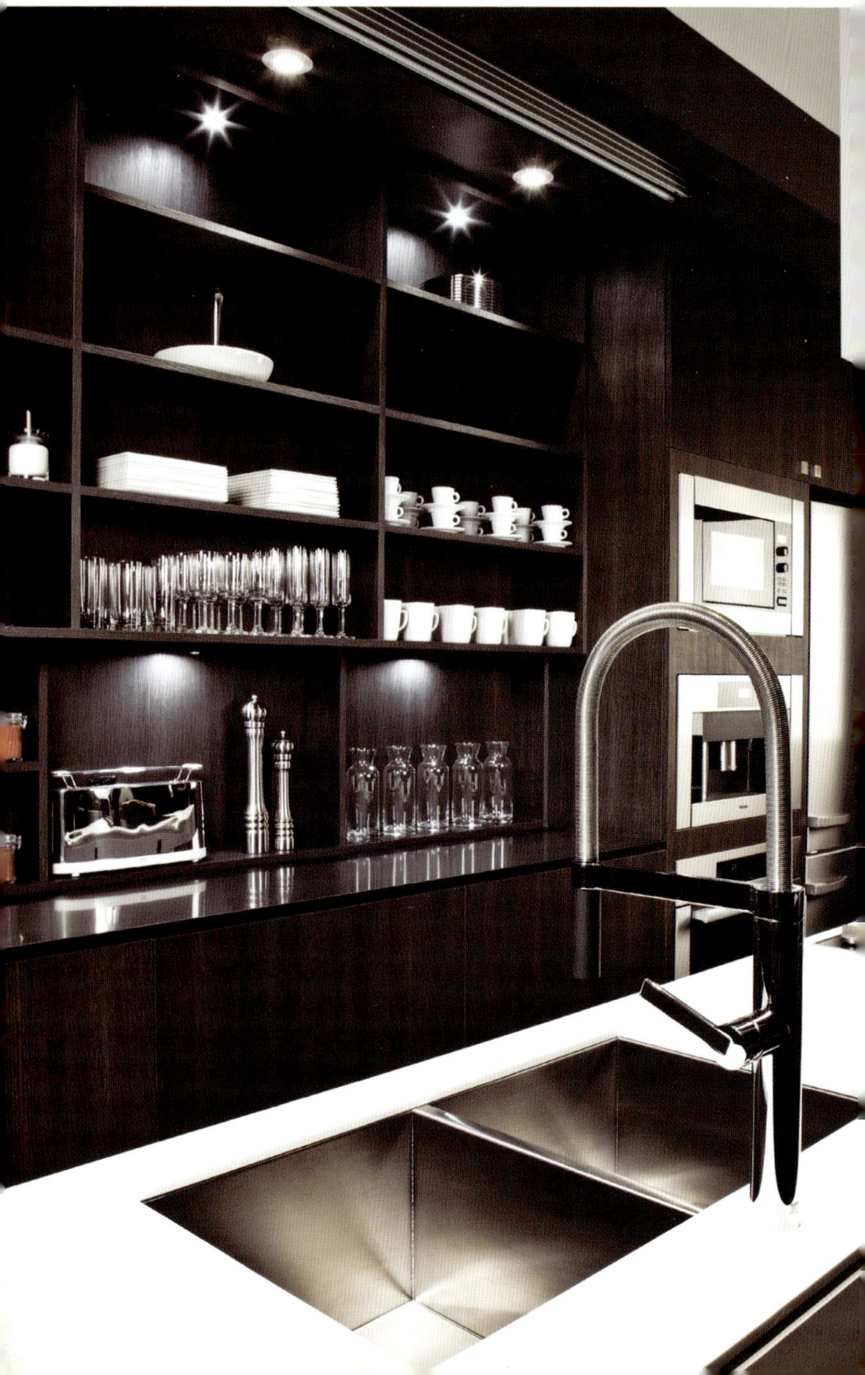

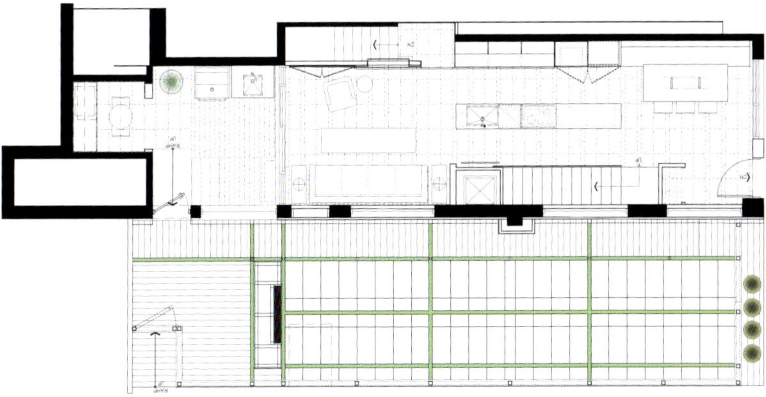

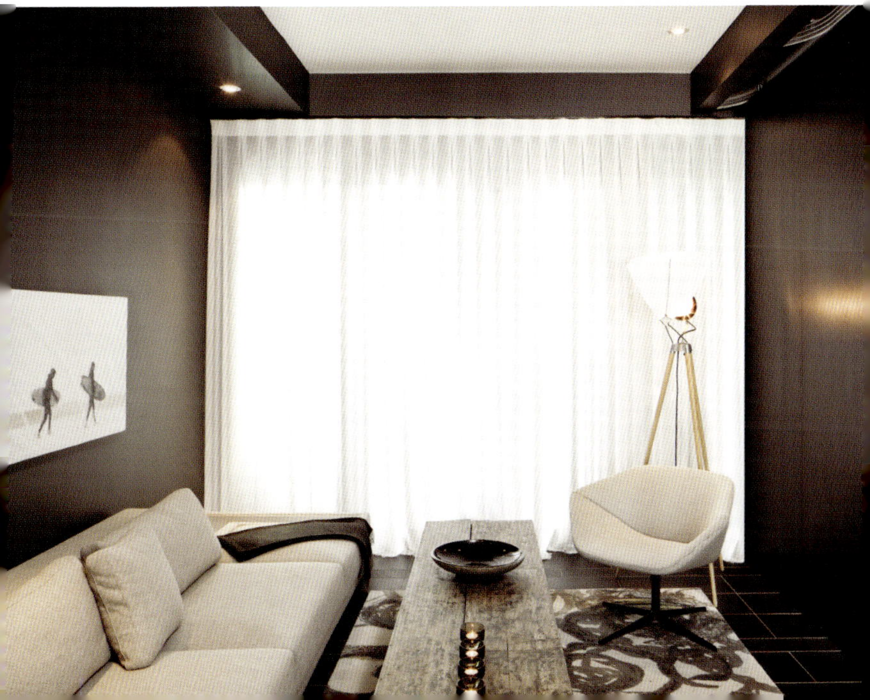

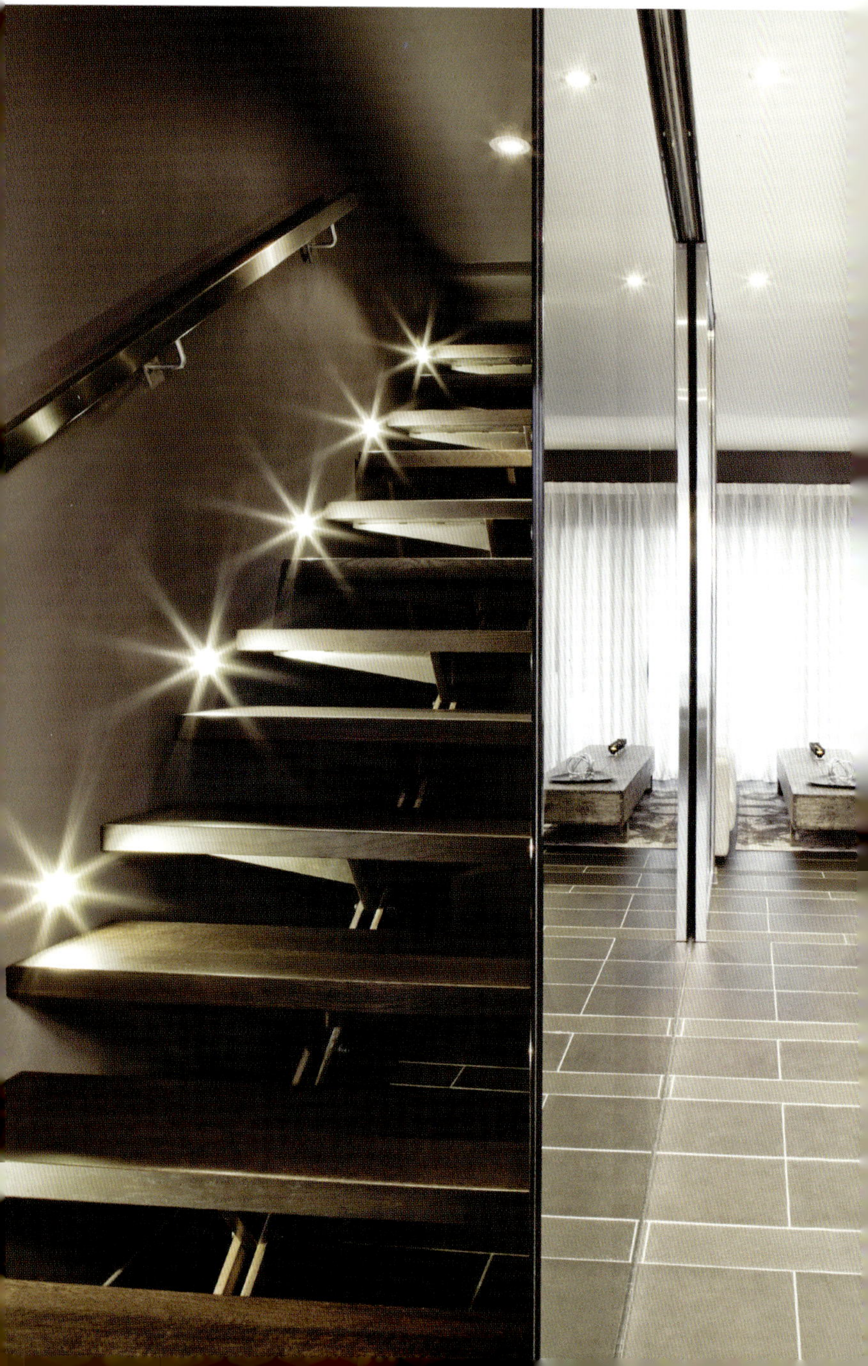

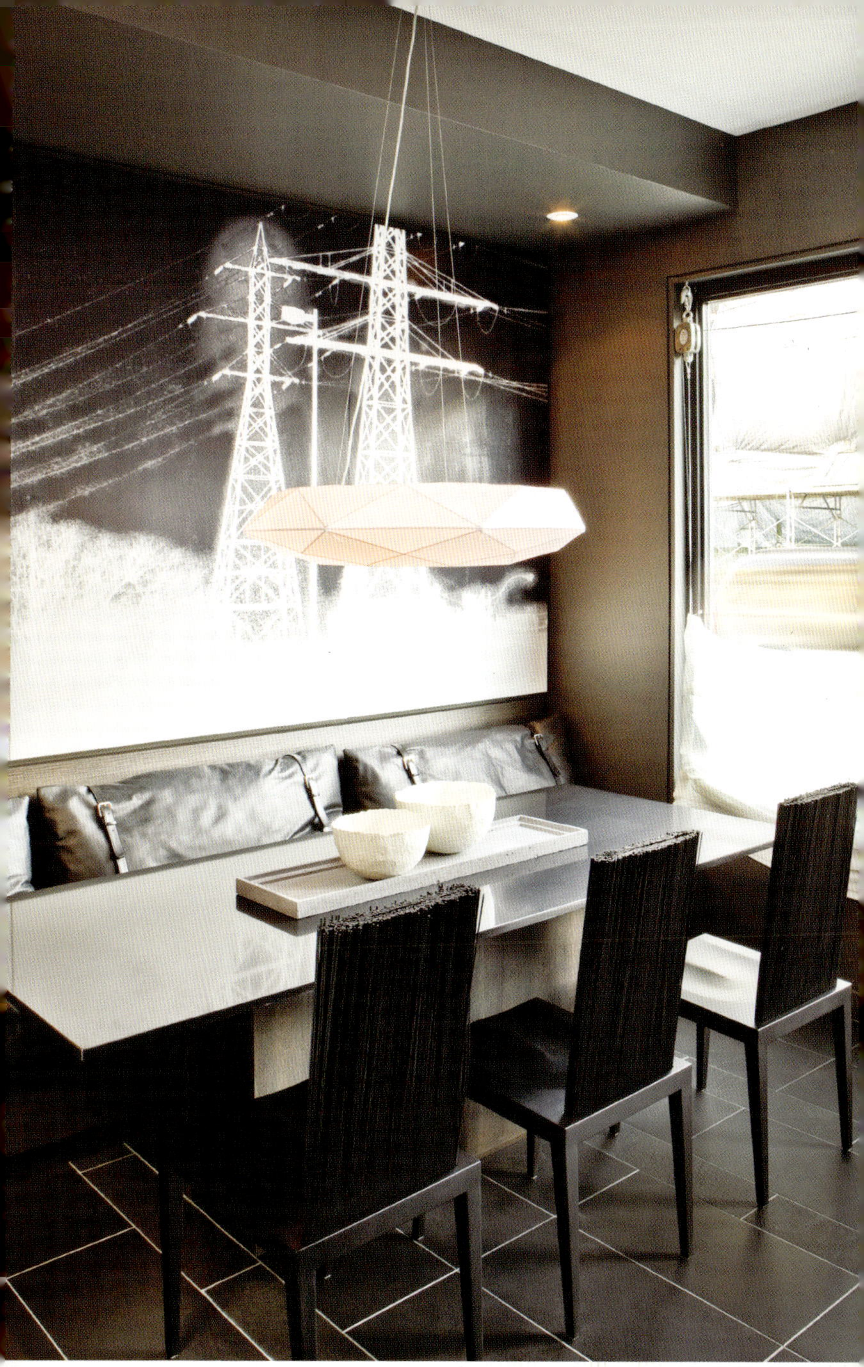

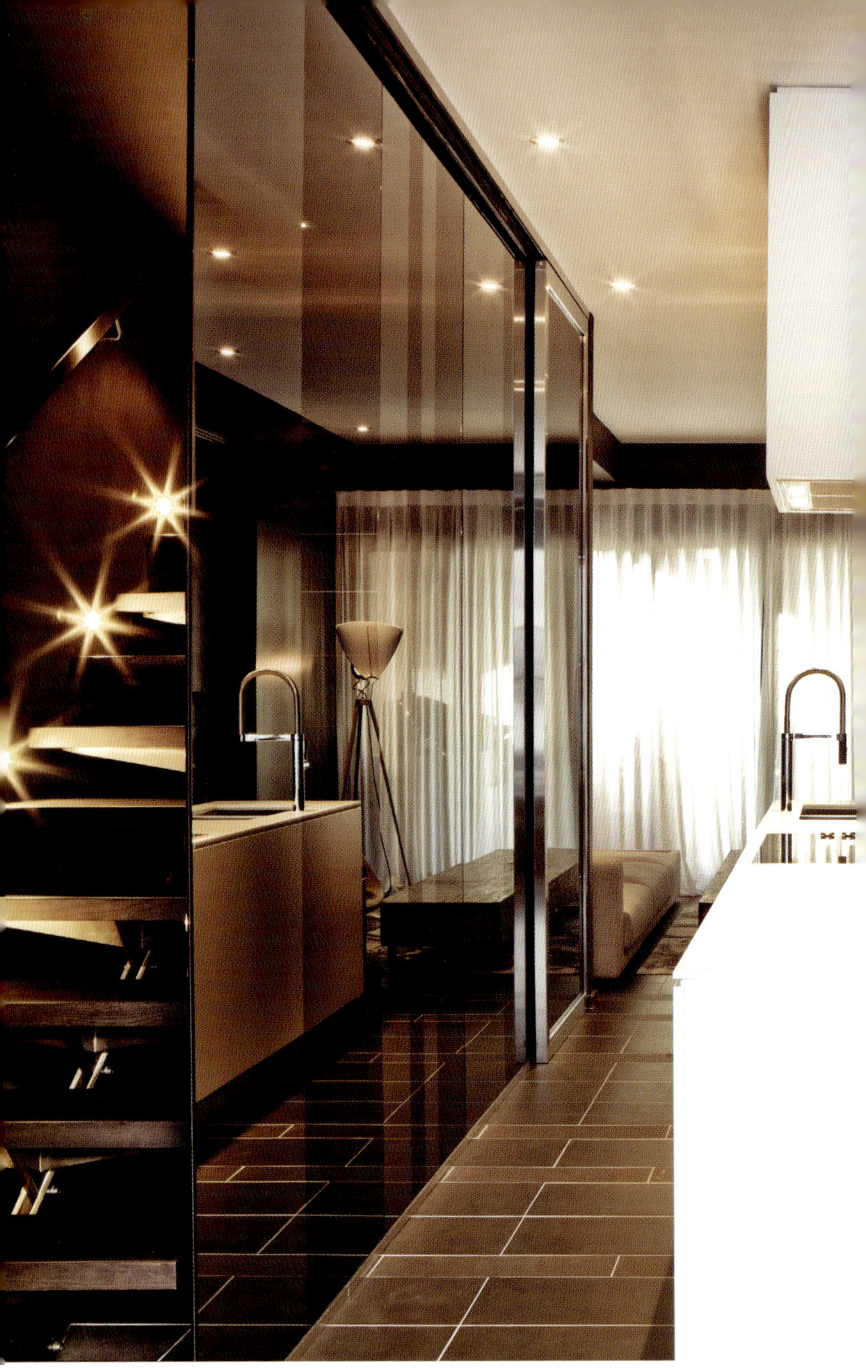

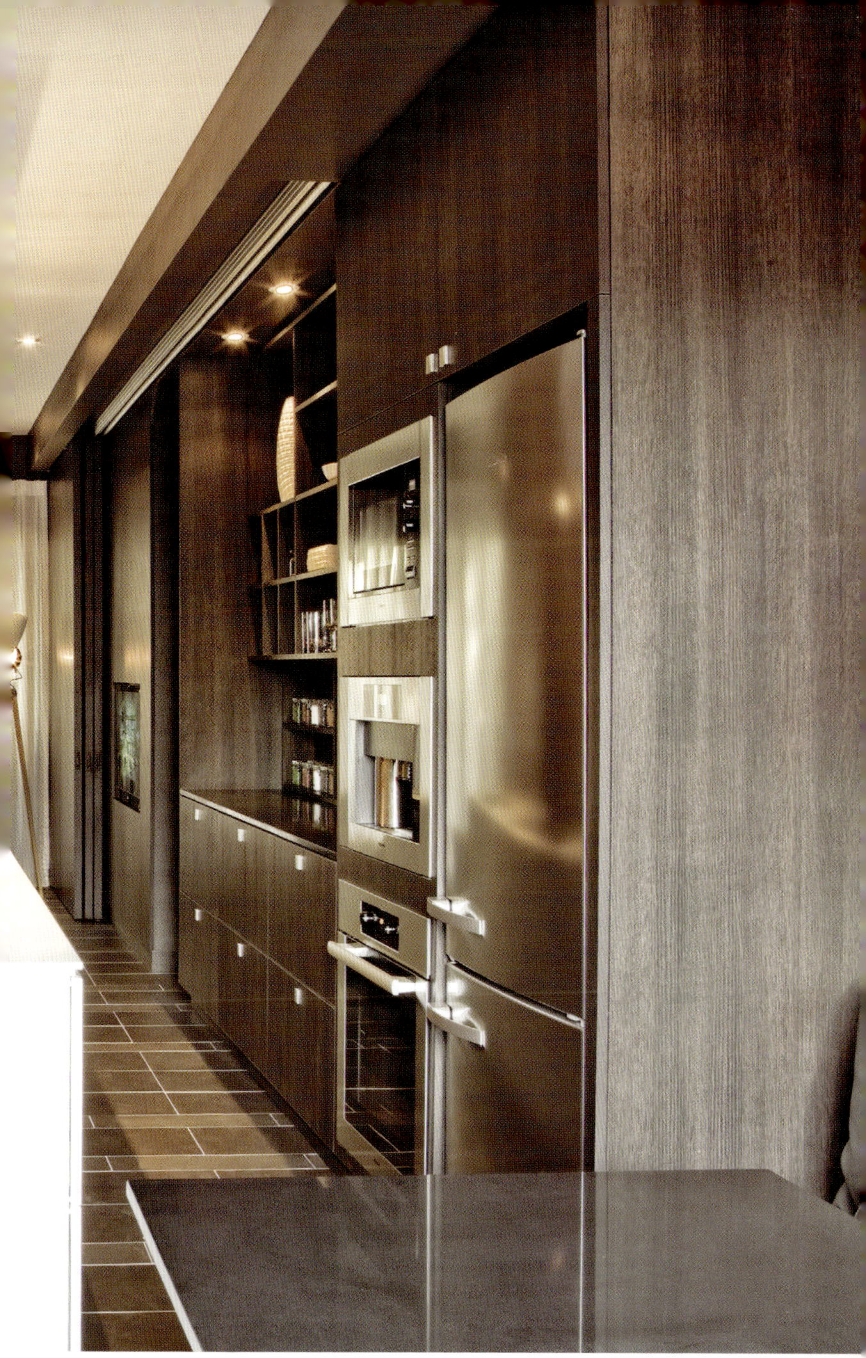

274 | **Casa Rizza** | Vacallo, Ticino | Studio Inches architettura

An existing volume **from the** 19th century, excavated **to create a liberated**, tower-like living **space**

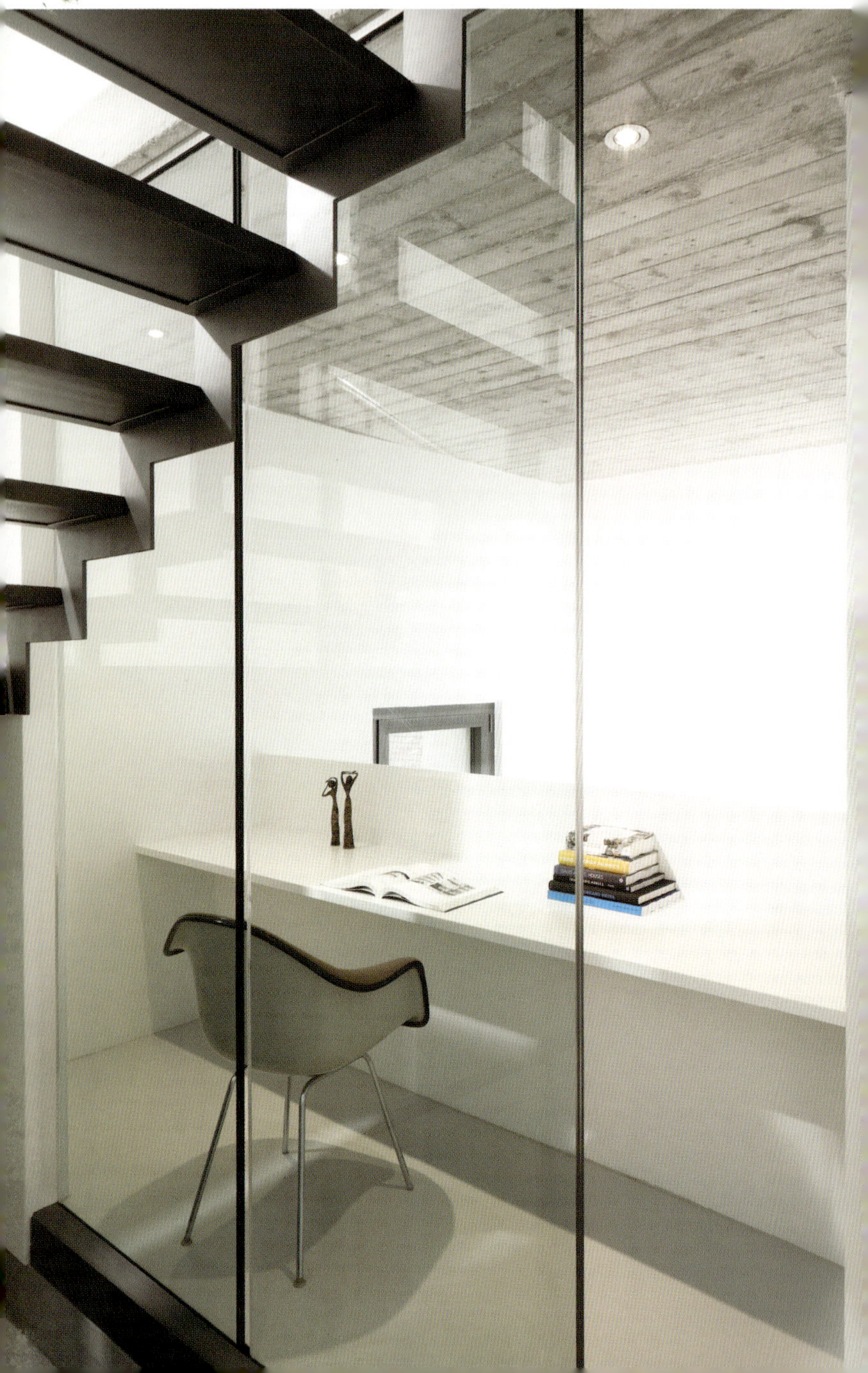

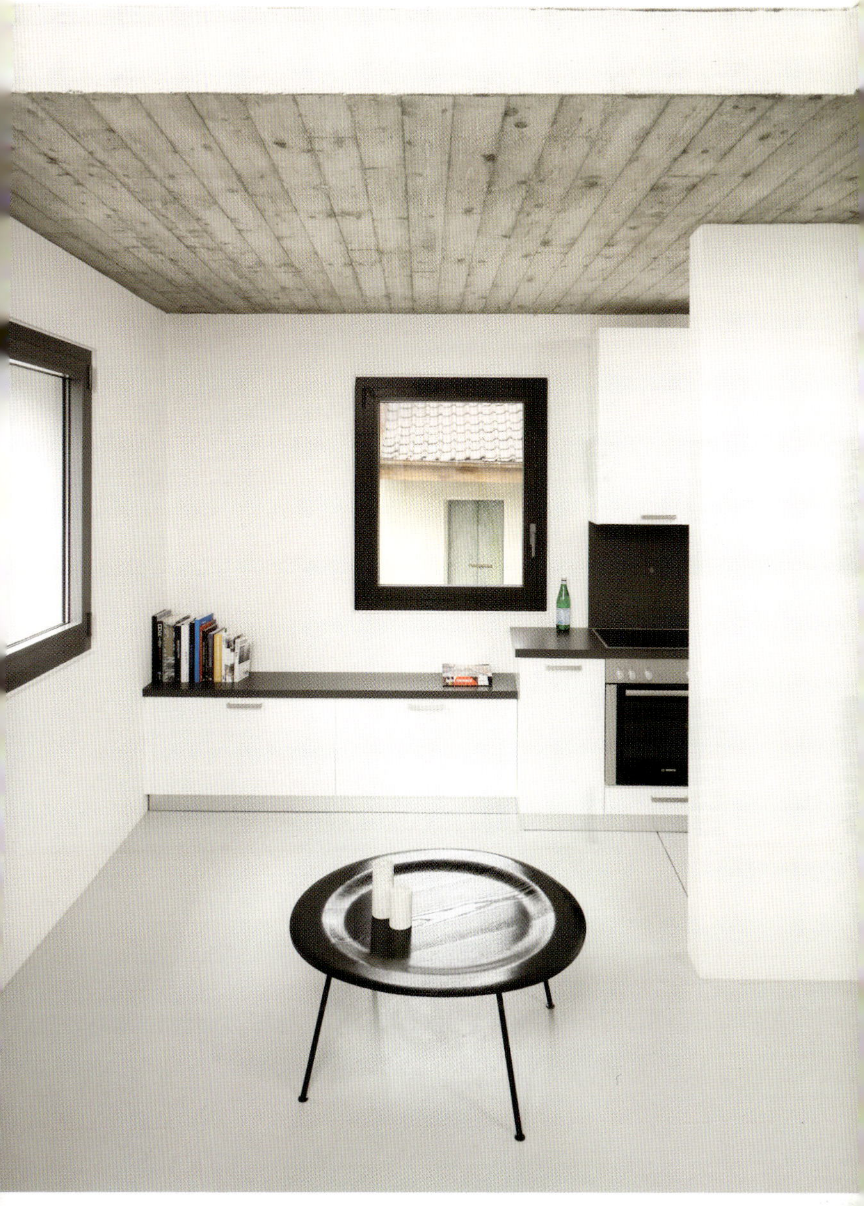

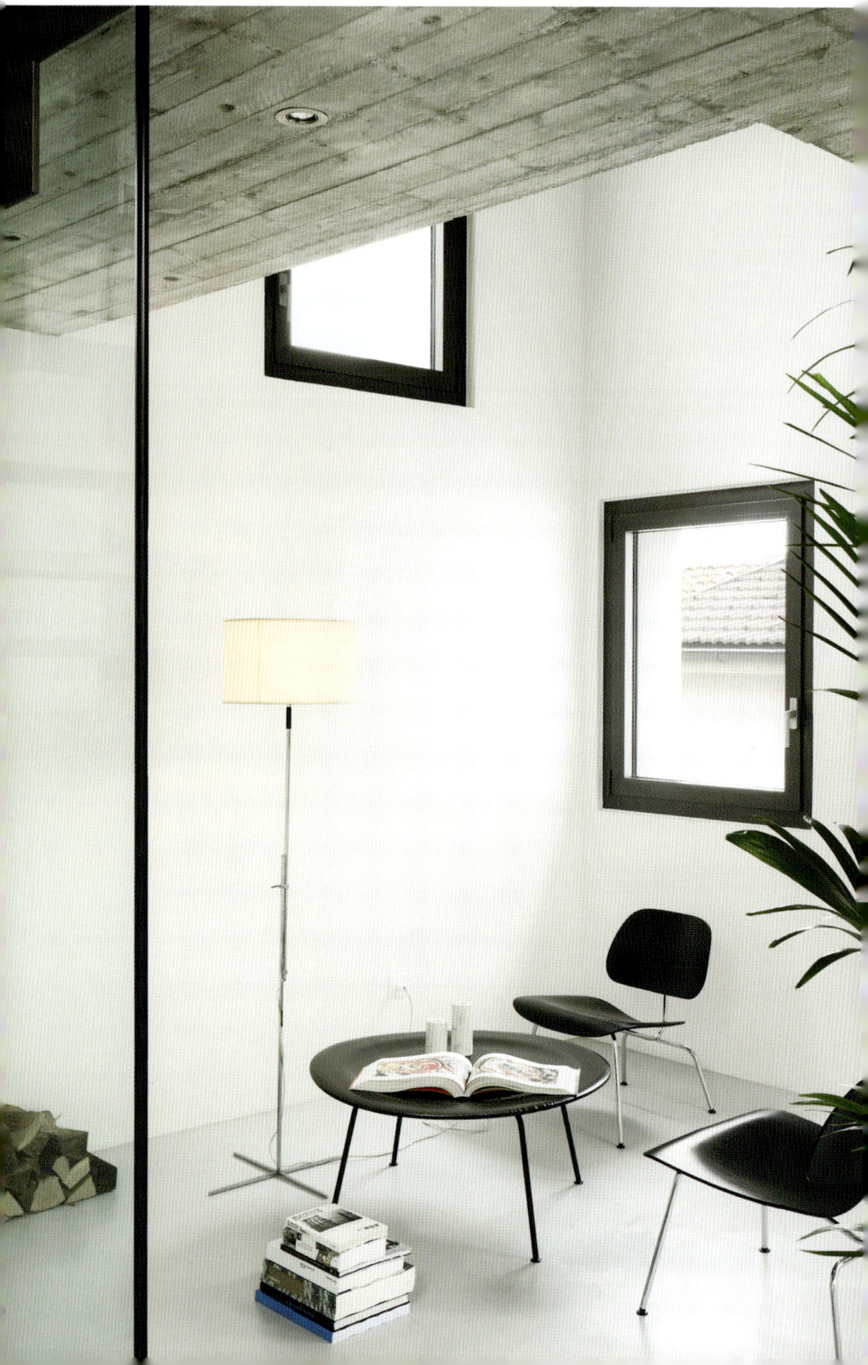

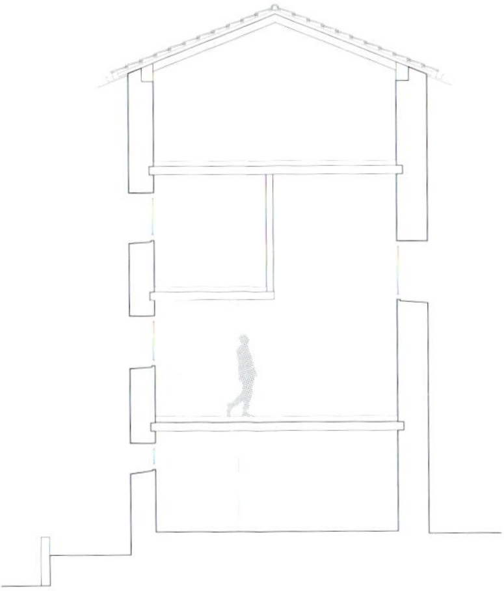

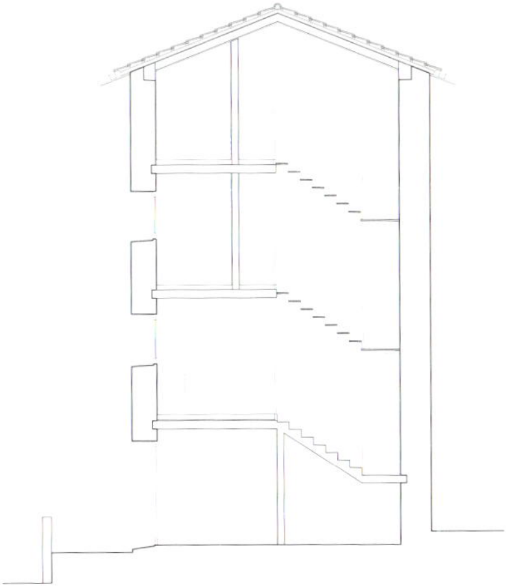

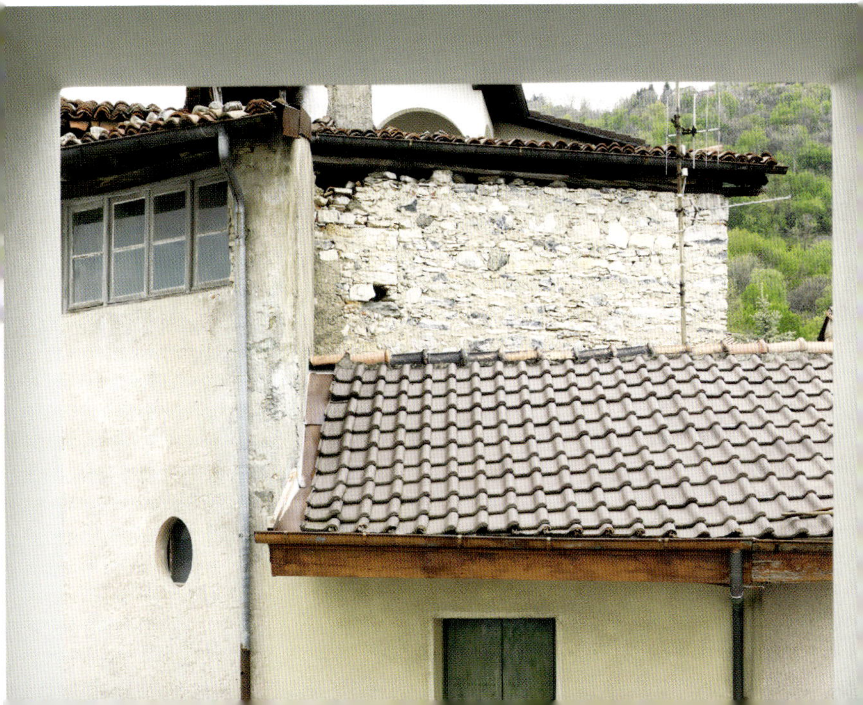

280 | **Vedbæk House** | Vedbæk | Norm. Architects

A former fishermen's cottage carved out to create a cozy, light-filled home

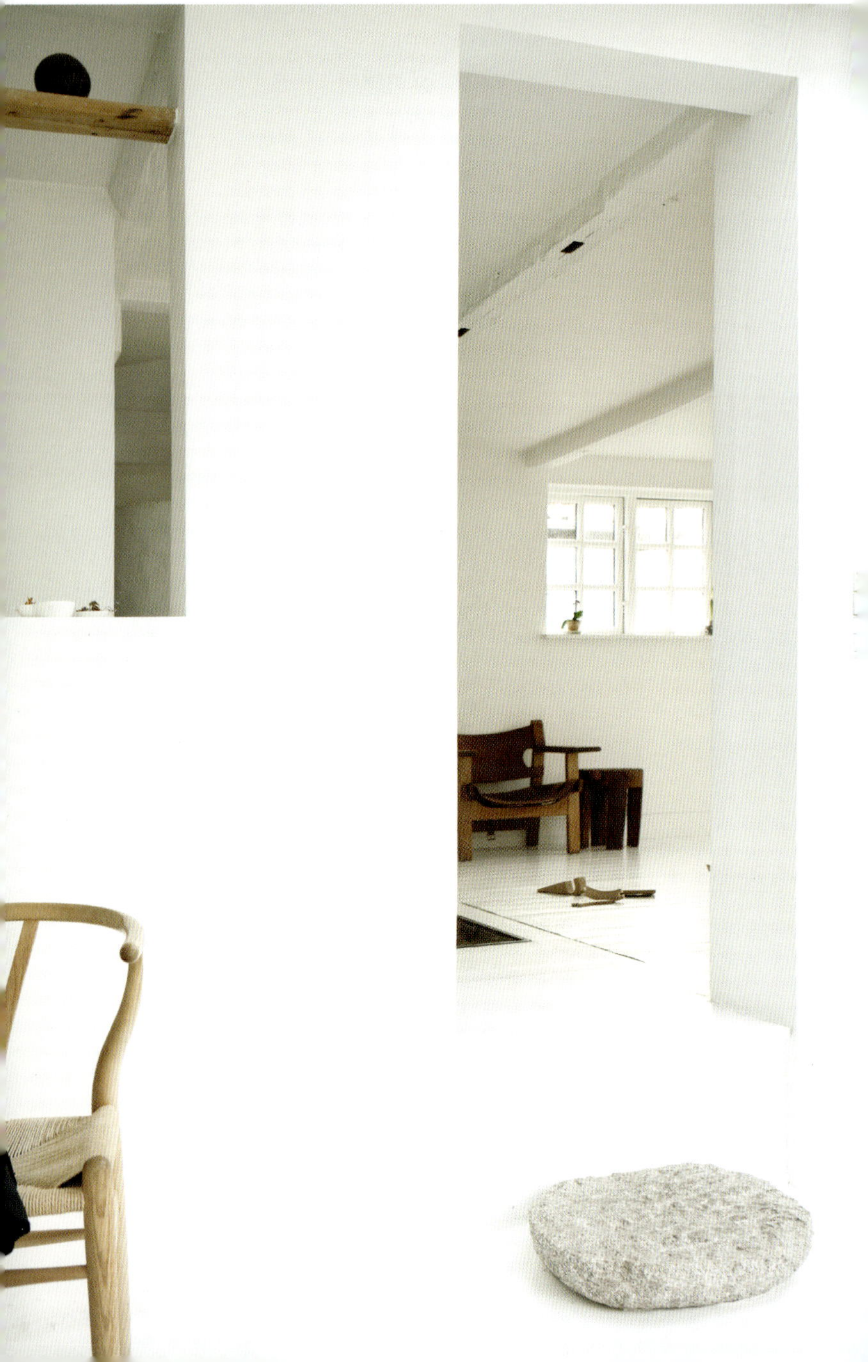

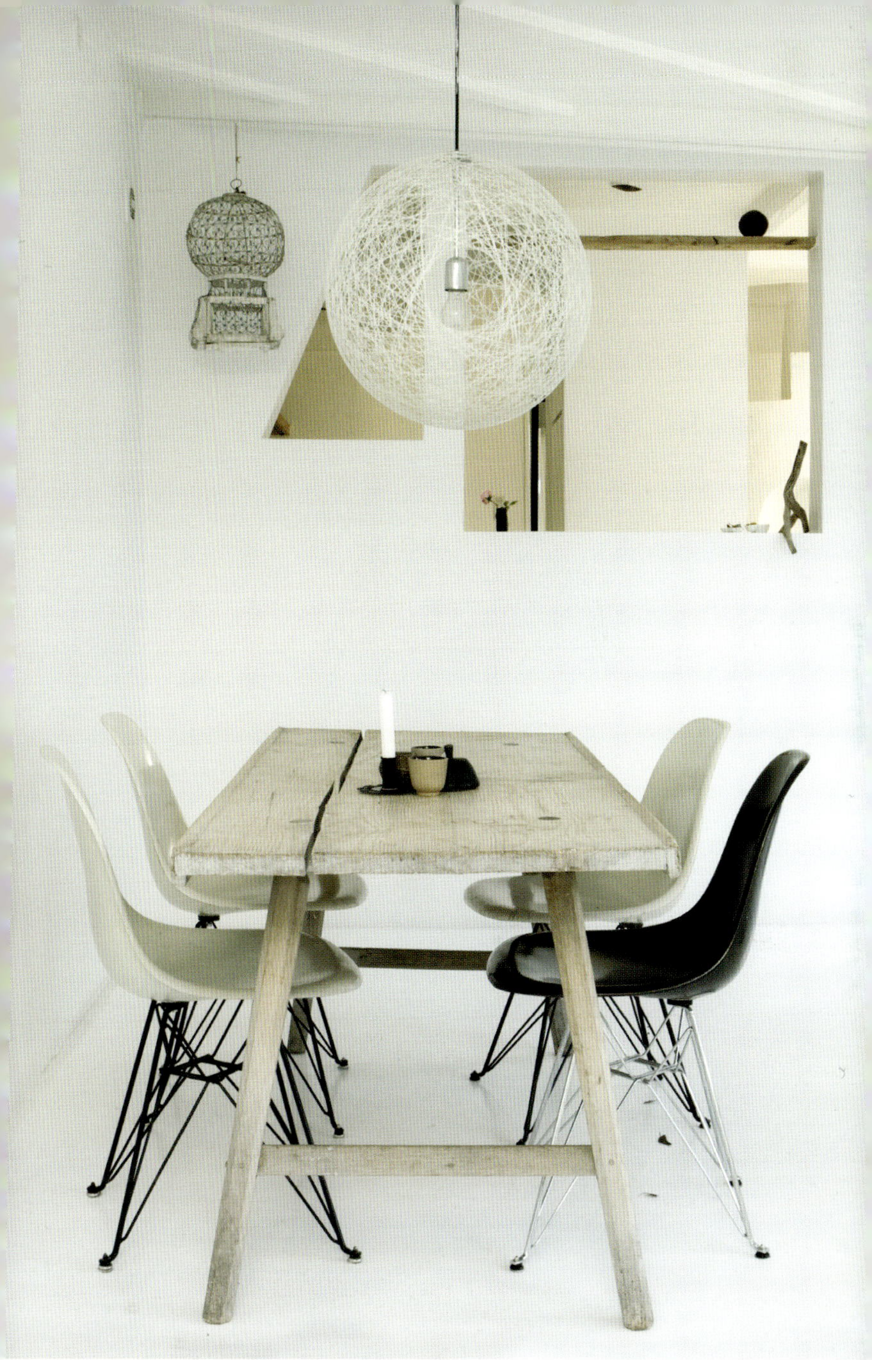

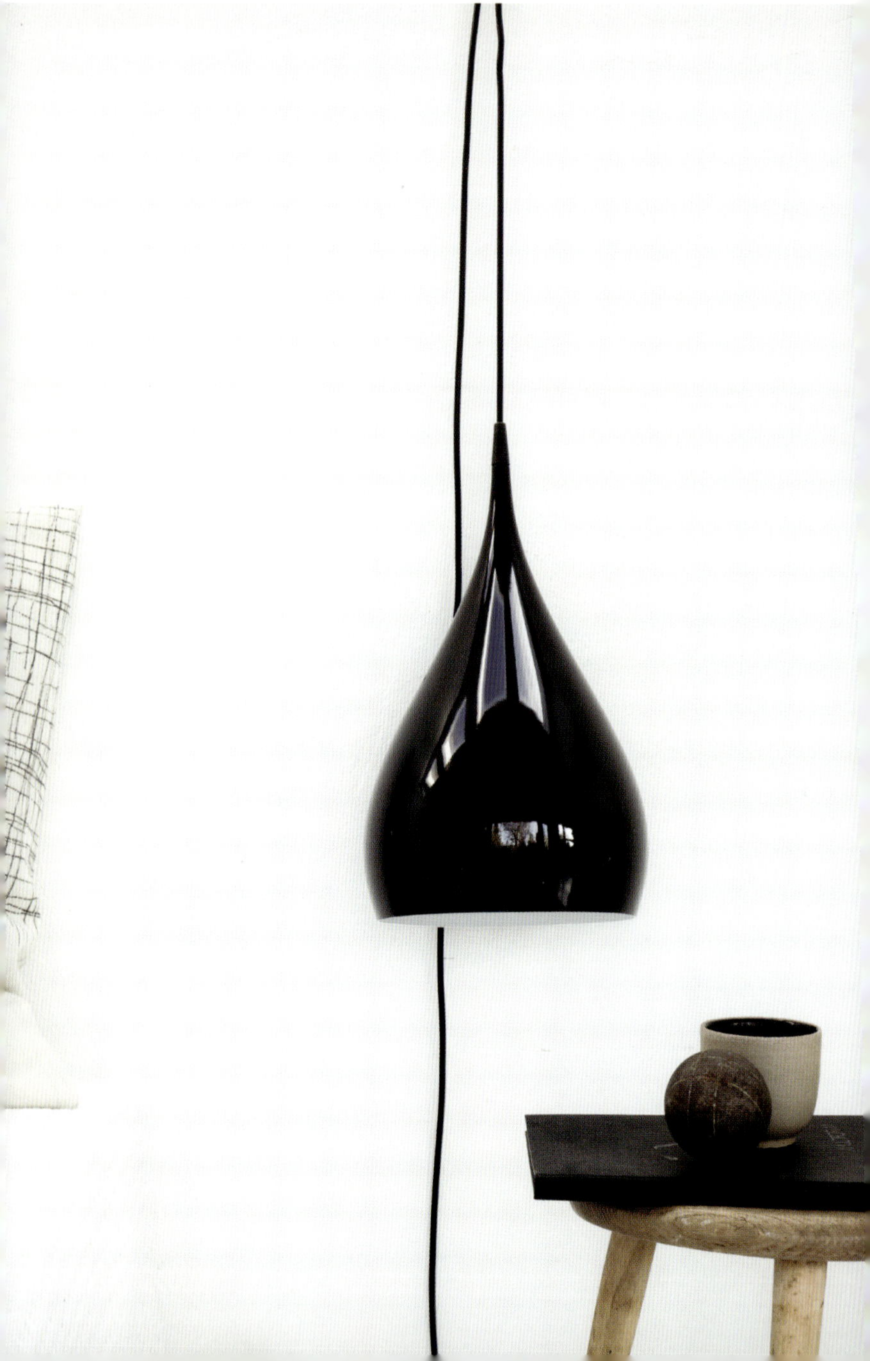

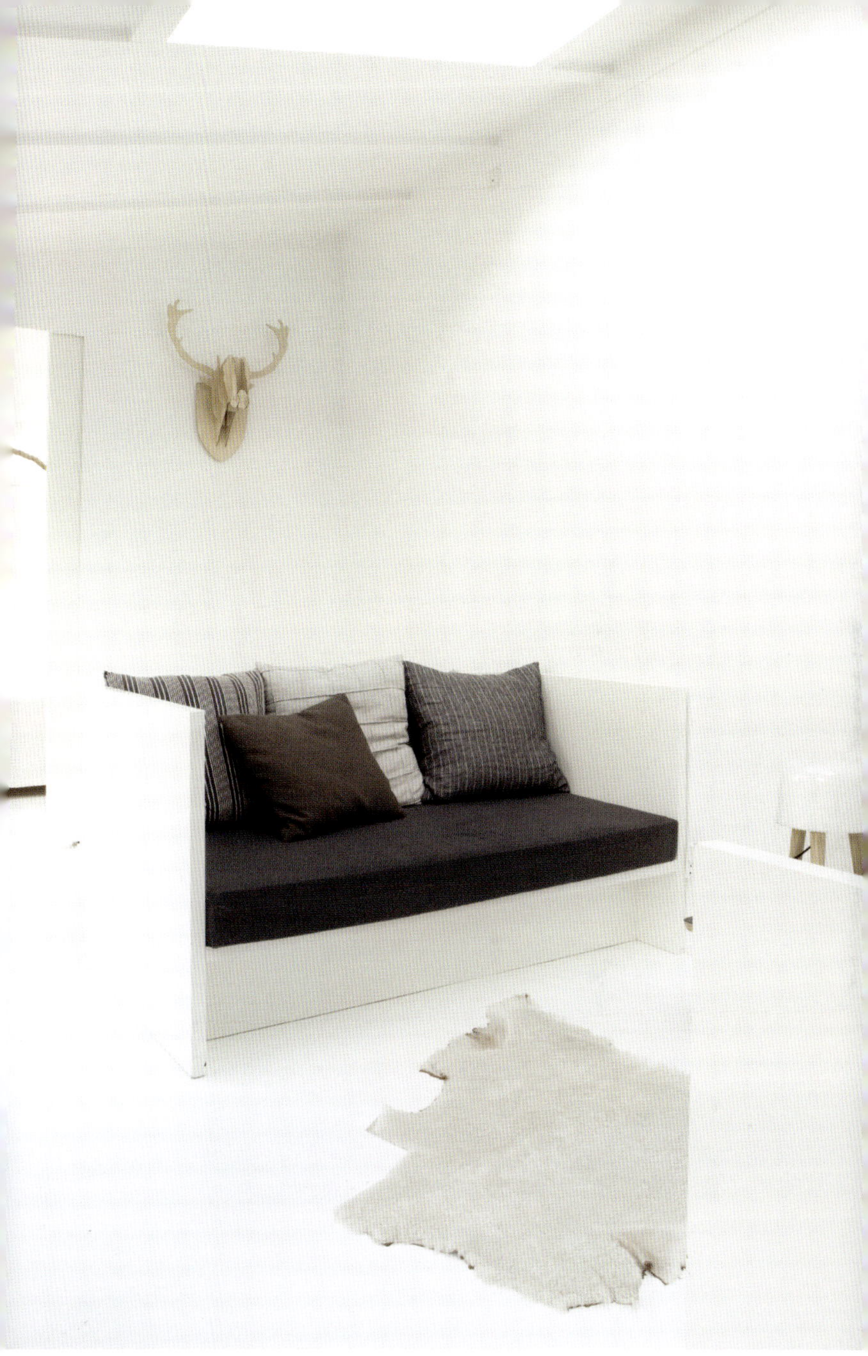

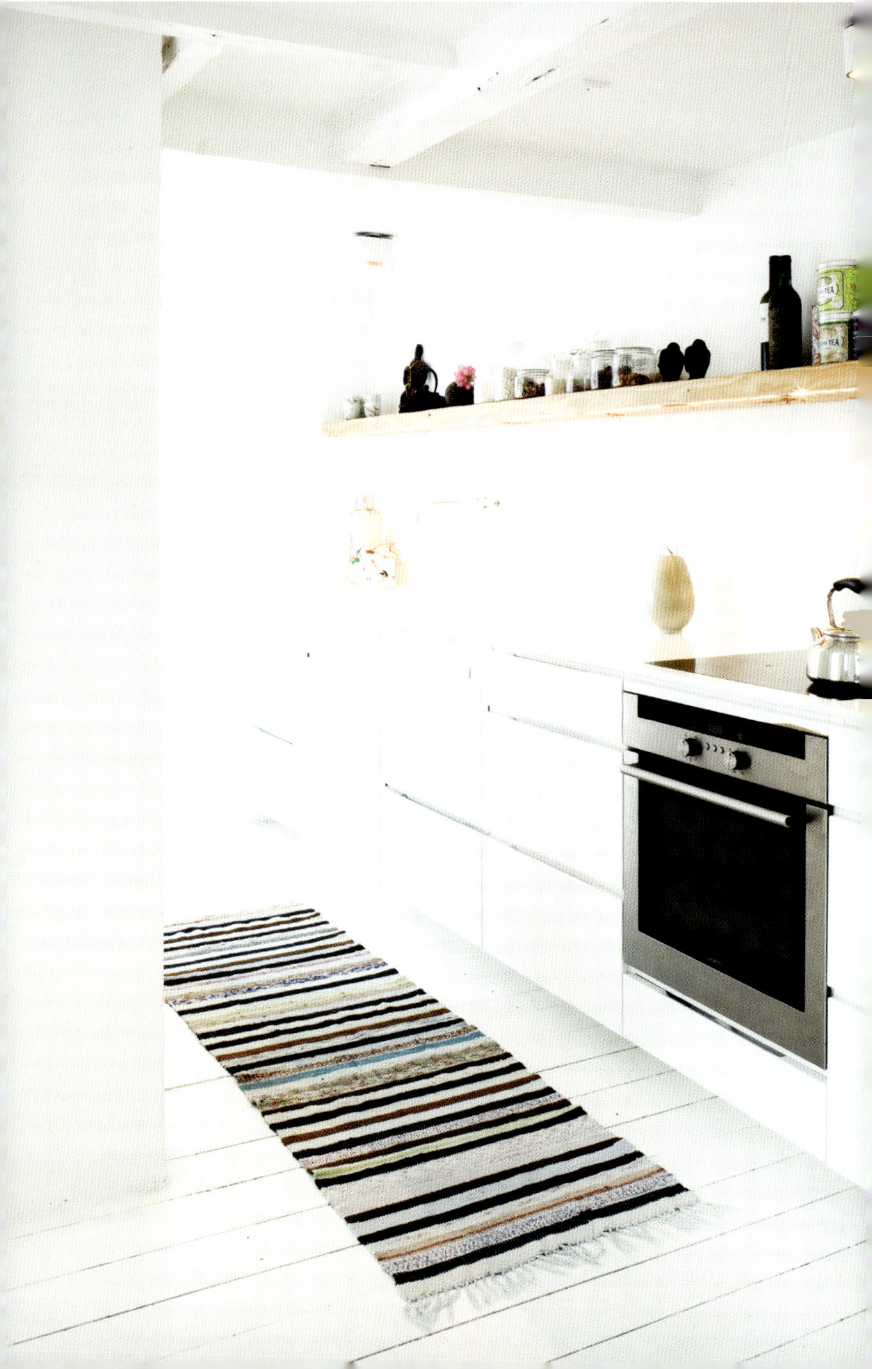

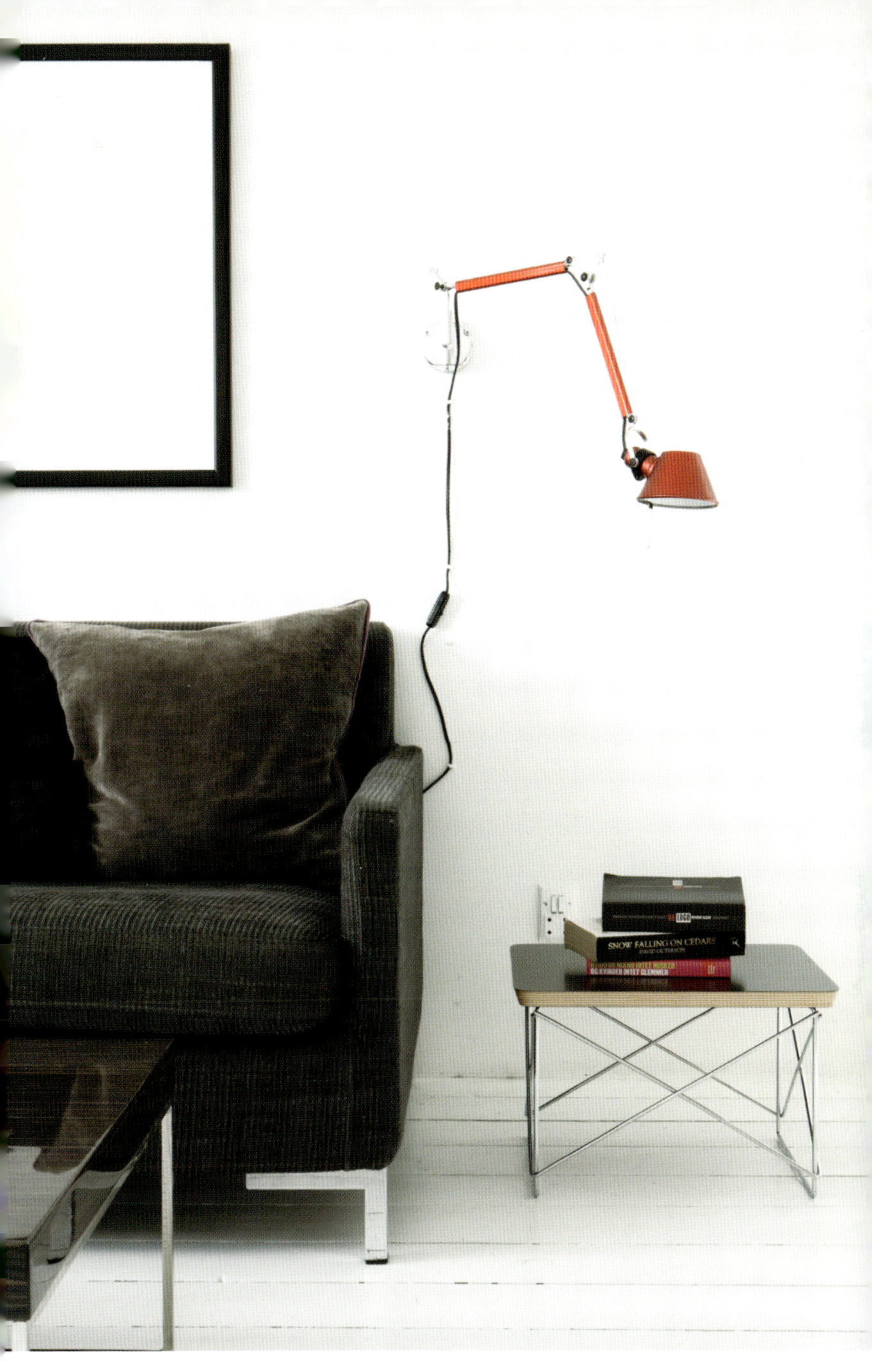

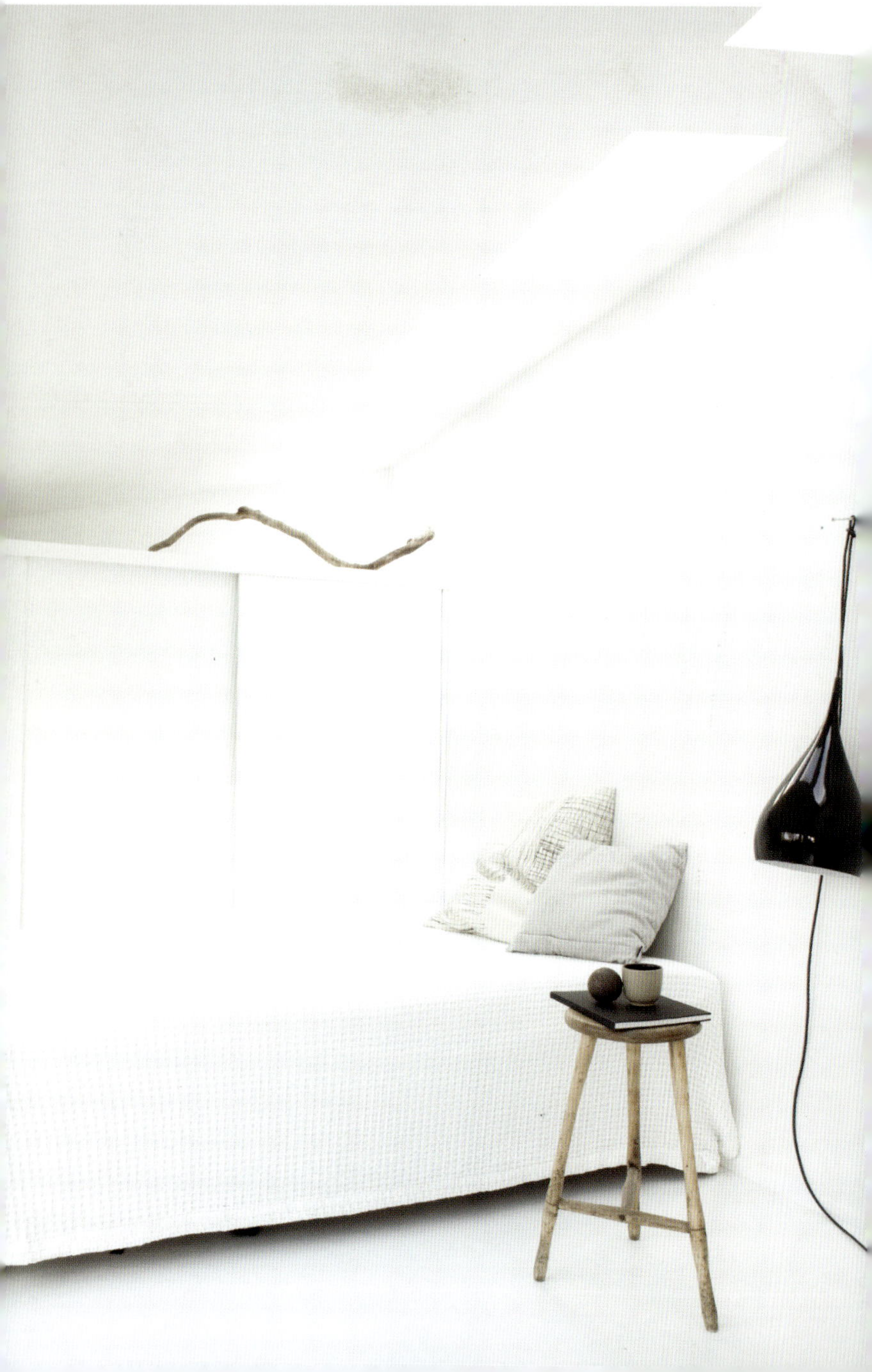

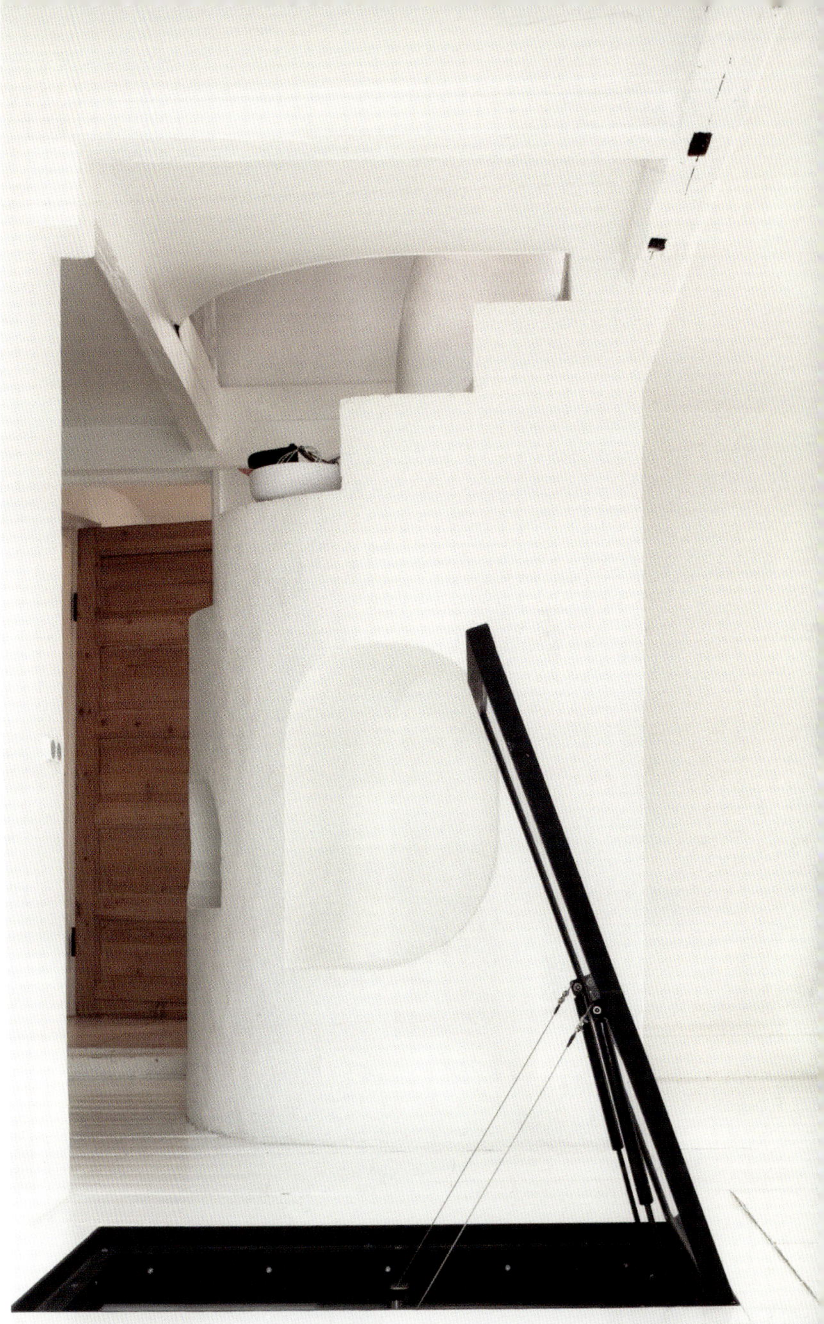

The Wilton Residence | Wilton | UXUS Design

The interiors of a traditional 1930s hunting lodge were transformed into an eclectic mix of European design & the classic American style.

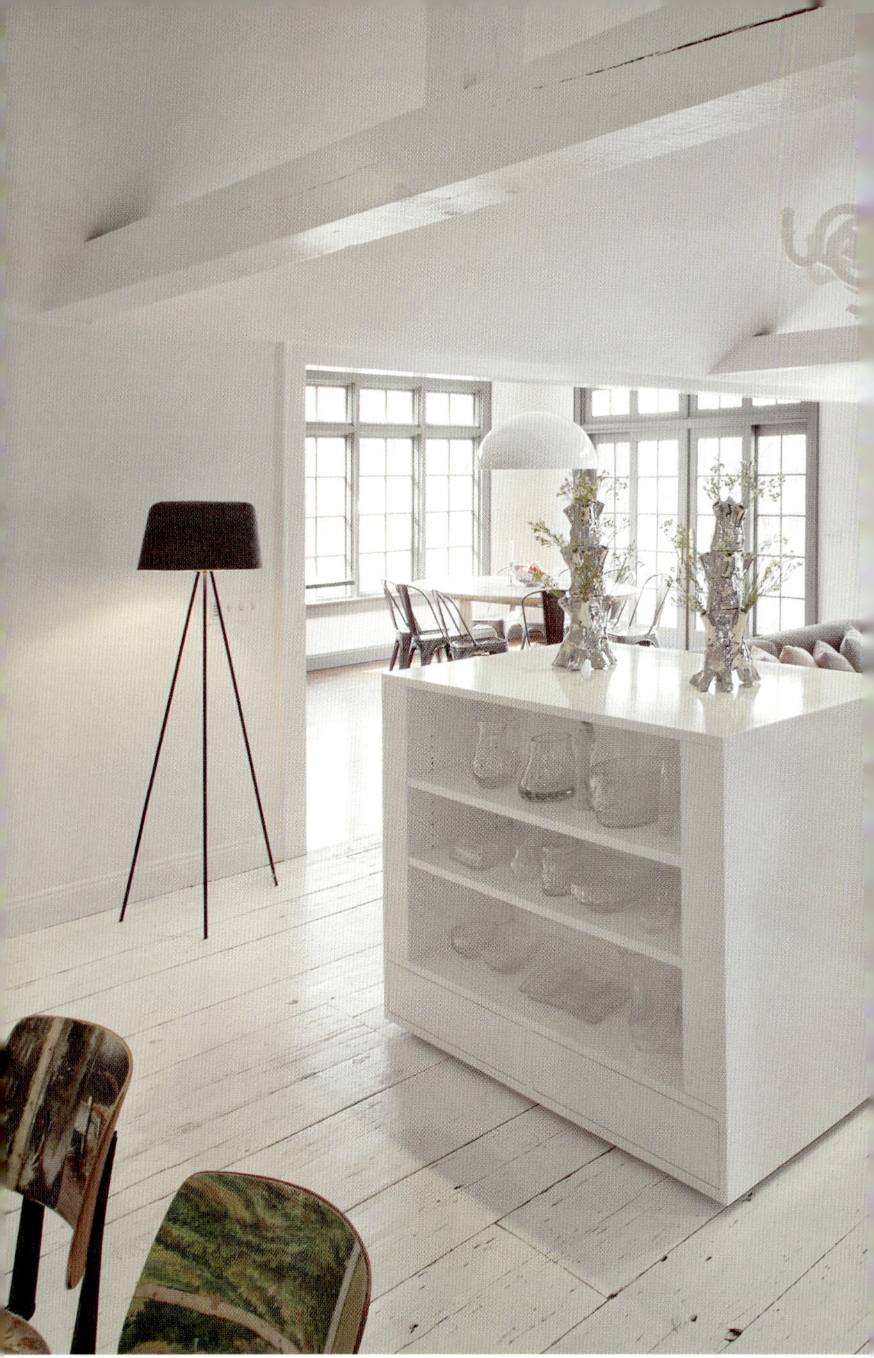

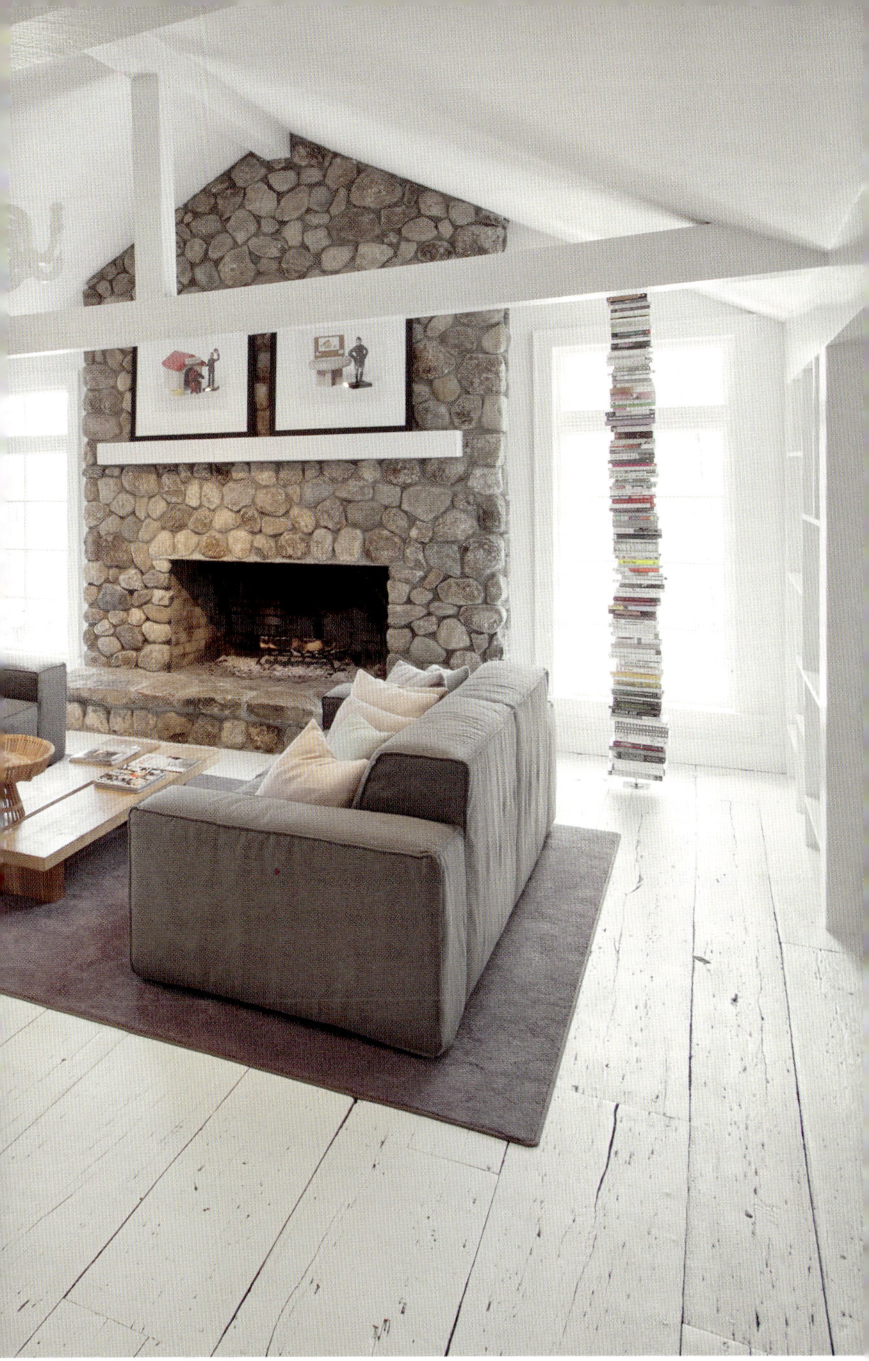

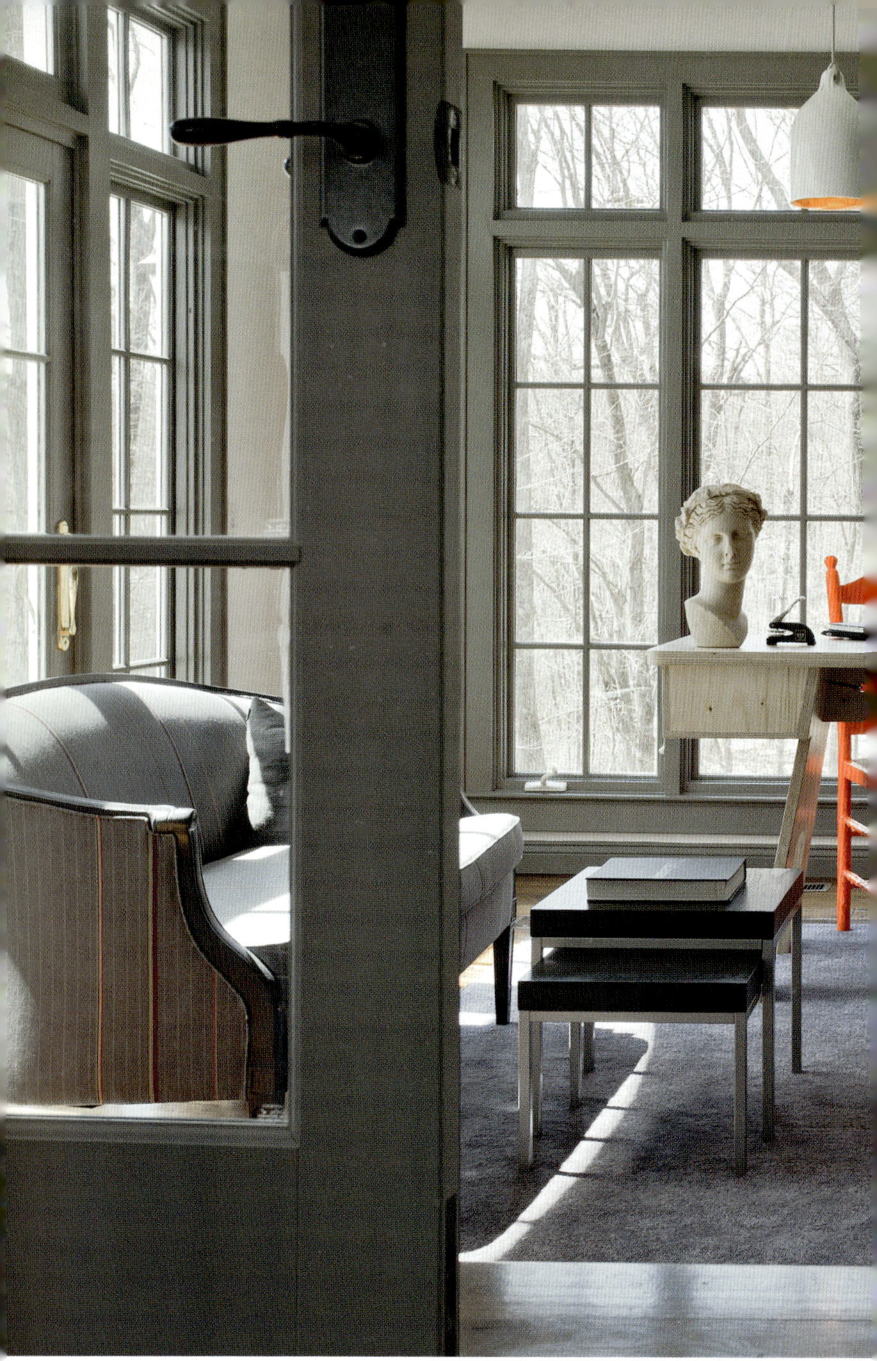

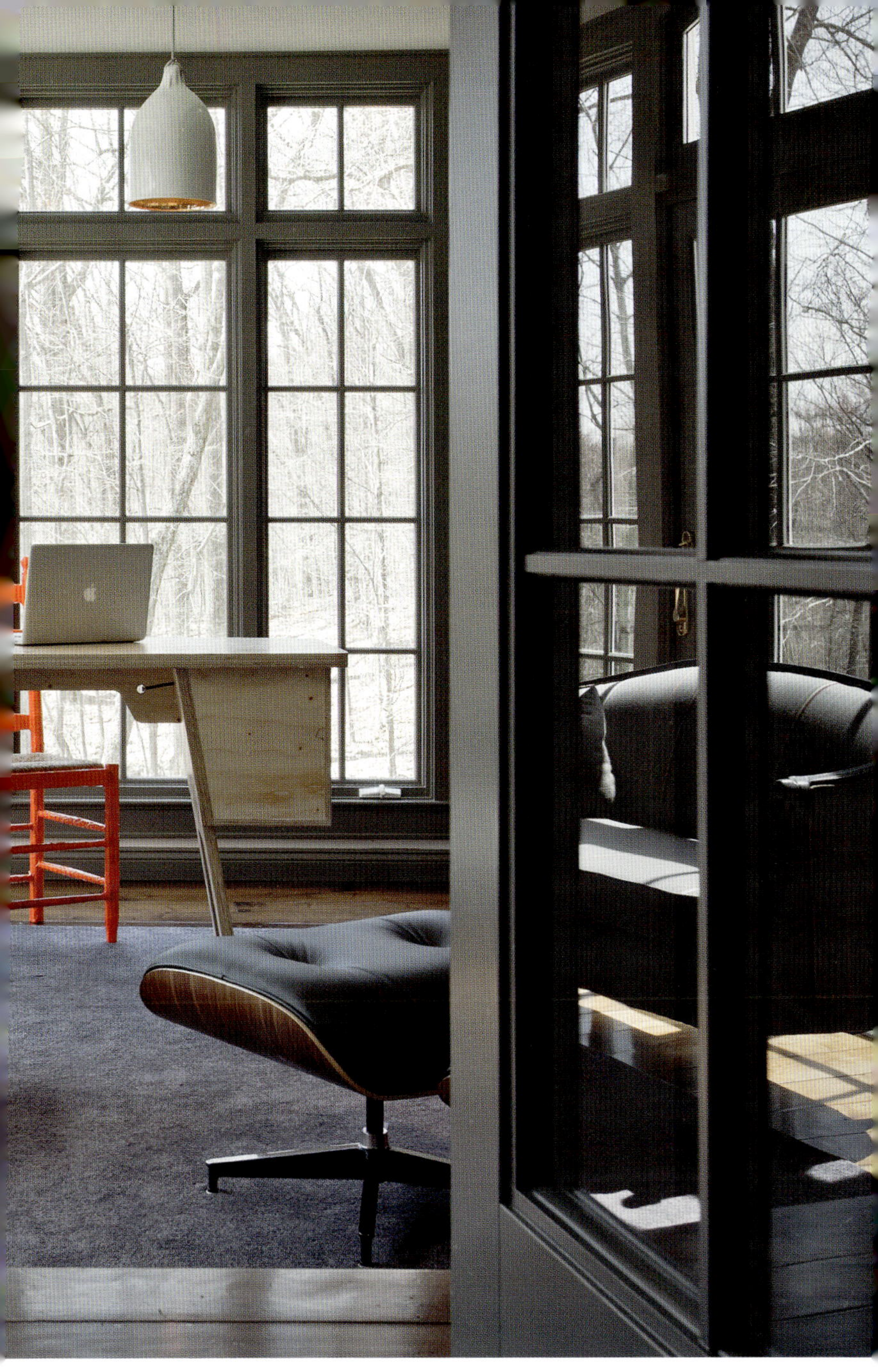

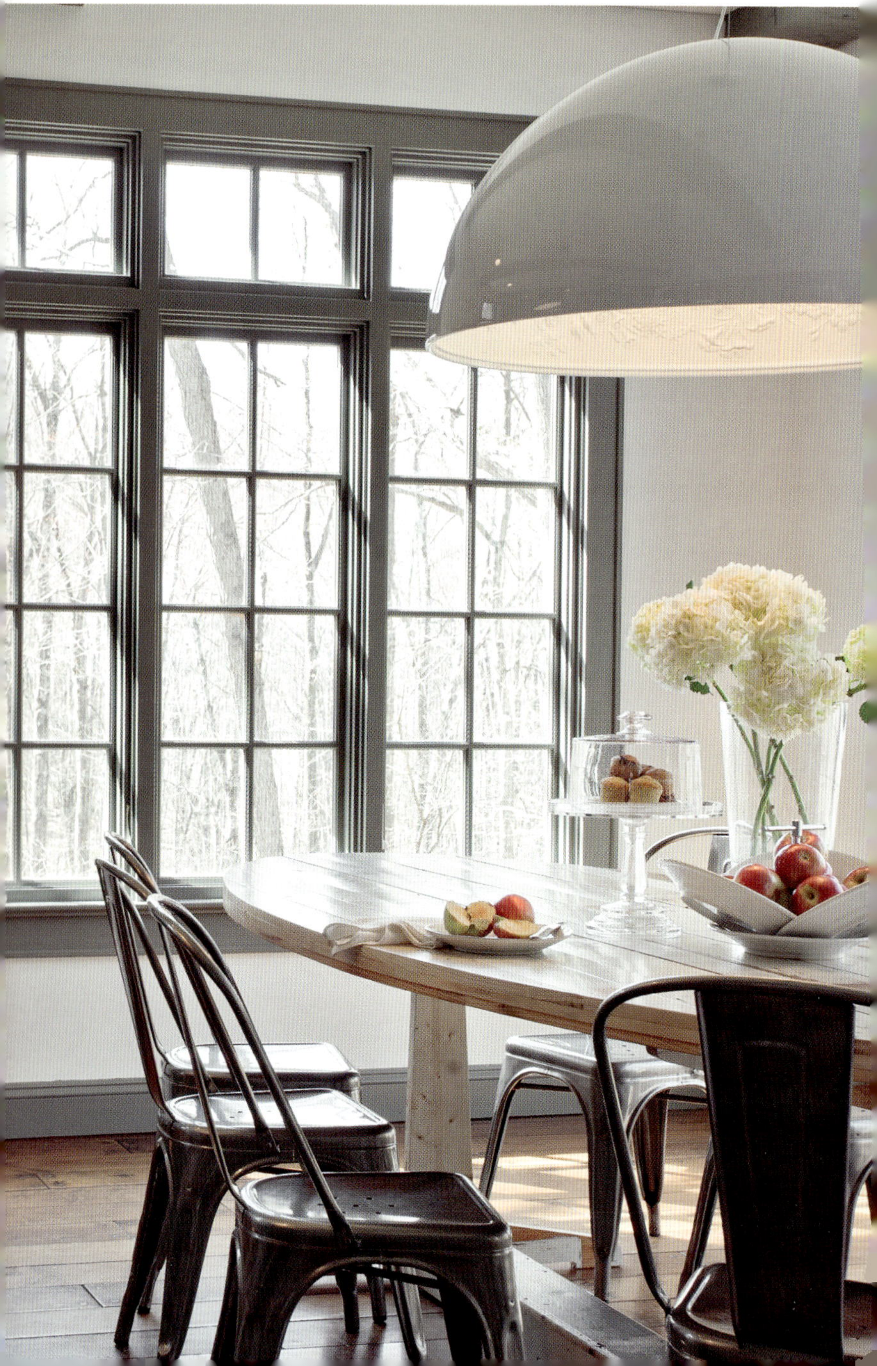

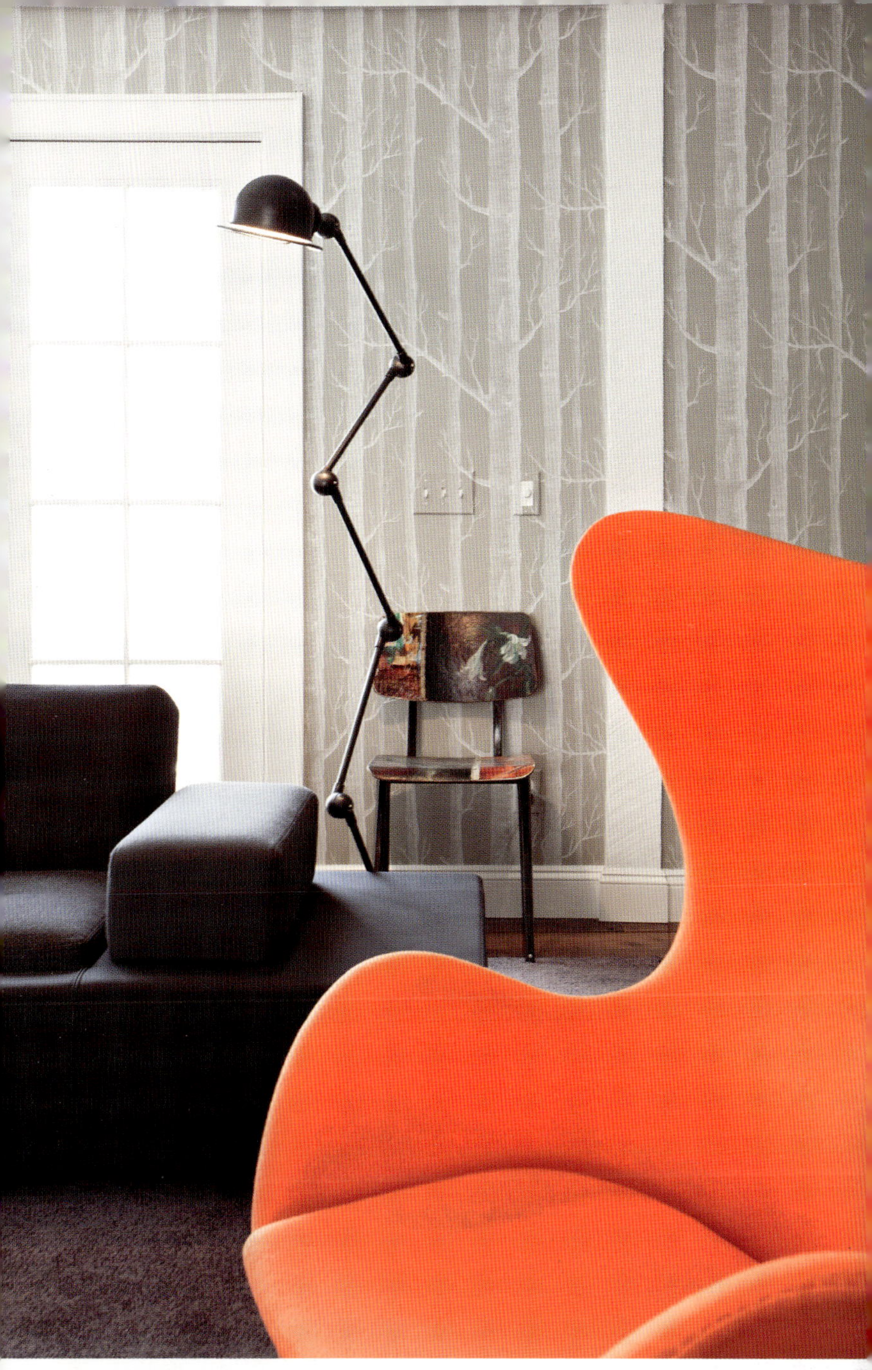

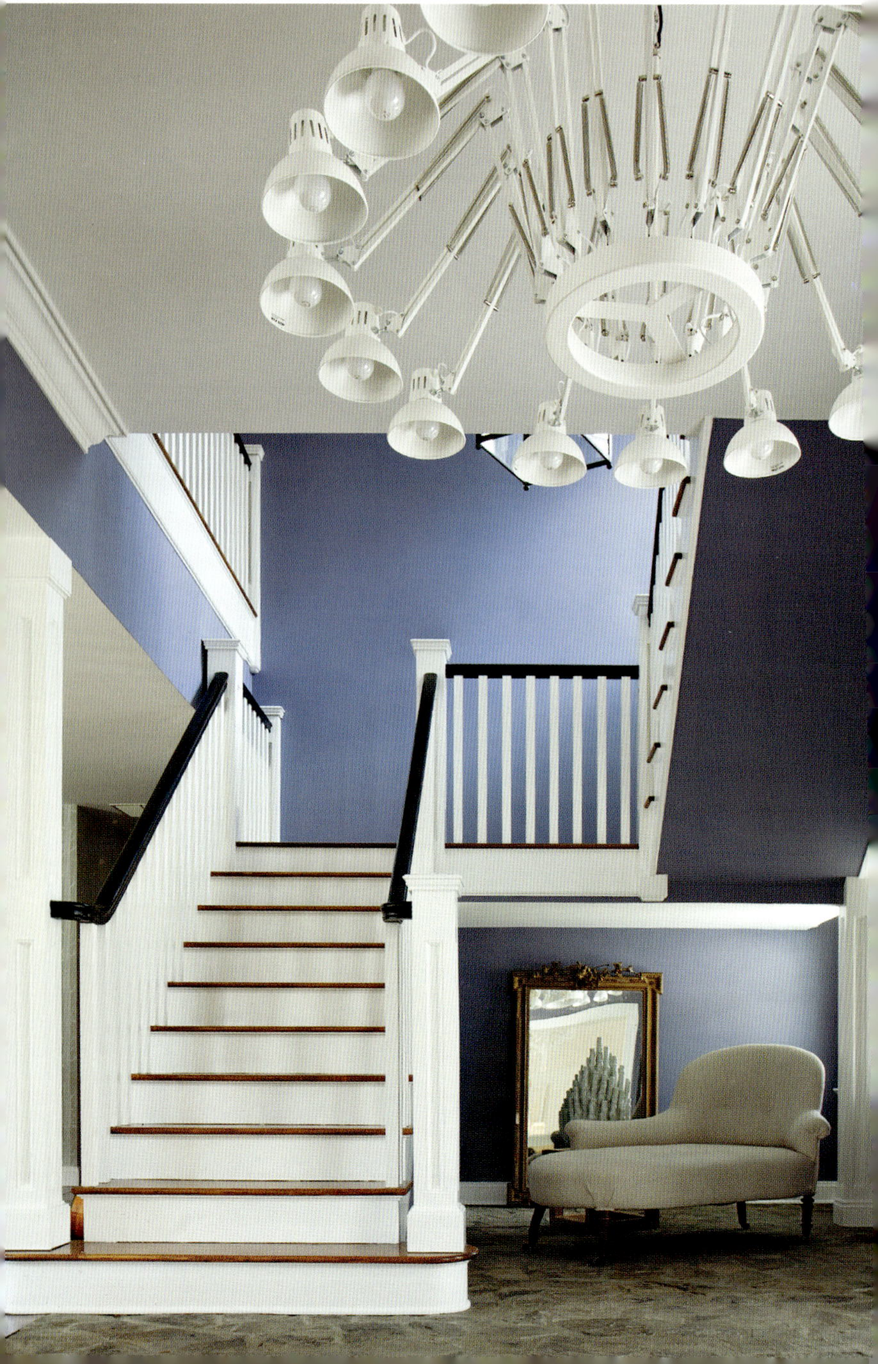

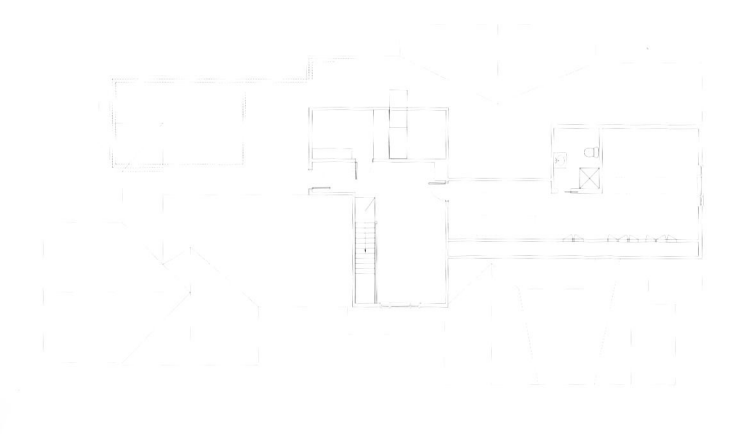

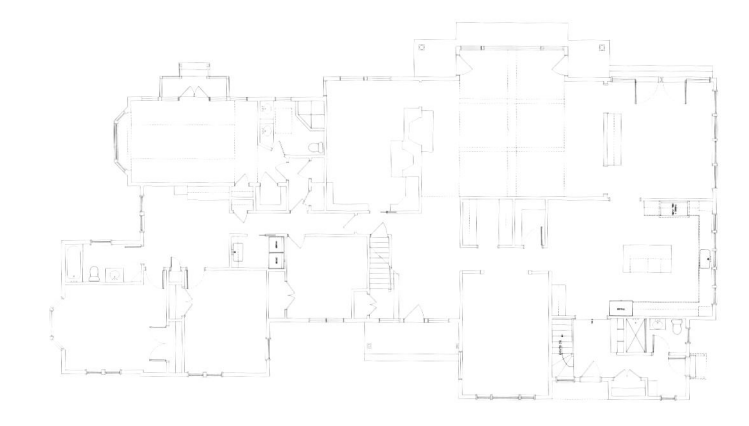

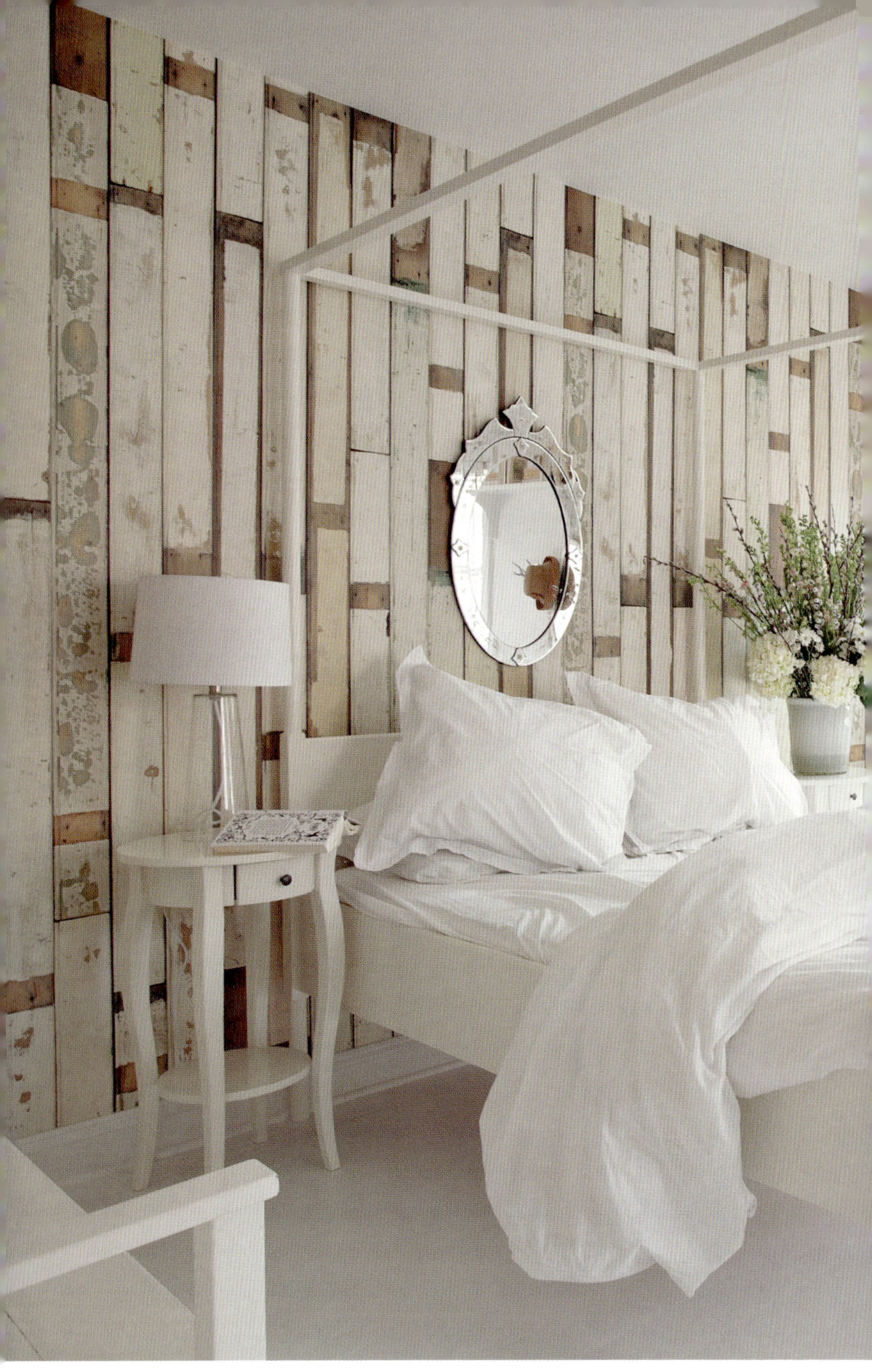

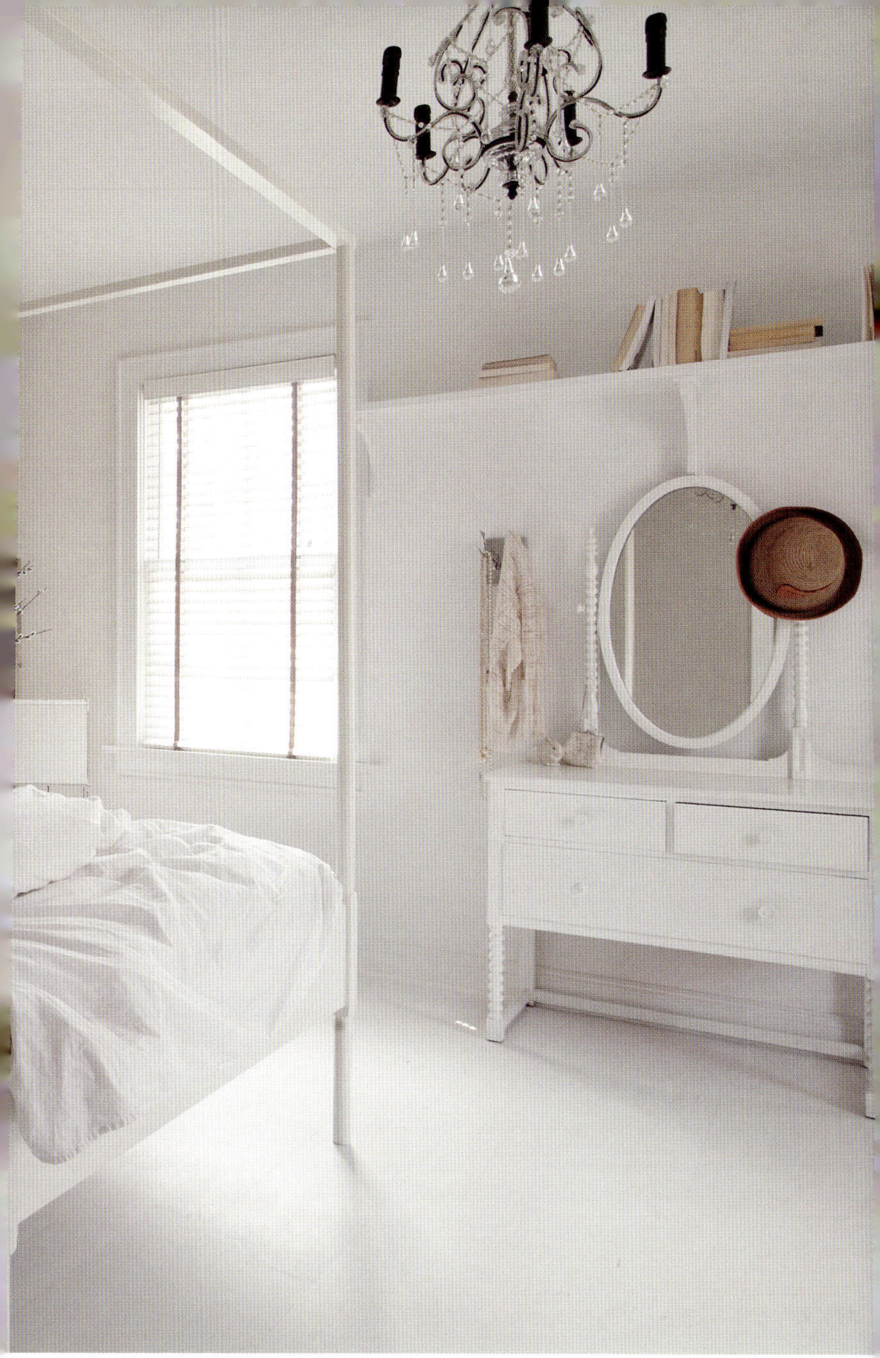

Architects Index

Àbaton Arquitectura
www.abaton.es ► 44

Peter Benoit ► 58

Alexander Brenner Architekten
www.alexanderbrenner.de ► 74, 240

Filippo Caprioglio – Caprioglio Associati Studio di Architettura
www.caprioglio.com ► 118

Cecconi Simone
www.cecconisimone.com ► 266

David Kohn
www.davidkohn.co.uk ► 160

Enoki (interiors) ► 10

Fujiwaramuro Architects
www.aplan.jp ► 170

Studio Garneau
www.studiogarneau.com ► 148

graciastudio
www.graciastudio.com ► 246

Felipe Hess
www.felipehess.blogspot.de ► 212

Studio Inches architettura
www.inches.ch ► 274

Mikel Irastorza
www.mikelirastorzainteriorismo.com ► 196

Marilyn Katsaris ► 256

Kokaistudios
www.kokaistudios.com ► 234

LASC Studio
www.lascstudio.com ► 176

Linea Studio/Kathryn Tyler
www.linea-studio.co.uk ► 66

Paul McAneary Architects
www.paulmcaneary.com ► 84

Naturehumaine
www.naturehumaine.com ► 126

Norm. Architects
www.normcph.com ► 280

Openstudio Architects
www.openstudioarchitects.com ► 78

Oskar Fabian Architecture Studio
www.oskarfabian.com ► 22

Padovani Maurice
www.padovani.fr ► 108

Palimpsest | Architects + Engineers office/Yannis A. Kaklamanis
www.palimpsest.gr ► 186

Paz arquitectura
www.pazarquitectura.com ► 132

Sergi Pons
www.sergiponsarchitect.com ► 18

SchappacherWhite
www.schappacherwhite.com ► 140

su11 architecture + design
www.su11.com ► 154

Sub Estúdio
www.subestudio.com.br ► 206

Troppo Architects
www.troppoarchitects.com.au ► 10

UXUS Design
www.uxusdesign.com ► 290

Walker Workshop Design Build
www.walkerworkshop.com ► 92

WHYDESIGN / Guto Requena, Maurício Arruda and Tatiana Sakurai
www.gutorequena.com.br ► 220, 226

Wiegand/Hoffmann Architektur & Intérieurs
www.wiegandhoffmann.de ► 32

Workstead
www.workstead.com ► 38

XTEN Architecture
www.xtenarchitecture.com ► 100

Yakusha design
www.yakusha.com.ua ► 52

Zege architects
www.zege.gr ► 256

Picture Credits

ÁBATON Architecture	44–51	Xia, Charlie	234–239
Ambrosetti, Tonatiuh	274–279	Yano, Ttoshiyuki	170–175
Asturias, Andres	132–139		
Avdeenko, Andrej	52–57		
Balsem, Dim	290–301	Cover	
Belvedere, Paolo	118–125	Balsem, Dim	
Braun, Zooey	74–77, 240–245		
Bryant, Richard / Arcaid	78–83		
Cole, Ty	154–159		
Cope, Nicolas Alan	92–99		
Droz, Daniela	274–279		
Engel, Gerret	22–31		
García, Luis	246–255		
Garriga Grau, Montse	196–205		
Görner, Reinhard	32–37		
Goula, Adrià	18–21		
Hobbs, Alexi	126–131		
Ibsen, Thomas	176–185		
Imaz, Belén	44–51		
Kelly, Drew	58–65		
King, Steve	100–107		
Knowler, James	10–17		
Kontor, Stamers	176–185		
Kordakis, Yiorgos	256–265		
Ladouce, Paul	108–117		
Lindberg, Jason	140–147		
Magnani, Marcelo	220–225, 226–233		
Marinescu, Ioana	160–169, 280–289		
Mastallier, Erwin	256–265		
McAneary, Paul Architects	84–91		
Meredith, Andrew	66–73		
Michiels, Bart	148–153		
Parente, Fran	206–211, 212–219		
Pryce, Will	280–289		
Scott, Mark	186–295		
Tiedemann von, Joy	266–273		
Williams, Matthew	38–43		